VARIETIES OF TRANSCENDENTAL EXPERIENCE
A Study in Constructive Postmodernism

Donald L. Gelpi, S.J.

A Michael Glazier Book
THE LITURGICAL PRESS
Collegeville, Minnesota

A Michael Glazier Book published by The Liturgical Press

Cover design by David Manahan, O.S.B. Illustration: *Morning in the Tropics* by Frederic Edwin Church (1826–1900). Gift of the Avalon Foundation, National Gallery of Art, Washington, D.C.

1	2	3	4	5	6	7

Library of Congress Cataloging-in-Publication Data

Gelpi, Donald L., 1934–
   Varieties of transcendental experience : a study in constructive postmodernism / Donald L. Gelpi.
      p.   cm.
   "A Michael Glazier book."
   Includes bibliographical references and index.
   ISBN 0-8146-5949-7 (alk. paper)
   1. Postmodernism—United States. 2. Transcendentalism—History.
  3. Postmodernism—Religious aspects—Christianity. I. Title.

B831.2.G45 2000
141'.3'0973—dc21   99-057869

CONTENTS

PREFACE: ENLIGHTENMENT, MODERNITY, AND POSTMODERNITY

History does not repeat itself; however, as Mark Twain once wisely remarked, history does rhyme. Moreover, those who overlook historical rhymes usually end by condemning themselves to relive the mistakes of the past. This study retrieves a neglected part of the religious and intellectual history of the United States. It tells the story of the emergence of Enlightenment religion and of the Transcendental critique of Enlightenment religion. I tell the following story because it throws light on the current debate over postmodernism.

Because we have institutionalized the education of the young by segregating them in academic institutions largely divorced from the rest of life, the academy sometimes succumbs to intellectual faddishness. The latest fad to rattle the branches in the groves of academe calls itself postmodernism. The term "postmodernism" means very different things to different people with the result that it ranks high on any contemporary list of weasel words. Weasel words have so many meanings that one finds oneself hard put to identify the word's real referent. In general, postmoderns are all trying to get beyond what they call "modernity." The term "modernity," of course, ranks right up there with "postmodernism" as a first-class weasel word. In the current debate over modernity and postmodernity, however, the term "modernity" usually connotes the presuppositions of Enlightenment thinking.[1] Postmoderns tend to scoff at the omnipotence of technology. They question unlimited human perfectibility. They sniff

---

[1] See Ernst Cassirer, *The Philosophy of the Enlightenment,* trans. C. A. Koellen (Princeton, N.J.: Princeton University Press, 1951); Norman Hampson, *The Enlightenment* (New York: Viking Penguin, 1968); Geoffrey Clive, *The Romantic Enlightenment* (New York: Meridian, 1960); Peter Gay, *The Enlightenment: An Interpretation* (New York: Vintage Books, 1966); Adrienne Koch, ed., *The American Enlightenment* (New York: Brazillier, 1965); Adrienne Koch, "Power and Morals and the Founding Fathers," *Review of Politics* 25 (1953) 470–90; Adrienne Koch, "Pragmatic Wisdom and the American Enlightenment," *William and Mary Quarterly* 18 (1961) 313–29; G. A. Koch, *The Religion*

suspiciously at universalizing generalizations, scientific and otherwise. They deplore Enlightenment individualism.[2]

Some scholars find postmodern themes developed by major thinkers in the classical American philosophical tradition.[3] In what follows I shall argue that among classical American thinkers, Orestes Brownson, Francis Ellingwood Abbot, and C. S. Peirce did indeed deconstruct fundamental presuppositions of Enlightenment thinking and replace them with a metaphysical realism. The mature Josiah Royce endorsed Peirce's version of pragmatism and developed many of Peirce's best insights. In my judgment, however, William James's therapeutic individualism as well as his nominalism both put him well within the ballpark of Enlightenment thinking. So did the nominalism of process philosophers like Alfred North Whitehead and his principal commentator, Charles Hartshorne.

Most people think of Transcendentalism as a movement which flowered in the third decade of the nineteenth century. In fact, Transcendentalism developed in a series of intellectual waves. A different thinker rode each wave. In the 1830s, Ralph Waldo Emerson reluctantly carried the torch of Transcendental intellectual leadership. In the 1840s, just as Emerson was having serious second thoughts about the naive optimism of his own Transcendental "saturnalia of faith," Theodore Parker took up the militant leadership of the movement. During the same decade, Orestes Brownson found himself converting from a naive Enlightenment faith in human innocence and perfectibility to Roman Catholicism. While Brownson had moved on the fringes of the inner circle of New England Transcendentalism, he did not actually formulate his personal brand of Transcendentalism until after he had embraced the Catholic faith. Through his *Brownson's Quarterly Review* and other publications he gave robust intellectual leadership to Transcendentalism in the 1840s, 50s, and 60s.

---

of the American Enlightenment (New York: Thomas Y. Crowell, 1963); Frank Manuel, *The Eighteenth Century Confronts the Gods* (Cambridge, Mass.: Harvard University Press, 1959); F. W. Voget, "Anthropology in the Age of Enlightenment," *Southwestern Journal of Anthropology* 24 (1968) 321–45; C. W. Hendel, "The Eighteenth Century as an Age of Ethical Crisis," *Ethics* 72 (1962) 202–14; N. Jacobson, "Political Realism and the Age of Reason: The Anti-Rationalist Heritage in America," *Review of Politics* 15 (1953) 446–69; R. Darnton, "In Search of the Enlightenment: Recent Attempts to Create a Social History of Ideas," *Journal of Modern History* 43 (1971) 112–32.

[2] See Albert Borgmann, *Crossing the Postmodern Divide* (Chicago: University of Chicago Press, 1992).

[3] See David Ray Griffin, John B. Cobb, Marcus P. Ford, Pete A. Y. Gunter, and Peter Ochs, *Founders of Constructive Postmodern Philosophy: Peirce, James, Bergson, Whitehead, and Hartshorne* (Albany, N.Y.: SUNY, 1993); Robert Cummings Neville, *The Highroad Around Modernism* (Albany, N.Y.: SUNY, 1992).

The first Transcendentalists shared a common theological and philosophical concern. They all wanted to get beyond, to transcend, if you will, the limitations of Enlightenment religion. Moreover, they all adopted an analogous strategy. They sought to rescue religious experience from the skeptical consequences of Enlightenment nominalism by developing an account of religious intuition. Emerson's theory of intuition rested on simplified and extremely dualistic Neo-Platonic foundations. Parker defended the subjective intuition of the objective truth of Enlightenment religion and in the process became the first systematic Enlightenment fundamentalist. Brownson's philosophical vitalism attempted to avoid the dualisms which marred Emerson's account of intuitionism, and Brownson's own theory of intuitive religious knowing rested on a robust theological incarnationalism.

Enlightenment religion shaped two major institutions in the United States: the federal government and the Unitarian church. Not surprisingly, then, all of the early Transcendentalists began their intellectual careers as Unitarian ministers. Emerson resigned his Unitarian pulpit; Parker battled to keep his ministerial standing in the Unitarian Church. Brownson received orders in the Universalist Church, which eventually blended with Unitarianism. Moreover, Emerson, Parker, and Brownson all wrestled with the meaning and destiny of the American republic. Emerson envisioned the nation as a theocratic democracy of creative individualists. Parker invoked Enlightenment fundamentalism in order to declare war on slavery and sexism. In the wake of the Civil War, Brownson, formerly a states righter, found himself forced by the tragedy of war to rethink his vision of the American Republic. In the course of doing so, he revised the philosophical foundations of constitutional law and mounted a telling critique of American individualism.

With Francis Ellingwood Abbot Transcendental thinking entered a new phase. Abbot moved on the fringes of William James and C. S. Peirce's Metaphysical Club much as Brownson moved on the fringes of Emerson's Transcendental Club. Abbot began his religious and intellectual career as a convinced Emersonian intuitionist. Like James and Peirce, he encountered a formidable challenge to his religious beliefs in the positivism of Chauncey Wright. James responded to Wright's religious skepticism with his "will to believe." For a time Peirce decided to segregate science from religion. Abbot decided that he needed to reconcile Emerson's Platonized Transcendentalism with the claims of positive science.

A much neglected but important thinker, Abbot's scientific Transcendentalism anticipated in many ways the process philosophy of Alfred North Whitehead, but without acquiescing in Enlightenment nominalism as Whitehead would. Moreover, reading Abbot's *Scientific Theism* helped launch Peirce on the third phase in the development of his metaphysical logic and semiotic by convincing him of the possibility of bringing about the happy marriage of religion and science. Although Peirce repudiated the intuitionism of the early Transcendentalists, in his mature period he admitted to some slight intellectual kinship with them.

In fact, the mature Peirce finally accomplished what earlier Transcendentalists had set out to do. He systematically dismantled the least tenable aspects of both Transcendentalist and Enlightenment thinking. Moreover, Abbot's scientific theism failed finally as a defensible philosophical system partly because Abbot did not understand science from the inside in the way in which Peirce did and partly because Abbot had only a rudimentary grasp of logic, while in logical matters Peirce stood head and shoulders above any other American thinker of his time. The mature Royce built on the solid philosophical foundations which Peirce had laid and articulated both a systematic critique of Enlightenment individualism and a pragmatic understanding of Christian religious experience.

This study attempts, then, to document the fact that postmodern dissatisfaction with the presuppositions of modernity stretches deep roots into the religious and intellectual tradition of the United States. This study also argues that the development of the Transcendental and pragmatic critiques of Enlightenment thinking has a lot to teach deconstructionist postmodernists. In some of its formulations, deconstructionist postmodernism tries to deconstruct the subject of discourse. Drawing on continental, European deconstructionism, it often portrays language as floating signifiers without a real referent. In deconstructionist postmodernism suspicion of universal generalization often degenerates into a subjectivistic conceptual nominalism[4] philosophically akin to the subjectivistic nominalism of those lights of the Enlightenment: John Locke, David Hume, and Immanuel Kant.[5] Finally, this study endorses the position put forward by Robert

[4] I use the term "conceptual nominalism" in the same sense as C. S. Peirce. Peirce distinguished classical from conceptual nominalism. Classical nominalism reduced universals to the *flatus vocis,* i.e., to the repeated application of the same concrete word to many concrete, sensible objects. Classical nominalism did not then allow the universality of conceptions. Conceptual nominalism concedes the universality of ideas but denies any generality in the reality the mind grasps. Conceptual nominalism reduces the objects of knowledge to concrete sensibles. See Charles Sanders Peirce, *Collected Papers,* ed. Charles Hartshorne and Paul Weiss, vol. 1 (Cambridge, Mass.: Harvard University Press, 1931) 6–27.

[5] See Madan Sarup, *An Introductory Guide to Post-Structuralism and Post-Modernism* (Athens: University of Georgia Press, 1993); Philippa Berry and Andrew Wernick, eds. *Shadow of Spirit: Postmodernism and Religion* (New York: Routledge, 1992); Huston Smith, *Beyond the Post-Modern Mind* (Wheaton, Ill.: Theosophical Publishing House, 1989); Joe Holland, *The Birth of Postmodern Culture: Challenge to Catholic and American Identities and Conservative and Liberal Explorations of the Postmodern Stage of the Human* (South Orange, N.J.: The Warwick Institute, 1989); Alan N. Olson, "Postmodernity

Cummings Neville in *The Highroad Around Modernism*,[6] but it focuses on those thinkers who laid the foundations for the road which Neville charts.

The Transcendental critique of Enlightenment religion also throws considerable light on the two weasel words which lie at the heart of contemporary debate about modernism and postmodernism because it highlights the least tenable presuppositions of Enlightenment thinking with greater precision than contemporary European deconstructionism. While deconstructionist postmodernists repudiate all forms of ontological metaphysical thinking, the scientific metaphysical realism which characterizes Peirce's mature semiotic unmasks that repudiation as precisely the kind of hasty universal generalization which deconstructionist postmoderns say one must never make. Deconstructionists who reject indefensible forms of foundational, ontological thinking need, in my judgment, to learn that foundational, metaphysical thinking comes in many forms, including forms which avoid the fallacies of classical ontologies. The Transcendental critique of Enlightenment thinking calls into question its nominalism, its individualism, its naive claims for what scientific rationality can accomplish, its groundless promise of limitless technological progress, its dualism. Moreover, as the Transcendental debate about the limits of modernity progressed, it produced an increasingly defensible metaphysical alternative to Enlightenment thinking which avoids all the fallacies which make aspects of modernity unacceptable. As a consequence, the American debate over modernity provides postmodern thinking with a new kind of metaphysical foundationalism which promises to survive long after deconstructionist postmodernism has, as it inevitably must, deconstructed itself.

One can read this study from three interrelated viewpoints. First of all, one can interpret it as an attempt to contribute something positive to the current debate over modernity and postmodernity. That debate raises a number of philosophical and theological issues. This study argues that the classical North American speculative tradition offers creative and fruitful alternatives to deconstructionist postmodernism.

---

and Faith," *Journal of the American Academy of Religion* 58 (1990) 37–50; Thomas Guarino, "Postmodernity and Five Fundamental Theological Issues," *Theological Studies* 57 (1996) 654–85; Janice Radway, ed., *American Quarterly* 39 (1987); Gerald Early, "American Education and the Postmodern Impulse," *American Quarterly* 45 (1993) 220–9; Paul Lakeland, *Postmodernity: Christian Identity in a Fragmented Age* (Minneapolis: Fortress Press, 1997); Bruce J. Nichols, ed., *Evangelical Review of Theology: Christ, Modernity, and Post-Modernity* 22 (1998).

[6] Robert Cummings Neville, *The Highroad Around Modernism* (Albany: State University of New York Press, 1987).

One could also read this study as a contribution to the history of religious and philosophical thought in the United States. In what follows, I shall analyze a variety of thinkers and the frames of reference which each developed for dealing with life and reality. One may, however, handle the events of history with a variety of methods. I myself, however, do not conceive what follows as strictly speaking a history of ideas.

Historians face two basic tasks. They need first to establish an accurate chronology of events, then they need to provide a causal explanation of why events turned this way rather than that. In dealing with the history of ideas, therefore, a strictly historical account of thinkers examined in the following chapters would have to spend much more time than I do contextualizing the thought of each person in its sources and providing a much more detailed account of why each thinker developed in the way in which he did.

In what follows, I have indeed taken into account what historians of the American intellectual tradition have to say about each of the figures studied. I, for my part, have preferred to approach the topic here discussed as a dialectician rather than as a historian. I use the term "dialectics" in Bernard Lonergan's sense of that term. Dialectics compares and contrasts the strengths and limitations of interpretative frames of reference. Rather than give a strict causal account of the development of a person's thought, the dialectician looks for areas of agreement and disagreement and assesses the interpretative adequacy of one frame of reference in comparison with another. A dialectical approach to the development of a speculative tradition prepares the ground for laying new foundations for constructive thinking. In what follows, I shall argue that C. S. Peirce brought the critique of Enlightenment modernism to a climax and laid solid foundations for postmodern thinking, foundations which fall under none of the strictures which many contemporary postmodern critics lodge against foundational thinking.

Even though I am approaching my subject dialectically, I have deemed it important to offer some contextualization for each of the interpretative frames of reference which I subject to comparative analysis in the following pages. I have therefore prefaced each dialectical analysis with basic biographical information about the thinker or thinkers studied in any given chapter. I have not integrated the biographical material into the dialectical analysis which follows lest I mislead the reader into thinking that I am attempting to write intellectual history as such. Separating biography from the dialectical analysis which follows it allows each frame of reference to stand on its own and facilitates the kind of comparison which dialectical thinking seeks to advance.

Some readers may wonder why a study which treats of the pragmatism of Charles S. Peirce and of its transformation in the thought of the mature Josiah Royce fails to deal in greater detail with the pragmatisms of William James and of John Dewey. The subtitle to this work suggests the explanation for this omission. This work studies how the Transcendental critique of Enlightenment modernism culminated in the thoughts of Peirce and Royce. In contrast to the constructive postmodernism of Peirce and of Royce, the pragmatisms of James and of Dewey remained mired in some of the least tenable aspects of Enlightenment modernism.

James helped endow Enlightenment individualism and subjectivism with the therapeutic introspection which North American culture systematically inculcates. While one might argue that James's nominalistic reading of Peirce's pragmatic maxim resulted in part from Peirce's own failure during his middle period to extricate himself fully from nominalistic presuppositions, the fact remains that the mature Peirce did mount a telling critique of Enlightenment nominalism and did finally defend a robust metaphysical realism, whereas James never did. Despite the elder James's intuitive flirtations with the compounding of consciousness, he remained to the end of his life a kind of Lockean nominalist who recognized a mysterious "more" to religious experience which his own philosophical presuppositions left him at a loss to explain. In what concerns Peirce's logic and triadic metaphysical realism, James never had a clue.

One may legitimately argue that Dewey managed to avoid the fallacies of Enlightenment nominalism, but Dewey's pragmatic instrumentalism, in my judgment, both endorsed the shallow rationalism of the eighteenth-century Enlightenment and acquiesced in the Enlightenment's naive and facile belief in human reason's capacity to effect virtually unlimited human progress. A questionable Enlightenment optimism about the integrity of human nature helped motivate Dewey's humanistic quest for more and better shared consummatory experiences. Nor does one find in Dewey the kind of openness to both the complexity and the realism of Christian religious experience which one finds in both Royce and Peirce. When confronted with religious experience, Dewey, understandably revolted by the pedantry and blindness of Christian fundamentalists, finally just blinked. In his assessment of the Christian tradition, Dewey manifested neither the hostility of the militant American Deists nor the benign tolerance of a Benjamin Franklin, only an obtuseness largely motivated by his uncritical acquiescence in the dialectical religious imagination which the American Enlightenment derived from the Calvinism against which it rebelled.

In other words, while I recognize the philosophical genius of both James and Dewey as well as the important positive contributions which both have made to the intellectual tradition in the United States, in my judgment neither thinker made a sufficiently significant contribution to the kind of constructive postmodernism which this study ponders. On the contrary, important strains in the thought of both men reinforce some of the least tenable aspects of the contemporary Enlightenment fundamentalism in which so much contemporary American secular culture languishes. At the same time the best insights of Peirce and of the mature Royce offer, in my assessment, a constructive alternative to such modernist fallacies.

Finally, one can read the present work as yet another contribution to the theological project on which I have been working since joining the Jesuit School of Theology. In the course of developing a thoroughly inculturated North American theology, I have drawn broadly on the philosophical tradition in the United States in order to formulate a fallibilistic metaphysics of experience. This study introduces some of the influential figures who have shaped my thought to those who might feel curious about the precise sources in the American philosophical tradition on which I draw.

The study which follows divides roughly into three parts. Part One describes the emergence of Enlightenment religion in the United States during the latter part of the eighteenth and in the early decades of the nineteenth century. Part Two describes the critique of Enlightenment modernity mounted by the first generation of Transcendental thinkers: Emerson, Parker, and Brownson. Part Three describes the completion of the Transcendental project of moving beyond the presuppositions of Enlightenment modernism accomplished in the work of Abbot, Peirce, and the mature Josiah Royce.

I owe a debt of gratitude to Evan Howard and to Jay Johnson for their excellent help in identifying important secondary sources for this study. The following students also assisted me with documentation: Andrea Giovanni, Christina K. Hutchins, Matthew Eddy, Nate Hinerman, Diana Walsh, Brian Lehane, and Gregory Zuschlag. I would also like to thank Frank Oppenheim, S.J., for his helpful suggestions for improving the chapter on Josiah Royce, as well as the members of the John Courtney Murray Group for their insightful and constructive input. I also thank my brother, Albert Gelpi, for his critical and constructive reading of the entire manuscript and for innumerable fruitful conversations concerning the American proposition.

Donald L. Gelpi, S.J.
The Jesuit School of Theology at Berkeley

PART ONE:
ENLIGHTENMENT RELIGION

Chapter 1

THE EMERGENCE OF ENLIGHTENMENT RELIGION: BENJAMIN FRANKLIN

O Creator, O Father, I believe that thou art Good,
and that thou art pleas'd with the Pleasure of thy Children.

—Benjamin Franklin

I

Clerics dominated thought in the early days of the American colonies. Not until the middle of the eighteenth century did the laity find a representative voice. That voice spoke in salty aphorisms about virtue, religion, politics, and wealth. The voice called itself "Poor Richard." It stood for reason, trade, science, prudent social and educational reform. Eventually, that voice supported revolution and the formation of a constitutional government. In real life the voice belonged to Benjamin Franklin.

Benjamin Franklin first saw the light on January 17, 1706. After two years of elementary schooling, young Benjamin served as an apprentice to his candle-making father, Josiah. In 1717, however, his brother James returned from England in order to establish a printing house in Boston. The following year young Benjamin became his brother's indentured apprentice.

The precocious Franklin became an autodidact. He found Cotton Mather's *Essays to Do Good* edifying,[1] and he relished the crackling prose of Addison and Steele.[2] In 1722 he assumed the pseudonym "Silence Do-good" and began publishing short pieces in his brother's newspaper, *The New England Courant.*

[1] See Virginia Bernhard, "Cotton Mather and the Doing of Good: A Puritan Gospel of Wealty," *New England Quarterly* 49 (1976) 225–41.

[2] See Albert Furtwangler, "Franklin's Apprenticeship and the Spectator," *New England Quarterly* 52 (1979) 377–96.

A cantankerous man, James Franklin angered the Boston establishment by his journalistic contempt for authority. His irascibility earned him a short prison term, during which young Benjamin managed the paper alone. The success of this editorial experiment convinced the youth of his own professional competence. In 1723 he broke his indenture and journeyed to Philadelphia to make his own way in the world. A printer named Samuel Keimer hired Benjamin. An exiled Camisard, Keimer had the temper of a religious fanatic.

In 1724 young Franklin made the personal acquaintance of Cotton Mather[3] and felt flattered by the courteous attention of Governor Burnett of New York. He began to move with greater ease in the presence of celebrated personages.

In 1725 Franklin published an attack on William Wollaston's *The Religion of Nature Delineated.* Franklin called his treatise *A Dissertation on Liberty and Necessity, Pleasure and Pain.* In it he attacked the Calvinist doctrine of universal depravity. Fearful that he had overstated his position, he withdrew the pamphlet from circulation.

In 1730 Franklin bought out Keimer's printing establishment. He began publishing the *Pennsylvania Gazette.*[4] During the year before the purchase, Franklin, inspired by Cotton Mather's neighborhood self-help organizations, founded the Junto, a humanitarian club dedicated to "mutual improvement."[5] That same year Franklin married Deborah Reed. The following year he launched his first major humanitarian venture: the Philadelphia Library Company, the first subscription library in the English colonies.

Franklin began publishing *Poor Richard's Almanac* in 1732. Poor Richard's homespun wit and wisdom boosted sales of the Almanac and helped make Franklin's name popular throughout the colonies. In 1735 he used the *Pennsylvania Gazette* in order to defend the preaching of Samuel Hemphill, a Presbyterian minister whose Deistic sermons had cost him his pulpit. In 1736 Franklin established the first Fire Department in Philadelphia. In the same year the people of that state elected him clerk of the General Assembly. In 1737 he assumed office as Philadelphia's Postmaster General.

When George Whitefield brought the Great Awakening to the English colonies, Franklin made his acquaintance. He found Whitefield a powerful preacher and admired the trans-sectarian appeal of the "new light"

---

[3] See Mitchell Robert Breitwieser, *Cotton Mather and Benjamin Franklin: The Price of Representative Personality* (Cambridge: Cambridge University Press, 1984); Phillis Franklin, *Show Thyself a Man* (Paris: Mouton, 1969).

[4] See Ralph Fresia, "From Apprentice to Journeyman to Partner: Benjamin Franklin's Workers and the Growth of the Early American Printing Trade," *Philadelphia Magazine of History and Biography* 114 (1990) 229–48.

[5] See Campbell Tatham, "Benjamin Franklin, Cotton Mather, and the Outward State," *Early American Literature* 6 (1972) 223–33.

preachers. Franklin published some of Whitefield's sermons and helped the revivalist raise funds for some of his humanitarian ventures. With time, however, he came to regard both Whitefield's religious zeal and the Awakening itself with jaundiced eyes.[6]

In 1742 Franklin invented the stove which bears his name. In 1744 he founded The American Philosophical Society and served as the organization's first secretary. Two years later, the Philadelphia Library Company received a Leyden jar as a gift from Peter Collison. Franklin began his private study of the properties of electricity.

Franklin continued to write and publish popular tracts. In 1747 he issued *Plain Truth,* a pamphlet urging public support for a militia in Philadelphia for defense against Native American attacks. The public responded positively and Franklin busied himself with recruitment. This victory over the pacifist Quaker establishment in Pennsylvania transformed Franklin into a major player in colonial politics. The following year he published *Advice to a Young Tradesman,* homespun hints about how to achieve financial success. In 1749 he began a series of tracts entitled *Proposals Relating to the Education of Youth in Pennsylvania.* In the same year he founded an academy of learning which eventually evolved into the University of Pennsylvania.

In 1751 Franklin brought out the first edition of his *Experiments and Observations on Electricity.* Probably in 1752 his famous kite experiment established the identity of electricity and lightning.[7] In addition to scientific interest, the desire to debunk Calvinist use of thunder and lightning as a theophany probably motivated Franklin's study of electricity. In the same year as the kite experiment Franklin founded the first fire insurance company in the English colonies. In 1753 he received the Copley medal from the Royal Society in London for his work in electricity. Both Harvard and Yale gave him honorary degrees. In 1755 he helped organize the Pennsylvania militia and assisted the commissar in General Braddock's disastrous expedition against the French and Native Americans.[8] The

---

[6] See Frank Lambert, "'Peddlar in Divinity': George Whitefield and the Great Awakening, 1737–1745," *Journal of American History* 77 (1990) 812–37; Jon Butler, "Whitefield in America: A Two-Hundred Fiftieth Commemoration," *Philadelphia Magazine of History and Biography* 113 (1989) 515–26.

[7] See Bruce Granger, *Benjamin Franklin: An American Man of Letters* (Ithaca, N.Y.: Cornell University Press, 1964); I. Cohen, *Franklin and Newton* (Philadelphia: American Philosophical Society, 1956); I. Cohen, ed., *Benjamin Franklin's Experiments* (Cambridge, Mass.: Harvard University Press, 1941); M. W. Jergenan, "Benjamin Franklin's 'Electrical Kite' and Lightning Rod," *New England Quarterly* 1 (1928) 180–96; B. S. Finn, "Appraisal of the Origins of Franklin's Electrical Theory," *Isis* 60 (1969) 362–9; A. O. Aldridge, "Benjamin Franklin and Jonathan Edwards on Earthquakes," *Isis* 41 (1950) 162–4.

[8] See R. L. Ketcham, "Conscience, War, and Politics in Pennsylvania," *William and Mary Quarterly* 20 (1963) 416–39.

following year Franklin supervised the construction of defensive forts throughout Pennsylvania.

The year 1757 saw both the publication of *The Way to Wealth*[9] and Franklin's appointment as colonial agent for the province of Pennsylvania. The post took him to London where he continued his electrical experiments. In 1759 the Philosophical Society of Edinburgh elected him an honorary member; in 1764 the province of Pennsylvania authorized him to submit a petition to change the province's charter from a proprietary one to royal status. The following year he presented to the Grenville government Pennsylvania's formal protest against the Stamp Act. His formal examination before the House of Commons concerning the repeal of the Stamp Act put him in the limelight of colonial affairs. Personally disconcerted with the growing violence of colonial protest against English misrule, Franklin nevertheless argued the colonies' case with wit and persuasion. In 1768 Franklin wrote a preface for John Dickenson's *Letters from a Farmer in Pennsylvania*. Dickenson had authored the *Declaration of Rights and Grievances* at the Stamp Act Congress. Dickenson's subsequent attack on the Townshend Acts placed him for a brief time in the forefront of colonial revolutionary protest, until the more strident voices of professional revolutionaries swept his staid legal arguments aside.

Franklin's appointment as London agent by the colonies of Georgia and New Jersey in 1769 testified to his growing reputation in the British colonies. In the same year The American Philosophical Society elected him its president. In 1771 he met David Hume.

Dismissed in 1774 from his post as deputy postmaster for the colonies for leaking the confidential Hutchinson-Oliver correspondence to knowledgeable revolutionaries back home, he began to despair of reconciling colonial and English interests. The same year saw the death of his wife. In 1775 Franklin returned to Pennsylvania, where he joined the revolutionary Philadelphia Committee of Safety, published an account of his London mission, and joined a revolutionary Committee of Secret Correspondence.

In 1776 he presided over the Constitutional Convention in Philadelphia and served on the committee which drafted the Declaration of Independence. In the same year, the Continental Congress appointed him one of three commissioners to the French court. Three years later in Paris he assumed the responsibilities of Minister Plenipotentiary to the French court where he schemed with both success and popularity to secure French military support for the colonies and against England.[10] In 1781 he functioned

[9] See C. W. Miller, "Benjamin Franklin's Way to Wealth," *Bibliographical Society of America Papers* 63 (1969) 231–46.

[10] Franklin's understanding of virtue as enlightened self-interest did not prevent him from womanizing when it served his personal, diplomatic, and political ends: see Claude

as one of the commissioners of the victorious colonies who negotiated peace and national independence from England. In 1782, together with John Jay and John Adams, he signed the treaty of Paris which terminated the American revolution.[11]

In 1785 Franklin resigned his post at the French court and returned to Philadelphia. Two years later he served as a delegate to the Constitutional Convention. In 1771 he began work on his autobiography. Seventeen years later he resumed the task. He never finished the story. He died quietly in Philadelphia on April 17, 1790.[12]

II

Journalist, factotum, diplomat, amateur moralist, scientist, author—Benjamin Franklin came to symbolize in many ways the hopes and aspirations of enlightened, middle-class colonial America during the eighteenth century. He had risen from the ranks of the hoi polloi to receive international honor in the courts of Europe. Elected as a member of academies of science and letters, Franklin embodied success, wit, tolerance, social progress, and bourgeois virtue. He used his popularity to render both revolution and Enlightenment philosophy socially respectable.

Through his inventions and entrepreneurial enterprise, Franklin made numerous practical contributions to life in the English colonies. Some of them—lightning rods, lending libraries, Franklin stoves—continue to touch our lives even today. A pioneer in American journalism, he championed

---

Lopez, *Mon Cher Papa: Franklin and the Ladies of Paris* (New Haven, Conn.: Yale University Press, 1966). See also Alfred Aldridge, *Benjamin Franklin and His French Contemporaries* (New York: New York University Press, 1957); R. Newcomb "Benjamin Franklin and Montaigne," *Modern Language Notes* 72 (1957) 489–91; Catherine M. Prelinger, "Benjamin Franklin and the American Prisoners of War in England During the American Revolution," *William and Mary Quarterly* 32 (1975) 261–94.

[11] See Esmond Wright, *Benjamin Franklin and American Independence* (London: English Universities Press, 1966); Gerald Stourzh, *Benjamin Franklin and American Foreign Policy* (Chicago: University of Chicago Press, 1954); Gerald Stourzh, "Reason and Power in Benjamin Franklin's Thought," *American Political Science Review* 47 (1953) 1092–115; Malcolm Eiselen, *Franklin's Political Theories* (Garden City, N.J.: Doubleday, 1928); Paul Connor, *Poor Richard's Politics* (New York: Oxford University Press, 1955); William Clark, *Ben Franklin's Privateers* (Baton Rouge: Louisiana State University, 1956); Eduard Baumbarten, *Benjamin Franklin: Der Lehrmeister der Amerikanischen Revolution* (Frankfurt am Main: V. Klostermann, 1936).

[12] See Carl van Doren, *Benjamin Franklin* (New York: Viking Press, 1938); Ronald W. Clark, *Benjamin Franklin* (New York: Random House, 1983); David Freeman Hawke, *Franklin* (New York: Harper & Row, 1976); Esmond Wright, *Franklin of Philadelphia* (Cambridge, Mass.: Belknap, 1986); Alfred Owen Aldridge, *Benjamin Franklin: Philosopher and Man* (Philadelphia: Lippincott, 1965).

educational reform in the colonies and played a significant role in the establishment of our national government.

Did Franklin contribute anything to the American mind? Today, some critics belittle his experiments with electricity as amateurish dabbling; but the scientists of his day took his work very seriously indeed. Franklin's study of electricity does not, however, constitute his most important contribution to culture in the United States. Perhaps one can best put Franklin into religious and philosophical perspective by contrasting him with his contemporary, Jonathan Edwards, the great puritan divine and defender of the Great Awakening.[13]

Like Edwards, Franklin's intellectual career began with a religious conversion. Edwards converted by acquiescing in the mysteries of Calvinist theology. Franklin converted to Deism. Raised a Presbyterian, Franklin found himself increasingly troubled by the Calvinist doctrines of predestination, election, and reprobation. He wrote in his autobiography:

> My parents had early given me religious impressions, and brought me
> through my childhood piously in the Dissenting way. But I was scarce fifteen,
> when after doubting by turns several points, as I found them disputed in dif-
> ferent books I read, I began to doubt of Revelation itself. Some books against
> Deism fell into my hands; they were said to be the substance of sermons,
> which had been preached at Boyle's lectures. It happened, that they wrought
> an effect on me quite contrary to what was intended by them. For the argu-
> ments of the Deists, which were quoted to be refuted, appeared to me much
> stronger than the refutations; in short I soon became a thorough Deist.[14]

In fact, theological disputation left Franklin not only dubious but bored. He regarded the squabbling of divines at best as the sterile dissection of dead religious issues, at worst as the product of the kind of narrow, sectarian spirit which had fueled both the wars of religion and religious persecution. Ministerial intolerance of other sects only settled him in an attitude of universal tolerance toward all forms of "reasonable" piety.[15] He deemed authentic religion a much simpler matter than the logic-chopping, flint-nosed theologians had made it. It sufficed to believe in a benevolent and providential creator who had made humans to worship him, to serve

---

[13] See I. W. Ward, "Who Was Benjamin Franklin?" *The American Scholar* 32 (1963) 541–53.

[14] Jared Sparks, ed., *The Works of Benjamin Franklin*, 12 vols. (Boston: Hilliard and Gray & Co., 1840) 1:74–5, 102. See Kerry Walters, "A Note on Benjamin Franklin and the Gods," *Transactions of the Charles S. Peirce Society* 31 (1995) 793–805; Richard V. Pierard, "Faith of Our Fathers: Some Post-Bicentennial Reflections," *Covenant Quarterly* 35 (1977) 15–25.

[15] See Sparks, *The Works of Benjamin Franklin*, 1:102, 104; Leonard Larabee, ed., *The Papers of Benjamin Franklin*, 24 vols. (New Haven, Conn.: Yale University Press, 1959–84) 2:88.

one another in this life, and to reap the fruits of one's virtues and vices in the life to come. He regarded these simple tenets as common to all religions. He believed that they expressed a shared human religious experience. Given the existence of one God, bickering churches, sects, and creeds had, he felt, to represent not authentic religion but non-essential human accretions.[16] Ironically, the Protestant impulse to purify religion of human abuse fueled Franklin's Deistic piety. His conversion to Deism expressed a desire to get down to the essence of religious faith, to strip away the non-essential, and to restore religion to its pristine simplicity.

III

The young Franklin learned from his Presbyterian upbringing to sniff at human vanity and foppery. Franklin, however, enjoyed burlesquing from time to time the crochets and inconsistencies of the Protestant religious establishment.[17]

Franklin's involvement in the Hemphill case confirmed him in his mistrust of all forms of sectarian religion. Ordained in Ireland, Hemphill, who preached Deism, had journeyed to Philadelphia under the cloud of heresy. Far from an original thinker, Hemphill used his pulpit in order to popularize a moralizing, rational creed. Church authorities thought he ought to be saying more about grace and redemption. In 1735 they initiated censure proceedings against him and eventually defrocked him.

Hemphill's Deistic sermons seem to have inspired in Franklin a short-lived hope for the Presbyterian Church. The censure proceedings and defrocking of Hemphill left him disillusioned and outraged. The squabble convinced Franklin that a Christian doctrine of grace necessarily implied the Calvinist doctrines of human depravity and divine predestination. Predestination, however, deprives humans of moral responsibility for their own choices, while church membership reduces them to the intellectual slaves of bigoted clerics who seek by force or deception to enforce assent to indemonstrable theological fantasies. If, however, as Franklin and Hemphill believed, Christianity finds its true foundation in human nature alone, then one can reduce the essence of religion to simple moral precepts easily intelligible to the common man or woman. Such a religion stimulates virtuous behavior and promises suitable rewards and punishments both in this life and in the next.[18]

---

[16] Larabee, *The Papers of Benjamin Franklin,* 2:44.

[17] Ibid., 2:15, 18–19, 22, 30–1, 40, 42; see also A. O. Aldridge, "Religious Hoax by Benjamin Franklin," *American Literature* 36 (1964) 204–9; Charles Mabee, "Benjamin Franklin's Literary Response to Dogmatic Religion," *American Journal of Theology and Philosophy* 31 (1982) 60–8.

[18] Larabee, *The Papers of Benjamin Franklin,* 50–64.

Never attuned to the subtleties of theological argument, Franklin in his defense of Hemphill fought for three fundamental religious values: the individual right to decide one's own religious beliefs, intellectual tolerance in religious matters, and faith in God's universal salvific will. He found a better vindication of such beliefs in Deism than in Calvinism. Franklin assailed the idea that conversion gives one assurance of divine election as hypocritical religious self-righteousness. Salvation results, he argued, not from instant supernatural transformation, but from patient moral effort. Far better to portray religion as the inculcation of sound moral principles than to lead humans into the illusion of believing that God has predestined them to live virtuous lives. Far better to hold people responsible for their own choices than to dupe them into believing that an arbitrary divine decree has destined them irrevocably for either heaven or hell.[19]

Calvinism had, of course, distinguished justification from sanctification and had preached moral living and moral responsibility. Against some strains of "new light" rhetoric, Jonathan Edwards had insisted that Christian practice offers the ultimate sign that one is responding to the action of supernatural grace. Franklin, however, sensed a tension between Calvinist moralizing and a predestinationist creed. A rationalizing Arminian, Franklin saw that in a deterministic, predestinationist universe, only God in the last analysis exercises real freedom of choice and enjoys moral responsibility. Deny troublesome theological beliefs like depravity and predestination, and the tension disappears.

Franklin denounced Hemphill's trial as a Presbyterian version of the Catholic Inquisition. "The Reverend Inquisitors," he jibed, "go to Prayer, they call upon God to direct them in every [one] of their Censures (altho' they have unanimously determined to condemn all who are so unfortunate as to be call'd before them)." Franklin accused Hemphill's judges of the same injustice and hypocrisy. He flailed them for suppressing and falsifying evidence and for forcing the defendant to testify against himself. The desire to foment ignorance, error, mindless enthusiasm, and superstition motivated their animus against Hemphill. The purely rational religion which Hemphill preached condemned all of these vicious abuses of religious authority.[20]

Finally, Franklin argued that only natural religion can offer the hope of salvation to all people. If God really desires the salvation of all, Franklin argued, would the deity not have spoken his message of salvation through a medium accessible to all? No sectarian creed enjoys the same accessibility as the book of nature. The religion of grace and of predestining divine election propounded by Hemphill's judges in effect excluded

[19] Ibid., 52–7.
[20] Ibid., 64–7.

people of universal good will like Hemphill from the ranks of the Church. The restriction of divine election to Church members in good standing only rationalized narrow-minded, religious intolerance and bigotry.[21]

As a moment in the development of Presbyterianism in the United States, the Hemphill incident amounted to a tempest in a very small Philadelphia teapot, but it marked an important turning point in Franklin's religious development. It brought his disillusionment with sectarian religion to a culmination, convinced him that Calvinist theology simply rationalizes religious bigotry and intolerance, and confirmed him in his Deistic creed.[22]

IV

Much earlier Franklin had sown the seeds which bore fruit in his assault on the Presbyterian clergy of Philadelphia. Ten years before the Hemphill trial Franklin had first written then withdrawn his *Dissertation on Liberty and Necessity, Pleasure and Pain*. In defending Hemphill, he had vindicated the freedom of the individual conscience in religious matters. In the *Dissertation* he had argued against the possibility of freedom in a predestinationist universe. The argument in the *Dissertation* sought to dramatize the indefensibility of predestinationist theology. If God really enjoys omnipotence, argued the young Franklin, whatever the deity wills necessarily happens, no matter how theologians try to disguise the fact with nice, abstract distinctions. If, moreover, God exemplifies infinite goodness, then whatever happens as a result of the divine decree must also enjoy an analogous goodness. The creatures of an omnipotent and good God must, then, perform only good and virtuous acts. Jacobus Arminius, in his theological attempt to avoid the logical consequences of Calvinistic predestination, had argued for a modicum of freedom in fallen humanity. Franklin, probably with tongue in cheek, argued from belief in predestination to the impossibility of either freedom or sin.[23]

---

[21] Ibid., 117–22.

[22] See Alfred Aldridge, *Benjamin Franklin and Nature's God* (Durham, S.C.: Duke University Press, 1967); James Stifler, *The Religion of Benjamin Franklin* (New York: Appleton, 1925); Melvin H. Buxbaum, *Benjamin Franklin and the Zealous Presbyterians* (University Park: Pennsylvania State University Press, 1975); David Williams, "More Light on Franklin's Religious Ideas," *American Historical Review* 43 (1938) 803–13; Charles L. Sanford, "An American Pilgrim's Progress," *American Quarterly* 6 (1954) 297–310; I. Bernard Cohen, *Benjamin Franklin: His Contributions to the American Tradition* (Indianapolis: Bobbs-Merrill, 1953).

[23] See Larabee, *The Papers of Benjamin Franklin,* 1:465–6; A. Owen Aldridge, "Benjamin Franklin and Philosophical Necessity," *Modern Language Quarterly* 12 (1951) 292–309.

In his autobiography Franklin says that he withdrew the *Dissertation* because of shortcomings in its "metaphysical reasonings."[24] He probably realized that the vindication of human freedom and responsibility counted more than exposing contradictions in the Calvinist evangelical scheme. Franklin did not, however, repudiate every position which he developed in the *Dissertation.* Its second half pondered the relationship between virtue, on the one hand, and pleasure and pain, on the other. In the second half of the *Dissertation* Franklin argued that the avoidance of pain in the end motivates all human activity. He concluded therefore that humans lack the capacity to make completely disinterested choices.[25] The mature Franklin seems to have discarded the psychology of human action which he proposed in the *Dissertation* as simplistic; but he never discarded the idea that even virtuous action expresses self-interest. In the *Dissertation* Franklin taught that self-love exemplifies "the only and irresistible motive" for action.[26] Two years following the Hemphill incident, Poor Richard offered the following bit of doggerel to his fellow citizens:

> *Self Love* but serves the virtuous mind to wake,
> As the small Pebble stirs the peaceful Lake;
> The Centre mov'd, a Circle strait succeeds,
> Another still, and still another spreads,
> Friend, Parent, Neighbor, first it will embrace,
> His country next, and next all human race;
> Wide and more wide, th' o'erflowing of the Mind
> Takes every Creature in of every kind.[27]

Poor Richard had dissociated self-love from the determinism which the *Dissertation* defended, but self-love remained the stimulus to every form of virtuous activity.

Even as late as the autobiography Franklin continued to defend the identity between virtue and self-love. In recalling his life story he noted that he had projected but never written a book on "The Art of Virtue." Had he written it, he would have tried to demonstrate "that vicious actions are not hurtful because they are forbidden, but forbidden because they are hurtful." Virtuous activity always advances human good; and for that reason virtue must always exemplify enlightened self-interest. In desiring virtue one cannot help but desire one's own good. Franklin apparently found no difficulty in living with the ethical ambiguity which such a moral doctrine inculcates.

[24] Sparks, *The Works of Benjamin Franklin,* 1:75–6.
[25] Larabee, *The Papers of Benjamin Franklin,* 1:63–4.
[26] Ibid., 1:65.
[27] Ibid., 2:5.

Having equated virtue with enlightened self-interest, Franklin next enshrined virtue at the heart of religion. Shortly before the Hemphill incident Franklin conceived a "bold and arduous project of arriving at *moral perfection.*" By systematically cultivating virtue, Franklin believed that he could avoid ever making a morally vicious choice. This ambitious program of moral self-improvement rested on the Enlightenment's belief in the fundamental innocence and integrity of human nature. As humans proceed from the hand of God, they come fully equipped by nature to do good and avoid evil.[28]

Franklin especially prized two virtues: philanthropic benevolence and tolerance. One serves God best, Franklin believed, by serving other people. His various philanthropic ventures from the Philadelphia fire department to the University of Pennsylvania expressed this fundamental religious belief. At one point in his life Franklin even dreamed of founding a religious sect called "The United Party for Virtue" in order to promote similar benevolent projects. The attempt at church founding never got off the ground.[29]

The virtue of tolerance exemplified admirably for Franklin how the cultivation of virtue serves the virtuous person's own self-interest. The tolerant person makes an agreeable companion and affability supplies one of the important ingredients in cultivating worldly success. Franklin's tolerance extended to every religious creed. "Talking against Religion," Poor Richard warned, "is unchaining the Tyger; the Beast let loose may worry his deliverer."[30] He repeated the same advice to an unknown correspondent in 1757. The addressee, possibly Thomas Paine, had sent Franklin a manuscript attacking the idea of particular providences. Recalling perhaps his own *Dissertation,* Franklin discouraged publication. The work attacked a basic religious belief, Franklin counseled, and while he allowed that the true philosopher could practice virtue for its own sake without such doctrinal props, still most people needed the support of creedal formulas in order to lead virtuous lives.[31] Sectarian creeds have justification as long as they motivate virtuous living.[32]

Franklin's bourgeois benevolence toward the young prompted him to inculcate over and over those virtues which foster rapid financial

[28] Sparks, *The Works of Benjamin Franklin,* 1:104–16. See Norman S. Fiering, "Benjamin Franklin and the Way to Virtue," *American Quarterly* 30 (1978) 199–223.

[29] Sparks, *The Works of Benjamin Franklin,* 1:120.

[30] Larabee, *The Papers of Benjamin Franklin,* 4:96; 7:82.

[31] See R. L. Bushman, "On the Uses of Psychology: Conflict and Conciliation in Benjamin Franklin," *History and Theory* 5 (1966) 225–40.

[32] Larabee, *The Papers of Benjamin Franklin,* 7:294–5; Carol Van Doren, *Benjamin Franklin* (New York: World, 1948); Gladys Meyer, *Free Trade in Ideas* (New York: Kings Crown, 1941); Ralph Ketcham, *Benjamin Franklin* (New York: Washington Square, 1965); James Campbell, "The Pragmatism of Benjamin Franklin," *Transactions of the Charles S. Peirce Society* 31 (1995) 745–92.

advancement: industry, frugality, punctuality, honesty, truthfulness, discipline, and useful education.[33] He realized that happiness requires more than just financial success. Serenity of soul, peace of conscience, trust in God, health of mind and of body, the esteem of other persons—all these things enhance human contentment; but all these blessings follow upon the cultivation of basic bourgeois morality.[34]

Franklin's faith in the natural rewards of virtue confirmed him in his rejection of belief in supernatural, justifying faith. In 1764, Franklin wrote George Whitefield:

> Your frequently repeated Wishes and Prayers for my Eternal as well as temporal Happiness are very obliging. I can only thank you for them, and offer you mine in return. I have my self no Doubts that I shall enjoy as much of both as is proper for me. That Being who gave me Existence, and thro' almost threescore Years has been continually showering his Favours upon me, whose very chastisements have been Blessings to me, can I doubt that he loves me? And if he loves me, can I doubt he will go on to take care of me not only here but hereafter? This to some may seem Presumption; to me it appears the best grounded Hope; Hope of the Future; built on Experience of the Past.[35]

Franklin's benevolent philosophical religion blended Deism with bourgeois morality. The American Deists who followed him, however, did not, as others have often noted, always emulate his tolerance of morally benign creedal religion.

V

Although contemporaries, Jonathan Edwards and Benjamin Franklin never met. Naming the issues which divided the two men, however, helps clarify Franklin's relationship to the religious establishment of his day. Franklin stood for a religion rooted in nature; Edwards, for one founded in supernatural grace. Franklin held for the possibility of universal salvation; Edwards, for an infralapsarian doctrine of divine predestination. Franklin believed that one could demonstrate the reasonableness of religious assent; Edwards discovered religious assent in cordial consent to the mystery of divine excellence incarnate. A Calvinist divine, Edwards defended the doctrinal integrity of sacramental worship; Franklin sought to free religion from its creedal and sacramental trappings by reducing it to its rational, philosophical essence. Both men believed in divine provi-

---

[33] Larabee, *The Papers of Benjamin Franklin,* 3:306–8, 352, 397–8, 480; 7:340–50; 8:124–30.

[34] Ibid., 1:262; 6:325.

[35] Ibid., 11:231–2.

dence. For Edwards, however, providence took the form of divine predestination, while Franklin reduced providence for all practical purposes to God's execution of a benevolent system of rewards and punishments for naturally cultivated virtues and vices. Edwards deemed conversion to the evangelical scheme an indispensable prelude to personal sanctification. Franklin thought religious conversion a non-essential but pragmatically justifiable aid to the cultivation of natural virtue. Franklin promoted the toleration of all morally sound religious beliefs as an aid to virtuous benevolence; Edwards demanded universal human assent to the mystery of God incarnate. Franklin believed that virtuous action always exemplifies enlightened self-interest; Edwards rejected Franklin's view of virtue as fallacious and defined "true virtue" as the cordial consent of being to Being-in-general. By that Edwards meant that only conformity of human consent to the holiness of divine consent rectifies the human conscience. Edwards conceded that human nature left to itself could consent to a limited number of natural goods, but Edwards denied that one could love with the universality which the gospel demands without the help of divine grace. Franklin affirmed the natural integrity of human nature in religious as well as in secular matters. Edwards defended the Great Awakening and insisted that the greater part of religion consists of graced affections. In the wake of the Great Awakening, Poor Richard warned: "If *Passion* drives, let Reason hold the Reins."[36] A convinced Calvinist, Edwards nevertheless saw himself defending the shared faith of Christians throughout the ages, as his *History of Salvation* makes clear. Franklin regarded religious belief as a matter of individual preference.[37]

---

[36] Ibid., 3:340.

[37] See David Levin, ed., *The Puritan in the Enlightenment: Franklin and Edwards* (Chicago: Rand McNally, 1963); Perry Miller, *Jonathan Edwards* (New York: Sloan Associates, 1949); David D. Brand, *Profile of the Last Puritan: Jonathan Edwards, Self-Love, and the Dawn of the Beatific* (Atlanta: Scholars Press, 1991); Edward H. Davidson, *Jonathan Edwards: The Narrative of a Puritan Mind* (Boston: Houghton Mifflin, 1966); Elizabeth D. Dodds, *Marriage to a Difficult Man: The "Uncommon Union" of Jonathan and Sarah Edwards* (Philadelphia: Westminster Press, 1971); Douglas J. Elwood, *The Philosophical Theology of Jonathan Edwards* (New York: Columbia University Press, 1960); Joseph A. Conforti, *Jonathan Edwards, Religious Tradition, and American Culture* (Chapel Hill: University of North Carolina Press, 1995); Norman Fiering, *Jonathan Edwards's Moral Thought and Its British Context* (Chapel Hill: University of North Carolina Press, 1981); Edwin M. Griffin, *Jonathan Edwards* (Minneapolis: University of Minnesota Press, 1971); "Edwards and the Ethical Question," Harvard Theological Review 60 (1967) 163–75; Clyde A. Holbrook, *The Ethics of Jonathan Edwards: Morality and Aesthetics* (Ann Arbor: University of Michigan Press, 1973); Iain H. Murray, *Jonathan Edwards: A New Biography* (Edinburgh: Banner of Truth Trust, 1987); Gerald R. McDermott, *One Holy and Happy Society: The Public Thought of Jonathan Edwards* (University Park: Pennsylvania

Franklin also dramatizes why middle-class Americans began to turn to Deism in the latter part of the eighteenth century. Franklin felt fed up with the clericalism of the established churches as well as disgusted with Christianity's sectarian fragmentation and with the intolerance of self-proclaimed Christians. Religious persecution among Christians and the wars of religion caused him to associate supernatural faith with irrationality and vice.

Besides these passionate attitudes of the heart, Franklin had intellectual reasons for embracing Deism. He had seen through the least tenable doctrines of Calvinistic Augustinianism: total human depravity, divine predestination, the necessitarian denial of freedom of choice. Franklin, moreover, turned classical Protestant criticism of institutionalized hypocrisy

---

State University Press, 1992); Paula M. Cooey, *Jonathan Edwards on Nature and Destiny: A Systematic Analysis* (Lewiston, N.Y.: Edwin Mellen Press, 1985); Robert W. Jensen, *America's Theologian: A Recommendation of Jonathan Edwards* (New York: Oxford University Press, 1988); Harold P. Simonson, *Jonathan Edwards: Theologian of the Heart* (Grand Rapids, Mich.: Eerdmans, 1974); Clyde A. Holbrook, *Jonathan Edwards, The Valley and Nature* (Cranbury, N.J.: Associated University Presses, 1987); James Carse, *Jonathan Edwards and the Visibility of God* (New York: Scribner's, 1967); Nathan O. Hatch and Harry S. Stout, eds., *Jonathan Edwards and the American Experience* (Amherst: University of Massachusetts Press, 1980); James Playsted Wood, *Mr. Jonathan Edwards* (New York: Seabury Press, 1968); Stephen R. Yarborough and John C. Adams, *Delightful Conviction: Jonathan Edwards and the Rhetoric of Conversion* (Westport, Conn.: Greenwood Press, 1993); John Opie, ed., *Jonathan Edwards and the Enlightenment* (Lexington, Mass.: Heath, 1969); Patricia Tracy, *Jonathan Edwards, Pastor: Religion and Society in Eighteenth-Century Northampton* (New York: Hill and Wang, 1979); Roland Delattre, *Beauty and Sensibility in the Thought of Jonathan Edwards* (New Haven, Conn.: Yale University Press, 1968); Mark Valeri, "The Economic Thought of Jonathan Edwards," *Church History* 60 (1991) 37–54; John F. Jamieson, "Jonathan Edwards's Change of Position on Stoddardeanism," *Harvard Theological Review* 74 (1981) 79–99; Donald L. Weddle, "The Melancholy Saint: Jonathan Edwards's Interpretation of David Brainerd as a Model of Evangelical Spirituality," *Harvard Theological Review* 81 (1988) 297–318; Janice Knight, "Learning the Language of God: Jonathan Edwards and the Typology of Nature," *William and Mary Quarterly Review* 48 (1991) 531–51; Gordon Miller, "Edwards's Sublime Book of Nature," *History Today* 46 (1996) 29–35; Robert Lee Stuart, "Jonathan Edwards and the Cheerfulness of Pleasantness," *American Literature* 48 (1976) 46–59; Norman Pettit, "Prelude to Mission: Brainerd's Expulsion from Yale," *New England Quarterly* 59 (1986) 28–50; James E. Hamilton and Edward H. Madden, "Edwards, Finney, and Mahan on the Derivation of Duties," *Journal of the History of Philosophy* 13 (1975) 347–60; Sang Hyun Lee, *The Philosophical Theology of Jonathan Edwards* (Princeton, N.J.: Princeton University Press, 1988); Allen C. Guelzo, "From Calvinist Metaphysics to Republican Theory: Jonathan Edwards and James Dana on Freedom of the Will," *Journal of the History of Ideas* 56 (1995) 399–418; Ava Chamberlain, "The Grand Sower of the Seed: Jonathan Edwards's Critique of George Whitefield," *New England Quarterly* 70 (1997) 368–85; Hans Oberdiek, "Jonathan Edwards," *American Philosophy,* ed. Markus Singe (Cambridge, Mass.: Cambridge University Press, 1985) 191–213.

in the Roman Church on the now long established mainline Protestant churches. In the process, Franklin secularized Protestant reforming zeal and claimed the higher moral ground for a naturalized, rational religion.

In addition to having emotional, rational, and religious appeal, Franklin's Deism had social motives as well. The case of Franklin makes it clear that Deism fitted well the conscious religious preferences of an emerging American bourgeoisie. Deism simplified religion and dispensed with the rigors (and, from a lay standpoint, with the tedium) of theological thought and disputation. Anyone could understand the rather simplistic Deistic creed and could do so without much thinking. Deism's bland reasonableness also took the terror out of any converted religious encounter with the *tremendum et fascinosum* and it endowed a shallow bourgeois morality with a fallacious religious aura. Franklin's Deism assured an increasingly prosperous middle class to regard financial and political success as the natural rewards of virtuous religious living, and Poor Richard's disciples learned to deny any distinction between virtuous action and the enlightened pursuit of one's own individual, personal interests. Belief in human perfectibility also appealed to shallow middle-class optimism.

Chapter 2

THE RELIGION OF REVOLUTION

When a man seriously reflects on the idolatrous
homage which is paid to the persons of Kings,
he need not wonder that the Almighty,
ever jealous of his honor,
should disapprove of a form of government
which so impiously invades
the prerogatives of heaven.

—Thomas Paine

I

The architects of the Constitution of the United States endorsed the proposal of Baron de la Brede et de Montesquieu that the powers of government ought to divide into the executive, the legislative, and the judiciary. More than any other thinker, however, John Locke's *Two Treatises of Government,* published in 1690, enunciated the Enlightenment principles which lie at the basis of government in the United States.

Locke's two treatises targeted two very different adversaries: Sir Robert Filmer and Thomas Hobbes. In 1680 Filmer, in a study entitled *Patriarcha,* proposed a flimsy theological justification of the divine right of kings. He derived the absolute power of monarchs from the allegedly "paternal authority" which Adam exercised over the whole human race and which he derived directly from God.[1] Locke's first treatise demolished

---

[1] See Sir Robert Filmer, *Patriarcha and Other Political Works,* ed. Peter Laslett (Oxford: Blackwell, 1949); B. King, "Dryden's Ark: The Influence of Filmer," *Studies in English Literature* 7 (1967) 403–14. For the relationship between Filmer and Hobbes see G. J.

Filmer's exegetical fantasies with comparative ease,[2] but he found a more formidable adversary in Thomas Hobbes. In *Leviathan,* Hobbes combined a mechanistic theory of human activity with belief in human moral depravity in order to frame a classic argument for the necessity of totalitarian government. In Hobbes's mythology of government, the human race in the beginning lived in a state of pure nature characterized by the human propensity to promote individual self-interest. Conflicting self-interests transformed the state of nature into a state of war until a social contract terminated both states by ceding to an absolute ruler power to impose order and stability on natural human chaos.[3]

Locke replaced Hobbes's dark myth of governmental origins with a more optimistic myth of his own. He endorsed Hobbes's belief in a natural state prior to the creation of political authority, but Locke replaced Hobbes's sinister portrait of human natural selfishness and violence with a sunnier depiction of human reasonableness. In the state of nature, reason, not selfish depravity, characterized human activity. Reasonable shared interests motivated the social contract, namely, the protection of

Schochet, "Thomas Hobbes on the Family and the State of Nature," *Political Science Quarterly* 82 (1967) 427–45.

[2] See H. H. Rowern, "Second Thoughts on Locke's First Treatise," *Journal of the History of Ideas* 17 (1956) 130–2.

[3] See J. Watkins, *Hobbes's System of Ideas: A Study in the Political Significance of Philosophical Ideas* (London: Hutchinson, 1965); Crawford Macpherson, *The Political Theory of Possessive Individualism: Hobbes and Locke* (Oxford: Clarendon Press, 1962); Howard Warrender, *The Political Philosophy of Thomas Hobbes* (Oxford: Clarendon Press, 1957); Leo Strauss, *The Political Philosophy of Hobbes* (Chicago: University of Chicago Press, 1952); F. McNeilly, *The Anatomy of Leviathan* (New York: St. Martin's Press, 1968); Samuel Mintz, *The Hunting of Leviathan: Seventeenth-Century Reactions to the Materialism and Moral Philosophy of Thomas Hobbes* (Cambridge: Cambridge University Press, 1962); Raymond Polin, *Politique et philosophie chez Thomas Hobbes* (Paris: Presses Universitaires de France, 1953); Raymond Polin, "La nature humaine selon Hobbes," *Revue Philosophique* 142 (1952) 31–52; Eugène Roesch, *The Totalitarian Threat* (New York: Philosophical Library, 1963); A. Levy, "Economic Views of Thomas Hobbes," *Journal of the History of Ideas* 15 (1954) 589–95; H. Warrender, "Political Philosophy of Hobbes: His Theory of Obligation," *Political Studies* 5 (1956) 389–405; C. Williamson, "Contradiction in Hobbes' Analysis of Sovereignty," *Canadian Journal of Economic and Political Science* 32 (1966) 202–19; Charles D. Tarlton, "Levitating Leviathan: Glosses on a Theme in Hobbes," *Ethics* 88 (1977) 1–19; Gregory S. Kavka, "Hobbes's War of All Against All," *Ethics* 93 (1983) 291–310; Robert A. Grover, "The Legal Origins of Thomas Hobbes's Doctrine of Contract," *Journal of the History of Religion* 18 (1980) 177–207; Ronald Beiner, "Machiavelli, Hobbes, and Rousseau on Civil Religion," *Review of Politics* 54 (1992) 5–33; Donald W. Hanson, "Reconsidering Hobbes's Conventionalism," *Review of Politics* 53 (1991) 627–51; Mark C. Murphy, "Was Hobbes a Legal Positivist?" *Ethics* 105 (1995) 846–73.

life, liberty, and property. Because people create governments, no government in fact enjoys absolute authority. The executive branch must obey the legislative, which submits in turn to popular control by those governed. When despotic and tyrannical rulers exceed the limits placed on their authority, then power reverts to the people to create a new government which better serves their needs.[4]

In Lockean political theory, the social contract creates human social and political relationships. Such a theory implicitly portrays social relations as artificial and therefore replaceable, and it tends to conceive individuals prior to the social contract as isolated and unrelated.

If thinkers like Locke and Montesquieu gave the American revolution its mind; the Great Awakening probably helped give it its heart. The leaders of the American revolution included Deists like Benjamin Franklin, Tom Paine, and Thomas Jefferson, but among the clergy those inclined to Enlightenment religion tended as a group to ally themselves with colonial moneyed interests, and those interests tended in politics to remain royalist and Tory rather than to turn nationalist and revolutionary. Those same liberal,

---

[4] See John Locke, *The Second Treatise of Government,* ed. Thomas Peardon (New York: Bobbs Merrill, 1952); Daniel O'Connor, *John Locke: A Critical Introduction* (London: Penguin, 1952); Raymond Poulin, *La politique morale de John Locke* (Paris: Presses Universitaires de France, 1960); M. Seliger, *The Liberal Politics of John Locke: An Historical Account of the Argument of the Two Treatises of Government* (London: Cambridge, 1969); M. Seliger, "Locke's Theory of Revolutionary Action," *Western Political Quarterly* 16 (1963) 548–68; J. E. Parsons, "Locke's Doctrine of Property," *Social Research* 36 (1969) 389–411; H. Moulds, "Private Property in John Locke's State of Nature," *American Journal of Economics and Sociology* 23 (1964) 179–88; A. Ryan, "Locke and the Dictatorship of the Bourgeoisie," *Political Studies* 13 (1965) 107–16; B.Wishey, "John Locke and the Spirit of '76," *Political Science Quarterly* 73 (1958) 413–25; J. W. Yolston, "Locke on the Law of Nature," *Philosophical Review* 67 (1958) 477–98; M. J. Osler, "John Locke and the Changing Ideal of Scientific Knowledge," *Journal of the History of Ideas* 31 (1970) 3–16; C. Thompson, "John Locke and New England Transcendentalism," *New England Quarterly* 35 (1962) 435–57; Richard Cox, *Locke on War and Peace* (Oxford: Clarendon Press, 1960); John Dunn, *The Political Thought of John Locke: An Historical Account of the Argument of the Two Treatises of Government* (Cambridge: Cambridge University Press, 1969); S. Edwards, "Political Philosophy Belimed: The Case of John Locke," *Political Studies* 17 (1969) 273–93; Walter Euchner, *Naturrecht und Politik bei John Locke* (Frankfurt am Main: Europaische Verlaganstalt, 1969); John Gough, *John Locke's Political Philosophy* (Oxford: Clarendon Press, 1956); Samuel Hefelbower, *The Relation of John Locke to English Deism* (Chicago: University of Chicago Press, 1918); H. Kelsen, "Foundations of Democracy: Property and Freedom in the Natural Law Doctrine of John Locke," *Ethics* 66 (1955) 86–90; Willimoore Kendall, *John Locke and the Doctrine of Majority Rule* (Urbana: University of Illinois Press, 1941); John Kraus, *John Locke: Empiricist, Atomist, Conceptualist, Agnostic* (New York: Philosophical Library, 1968); Sterling Lamprecht, *The Moral and Political Philosophy of John Locke* (New York: Russell & Russell, 1962); Crawford Macpherson, *The Political Theory of Possessive Individualism: Hobbes and Locke* (Oxford:

rationalizing ministers had opposed the Great Awakening, but the "new light" ministers who had preached the Great Awakening identified with the unwashed masses they evangelized. As a group, "new light" ministers demanded of civil servants the same ideals of selfless public service which they expected of their fellow clergymen. In the course of preaching the Awakening they had accustomed themselves to resisting the establishment. As a group they tended to ally themselves with those colonists who opposed tyranny and oppression.[5]

In addition, the more theologically conservative ministers endorsed belligerency more freely than their more liberal counterparts who flirted with some form of Enlightenment theology but feared that war with England would upset a healthy balance of trade.[6] Awakened ministers, by contrast, tended to hail the French and Indian War as an Armageddon, as a final, bloody scouring of Papist heresy from the American continent, and they invoked the curse of Meroz on those who shrank from the fight. Their opposition to the establishment of an Anglican bishop over all the colonies took the form of a crusade for religious liberty. Subsequent British encroachments on colonial liberty together with incidents like the Boston massacre tended to confirm conservative Calvinist ministers in their belief that the king and those who served him had allied themselves with the selfish interests of the moneyed and the unconverted. When revolution finally dawned, the conservative Calvinist ministers served first and longest

---

Clarendon Press, 1962); F. Marini, "John Locke and the Revision of Classical Democratic Theory," *Western Political Quarterly* 22 (1969) 5–18; H. Moulds, "John Locke and Rugged Individualism," *American Journal of Economics and Sociology* 24 (1965) 97–109; Barbara Arneil, *John Locke and America: The Defense of Colonialism* (Oxford: Clarendon Press, 1996); A. John Simmons, *The Lockean Theory of Rights* (Princeton, N.J.: Princeton University Press, 1992); A. John Simmons, *On the Edge of Anarchy: Locke, Consent, and the Limits of Society* (Princeton, N.J.: Princeton University Press, 1993); James Tully, *An Approach to Political Philosophy: Locke in Context* (Cambridge: Cambridge University Press, 1993); Edward J. Harpham, *John Locke's Two Treatises of Government: New Interpretations* (Wichita: University Press of Kansas, 1992); David Foster, "Taming the Father: John Locke's Critique of Patriarchal Fatherhood," *Review of Politics* 56 (1994) 641–70; Mary B. Walsh, "Locke and Feminism on Private and Public Realms of Activity," *Review of Politics* 56 (1995) 252–77; John Kilcullen, "Locke on Political Obligation," *Review of Politics* 45 (1983) 323–44; Jeremy Waldron, "John Locke: Social Contract Versus Political Anthropology," *Review of Politics* 51 (1989) 3–28; Joshua Mitchell, "John Locke and the Theological Foundations of Liberal Toleration: A Christian Dialectic of History," *Review of Politics* 52 (1990) 64–83.

[5] See Emory Elliot, "The Dove and the Serpent: The Clergy in the American Revolution," *American Quarterly* 31 (1979) 187–203.

[6] See Conrad Wright, *The Beginnings of Unitarianism in America* (Boston: Beacon Press, 1955); Conrad Wright, *The Liberal Christians* (Boston: Beacon Press, 1970).

The Religion of Revolution 23

in the field, urging the troops to win their freedom by responding to God's clear call to arms.[7]

In 1765 John Adams expressed the sense of high moral and religious purpose which opposition to the crown could stir in colonial hearts. In his *Dissertation on the Canon and the Feudal Law,* Adams discovered the same sort of tyranny operative in both legal systems. The Protestant reformation had, he claimed, overthrown the despotic pretensions of the canonical code by declaring independence from papal domination. The Puritans had subsequently laid the foundations for an ideal Protestant commonwealth in America, but monarchical tyranny still threatened that high religious and social ideal. Colonial opposition to royal oppression and the overthrow of a monarchical feudal system would, therefore, complete the great work that the Protestant reformation had begun.[8]

Adams exhorted the Protestant churches to sound the trumpet of liberation from all forms of religious and medieval tyranny:

> Let the pulpit resound with the doctrines and sentiments of religious liberty. Let us hear the danger of thraldom to our consciences from ignorance, extreme poverty, and dependence, in short from civil and political slavery. Let us see delineated before us the true map of man. Let us hear the dignity of his nature, and the noble rank he holds among the works of God,—that consenting to slavery is a sacrilegious breach of trust, as offensive in the sight of God as it is derogatory from our own honor or interest or happiness,— and that God Almighty has promulgated from heaven, liberty, peace, and good-will to man![9]

In point of fact, feudalism, while far from perfectly just, had functioned in less tyrannical ways than the absolute monarchies of the eighteenth century, but the rhetoric of revolution rarely troubles with such

---

[7] See Alan Heimert, *Religion and the American Mind: From the Great Awakening to the Revolution* (Cambridge: Harvard University Press, 1966); Alan Heimert and Perry Miller, *The Great Awakening: Documents Illustrating the Crisis and Its Consequences* (Indianapolis: Bobbs-Merrill, 1967).

[8] See Leonard Kriegel, ed., *Essential Works of the Founding Fathers* (New York: Bantam Books, 1964) 6–22. For an assessment of the impact of biblical thinking on the American revolution see Mark A. Noll, "The Bible in Revolutionary America," *The Bible in American Law, Politics, and Political Rhetoric,* ed. James Turner Johnson (Philadelphia: Fortress Press, 1985) 39–60.

[9] Kriegel, ed., *Essential Works of the Founding Fathers*, 20. See Andrew Rec, "The Philosophical Background of the American Constitution(s)," *American Philosophy,* ed. Markus Singe (Cambridge, Mass.: Cambridge University Press, 1985) 273–93; David M. Post, "Jefferson's Revisions of Locke: Education, Property Rights, and Liberty," *Journal of the History of Ideas* 47 (1986) 147–57; John G. Buchanan, "The Justice of America's Cause: Revolutionary Rhetoric in the Sermons of Samuel Cooper," *New England Quarterly* 50 (1977) 101–24.

niceties. Moreover, the chord which Adams struck in 1765 found resonance in the revolutionary writings of Thomas Paine. More than any other individual perhaps, Tom Paine fused the mind and the heart of the American revolution and consecrated both of them on the altar of national independence, and during the darkest hours of the revolution his writings kept the flickering flame of resistance from dying out.

II

Thomas Paine was born on January 29, 1737, in Thetford, England. He was raised a Quaker, but already as a child he had rejected a Calvinist theology of atonement. He left grammar school at the age of thirteen and in his teens he served aboard a British privateer, *The King of Prussia.* At twenty he took up the trade of stay-making in London. He married Mary Lambert on September 21, 1759, but she died within a few months. Admitted into the civil service, he found himself first dismissed for negligence and subsequently restored to office. In 1767 he taught in Kensington. Two years later he took a second wife, Elizabeth Ollive, but they separated in 1774, probably because of Paine's mounting debts.

In October of the same year Paine set sail for the American colonies. There he found his true metier: journalism. Until 1775 he edited the *Pennsylvania Magazine.* In it on March 8, 1774, Paine published an article attacking the institution of slavery, and in a series of articles entitled "Common Sense" he argued the case for colonial independence from England. During the revolution his *Crisis* tracts sustained the morale of the beleaguered colonial troops. In 1781 Paine participated without distinction in an embassy to Paris and subsequently returned to America.[10]

After the American revolution Paine's public image suffered as a result of his support for unpopular tax measures. He withdrew temporarily from politics and began to promote the construction of span bridges. With this engineering feat as his goal, he set sail for France in 1787, where he found himself increasingly embroiled in revolutionary activity. In February 1791 he wrote *The Rights of Man,* a reply to Edmund Burke's attack on the French revolution.[11] Robespierre rewarded him with French citizenship, and in 1792 Paine successfully gained a seat in the National Assembly. There his voice joined the handful who opposed the trial and execution of the French king.

[10] Stuart Andrews, "Paine's American Pamphlets," *History Today* 31 (1981) 7–11.

[11] See R. Fennessy, *Burke, Paine, and the Rights of Man* (The Hague: M. Nyhoff, 1963); Ray Browne, ed., *The Burke-Paine Controversy: Texts and Criticism* (New York: Harcourt, Brace & World, 1963); S. B. Purdy, "Note on the Burke-Paine Controversy," *American Literature* 39 (1967) 373–5.

Paine's disillusionment with the excesses of the French revolution grew, and he published *The Age of Reason* partly in order to combat on Deistic grounds the growth of irreligion in France. Paine scarcely had time to smuggle the manuscript to Joel Barlow before the gendarmes arrested him and marched him off to the Luxemburg Prison. There he languished with fever and only by chance escaped the guillotine. On November 4, 1794, James Monroe secured his release.[12] He regained his seat in the National Assembly and served there until the adoption of the new French constitution. Between 1795 and 1796 he published Agrarian Justice and other political and economic tracts.[13] Cantankerous to the end, in an open letter he accused George Washington of having conspired in his arrest and imprisonment. In 1802, at the invitation of President Jefferson, Paine returned to the United States only to find that his Deistic writings and his attack on Washington had transformed him into something of a pariah. He retired to New York, where in July 1806, he suffered an apoplectic seizure. He died on June 8, 1809, a lonely and a broken man.[14]

A quarrelsome man, Paine possessed the temperament of a revolutionary. A convinced Deist, Paine the propagandist did not hesitate to play on popular religious feelings when it suited his political purposes. In *Common Sense* and in *The Crisis,* he appealed to the millenarian expectations of the American people by promising them a new era of peace and prosperity once they had purged the land of British corruption. He invoked the authority of the Bible in order to convict the crown of villainy and in order to establish the righteousness of the colonial cause. He spoke of the predestined march of history, whose progress the divine enemy of all popery and tyranny had decreed. He proclaimed the overthrow of royal authority a holy cause and those who gave their lives for it martyrs for a sacred truth.

In his argument with the crown Paine cited the Bible in support of his position. Indeed, he waxed most biblical in denouncing the corruption of

[12] See A. O. Aldridge, "Thomas Paine's Plan for a Descent on England," *William and Mary Quarterly* 14 (1957) 74–84.

[13] See P. F. Nursey-Bray, "Thomas Paine and the Concept of Alienation," *Political Studies* 16 (1968) 223–42; A. O. Aldridge, "Why Did Thomas Paine Write on the Bank?" *Proceedings of the American Philosophical Society* 93 (1949) 309–15.

[14] See Robin McKown, *Thomas Paine* (New York: Putnam's, 1962); A. O. Aldridge, *Man of Reason: The Life of Thomas Paine* (Cornwall: Cornwall, 1959); Moncure Conway, *The Life of Thomas Paine* (New York: Putnam's, 1892); David Powell, *Tom Paine: The Greatest Exile* (New York: St. Martin's Press, 1985); David Freeman Hawke, *Paine* (New York: Harper & Row, 1974); Audrey Williamson, *Thomas Paine: His Life, Work, and Times* (New York: St. Martin's Press, 1973); Jerome D. Wilson and William F. Ricketson, *Thomas Paine* (Boston: Twayne Publishers, 1989); Mary A. Best, *Thomas Paine, Prophet and Martyr of Democracy* (New York: Harcourt, Brace & Co., 1927); Eric Foner, *Tom Paine and Revolutionary America* (New York: Oxford University Press, 1976).

monarchical government. Scripture convicts every government of corruption, he warned with Quaker fervor, but of all governmental forms the Bible especially brands monarchy as sinful. Had not the monarchy led the ancient Hebrews into sinful unbelief? Monarchical pretensions had corrupted the papacy. In the latter part of the eighteenth century one had not far to look for an example of monarchical sinfulness. Witness the case of King George who claimed the right to bind free men "in all cases," a right which in the end belongs only to God. Surely, God sanctioned revolutionary opposition to such sinful arrogance.[15]

After cataloguing Old Testament denunciations of monarchy, Paine concluded:

> These portions of scripture are direct and positive. They admit of no equivocal construction. That the Almighty hath here entered his protest against monarchical government, is true, or the scripture is false. And a man hath good reason to believe that there is as much of king-craft, as priest-craft, in withholding the scripture from the public in Popish countries. For monarchy in every instance is the Popery of government.[16]

Moreover, Paine urged, the fatal march of history had been moving the American people with moral inevitability toward mortal conflict with the English crown. With each passing day the English government showed itself bloodier, more selfish, more intransigent in its demands. Each day, therefore, the crown proved itself less and less suited to rule over the hearts of peace-loving, freedom-loving Americans. Did not the fatal, inexorable march of events manifest that they followed an inevitable divine decree and that God himself espoused the righteous cause of the colonies? Even geography supported Paine's reading of God's providential plan for the American colonies. Had the God of nature wanted Americans to remain subjects of the crown, the deity would never have separated England from America by the vast gulf of the Atlantic ocean.[17]

In the course of rallying his fellow countrymen to a holy war, Paine used his rhetorical skill to create the myth of "Young America." Recent plantations in a new world, the colonial governments should regard their relative youth as proof of America's national innocence. The moral and political corruption of old world politics had already involved the colonies unwillingly in wars with British enemies. If, then, the American people had sinned, they had done so by submitting for so long to the yoke of

[15] See Thomas Paine, *Common Sense and the Crisis* (Garden City, N.Y.: Doubleday, 1960) 13–16, 20–2, 69, 81, 177. See also Joyce Appleby, "The Social Origins of American Revolutionary Ideology," *The Journal of American History* 64 (1978) 935–58.

[16] See Kriegel, ed., *Essential Works of the Founding Fathers,* 143.

[17] Ibid., 35–7, 43, 69–70, 86, 99.

monarchical tyranny. Still, as a united people bound together in a single nation, British colonials had yet to eat of the corrupting tree of the knowledge of good and evil. In proof of national innocence, Paine cited the patient persistence with which the American colonies had sought to avoid revolt despite repeated royal rebuffs.[18]

The free and selfless sacrifices which the American cause inspired also proved its purity. In Paine's mythical America, every citizen had fortified mind and heart against the forces of British violence and oppression. The free-spirited citizenry spontaneously supported the cause of rebellion, and the war against English oppression expressed a "splendid" passion in which every emotion but despair conspired to sustain the people in commitment to the cause of freedom and in bitter opposition to the hated English.[19]

Moreover, the God of revolution had raised up as his chosen leader George Washington. God's elect leader would preside over a final bloody expiation of the corruption which monarchy had visited upon the American people. Thus purified, the nation would emerge from the crucible of revolutionary suffering having earned the right to establish a regime of peace in a land in which law, not kings, ruled over human hearts.[20]

Of Washington, Paine wrote in *The Crisis:*

> Voltaire has remarked that King William never appeared to full advantage but in difficulties and in action; the same remark may be made of General Washington, for the character fits him. There is a natural firmness in some minds which cannot be unlocked by trifles, but which, when unlocked, discovers a cabinet of fortitude; and I reckon it among those kinds of public blessings, which we do not immediately see, that GOD hath blest him with uninterrupted health, and given him a mind that can even flourish upon care.[21]

God blessed the American struggle for national independence, but the new order which would emerge from colonial victory would have a political, not a sectarian, religious nature. Still, in Paine's eyes, the American who opposed British tyranny deserved the title "Defender of the Faith."[22]

---

[18] Ibid., 69–70.

[19] Ibid., 88, 126, 192, 198, 214–5.

[20] Ibid., 27–8, 69–70, 72, 86, 99, 104, 125, 135, 137–8, 142–4, 175, 225–8; see also William Van der Weyde, *Thomas Paine on War and Monarchy* (New York: Thomas Paine National Historical Association, 1915); Rudolf Böhringer, *Die Propaganda Thomas Paines während des amerikanischen Unabhaenginkeitskampfes* (Berlin: Junker und Dünnhaupt, 1938); Dominic Elder, "The Common Man Philosophy of Thomas Paine" (master's thesis, University of Notre Dame, 1951); F. E. Pettit, "Tom Paine," *Contemporary Review* 214 (1969) 47–8.

[21] See Kriegel, ed., *Essential Works of the Founding Fathers,* 196.

[22] Prior to Henry VIII's conflicts with the papacy, the pope had awarded the young king this title for his zeal in defending the faith against Protestant attacks.

In appealing to "common sense," Paine invoked the sane reasonableness of the common citizen. As an Enlightenment prophet of revolution, he insisted on the complete divorce between sectarian religion and politics as an essential precondition for establishing a just social order in the new nation.[23]

III

When Thomas Jefferson dispatched an American frigate to bring Paine back to the United States after his ordeal in France, the President acted with a profound sense of the debt which the nation owed to Paine and to his eloquent pen. At a time when others had hesitated to speak, he had trumpeted the call to independence from British rule. Without Paine, the Declaration of Independence and the events which it precipitated might have ended very differently.[24]

The Declaration itself had ideological as well as political consequences. As a document it claimed to represent a national consensus, and the events which it set in motion tended to transform it into precisely that. As a national creed the Declaration enshrined in the minds and hearts of Americans basic principles of Lockean political philosophy: that all men[25] stand as equals under God, that they enjoy certain inalienable rights, including the right to life, to liberty, and to the pursuit of happiness. Moreover, the Declaration endowed these principles with an epistemological self-evidence which placed them beyond debate.

The principal architect of the Declaration, Jefferson believed devoutly in the self-evidence of moral truth, so devoutly indeed that he enshrined it in the document which eventually came to function like a national creed. Through its idealization in the popular American mind, the Declaration helped disseminate, therefore, the individualistic model of conscience which typified Jeffersonian ethics. Jefferson, like the other *philosophes* of the eighteenth century, assumed that the laws of morality, like the laws of nature, remain essentially immutable and fixed. One discovered the laws of nature through controlled experimentation, but one discovered the laws of morality by retiring within oneself and listening to the divine voice of moral sentiment which spoke clearly to each individual in the depths of

[23] Kriegel, ed., *Essential Works of the Founding Fathers*, 78, 166–7; see also Harry Clark, "Thomas Paine's Theories of Rhetoric," *Transactions of the Wisconsin Academy of Science, Arts, and Letters* 28 (1933) 307–39; Henry Leffman, "The Real Thomas Paine, Patriot and Publicist," *Pennsylvania Magazine of History and Biography* 46 (1922) 81–99; Margarte M. Vanderhoar, "Whitman, Paine, and the Religion of Democracy," *Walt Whitman Review* (1970) 14–22.

[24] See William Woodward, *Tom Paine: America's Godfather* (New York: Dutton, 1945); Lemuel Washburn, *America's Debt to Thomas Paine* (Boston: Colburn Bros., 1878).

[25] The Declaration's principles did not include women or slaves.

the soul, just as the Holy Spirit was supposed to speak directly to the individual Calvinist conscience. Through the secret inner voice of conscience, the God of nature had chosen to communicate his eternal and immutable will to each individual. In other words, to the "popish" corruptions of monarchy, Jefferson's "enlightened" religious and ethical rhetoric opposed the self-evident inner light of the individual human conscience.[26]

IV

After the American revolution, the framers of the national constitution faced a more formidable constructive task than those who had precipitated and supported armed resistance to the crown. They had to frame a government which guaranteed political stability to an emerging nation without betraying the aspirations of the revolution itself. Moreover, not a few Americans who had suffered for the cause of freedom felt loathe to abdicate their newly won liberty to yet another legal bureaucracy. In New York especially, sectional feeling gave added impetus to the cause of non-ratification.[27]

To meet this crisis, Alexander Hamilton, James Madison, and John Jay combined their wits to write *The Federalist Papers,* a series of leisurely political tracts extolling the virtues and reasonableness of each major section of the proposed national constitution. Hamilton bore the brunt of the labor; but all three men signed their essays with the same pseudonym: Publius. The extent to which *The Federalist Papers* successfully secured New York's support of the new constitution remains debatable. The fact that Washington and Franklin came out publicly for ratification very likely swayed the masses more than Publius's reflective philosophical arguments. Nevertheless, the three men who authored *The Federalist Papers* stole a march on other political theorists. Even prior to the constitution's ratification, they produced a classic commentary upon it which profoundly influenced jurisprudence in the United States.[28]

[26] See David Hawke, *A Transaction of Free Men: The Birth of the Declaration of Independence* (New York: Scribners, 1964); Edward Dumbauld, *The Declaration of Independence and What It Means Today* (Norman: University of Oklahoma Press, 1950); Carl Becker, *The Declaration of Independence* (New York: Knopf, 1942); Garry Wills, *Inventing America: Jefferson's Declaration of Independence* (New York: Doubleday, 1978); Robert W. Tucker, *Empire of Liberty: The Statecraft of Thomas Jefferson* (New York: Oxford University Press, 1990); Peter S. Onufed, *Jeffersonian Legacies* (Charlottesville: University Press of Virginia, 1993); Wilham Penak, "The Declaration of Independence: Changing Interpretations and a New Hypothesis," *Pennsylvania History* 57 (1990) 225–35.

[27] See Linda DePauw, *The Eleventh Pillar: New York State and the Federal Constitution* (Ithaca, N.Y.: Cornell University Press, 1966).

[28] See Saul Padover, ed., *The Mind of Alexander Hamilton* (New York: Harper, 1958); C. M. Kenyon, "Alexander Hamilton: Rousseau of the Right," *Political Science Quarterly*

The Federalist Papers represent, therefore, an important interpretative consolidation and institutionalization of American revolutionary sentiment. Those who precipitated the revolution seem to have sensed that they had set loose historical forces whose consequences they could only dimly foresee. Those who supported the revolution felt themselves swept along by the course of momentous events. Paine had exploited that feeling in order to lend divine providential sanction to the American struggle for independence. Now the Federalists exploited the same religious feeling in order to endow the new constitution with an aura of fatalistic credibility. The aspiration to order which the constitution expressed brought the historical forces which had fueled the revolution to their culminating moment.[29] Madison put the question this way:

> Was, then, the American Revolution effected, was the American Confederacy formed, was the precious blood of thousands spilt, and the hard earned substance of millions lavished, not that the people of America should enjoy peace, liberty, and safety, but that the governments of the individual States, that particular municipal establishments, might enjoy a certain extent of power and be arrayed with certain dignities and attributes of sovereignty?[30]

To Federalist eyes, present national union offered the only realistic peace-time guarantee of the ideals which had inspired the revolution: ideals like inter-colonial peace, the guarantee of the rights of individuals, and security from foreign encroachment. To such high-minded ideals they opposed the sectarian spirit of non-ratification: a spirit of narrow regionalism and selfish factionalism.[31] In Federalist rhetoric, regionalism and factionalism had the same negative connotations as religious sectarianism enjoyed in Enlightenment anti-Christian diatribes.

The Federalists, moreover, viewed the masses of the people through a lens tinged with something akin to Calvinistic pessimism. Philosophers

---

73 (1958) 161–78; Adrienne Koch, "Hamilton, Adams, and the Pursuit of Power," *Review of Politics* 16 (1954) 37–66; F. W. Meyer, "Note on the Origins of the Hameltonian System," *William and Mary Quarterly* 21 (1964) 579–88; B. Mitchell, "The Secret of Alexander Hamilton," *Virginia Quarterly Review* 29 (1953) 595–609; D. Adair and M. Harvey, "Was Alexander Hamilton a Christian Statesman?" *William and Mary Quarterly* 12 (1955) 308–29; J. E. Davies, "Alexander Hamilton: His Politics and Policies," *Southwestern Social Science Quarterly* 42 (1961) 233–9; T. P. Govan, "The Rich, the Well-Born and Alexander Hamilton," *The Mississippi Valley Historical Review* 36 (1950) 675–80; John Miller, *Alexander Hamilton and the Growth of the New Nation* (New York: Harper, 1959); D. O. Dewey, "Madison's Views on Electoral Reform," *Western Political Quarterly* 15 (1963) 140–5.

[29] See Clinton Rossiter, ed., *The Federalist Papers* (New York: New American Library, 1961) 37–41, 289–95.

[30] Ibid., 284.

[31] Ibid., 43–71.

might follow the clear light of reason, but the great masses of the people could and often enough did remain egotistical, jealous, and unfaithful to the principles of law and of justice. Federalist political philosophy therefore feared pure democracy as the institutionalization of mob rule. At the same time, it abhorred monarchy as institutionalized tyranny. Federalism claimed the middle ground between these extremes: a representative, republican government strengthened by a strong executive and by a strong court system.[32]

Only a strong federal government could ensure peace among the member states which constituted the federal republic, for the same selfish passions which mar the social dealings of individuals cast a blight upon the international dealings of loosely confederated member states. As a consequence, without the counterbalance of a strong national government the member states would soon subordinate the common national good to local and sectional interests.[33] In addition, the wily intrigues of foreign powers could all too easily divide an only loosely confederated group of states. The corrupt monarchies of Europe would quickly exploit American sectionalism in order to divide and conquer.

In the face of all these internal and external threats, the federal government must own and use the power to defend the national interest against internal fragmentation and against foreign encroachment. The federal government should achieve these ends through diplomacy when possible, through force when necessary. Creating centralized, national institutional structures which would ensure stability, social balance, and equilibrium in the body politic defined one of Federalists' overriding goals.[34]

The common pseudonym "Publius" concealed to all but the careful reader a certain number of significant divergences among the authors of *The Federalist Papers*. Since Jay penned only five of the eighty-five tracts, the principal disagreements occurred between Hamilton and Madison. Hamilton, for example, viewed the ratification of the constitution as the free consent of the people at large to the federal system of government. Madison portrayed ratification as a contract among sovereign states.

[32] Ibid., 46–9, 56, 78–82, 116, 139–40, 150–1, 168, 194, 379, 423–57, 465–91; see also Gottfried Dietze, *The Federalist* (Baltimore: Johns Hopkins University Press, 1960) 105–71; B. F. Wright, "The Federalist on the Nature of Political Man," *Ethics* 59 (1949) 1–31; M. Smith, "Reason, Passion, and Political Freedom in *The Federalist*," *Journal of Politics* 22 (1960) 525–44; J. P. Scanlan, "The Federalist and Human Nature," *Review of Politics* 21 (1959) 657–77.

[33] Rossiter, ed., *The Federalist Papers,* 54, 69, 71–3, 84–9, 174–5, 178, 201, 206–11, 215–6, 269, 347; Dietze, *The Federalist,* 177–218.

[34] Rossiter, ed., *The Federalist Papers,* 42–4, 50–3, 115, 182–4, 188–93; Dietze, *The Federalist,* 219–52.

Madison expected the checks and balances within the federal system to protect the rights of states in the federation from encroachment by federal power. Hamilton's federalism put federal authority in the driver's seat by concentrating power in the central, national government.[35] Vagueness on all these points of disagreement within the federal system set the stage for the debate over national union vs. states' rights, which erupted finally in the Civil War.

Still, Hamilton and Madison found themselves in basic agreement on a broad spectrum of questions. Both possessed a rather dim view of human nature and looked to the external structures of government to check the spontaneous selfishness of individual and regional factionalism. Both recognized the inadequacy of the Articles of Confederation under which the Continental Congress had struggled during the revolution.[36] Both regarded government as the creation of free social compacts among individuals or sovereign states. Both affirmed government's dependence on the will of the people. Both insisted on the need for the people at large to participate in government. Both asserted that government exists in order to secure individual rights and in order to protect the common interest. Both expected national unity to foster peace, security, and individual freedom.

Federalism, however, consciously set out to divert the passion of the revolution into controlled governmental channels. The Federalists feared that baser popular passions might subvert the ideals of peace, security, and freedom for which so many Americans had fought and died. Federalist philosophy viewed the formation of new governmental structures as the normal sequel to the revolutionary overthrow of tyranny. Hence, in pushing for governmental checks to popular sentiment and vested self-interest, the Federalists believed that they were in fact leading the revolution to its institutional fulfillment. In the eyes of their critics, their mistrust of human nature and reliance on centralized political power betrayed the very democratic ideal for which Americans had fought and died.[37] At least, so it seemed to Thomas Jefferson.

[35] See Rossiter, ed., *The Federalist Papers,* 153–4, 161, 163; Dietze, *The Federalist,* 256–70.

[36] See Edmund Burnett, *The Continental Congress* (New York: Norton, 1964); Andrew McLaughlin, *The Confederation and the Constitution* (New York: Collier Books, 1967).

[37] See John Lewis, ed., *Anti-Federalist vs. Federalist: Selected Documents* (Scranton, Pa.: Chandler, 1961); S. Lynd, "Capitalism, Democracy and the United States Constitution," *Science and Society* 27 (1963) 385–414; Morton J. Frisch, *Alexander Hamilton and the Political Order: An Interpretation of His Political Thought and Practice* (Lanham, Md.: University Press of America, 1991); Richard Loss, *The Modern Theory of Presidential Power: Alexander Hamilton and the Corwin Thesis* (New York: Greenwood Press, 1990); Leslie Wharton, *Polity and the Public Good: Conflicting Theories of Government in the*

V

Thomas Jefferson drew his first breath on April 13, 1743. The son of a prosperous planter, young Thomas received the benefits of a classical education. In 1764 he began to doubt the historicity of the Bible. Those doubts started his gradual drift into Deism. He decided upon a career in law and graduated from William and Mary in the spring of 1762. Ten years later he married Martha Skelton. They settled at Monticello, then still under construction.

Patrick Henry's impassioned opposition to the Stamp Act left a deep impression on Jefferson. After the burning of the British cutter *Gaspee,* the two men, alarmed by the crown's threats against those suspected of the deed, organized colonial committees of correspondence as a protection against further British encroachment.

In August 1774 a temporarily-ailing Jefferson submitted *in absensia* to the Virginia Convention at Williamsburg a document later published under the title "A Summary View of the Rights of British America." The delegates never debated the document and, if they had, would probably have viewed Jefferson's manifesto as too extreme, too revolutionary for adoption. Published anonymously as a political tract, "A Summary View" enjoyed wide circulation, and by word of mouth its true author received deserved recognition. During the Second Continental Congress at Philadelphia, the popular success of "A Summary View" made Jefferson a logical choice for drafting the Declaration of Independence. The Congress adopted his draft of the Declaration with some amendments on July 4, 1776.[38]

In the same year, Jefferson returned to the Virginia house of Delegates where he labored on the systematic revision of the state legal code.

New Nation (Ann Arbor: University of Michigan Research Press, 1980); Neal Riemer, *James Madison: Creating the American Constitution* (Washington, D.C.: Congressional Quarterly, 1986); Richard K. Matthews, *If Men Were Angels: James Madison and the Heartless Empire of Reason* (Lawrence: University Press of Kansas, 1995); Lance Banning, "James Madison and the Nationalists, 1780–1783," *William and Mary Quarterly* 40 (1983) 227–55; Ralph Ketcham, "James Madison: The Unimperial President," *Virginia Quarterly Review* 54 (1978) 116–36; Peter Augustine Lawler, "James Madison and the Metaphysics of Modern Politics," *Review of Politics* 48 (1986) 92–115; Donald F. Swanson and Andrew P. Trout, "Alexander Hamilton, the Celebrated Mr. Necker, and Public Credit," *William and Mary Quarterly* 47 (1990) 422–30; "Alexander Hamilton's Hidden Sinking Fund," *William and Mary Quarterly* 49 (1992) 108–16; Doron Ben Atar, "Alexander Hamilton's Alternative: Technological Piracy and the Report on Manufactures," *William and Mary Quarterly* 52 (1995) 389–414; William A. Smith, "Henry Adams, Alexander Hamilton, and the American People as a 'Great Beast,'" *New England Quarterly* 48 (1975) 216–30.

[38] See Julian P. Boyd, "Jefferson's Expression of the American Mind," *Virginia Quarterly Review* 50 (1974) 538–62.

Eventually, a number of his proposals found their way into the Virginia constitution. In 1775 he had introduced a "Bill Establishing Religious Freedom." The bill sanctioned the disestablishment of all religions and passed with minor modifications in 1778.[39] In 1779 Jefferson was elected governor of Virginia and served two terms. As governor he spent much of his time provisioning the Virginia militia serving in the colonial army.

His wife died in 1782. The following year saw him elected delegate to the Confederation Congress in Philadelphia. Two years later he joined Benjamin Franklin and John Adams in Paris as a minister plenipotentiary for the negotiation of European trade agreements. In 1785, after Franklin's departure, Jefferson remained in Paris as the minister plenipotentiary to the court of France. In Paris, Jefferson joined the diplomatic circle which surrounded Lafayette. Unlike Paine, Jefferson thoroughly enjoyed the social and cultural life of the European continent. He even seems to have experienced one minor affair of the heart; and he followed with optimistic approval the early events of the French revolution.[40]

In 1789 Jefferson resigned his post in Paris and returned to the United States, only to discover that President Washington had chosen him to serve as the first Secretary of State. After he assumed office, Jefferson found himself increasingly shocked and disturbed by Federalist thinking, which sounded in his ears like a betrayal of the revolution and a return to monarchicalist principles of government. He drifted into an increasingly embittered dispute with Alexander Hamilton, then Secretary of the Treasury. Hamilton passionately believed in the need to ground the new republic on a sound financial basis. Hamilton's deference, however, toward business interests filled the Secretary of State with alarm, and his meddling in questions of state peeved the Virginian.[41]

---

[39] For a thorough contextualization of bill's passage see Thomas E. Buckley, *Church and State in Revolutionary Virginia: 1776–1787* (Charlottesville: University Press of Virginia, 1977).

[40] See S. Andrews, "Jefferson and the French Revolution," *History Today* 18 (1968) 299–306; Eleanor Berman, *Thomas Jefferson among the Arts* (New York: Philosophical Library, 1947); Edwin Martin, *Thomas Jefferson: Scientist* (New York: H. Schuman, 1952); S. G. Brown, "The Mind of Thomas Jefferson," *Ethics* 73 (1963) 79–99; Charles Browne, *Thomas Jefferson and the Scientific Trends of His Time* (New York: G. E. Stechert, 1944).

[41] See Lynton Caldwell, *The Administrative Theories of Hamilton and Jefferson* (Chicago: University of Chicago Press, 1944); Caleb Peterson, *The Constitutional Principles of Thomas Jefferson* (Austin: University of Texas Press, 1953); Adrienne Koch, *Jefferson and Madison: The Great Collaboration* (New York: Knopf, 1950); A. H. Bowman, "Jefferson, Hamilton, and American Foreign Policy," *Political Science Quarterly* 71 (1956) 18–41; Lance Banning, "Jeffersonian Ideology Revisited: Liberal and Classical Ideas in the New American Republic," *William and Mary Quarterly* 43 (1986) 3–19.

In 1794 Jefferson, after a stressful year marked by the Citizen Genet affair, resigned as Secretary of State and retired to Monticello to read, reflect, and philosophize. He found his peace disturbed in 1796 when the Democratic Republican Party, the fruit of his break with Federalism, drafted him to run against John Adams, the Federalist candidate for President. Jefferson lost in the electoral college by only three votes, and, under the prevailing political system, he assumed office as vice-president. He and Adams made an ill-matched political team. Jefferson experienced increasing alarm over administration policies. The vice-president regarded the Alien and Sedition Acts, not without reason, as an assault against freedom of speech and freedom of the press.

Although in 1801 neither Jefferson nor Adams campaigned actively for the presidency, the campaign bristled with mudslinging and mutual recrimination on the part of both Federalists and Republican Democrats. After an indecisive electoral vote, the House of Representatives elected Jefferson the third president of the United States.[42] On May 2, 1803, he signed the Louisiana Purchase. By a stroke of the pen Jefferson had more than doubled the territory of the United States. The following year he dispatched Lewis and Clark to explore the new territory. During his second term as president, he found himself bedeviled by head-splitting problems: the Burr conspiracy, growing British interference in United States trade, the Embargo Act.[43]

At the age of sixty-six, he returned with relief to Monticello, where eleven years later he wrote his autobiography. His reconciliation with John Adams led to a long and friendly correspondence between the two elder statesmen.[44] During this period, he devoted most of his energies to designing and organizing the University of Virginia. It opened in 1825, the

[42] J. Charles, "Adams and Jefferson: The Origins of the American Party System," *William and Mary Quarterly* 12 (1955) 410–30; Susan Dunn, "Revolutionary Men of Letters and the Pursuit of Radical Change: The Views of Burke, Tocqueville, Adams, Madison, and Jefferson," *William and Mary Quarterly* 53 (1996) 729–54; Michael Drury, "Thomas Paine's Apostles: Radical Emigrés and the Triumph of Jeffersonian Republicanism," *William and Mary Quarterly* 44 (1987) 661–8.

[43] See Claude Bowers, *Jefferson in Power: The Death Struggle of the Federalists* (Boston: Houghton Mifflin, 1936); J. E. Prince, "The Passing of Aristocracy: Jefferson's Removal of the Federalists, 1801–1805," *Journal of American History* 57 (1970) 563–75; William G. McLoughlin, "Thomas Jefferson and the Beginning of Cherokee Nationalism, 1806–1809," *William and Mary Quarterly* 32 (1975) 547–80; Douglas L. Wilson, "Jefferson vs. Hume," *William and Mary Quarterly* 46 (1989) 49–70; Robert Kelley, "Ideology and Political Culture from Jefferson to Nixon," *The American Historical Review* 82 (1977) 531–62.

[44] See John Allison, *Adams and Jefferson: The Story of a Friendship* (Norman: University of Oklahoma Press, 1966).

year before his death. Both Jefferson and Adams died within hours of one another on July 4, 1824, the forty-eighth anniversary of the Declaration of Independence.

Thomas Jefferson lies buried in Monticello beneath a monument of his own design. He also composed the inscription: "Here lies buried Thomas Jefferson, Author of the Declaration of American Independence, of the Statute of Virginia for religious liberty, and Father of the University of Virginia."[45]

Jefferson's strong disagreement with the Federalists sprang from deeply held convictions. He believed that their pessimistic view of human nature, their preoccupation with governmental checks upon popular sentiment, and their predilection for moneyed interests all betrayed the best ideals of the American revolution. Jefferson did not espouse a naively optimistic view of human nature. He acknowledged human blindness and imperfection. He recognized the evils and injustices which plague human society. Still, Jefferson believed humanity to be instinctively moral and he held that, with proper education, people will follow the benevolent impulses which "nature hath implanted in our breasts."[46]

Jonathan Edwards discovered true virtue in heartfelt consent to the divine excellence manifest in the incarnation and in nature. Franklin equated virtue with the cultivation of enlightened self-interest. Jefferson, the patrician planter, grounded virtue in an innate moral sense of duty. He described the moral sense as "a sense of duty [to others] . . . which prompts us irresistibly to feel and succor their distress."[47] The *noblesse oblige* of the southern, patrician, planter class had bred such sentiments into Jefferson's bones, but he believed that every human possesses identi-

---

[45] See Roy Honeywell, *The Educational Work of Thomas Jefferson* (Cambridge: Harvard University Press, 1931); James Conant, *Thomas Jefferson and the Development of American Public Education* (Berkeley: University of California Press, 1962). For general biographies of Jefferson see Dumas Malone, *Jefferson and His Times,* 6 vols. (Boston: Little, Brown, 1948–81); Noble Cunningham, *In Pursuit of Reason: The Life of Thomas Jefferson* (Baton Rouge: Louisiana State University Press, 1987); Edwin Thomas Martin, *Thomas Jefferson, Scientist* (New York: H. Schuman, 1952); Karl Lehman, *Thomas Jefferson: American Humanist* (New York: Macmillan, 1947); and Fawn Brodie's controversial study *Thomas Jefferson: An Intimate Biography* (New York: Norton, 1974); Eugene F. Miller, "On the American Founders' Defense of Liberal Education in a Republic," *Review of Politics* 46 (1984) 65–90.

[46] See Andrew Lipscomb, ed., *The Writings of Thomas Jefferson,* 20 vols. (Washington, D.C.: The Thomas Jefferson Memorial Association, 1904) 14:141–2; Gilbert Chinard, *Thomas Jefferson: The Apostle of Americanism* (Ann Arbor: University of Michigan Press, 1960); Paul A. Rahe, "Thomas Jefferson's Machiavellian Political Science," *Review of Politics* 57 (1995) 449–81.

[47] Lipscomb, ed., *The Writings of Thomas Jefferson,* 14:139–40, 257.

cally the same moral sense. He had appealed to that moral sense in writing the Declaration of Independence. One need only proclaim man's inalienable right to life, to liberty, and to the pursuit of happiness for the rest of thinking men to recognize within their own consciences the self-evidence of these moral truths. Jefferson's faith in a universal moral sense also motivated his opposition to Federalist philosophy and to Federalist national policy. Jeffersonian democracy stood or fell on the ability of free men everywhere to consult their private, individual sense of right and of wrong and to follow the immutable, self-evident, universally binding principles which they discovered there. In a very real sense, therefore, Jeffersonian democracy presupposed a naturalized, secular "inner light" which yielded an individual, subjective, self-evident grasp of the unchanging, universal principles of moral action. Jefferson's moral vision gave concrete philosophical meaning to Paine's dream of a democratic society in which each individual submits spontaneously to the rule of law.[48]

Jefferson acknowledged possible objections against this theory of a uniform, universal, human moral sense. He conceded that in fact not all individuals and nations subscribe to the same moral codes; however, he attributed such differences not to the moral sense as such, but to a lack of education and to the need to apply the unchanging principles of moral conduct to divergent moral situations. This sense of de facto ethical pluralism plus the utilitarian bent of his mind eventually led him to invoke "utility" as a supplement to the moral sense in judging virtuous action. Needless to say, "utility" cloaks a multitude of ambiguities which Jefferson never clarified.

At the same time, Jefferson's belief in a moral sense did enable him to reformulate Franklin's critique of established religion in more systematic terms than Franklin himself. Both men discovered at the basis of all religion a philosophical least common denominator. Both rejected religious creeds as divisive, but Jefferson's espousal of the cause of religious disestablishment brought him into an increasing number of conflicts with the clergy. Their embittered personal attacks upon him led him to regard them collectively as the bigoted enemies of freedom and of tolerance.[49]

For Jefferson, nature rather than supernatural grace grounds religious belief and practice, and within human nature the moral sense supplies the

---

[48] See Adrienne Koch, *The Philosophy of Thomas Jefferson* (Gloucester, Mass.: Peter Smith, 1957) 15–22; Adrienne Koch, *Jefferson and Madison: The Great Collaboration* (New York: Oxford University Press, 1969); Steward Gerry Brown, "The Mind of Thomas Jefferson," *Ethics* 73 (1963) 79–99; Charles A. Miller, *Jefferson and Nature: An Interpretation* (Baltimore: Johns Hopkins University Press, 1988).

[49] Lipscomb, ed., *The Writings of Thomas Jefferson,* 10:78, 175; 11:428; 13:253, 400; 14:127, 233.

basic precepts of natural religion. In a letter to Peter Carr written from Paris in 1787, Jefferson advised the younger man to subject every belief to rigorous rational doubt and scrutiny, including belief in the existence of God. Only pitiless rational criticism could, Jefferson felt, endow belief with the sincerity God expects of humans. "Your own reason," he warned, "is the only oracle given you by heaven, and you are answerable, not for the rightness, but for the uprightness of the decision." Moreover, even one who denies the existence of God can continue to live virtuously, and morality—staunch republican fidelity to the duties disclosed by the moral sense—constitutes the very essence of religion.[50]

Despite Jefferson's radical advice to Carr, he himself harbored no doubts concerning God's existence. Indeed, he believed that "when we take a view of the universe, in its parts, general or particular, it is impossible for the human mind not to perceive and feel a conviction of design, consummate skill, and indefinite power in every atom of its composition." Of God's nature, however, he professed ignorance.[51] Far better, he believed, to concentrate on those religious truths which enjoy not only intelligibility but self-evidence—namely, the truths of moral living. Paradoxically, then, Jefferson's view of the deity bore a remarkable similarity to that of Puritan federal theologians. For both, God remained incomprehensible in himself but had revealed himself to humans in rationally comprehensible moral precepts. Needless to say, the Enlightenment philosophers and the Calvinist divines also differed. Jehovah spoke to Puritan federal theologians through Moses and Jesus, while the creator of the universe spoke to the Jeffersonian conscience through the personal, inner light of universally uniform, self-evident moral truths.

At the same time, Jefferson believed that universal ethical truth had found its most sublime expression in the morality proclaimed by Jesus. Jefferson denied, of course, the divinity of Jesus and the trinitarian theology which it reveals. Jefferson dismissed the trinity cavalierly as a "hocus pocus phantom" which reduces God to a three-headed Cerberus.[52]

On April 21, 1803, after reading with approval Joseph Priestly's comparison between the ethical doctrines of Jesus and of Socrates, Jefferson sketched an outline of the Christian ethics which he had ambitions of writing. He noted with approval that the great moralists of antiquity—Pythagoras, Socrates, Epicurus, Cicero, Epictetus, Seneca, and Antoninus—had all inculcated the pursuit of mental tranquility through control of the passions. They had also preached fidelity to one's duties to friends, kin-

[50] Ibid., 6:61; 12:236–7, 315.
[51] Ibid., 15:426–7.
[52] Ibid., 15:408–9.

dred, and country. They had failed, however, to inculcate universal benevolence toward all people, as Jesus had. Jefferson found Jewish morality fundamentally Deistic but narrowly nationalistic in its tone and marred by hostility toward the Gentile nations.[53]

Like other Enlightenment philosophers, Jefferson found analogies between Jesus and Socrates. Neither had written down any doctrine. Both met opposition in the learned of their day. Both fell victim to altar and throne. Jefferson believed that the New Testament preserved Jesus' teachings in mutilated form, but he also believed that when purged of theological superstition, Jesus' teachings purified the Jewish conception of God, preached survival after death as an incentive for moral conduct, and inculcated the duty of universal benevolence to all people. Jefferson's Jesus, like the Jesus presented by other Enlightenment thinkers, resembled an eighteenth-century *philosophe* not unlike Jefferson himself, at least in his more idealistic moments. Jefferson's Jesus in his preaching appeals, like Jefferson himself, to the self-evident inner light of the conscience.[54]

Jefferson never wrote the moral treatise he projected. Perhaps he made his closest approach to doing so in his demythologizing editing of the Gospels. His editorial scissors reduced the Gospels to their pure "moral essence" by snipping out allegedly theological and mythical elements from gospel text. Jefferson produced his demythologized New Testament "by cutting the texts out of the book, and arranging them on the pages of a blank book in a certain order of time or subject." He pronounced himself pleased with the result. He wrote to John Adams in 1813:

> A more beautiful or precious morsel of ethics I have never seen; it is a document in proof that I am a real Christian, that is to say, a disciple of the doctrines of Jesus very different from the Platonists who call me infidel and themselves Christians and preachers of the gospel, while they draw all their characteristic dogmas from what its Author never said nor saw.[55]

Indeed, Jefferson felt sure enough of his "real Christianity" to defend Jesus, the Jeffersonian ethician, from his "pseudo-followers," the Calvinists.[56] Jefferson espoused a Lockean nominalism. He had little speculative use for Plato and for the Augustinian tradition. Indeed, Jefferson blamed Plato for many of the theological abuses present in Calvinist Christianity.

[53] Ibid., 10:381–2.
[54] Ibid., 10:383–5.
[55] Ibid., 14:385–6; see also Gilbert Chinard, ed., *The Literary Bible of Thomas Jefferson* (Baltimore: Johns Hopkins University Press, 1928); Lee Quimby, "Thomas Jefferson: The Virtue of Aesthetics and the Aesthetics of Virtue," *The American Historical Review* 87 (1982) 337–56.
[56] Lipscomb, ed., *The Writings of Thomas Jefferson,* 15:257.

He found the dualistic caste of Platonic thought most abhorrent. He countered Platonic "spiritualism" with a thorough-going materialism. The presuppositions of Lockean empiricism led, he believed, to such a conclusion. In 1820 he confided to John Adams: "When once we quit the basis of sensation all is in the wind. To talk of immaterial existence is to talk of nothing. To say that the human soul, angels, God, are immaterial, is to say, they are nothings, or that there is no God, no angels, no soul."[57] Jefferson deemed "real Christianity" compatible with materialism. He saw no contradiction in the idea that God might endow matter with thought or that God might not enjoy material existence.[58] When it came to Jesus' espousal of materialism, Jefferson wavered. On April 20, 1820, in writing to William Short, he characterized Jesus as a "spiritualist." Four months later, however, in a letter to Adams, he toyed with the idea that Jesus' doctrine may have approached more nearly to materialism than he had suspected. Jefferson's capacity for biblical eisegesis knew few limits.[59]

Jefferson rejected more than the spiritualistic tendencies in Platonism and in Calvinism. He dismissed the body of Calvinistic doctrine as diametrically opposed to "real Christianity." As in the case of Franklin, however, Jefferson's presentation of the Calvinist position reads like a crude and shallow parody:

> The doctrines of Jesus are simple and tend all to the happiness of man. 1. That there is one only God, and he all perfect. 2. That there is a future state of rewards and punishments. 3. That to love God with all thy heart and thy neighbor as thyself is the sum of religion. These are the great points on which He endeavored to reform the religion of the Jews. But compare with these the demoralizing dogmas of Calvin. 1. That there are three Gods. 2. That good works, or the love of our neighbor are nothing. 3. That faith is everything, and the more incomprehensible the proposition, the more merit in its faith. 4. That reason in religion is of unlawful use. 5. That God from the beginning elected certain individuals to be saved, and certain others to be damned; and that no crimes of the former can damn them; no virtues of the latter save.[60]

At the same time, Jefferson conceded some foundation for Calvinist doctrine in the teachings of Jesus, especially in the latter's doctrine of the "efficacy of repentance towards the forgiveness of sin."[61]

Of all the American Deists and revolutionaries, Jefferson stood out for his single-minded opposition to the political establishment of religion.

[57] Ibid., 15:274.
[58] Ibid.
[59] Ibid., 15:244.
[60] Ibid., 15:383–4.
[61] Ibid., 15:244; see also Henry Wilder Foote, *The Religion of Thomas Jefferson* (Boston: Beacon Press, 1947); Adrienne Koch, *The Philosophy of Thomas Jefferson* (New

Religious establishment meant that a particular church enjoyed recognition and protection by the political sovereign as the official religion of the state. In different colonies, state protection of a particular church had entailed to varying degrees the following legal practices: (1) the restriction to church membership of the right to vote and hold office; (2) imprisonment and fines for convicted unbelievers; (3) the right to expel dissenters from the commonwealth; (4) financial support of the established church derived from taxes levied on all citizens, both members and non-members of the established church; and (5) restriction to the established church of the right to hold public worship, evangelize, or perform marriages and burials.

Besides official establishment, the colonial churches and civil governments had worked out other areas of cooperation and accommodation. They included the following: (1) the lease and use of public lands for religiously oriented education; (2) civil statutes punishing blasphemy and violations of the sabbath; (3) civil proclamation of days of fast, thanksgiving, and prayer; (4) the civil incorporation of churches and other religious bodies; and (5) the participation of ministers in the processes of civil government.[62]

In the bill for religious disestablishment which he memorialized on his own tombstone, Jefferson had called for an end to special civil recognition of a particular church, for an end to the special privileges granted its ministers, and for the termination of across-the-board tax support for parishes. When understood in context, Jefferson's bill did not represent a comprehensive piece of legislation. In Jefferson's mind, however, the disestablishment of religion raised more than legal issues. In seeking to separate the religious from the political forum, he was, he believed, acting in the best interests of true Christian religion as he had come to understand it. Religious establishment gave legal sanction to the attempt of one sect to impose its beliefs on the consciences of others. Jefferson judged that such creedal intolerance failed to respect the private revelations of the moral sense, justified religious persecution, and inhibited both free religious inquiry and the spontaneous growth of natural belief.[63]

York: Columbian, 1943); Daniel Boorstin, *The Lost World of Thomas Jefferson* (Boston: Beacon Press, 1948); Charles B. Sanford, *The Religious Life of Thomas Jefferson* (Charlottesville: University of Virginia Press, 1984); Rem B. Edwards, *A Return to Moral and Religious Philosophy in Early America* (Washington, D.C.: University Press of America, 1982); Edwin Scott Gaustad, *Sworn on the Altar of God: A Religious Biography of Thomas Jefferson* (Grand Rapids, Mich.: Eerdmans, 1996).

[62] See Antineu Chester, *Freedom from Religious Establishment* (Milwaukee: Bruce, 1964) 1–31, 62–3.

[63] Thomas Jefferson, *The Papers of Thomas Jefferson*, ed. Julian Boyd, 17 vols. (Princeton, N.J.: Princeton University Press, 1950–65) 1:536–56; Frank Swancare, *Thomas Jefferson Versus Religious Oppression* (New York: University Books, 1969); S. G. Sandler,

Behind Jefferson's stand on religious disestablishment lay his conviction that the moral sense provides the true basis for religious living. Like Franklin, Jefferson proclaimed Deism more Christian in its tolerance than sectarian Christianity. By dissociating the forms of democratic government from the forms of sectarian belief and worship, Jefferson hoped to institutionalize Deistic tolerance. He did so, moreover, in the name of "true Christianity," which, of course, consisted in a Christianity purified by moral reason of all its superstitious, theological trappings. Moreover, for Jefferson, the disestablishment of religion reduced religious belief to its pure essence: the relationship of each individual to the God who spoke in the privacy of each individual conscience.

Finally, Jefferson provided democracy in the United States with a myth of national social genesis. The myth reflected the racism of colonial American culture. Though himself a slave-holder, Jefferson disapproved of the institution of slavery as an unjustifiable infringement of innate human freedom. In 1777 he proposed to the Virginia legislature a bill to prevent the further importation of slaves.[64] Jefferson sincerely deplored the plight of black slaves, but he conceded regretfully that the "empirical evidence" pointed to their essential racial inferiority to whites. In his *Notes on the State of Virginia* he observed: "The improvement of the blacks in body and mind, in the first instance of their mixture with the whites, has been observed by every one, and proves that their inferiority is not the effect merely of their condition of life."[65] The "every one" in question meant, of course, the white Virginia planter class. In 1801 Jefferson speculated to James Monroe about the possibility of transporting the freed slaves to the West Indies or, that failing, back to Africa itself. Massive deportation seemed to Jefferson the best practical way to preserve the racial purity of the American Anglo-Saxon.[66]

Racial pride entered constitutively into Jefferson's revolutionary creed. In his *Summary View* he had depicted America's revolutionary struggle as an attempt to return to the pure democratic ideal of government which had prevailed in Anglo-Saxon England prior to the establishment of

---

"Lockean Ideas in Thomas Jefferson's Bill for Establishing Religious Freedom," *Journal of the History of Ideas* 21 (1960) 110–16; S. E. Mead, "Thomas Jefferson's Fair Experiment: Religious Freedom," *Religion in Life* 23 (1954) 566–79; Robert Healy, *Jefferson on Religion in Public Education* (New Haven, Conn.: Yale University Press, 1962).

[64] Jefferson, *The Papers of Thomas Jefferson,* 2:22.

[65] Ibid., 2:194–7. See also Dorothy Medlin, "Thomas Jefferson, André Morellet, and the French Version of Notes on the State of Virginia," *William and Mary Quarterly* 35 (1978) 85–99.

[66] Jefferson, *The Papers of Thomas Jefferson,* 2:296–7, 326–7.

a corrupt, norman, feudal monarchy.[67] While serving on the committee which designed the national seal, Jefferson proposed that the national crest display

> the Children of Israel in the wilderness, led by a cloud by day and a pillar of fire by night; and on the other side Hengist and Horsa, the Saxon chiefs from whom we claim the honor of being descended and whose political principles and form of government we have assumed.[68]

In his reform of American education, Jefferson advocated the study of Anglo-Saxon as a means of putting Americans in contact with their primordial, democratic racial origins.[69]

In a sense the American revolution began with Locke's myth of human social origins and ended with Jefferson's racially proud myth of national origins. Moreover, patterns emerge in the development of Enlightenment revolutionary thinking. The Enlightened American revolution began by proclaiming itself the work of the God of Reason; it ended by endowing natural moral reason with subjective self-evidence. In the name of Reason, the Enlightened leaders of the revolution went about the task of creating a highly imaginative, quasi-religious myth of national genesis and of a divinely predestined national destiny. The Enlightenment attempt to reduce Christian religion to its pure philosophical essence contributed significantly to the secularization of life in the United States, but, at the same time, Enlightenment longing for a moral and religious social order purified of all historical abuse tended to endow the secular institutions of the United States' national government with a quasi-religious aura. Particularly in the thought of Jefferson, the subjective self-evident enlightenment of each individual conscience promised to mediate the kind of spontaneous consensus which reliance on the "inner light" of the Holy Spirit had failed to produce in Calvinism. All of these philosophical and theological motifs would significantly condition the first attempts of Transcendentalism to move beyond Enlightenment thinking.

---

[67] Ibid., 1:132–4.

[68] Ibid., 1:495.

[69] See Lipscomb, ed., *The Writings of Thomas Jefferson,* 16:42–3; 18:363–7, 386; see also Charles Galbraith, "Thomas Jefferson's Views on Slavery," *Ohio Archaeological and Historical Quarterly* 34 (1925) 184–202; W. Cohen, "Thomas Jefferson and the Problem of Slavery," *Journal of American History* 54 (1969) 503–26; Leonard Levy, *Jefferson and Civil Liberties: The Darker Side* (Cambridge: Belknap, 1963); Robert McColley, *Slavery and Jeffersonian Virginia* (Urbana: University of Illinois Press, 1964); Frederick Binder, *The Color Problem in Early National America* (Paris: Mouton, 1968); G. S. Wood, "The Problem of Jefferson," *Virginia Quarterly Review* 47 (1971) 137–41.

Chapter 3

MILITANT DEISM

Let reason, then, perform her faithful duty,
and ignorance, fanaticism, and misery
will be banished from the earth.
A new age, the true millennium, will then commence;
the standard of truth and of science
will then be erected among the nations of the world,
and man, the unlimited proprietor of his own person,
may applaud himself in the result of his energies,
and contemplate with indescribable satisfaction
the universal improvement and happiness of the human race.

—Elihu Palmer

I

American Deism developed in two discernible phases. The first Deists professed a condescending tolerance toward traditional creedal religions. Franklin discouraged attacks on Christian doctrines which fostered the cultivation of bourgeois virtue among the unenlightened masses. Franklin seems to have regarded the tolerance of any other person's faith as a matter of good breeding.[1] He even composed a "Parable against Persecution" in the literary style of the King James Bible. In the parable God admonished Abraham against persecuting any individual for fashioning a personal god.[2] Franklin delighted in confounding the salons of France by

[1] Leonard Larabee, ed., *The Papers of Benjamin Franklin,* 24 vols. (New Haven, Conn.: Yale University Press, 1959–84) 12:82–4, 294–5.
[2] Ibid., 6:122–3.

inserting the parable into a King James Bible and then reading it to the assembled group as the inspired word of God. Jefferson displayed somewhat more militancy: the lord of Monticello regarded his Deistic creed as "true Christianity" and defended it in his private writings against the distortions of Christian faith which a Platonized Calvinism had popularized. Still, Jefferson kept his antipathy toward Calvinism largely to himself and he admitted, somewhat grudgingly, that he had encountered some fine men among orthodox trinitarians.[3] Both Jefferson and Franklin tended to dismiss theological creeds and arguments as beneath serious intellectual or philosophical concern, but they did not attack them publicly.

The American revolution had, however, done more than create secular political structures. It had also fused philosophy and myth in order to endow those secular structures with quasi-religious significance. After these initial gains, American Deism tended to assume a more militant stance toward established religion. The Calvinist tradition came in for special criticism and attack. Because of Tom Paine's national notoriety, his diatribes against revealed religion in *The Age of Reason* probably caused the greatest shock waves, but Ethan Allen and Elihu Palmer also launched notable attacks upon the Calvinist evangelical scheme.

In *The Age of Reason* Paine announced that his rejection of evangelical religion went hand-in-hand with his repudiation of monarchical tyranny. The publication of *Common Sense,* he insisted, marked only the first step in an ambitious program to free the human spirit from all superstition and error.[4] The French Revolution had, Paine argued, advanced the cause of religious freedom "beyond" any consideration of religious tolerance. "The French Constitution hath," he declared, "abolished or renounced toleration, and intolerance also, and hath established UNIVERSAL RIGHT OF CONSCIENCE." After the American and French revolutions, in other words, one could tolerate no intermediaries whatever between the private conscience of individuals and their God. Deism, therefore, must undertake to purify religion of all sacramental or quasi-sacramental mediators and must allow each soul to stand in naked solitude before its creator.[5]

[3] Thomas Jefferson, *The Papers of Thomas Jefferson,* ed. Julian Boyd, 17 vols. (Princeton, N.J.: Princeton University Press, 1950–65)10:78; 11:428; Andrew Lipscomb, ed., *The Writings of Thomas Jefferson,* 20 vols. (Washington, D.C.: The Thomas Jefferson Memorial Association, 1904) 13:253; 14:233; 15:409–10.

[4] Thomas Paine, *The Age of Reason,* ed. Moncure Conway (New York: Putnam's, 1930). See also Thomas Osmond, "The Theological Works of Thomas Paine," *Methodist Quarterly Review* 8 (1854) 481–513; 9 (1855) 62–72; William C. Kashatus, "Thomas Paine: A Quaker Revolutionary," *Quaker History* 73 (1984) 38–61.

[5] Paine, *The Age of Reason,* 90–1.

In the profession of religious faith which prefaces *The Age of Reason* Paine announced, "My own mind is my own church."[6] In the pages of the book Paine acknowledged Jesus as "a virtuous and amiable man,"[7] but, with quasi-prophetic passion, Paine denounced all supernatural revelation as religious hypocrisy: "It [revelation] has set up a religion of pomp and of revenue in pretended imitation of a person whose life was humility and poverty."[8] Paine replaced a religion of revelation with a religion of reason and of science: "The Almighty lecturer, by displaying the principles of science in the structure of the universe has invited man to study and to imitation."[9] Paine contrasted the sweet reasonableness of Deism with Calvinist faith in a vengeful God who vents his wrath on his own innocent Son: "How different is this to the pure and simple profession of Deism! The true deist has but one Deity; and his religion consists in contemplating the power, wisdom, and benignity of the Deity in his works, and in endeavouring to imitate him in every thing moral, scientifical, and mechanical."[10] Paine replaced the "pious fraud" perpetrated by Christianity with the elemental human faith proposed by Deism: "The only religion that has not been invented, and that has in it every evidence of divine originality, is pure and simple deism. It must have been the first and will probably be the last that man believes."[11]

Sam Adams read *The Age of Reason* with shock and incredulity and he wrote Paine to protest against the "infidelity" which breathed from the latter's rhetoric. Hurt and offended, Paine replied: "What, my good friend, do you call believing in God infidelity?"[12] Later in the nineteenth century Moncure Conway sensed something of the religious feeling which motivated Paine's secular vision. In his introduction to *The Age of Reason* Conway observed: "Although Paine arraigned the union of Church and State, his ideal Republic was religious. . . . Paine's 'Reason' was only an expansion of the Quaker's 'inner light.'"[13] Conway overstated his case. He would have done better to say that Paine had secularized, naturalized, and contracted the Quaker inner light rather than expanded it, but Paine certainly believed that one must experience divine revelation immediately within the soul's privacy if one hopes to experience it at all.[14] This "rational"

[6] Ibid., 22.
[7] Ibid., 26.
[8] Ibid., 42.
[9] Ibid., 55.
[10] Ibid., 65.
[11] Ibid., 190.
[12] Ibid., 202–3.
[13] Ibid., 5.
[14] Ibid., 23. See also Robert P. Falk, "Thomas Paine: Deist or Quaker?" *Pennsylvania Magazine of History and Biography* 62 (1938) 52–63; Franklin K. Prochaska, "Thomas Paine's *The Age of Reason* Revisited," *Journal of the History of Ideas* 33 (1972) 561–76.

Deist could, therefore, dismiss any religious impulse ungrounded in subjective immediacy as "fabulous" and "superstitious." Paine found the word of God revealed in the immutable laws of nature, which the human mind grasps either scientifically, and therefore objectively, or subjectively, through the illumination of one's private conscience. The scientist grasps God's self-revelation in nature only imperfectly, but each individual enjoys immediate access to the deity through the inner light of the conscience.[15]

Paine concluded that supernatural revelation sought to set humanity at odds with nature, the true and immediate source of divine revelation, by filling the human spirit with fairy tales about human corruption, about the vindictive anger of God, and about the crucifixion of the deity. Calvinist supernaturalism played upon the fear of damnation in order to cow humans into submission to an unenlightened and manipulative clergy.[16] As a consequence, Deistic faith completed the purification of religion which the Protestant reformation had begun: "The very nature and design of religion, if I may so express it, prove even to demonstration that it must be free from every thing of mystery, and unencumbered with every thing that is mysterious."[17] The religious purification of Christianity required, therefore, the abandonment of faith in miracles, in prophecy, in anthropomorphic conceptions of deity, in redemption, in grace, in sacraments, in ecclesiastical authority, in the Bible, and in religious tradition in order that each individual conscience might stand solitary before its God. Paine's Deism allowed only "natural mysteries," that is, unexplained events in nature of which human reason would eventually give a rational account.[18]

Paine in his Deistic militancy repudiated the Bible as the *fons et origo* of everything in Christianity which most offended him. Aware that classical Protestantism opposed Scripture to tradition, Paine cleverly used the same opposition in order to undermine faith in the Bible. Had not, he asked, a corrupt Christian tradition proclaimed the divine inspiration of Scripture? If so, ought not those who reject tradition as corrupt also reject the divine inspiration of the Bible?[19] By the same token, had not Calvinism preferred the inner illumination of the Holy Spirit to the external forms of sacramental worship? A God who speaks immediately and directly to each individual conscience needs no external written account in order to communicate personally with each individual.[20] Classical Protestantism had attacked the

[15] Paine, *Age of Reason,* 45–6, 78.
[16] Ibid., 60, 74–5.
[17] Ibid., 76.
[18] Ibid., 77–81.
[19] Ibid., 32–3.
[20] Ibid., 33.

penitential practices of the Roman Church. Paine suggested wickedly that Calvinist theories of redemption and expiation derived not from the Bible, but from the very papist penitential practices which Calvinism had so passionately condemned. Theologians, he sneered implausibly, had developed the metaphor that Jesus had paid the price for sin from reflection on the papal sale of indulgences.[21] Finally, Paine drew on the stereotypical, anticlerical rhetoric of the French Enlightenment in order to tar all churchmen, both Protestant and Catholic, with the same lurid rhetoric with which classical Protestantism had denounced Roman clerical abuse.[22] As in the case of his attack on the English crown, Paine preferred ridicule to reason in his assault on Biblical faith.

Even in the excesses of his rhetoric, however, Paine displayed a sure sense of issues. He named the flaw which lay at the basis of a Protestant reworking of medieval atonement theory. How, Paine asked, could a supposedly merciful divine Father require the death of his innocent Son in order to satisfy his vindictive rage against a sinful humanity?[23] Paine, however, did more than reject medieval atonement christology; he jettisoned all traditional Christian doctrines: the Trinity, the incarnation, the virginal conception of Jesus, the resurrection. He found no more truth in these traditional Christian tenets than in the irrational myths of Greek and Roman religion.[24]

II

Paine wrote *The Age of Reason* in Paris in 1791. Four years earlier in the United States a writer with questionable intellectual credentials had published a similar Deistic broadside against the American religious establishment. The writer called himself Ethan Allen. He had gained some notoriety during the American Revolution by leading a band of ruffians called The Green Mountain Boys in a successful assault on the British forts at Ticonderoga and Crown Point. Because of Paine's public stature as a revolutionary, his Age of Reason created more stir in the new nation than did the writings of an obscure backwoodsman like Allen. Still, Allen

[21] Ibid., 42–3.
[22] Ibid., 32, 36, 89.
[23] Ibid., 65.
[24] Ibid., 26, 28, 50, 152, 164–5. See also Ira M. Thompson, *The Religious Beliefs of Thomas Paine* (New York: Vantage Press, 1965); Harry Hayden Clark, "An Historical Interpretation of Thomas Paine's Religion," *University of California Chronicle* 35 (1933) 56–8; Harry Hayden Clark, "Toward a Reinterpretation of Thomas Paine," *American Literature* 5 (1933–34) 133–45; Michael Payne, "Priestly, Paine, Blake, and the Tradition of English Dissent," *Pennsylvania English* 10 (1983) 5–13; Wallace P. Rusterholtz, "Thomas Paine and Liberal Religion," *Religious Humanism* 23 (1989) 88–94.

first gave voice in the United States to the new religious militancy which had begun to stir in Deistic circles.

Ethan Allen first saw the light in 1737 in the town of Roxbury, Connecticut. We know little of his childhood. Until the age of seventeen, however, Allen received no schooling. Shortly before his father's death in 1755 he went to study for a short time with Jonathan Lee, a Congregational minister. During the French and Indian War, he joined the militia but saw no active service. In January 1769 he married Mary Brownson. The union proved tempestuous. In 1783 Mary died, leaving Allen with five children. She had lost three other children in childbirth. After his wife's death Allen lived a footloose existence, wandering from one frontier town to another.

A profane, rollicking man, Allen drank heavily and once escaped (no one knows how) having his ears clipped and his tongue cut out for uttering blasphemy. Early in his career he dabbled in land speculation, a practice which eventually drew him into a protracted feud between New York and Vermont over some disputed land grants. As the political tide turned against Allen and the Vermonters, he organized The Green Mountain Boys, a gang of vigilantes who undertook to "discourage" New Yorkers from settling in the disputed lands. Allen successfully led this motley crew in the capture of Forts Ticonderoga and Crown Point because both British outposts had degenerated into sitting ducks. When the Green Mountain Boys got to Crown Point they found it a ruin defended by one sergeant and eight privates. Emboldened by two easy military coups, Allen led an ill-conceived assault on Montreal in 1776. It ended in disaster for Allen and the Green Mountain Boys. The British captured Allen, but they exchanged him as a prisoner of war two years later.

Allen's military escapades transformed him into a national folk hero and his flamboyant narrative of his captivity, published in 1779, the year after his release, did nothing to discourage his public notoriety.[25] After the revolution Allen resumed his land war with New York state and dabbled in politics.

Allen claimed that as a young man he had developed an interest in "matters of the mind," but at the time he probably confined his intellectual activity to reading the newspaper and picking the brains of Dr. Thomas Young, a frontier intellectual. In the autumn of his life, however, Allen turned to philosophy. In 1785 he published a speculatively pretentious Deistic tract entitled *Reason, the Only Oracle of Man*. In 1787 he amended this treatise with *An Essay on the Universal Plentitude of Being*. He died in Burlington, Vermont, on February 12, 1789.[26]

[25] Ethan Allen, *The Narrative of Colonel Ethan Allen,* ed. Brooke Hindle (New York: Corinth Books, 1961).

[26] See Henry Hall, *Ethan Allen* (New York: D. Appleton & Co., 1892); Steward H. Holbrook, *Ethan Allen* (New York: Macmillan, 1944); Charles Jellison, *Ethan Allen: The*

Those who knew Allen personally recognized his rough-hewn genius, and some speculated about the shape his career might have taken had he enjoyed the benefits of a formal education. Rough-edged and untutored, Allen's frontier philosophy did not lack intelligence.

In *Reason, the Only Oracle of Man,* Allen boasted that, raised Arminian, he had successfully resisted the attempt of a Calvinist clergyman to persuade him that one could accept the doctrine of imputed grace independently of the rest of Calvinist doctrine. The incident had convinced him of the systematic character of the Calvinist evangelical scheme. The orthodox Calvinist, he concluded, had to "concede to it entirely or not at all, or else believe inconsistently as the clergyman had argued."[27] Disprove one Calvinist dogma, Allen concluded, and the whole evangelical scheme came tumbling down like a pack of cards.

Allen regarded Calvinist belief in predestination as the most problematic doctrine of the evangelical scheme. The dogma demanded belief in a deterministic universe, and determinism, Allen argued, contradicted human experience. Calvinist divines might attempt endlessly to disprove a priori the fact of human freedom. They could argue from the certain foreknowledge of God to the impossibility of free human choice. In the end, however, Allen dismissed such theological hair-splitting as exercises in futility because experience of our own choices tells us that in fact we choose freely.[28] Allen deemed the idea of a deterministic universe both inconsistent and dangerous. In the deterministic world of Calvinist predestination, he argued, only God can function as a real moral agent; creatures serve as the passive instruments of the deity's immutable decrees. The experience of personal moral agency, however, teaches otherwise.[29] In addition, Allen argued that the Calvinist portrayal of the human will as necessarily determined in its activity confounds the realms of matter and of spirit. Material things follow mechanical laws, as Newtonian physics taught; but spiritual beings exercise free self-determination. Allen also feared that determinism had demoralizing consequences upon human activity. On the one hand it denied personal ethical responsibility for one's own choices; on the other hand determinism provided a ready rationalization for human viciousness by placing the ultimate responsibility for sin

Frontier Rebel (Syracuse, N.Y.: Syracuse University Press, 1969); John Pell, *Ethan Allen* (Boston: Houghton Mifflin, 1929).

[27] Ethan Allen, *Reason, the Only Oracle of Man* (Bennington, Vt.: Haswell & Russell, 1884) 388.

[28] Ibid., 102.

[29] Ibid., 101.

upon a predestining God.[30] Although he lacked the capacity to reply to the subtleties of Jonathan Edwards's argument in his *Freedom of the Will,* Allen rejected as finally contradictory any speculative attempt to reconcile freedom and necessitarianism.

Moreover, Allen understood well enough the implications of Calvinist theology in order to realize that, if the human will enjoys natural freedom, then it cannot, on Calvinist presuppositions, qualify as totally depraved. He concluded somewhat hastily, therefore, that the present state of humanity coincides with the state of innocence which Adam and Eve first enjoyed in the Garden of Eden.[31] Having appealed to experience in his vindication of human freedom of choice, Allen failed to respond to Jonathan Edwards's argument in his treatise on original sin that this Calvinist doctrine roots itself directly in human experience.[32]

Allen, however, realized that the denial of human depravity demands the reinstatement of human reason along with freedom of choice. Like Paine, Allen's account of human reason remained torn between a strict empiricism and an appeal to subjective sentiment. In what concerned the genesis of ideas, Allen accepted the broad outlines of Lockean psychology. He divided ideas into ideas of sensation and ideas of reflection, and he endorsed the Lockean principle that all reasoning concerns the former.[33] Allen had the wit to realize that a strict empiricist account of human experience severely limits what the human mind can know scientifically. If humans can know only sense objects, then they cannot know empirically the divine essence, disembodied spirits, or the rewards and punishments of the after life.[34]

Allen, therefore, looked to human subjectivity to ground belief in the basic tenets of Deistic religion. He grounded belief in God in a subjective, human sense of dependence on a greater power than oneself. Reason, he argued, need only demonstrate the impossibility of an infinite series of causes in order to transform this subjective sentiment into certitude. Similarly, Allen summoned his reader to endorse the freedom of human choices by consulting their "intuitive" grasp of their own subjective personal choices.[35]

Whatever problems attend Allen's account of human religious belief, this frontier *philosophe* saw clearly that the affirmation of humanity's natural innocence called into question the Calvinist affirmation of the ne-

[30] Ibid., 95, 102.
[31] Ibid., 359–61.
[32] Jonathan Edwards, *Original Sin,* ed. Clyde A. Holbrook (New Haven, Conn.: Yale University Press, 1970).
[33] Allen, *Reason, the Only Oracle of Man,* 210.
[34] Ibid., 135, 132–48, 157–59, 210–11, 344–5.
[35] Ibid., 25–35, 91, 210.

cessity of grace and redemption. One cannot consistently impute to a guiltless humanity either corrupting sinfulness or the consequent universal need for grace and redemption. Allen found the very idea of imputed merits or demerits unintelligible. How, he asked, can any moral individual assume responsibility for someone else's meritorious or sinful actions?[36]

Natural human innocence, Allen further argued, nullifies the entire redemptive order which the Calvinistic evangelical scheme requires. Given the fact of human innocence and integrity, what need have humans for justifying faith, the illumination of the Holy Spirit, and biblical revelation? The natural functioning of innocent human reason yields everything humans need to know. By the same token, miracles, prophecy, and the authority of the Bible must all yield to the judgment of rational religion.[37] Finally, without the need for grace and redemption one can also dispense with a redeemer. Rational religion has, therefore, no need for either the incarnation or the Trinity which the incarnation reveals.[38]

Having demonstrated to his satisfaction the indefensibility of the entire evangelical scheme, Allen targeted specific doctrines which he found particularly offensive. He especially called into question the notion of infinite atonement. This medieval theological theory taught that human sin required infinite suffering as an atonement because it had offended an infinite God. In his refutation of this doctrine, Allen invoked the principle that choice follows knowledge. If so, then the consequences of human choice can never transcend the finitude of human knowing. The irreducibly finite character of each human act precludes imputing to it an infinite burden of guilt. During the fourteenth century the English theologian John Duns Scotus had reached a similar conclusion. Allen further argued that both the blessings and sufferings of the next life must enjoy a finite duration. Hence, the soul after death must retain the capacity to change as readily as it does in this life. Here, Allen went beyond Scotus.[39]

Having demolished to his satisfaction the Calvinist evangelical scheme, Allen set about the task of religious reconstruction. The creed of his rational religion endorsed the three fundamental tenets of Deistic faith: (1) the existence of a benevolent and provident Creator, (2) the existence of an unchanging natural law and of a divinely ordained system of rewards and punishments, and (3) the existence of an afterlife in which the deity administers those same rewards and punishments.[40] Allen's instinctive

---

[36] Ibid., 385–420.

[37] Ibid., 177–8, 190, 199, 201, 210, 220, 225, 233–60, 274, 283–94, 302–10, 316, 361.

[38] Ibid., 344, 352, 416–20.

[39] Ibid., 25–50, 62, 115–21, 130, 164–73, 472–4. See also John Duns Scotus, *In 3 Sent.,* d. 19, q. 1; d. 20, q. 1.

[40] Ibid., 25–50, 62, 115–21, 130, 164–73, 472–4.

mistrust of inner light piety left him less inclined than Paine to appeal to the self-evident light of conscience,[41] but Allen's philosophical vision secularized other tenets of Calvinism. Like Calvin, Allen accepted the dualistic split in human nature between matter and spirit[42] and, like Jonathan Edwards, he believed that creation reveals the divine glory.[43] Moreover, together these two beliefs brought Allen to the brink of pantheism.

In *Reason, the Only Oracle of Man,* Allen repudiated the notion of creation in time. He viewed God as monarch of the universe in virtue of the divine nature itself. Allen's God exemplified the ultimate ruling power on which all things depend. For that reason, humans experience their relationship to God as a felt sense of dependence. Allen reasoned that, since human monarchs need subjects in order to exercise sovereign sway over them, the divine King too needs creatures subject to him in order to exist as God. Because the dependence of creatures on the deity entered into Allen's very definition of divinity, he concluded that God and creation must always co-exist. God's eternity, therefore, requires that creation, like God, exist from eternity.

In constructing this somewhat contrived and thoroughly inconclusive argument, Allen was, of course, thumbing his nose at the first chapter of Genesis, but not until after the publication of *Reason, the Only Oracle of Man* did Allen begin to understand what the co-eternity of the world and of God implied for one's understanding of the relationship between creature and creator.[44] Second thoughts about the nature of the human soul triggered his new theological insight. When writing *Reason, the Only Oracle of Man,* Allen's dualistic sundering of the human person into spirit and matter led him to deny that the soul could in any sense exist in a material place.[45] On reflection, however, he concluded that if the soul does in fact exist in a human substance, then it must exist somewhere. The soul must, therefore, interpenetrate the body.[46]

However, if the soul could penetrate matter, why not God? An infinite being must exist everywhere. Though not encompassed by any place, the infinite deity must nevertheless encompass every place. The universe, Allen concluded, confronts human reason as a divine "plenum" of intelligent being. The divine essence differs from the essence of finite creatures, but the

---

[41] Ibid., 225–6, 317.

[42] Ibid., 142, 154, 158, 165–70, 408.

[43] Ibid., 81.

[44] Ibid., 51–71.

[45] Ibid., 94.

[46] Ethan Allen, "Essay on the Universal Plenitude of Being and on the Nature and Immortality of the Human Soul and Its Agency," *Reason, the Only Oracle of Man,* 1–12.

divine essence nevertheless "pervades" finite intelligences. Like Jonathan Edwards, then, Allen in the end subscribed to a panentheistic understanding of the relationship between God and creation. Though distinct from the world, God interpenetrates all creation, which in turn exists in God.

Finally, Allen's Deism radicalized and secularized another dimension of the Calvinist tradition. Calvinism had sought to free Christianity from the corruptions of a decadent historical tradition. By grounding religion in the rational grasp of immutable natural laws, Allen's Deism sought to free religion from history itself. This final liberation of religion would, Allen fondly hoped, complete the project of the Protestant reformation and purify religious faith from all the abuses of a decadent past by rendering it ahistorical. Allen's assault on historical religion employed a variety of rhetorical gambits. He ridiculed the sectarian divisions of the Christian churches. The bickering of Protestants and Papists, of Christians and Muslims only dramatizes, he sneered, the corrupt and superstitious character of every religious tradition. Allen also dismissed the historical evidence for orthodox Christianity as too ambiguous to require religious assent. Finally, given the fallibility and limitations of the human mind, Allen questioned whether humans had the capacity to transmit a historical revelation from one generation to the next without corrupting and adulterating it.[47]

In his attempt to render religion ahistorical Allen unwittingly brought to something like a pure position Calvinism's own dualistic sundering of internal religious experience from its external, ritual expression. In *Reason, the Only Oracle of Man,* Allen observed:

> Most people place religion in arbitrary ceremonies, or mere positive institutions, abstractly considered from the moral rectitude of things, and in which religion does not and cannot consist, and thus delude themselves with an empty notion of religion, which in reality is made up of tradition and superstition and in which moral obligation is not concerned; not considering that a conformity to moral rectitude, which is morality in the abstract, is the sum of all religion, that ever was or can be in the universe; as there can be no religion in that in which there is no moral obligation; except we make religion to be void of reason, and if so, all argument about it is at an end.[48]

In other words, unless the individual conscience grasps the immutable principles of ethics rationally, the external forms of religion remain vain and empty. Once conscience has spoken, they become superfluous.[49]

---

[47] Allen, *Reason, the Only Oracle of Man,* 336–40, 423–4.

[48] Ibid., 469.

[49] Ibid., 445–63. See also B. T. Schantz, "Ethan Allen's Religious Ideas," *Journal of Religion* 18 (1938) 183–217; Dana Doten, "Ethan Allen's Original Something," *New England Quarterly* 11 (1938) 361–6; Clarence Gohdes, "Ethan Allen and His Magnum Opus,"

III

Despite a lack of schooling, Allen had grasped and articulated with remarkable clarity many of the fundamental presuppositions of Enlightenment religion. Deism in young America, however, found its most fervent evangelist in Elihu Palmer. Born on August 7, 1764, on his father's farm in Caterbury, Connecticut, Palmer attended Dartmouth College and succeeded so well in his studies that he underwent induction into Phi Beta Kappa. After college he studied divinity for a time with the Rev. John Foster. In 1788 he accepted a pulpit in Newton, Long Island, but he remained there only six months.

Under suspicion of heresy because of his Deistic tendencies, he moved to Philadelphia in 1789. There he joined the Baptist Church and accepted a pulpit in it, only to suffer excommunication as a heretic in 1791. Followed by a handful of parishioners, he accepted an invitation to minister to The Universal Society, a group founded by John Fitch, the inventor of the steamboat. Shortly thereafter, Palmer preached a sermon denying the divinity of Christ which so inflamed public sentiment in Philadelphia that Palmer found himself forced to flee the city in order to avoid physical attack. Palmer retired to his brother's home in western Pennsylvania. There, under his brother's direction, he read law. In 1793 Palmer returned to Philadelphia and joined the bar. Three months later both he and his wife fell victim to yellow fever. The disease claimed the life of Palmer's wife and left him blind.

His legal career nipped in the bud Palmer moved to New York, which became the center of his Deistic evangelization. He felt a call, despite his blindness, to spread the gospel of Deism among the masses of the American people. Shortly after his arrival in New York Palmer founded The Deistical Society. In 1800 the Society began publishing *The Temple of Reason*. Dennis Driscol, a defrocked Catholic priest, edited this weekly paper. It folded in 1802. In either 1801 or 1802 Palmer published *Principles of Nature or, A Development of the Moral Causes of Happiness and Misery Among the Human Species.*

Undaunted by the collapse of *The Temple of Reason,* Palmer founded a new weekly entitled *Prospect, or View of the Moral World.* On March 30, 1805, *Prospect* too collapsed for lack of financial backing. In 1806 Palmer came to Philadelphia for a lecture. There he contracted pleurisy and died on April 7.

Open Court 43 (1929) 148; George Pomeroy Anderson, "Who Wrote Ethan Allen's Bible," *New England Quarterly* 10 (1937) 685–96; Darlene Shapiro, "Ethan Allen: Philosopher-Theologian to a Generation of American Revolutionaries," *William and Mary Quarterly* 21 (1964) 236–55.

Palmer exemplified a curious blend of religious attitudes. Like Allen, he rejected revealed, supernatural, creedal religion, but Palmer injected into American Deism an element of aggressive, quasi-evangelical, "new light" fervor absent from tolerant freethinkers like Franklin and Jefferson. Add to this a heavy salting of popular republican religion and a flair for religious diatribe. Palmer believed passionately in the United States and in the republican form of government which it incarnated. The War for Independence, Palmer believed, had ushered in a millennium of unparalleled prosperity as long as Americans trusted their God-given natural powers in reaping the benefits of the dawning new age. Palmer's social gospel transmuted Paine's myth of American innocence into the promise of limitless social progress. The roots of social corruption, Palmer proclaimed with Rousseauvian fervor, lay in the structures of society, not in human nature. Reform those structures and education must of necessity usher in the millennium. Two forces opposed the combined power of reason, education, and progress: political despotism and organized religion. Palmer wrote in *Principles of Nature:*

> The double despotism of Church and state has borne so hard upon human existence that man is sunk beneath its dreadful weight; but resuscitated nations are about to teach kings and tyrants a lesson awfully impressive, in regard to the destiny which awaits the aggregate injustice of the world. The period is at hand, in which kings and thrones, and priests and hierarchies, and the long catalogue of mischiefs which they have produced, shall be swept away from the face of the earth, and buried in the grave of everlasting destruction. Then will arrive the era of human felicity, in which the heart of unfortunate man shall be consoled; then will appear the moment of national consolation, and universal freedom; then the empire of reason, of science, of virtue, will extend over the whole earth, and man, emancipated from the barbarous despotism of antiquity, will assume to himself his true predicament in nature, and become a standing evidence of the divinity of thought and of the unlimited power of human reason.[50]

In the pages of *Prospect* he took up the same theme:

> Let reason perform her faithful duty, and ignorance, fanaticism, and misery will be banished from the earth. A new age, the true millennium will then commence; the standard of truth and of science will then be erected among the nations of the world, and man, the unlimited proprietor of his own person, may applaud himself in the result of his energies, and contemplate with indescribable satisfaction the universal improvement and happiness of the human race.[51]

[50] Elihu Palmer, *Principles of Nature* (London: R. Carlile, 1823) 200.
[51] Elihu Palmer, "On Immortality," *Prospect* 10 (1803) 48; see also 10 (1804) 79.

In the name of Reason, Palmer turned the rhetoric of revivalist piety against revivalism itself. "The energy of thought," he warned, "will one day teach fanaticism that her native home is hell."[52] And again: "Revelation is a system of juggling, in which each dexterous imposter plays off a game of folly and fanaticism to accumulate interest, or gratify the enthusiastic feelings of the heart."[53]

In January 1804 Palmer began publishing in Prospect a series of Deistic homilies on Sacred Scripture. He ambitioned an exhaustive commentary on the sacred texts which would expose the superstitious and demoralizing character of the evangelical scheme. The biblical accounts of creation, the flood, the tower of Babel, the destruction of Sodom and Gomorrah, the sacrifice of Isaac, the Exodus, the Levitical code—each came under scornful commentary and scathing dismissal. One finds little reason and even less scholarly exegesis in Palmer's Scripture "commentaries." He had received only perfunctory theological training and, despite his fervid commitment to the cause of Reason, he himself found his forte more in rhetoric than in logic. Paradoxically, then, Palmer's odd fusion of Deistic faith with "new light," evangelical fervor ended by grounding the religion of pure reason more in passionate feeling than in rational argument.[54]

When Tom Paine returned from France to the nation his rhetoric had helped to create, he found himself ostracized from polite society not only by his public attack on the new nation's acknowledged "father," George Washington, but also by his own aggressive attacks on Christianity. Militant Deism had caused the mainline churches in the new nation to close ranks against an aggressive and identifiable enemy. Eventually, however, Enlightenment religion did acquire social respectability, but the religion of Reason did not win social acceptance without a struggle. In the end it found the social respectability it sought by institutionalizing itself as the Unitarian Church.

---

[52] Elihu Palmer, "Characters in the Christian Drama," *Prospect* 2 (1803) 7.
[53] Ibid., 18 (1804) 141.
[54] See Kerry S. Walters, "Elihu Palmer's Crusade for Rational Religion," *Religious Humanism* 24 (1990) 113–29.

Chapter 4

THE UNITARIAN COMPROMISE

Superstition contracts and darkens the mind;
but that living faith in moral and religious truth,
for which I contend as the highest culture of rich and poor,
is in no respect narrow or exclusive.

—William Ellery Channing

I

New England Congregationalism put to the test the fundamental principle on which English Congregationalism had taken a stand. That principle asserted that the supernatural enlightenment of the Holy Spirit would produce a spontaneous consensus of faith among converted Bible-reading Christians without the supervision of the ecclesiastical authority of the Anglican Church. As long as religious and political power remained wedded in New England, the law could enforce supernatural consensus, as both Roger Williams and Mistress Anne Hutchinson had discovered. With the replacement of the old colonial charter by a royal one, legal power to enforce orthodoxy passed from the hands of the New England clergy. Thereafter, orthodox ministers found themselves relatively helpless to counteract the fragmentation of religious belief.

The Mathers fulminated for many years against the Presbyterian tendencies of Solomon Stoddard, the unconventional uncle of Jonathan Edwards, whose pulpit Edwards assumed. With the spread of liberal views among the clergy, Cotton Mather, the self-appointed guardian of the Puritan tradition, began to see the wisdom of establishing a tighter control of ministerial sentiment than strict congregational principles allowed. Cotton

Mather's search for the political means to enforce orthodoxy brought him into conflict with the Rev. John Wise, the pastor of Chebacco.

The formation of the Brattle Street Church triggered the controversy between the two churchmen. Exercising the local autonomy granted it by the congregational principle, the Brattle Street community passed a series of resolutions concerning worship and discipline which disturbed orthodox opinion in Boston. Weary of seemingly endless biblical sermons, the bored congregation on Brattle Street declared the explication of sacred texts optional during Sunday worship. More alarming still to the orthodox leaders of the Congregational Church, the Brattle Street Church ceased to require conversion as a condition for church membership and extended the vote to all baptized, adult members of the community.

Increase Mather, that lion of New England orthodoxy and father of Cotton Mather, felt compelled to respond to the heretical doings at Brattle Street.[1] In 1700 he published *The Order of the Gospel*. The tract denounced the deviations emanating from the Brattle Street congregation. Not satisfied with verbal denunciation, in May of the same year the Mathers organized a general convention in order to repudiate the new licentiousness.

Finding the Brattle Street community unperturbed and even defiant, Cotton Mather attempted a new gambit. In 1705 he published a proposal for an association of ministers who would exercise effective control over church discipline. To John Wise, Mather's proposal clearly flew in the face of the basic principles of New England Congregationalism enunciated in the Cambridge Platform.[2]

---

[1] See Kenneth Murdock, *Increase Mather: The Foremost American Puritan* (Cambridge, Mass.: Harvard University Press, 1925).

[2] See Wendell Barrett, *Cotton Mather: The Puritan Priest* (New York: Dodd, Mead, 1891); Ralph and Louise Boas, *Cotton Mather: Keeper of the Puritan Conscience* (New York: Harper, 1928); E. Benz, "Ecumenical Relations between Boston Puritanism and German Pietism: Cotton Mather and Auguste Hermann Franke," *Harvard Theological Review* 54 (1961) 159–93; S. Bercovitch, "Delightful Examples of Surprising Prosperity: Cotton Mather and the American Success Story," *English Studies* 51 (1970) 40–3; S. Bercovitch, "New England Epic: Cotton Mather's *Magnalia Christi Americana*," *English Literary History* 33 (1966) 337–50; O. T. Beall and R. H. Shryock, "Cotton Mather: First Significant Figure in American Medicine," *Proceedings of the American Antiquarian Society* 63 (1953) 237–74; Phillis Franklin, *Show Thyself a Man* (Paris: Mouton, 1969); M. A. Isani, "Cotton Mather and the Orient," *New England Quarterly* 43 (1970) 46–58; David Levin, "The Hazing of Cotton Mather: The Creation of a Biographical Personality," *New England Quarterly* 36 (1963) 147–71; R. Middlekauff, "Piety and Intellect in Puritanism," *William and Mary Quarterly* 22 (1965) 457–70; A. K. Nelson, "King Philip's War and the Hubbard-Mather Rivalry," *William and Mary Quarterly* 27 (1970) 615–29; P. H. Smith, "Politics and Sainthood: Biography by Cotton Mather," *William and Mary Quarterly* 20 (1963) 186–206;

II

We do not know the date of John Wise's birth, but the Congregational Church baptized him on August 15, 1652. Wise received a master's degree from Harvard College. He served twice as a militia chaplain: once in 1676 and again in 1690. After filling two other pulpits, he accepted a call to Chebacco in 1680.

An outspoken defender of liberal causes, Wise served a term in prison for his outspoken opposition to the taxes imposed by Governor Andros. Wise also openly criticized General Walley's conduct of a disastrous expedition against Quebec in 1690. Wise had served as chaplain to the defeated and butchered troops. In 1692 Wise denounced the Salem witch trials and signed a petition in support of the Proctors, who had also opposed the Salem court only to fall victim to its judgment. In 1721 Wise publicly supported inoculation against smallpox, despite general fear of the practice. A colorful frontier figure and a physically powerful man, Wise enjoyed a popular reputation as a formidable wrestler; but his reputation rested on more than feats of physical prowess. In 1720 he published a short treatise on Church music, and Wise's attack on Mather's proposals for shoring up ministerial authority breathe with a wit and humor rare among New England Calvinist clergymen.

Wise published two tracts opposing Mather's proposals: *The Churches Quarrel Espoused* in 1710 and *A Vindication of the Government of New England Churches* in 1717. He arraigned the proposals satirically before a mock tribunal and convicted them of Presbyterianism, Prelacy, usurpation of rights, rebellion, and infidelity. In the spirit of Roger Williams, Wise rejected outright the clergy's right to wield political power and he denied the proposals any biblical justification.[3]

To all appearances, Wise's vindication of the Congregational principle defended the status quo. But when one reads it in the light of the growing fragmentation of orthodox Congregational belief his tract takes on a revolutionary character, for Wise chose to defend the principle of local church autonomy at the precise moment when local autonomy was subverting traditional beliefs and sacramental discipline. As a consequence, he gave orthodox justification to the right of local churches to entertain and adopt unorthodox theological views. Not only did Wise's defense of

---

Gustav van Cromphout, "Cotton Mather: The Puritan Historian as Renaissance Humanist," *American Literature* 49 (1977) 327–37; Philip F. Gena, "Cotton Mather's Life of Phips: 'A Vice with the Vizard of Vertue Upon It,'" *New England Quarterly* 50 (1977) 440–57; Maxine Van de Wetering, "A Reconsideration of the Inoculation Controversy," *New England Quarterly* 58 (1985) 46–67.

[3] See George Allan Cook, *John Wise: Early American Democrat* (New York: Crown Press, 1952) 107–23.

the Cambridge Platform embarrass Cotton Mather, but it also dramatized the impotence of orthodox Congregational ministers as they faced the threat of growing popular infidelity on the part of clergy and laity alike.[4]

III

The development of secular Deism in young America found a parallel in the gradual erosion of orthodoxy in a number of established congregations. Ministers of liberal bent like Charles Chauncy and Jonathan Mayhew repudiated one basic Calvinist dogma after another while preserving the external forms of orthodox Calvinist worship. In New England, the Great Awakening had dramatized the growing cleavage between clergy of orthodox and of liberal sentiment. Chauncy, the liberal, had engaged Jonathan Edwards, the eloquent defender of orthodoxy, in an open debate over the religious merits of the revival. Chauncy had denounced the "new light" preachers for fomenting disorder, for subverting the teaching authority of ordained ministers, for seeking to discredit "old light" preachers. Chauncy had defended pluralism in religious experience, had suggested purely natural explanations for supposedly graced, supernatural experiences, and had repudiated the "enthusiasm" of revivalist piety for a more "reasonable" form of Christianity.[5]

The debate between liberal and orthodox ministers centered on key doctrinal issues. Orthodox communities opted for a policy of closed communion in celebrating the Lord's supper. Liberal parishes gradually relaxed the requirements for participation in eucharistic communion. Initially, doctrinal debates focused on the issue of original sin. The popularity of John Taylor's *Scripture Doctrine of Original Sin* prompted Jonathan Edwards to undertake its systematic refutation. Edwards's argument set the terms of subsequent theological discussion. Edwards, like other Puritan divines, recognized that human nature left to itself could desire limited natural goods, but he quite reasonably questioned the capacity of human nature to love with the universality to which the gospel calls the human heart. In *Original Sin,* Edwards, probably motivated by the fallacies of Ramist logic, bound belief in human sinfulness and depravity to faith in grace, Calvinist determinism, and Christ's redemptive death. Like Allen, Edwards saw clearly that the Calvinist evangelical scheme which he defended formed a logical whole. Compromise on any key dogma undermined the entire doctrinal scheme.[6]

[4] See ibid.; C. Rossiter, "John Wise: Colonial Democrat," *New England Quarterly* 22 (1949) 3–32.

[5] See Norman W. Gibbs, "Charles Chauncy: A Theology of Two Portraits," *Harvard Theological Review* 83 (1990) 259–70.

[6] Jonathan Edwards, *Original Sin,* ed. Clyde Holbrook (New Haven, Conn.: Yale University Press, 1970). See also Donald L. Gelpi, "Conversion: Beyond the Impasses of Indi-

Liberal theological sentiment showed less concern than Edwards with intellectual rigor and more openness to theological compromise. However, the progress of liberal theology vindicated Edwards's theological instincts, for after jettisoning the doctrine of original sin liberal ministers found themselves yielding piecemeal every other key Calvinist belief. Liberal theology progressed with logical predictability from an Arminian denial of human depravity, to rationalism, to universalism, to Arianism, and finally to Unitarianism. Let us reflect on the motives for that progress.

In response to Edwards's vindication of a strict determinism of grace,[7] liberal ministers opted for belief in natural human freedom. In their eyes the classical Calvinist doctrine of total human depravity grossly exaggerated the evil of the human condition. Liberal clergymen recognized both good and evil tendencies in the human heart, but they refused to ascribe all human goodness to the action of divine grace. They regarded virtuous activity as the product of free human choice rather than of predestining grace. Having embraced a robust Arminian defense of human freedom, liberal divines next rehabilitated human reason. Moreover, they tended to acquiesce in a Lockean, nominalistic account of how human reason works. As a consequence, they also tended to assume that, if God communicates with the human race, the deity must respect the limits imposed on religious experience by Lockean nominalism. They therefore portrayed divine revelation as compensating for the relatively slow progress of rational, empirical investigations. In the process they implicitly conceded that human reason, left to its own resources, would eventually have discovered the truths contained in divine revelation. Only the importance of saving truth and the fallibility of the human mind had led God to resort to historical revelation. The deity had, moreover, confirmed that revelation with scientifically verifiable miracles. Thus, liberal, Arminian divines transformed the content of divine revelation into nature's law re-edited in a brighter, fairer edition.

Theological rehabilitation of human nature led liberal divines to question next the need for divine, supernatural election. Far from saving and damning souls arbitrarily in the manner of a Calvinist Jehovah, the God of liberal piety willed the salvation of all people. In his *Mystery Hid from Ages and Generations,* Charles Chauncy gave this new salvific optimism clear and radical formulation. No one, he declared, need fear Calvinist threats of eternal damnation. The Bible says nothing about the fate of individuals after death. Christians should, therefore, trust that an

---

vidualism," *Beyond Individualism: Toward a Retrieval of Moral Discourse in America,* ed. Donald L. Gelpi (Notre Dame: University of Notre Dame Press, 1989) 1–32.

[7] Jonathan Edwards, *Freedom of the Will,* ed. Paul Ramsey (New Haven, Conn.: Yale University Press, 1957).

infinitely good, wise, and benevolent God will bring about the saving reconciliation of every human being.

Belief in universal divine benevolence demanded in turn a reevaluation of Jesus' place in God's saving scheme. Calvinist soteriology blended medieval atonement theology with Augustinian belief in human depravity. On Calvinist principles the utter depravity of human nature made the incarnation necessary. Moreover, in Calvin's thought, Christ's atoning work consisted in absorbing the wrath which God vents on a sinful and corrupt humanity so that God can subsequently show mercy to sinners. Liberal divines reasoned hastily that, if God does not demand vindictive satisfaction for sin, as Calvinism had taught, then one need not assert the redemptive character of Jesus' death. Liberal Arminian piety still focused on the person of Jesus as an object of special veneration and love, but liberal divines tended more and more to preach an Arian Christ. Among God's creatures, Jesus deserved special veneration and praise, but only God deserved divine adoration. In 1653 John Biddle published *A Twofold Catechism* of Unitarian doctrine adapted to both adults and children. As a consequence, many regard him as the founder of American Unitarianism.

In England, the publication of John Locke's *Reasonableness of Christianity* had encouraged the cultivation of rational empiricism in religious circles. In the eighteenth century Theophilus Lindsey and Joseph Priestly emerged as the leaders of the Unitarian movement in England. When these philosophical and theological influences reached the colonies, they found a soil prepared to receive the seeds they sowed. As early as 1740 Ebinezer Gay began preaching against the doctrine of the Trinity. James Freeman, the pastor of Kings Chapel, seconded Gay's efforts and succeeded in leading the first Episcopal parish into the Unitarian fold. In 1794 Joseph Priestly brought his Unitarian message to Philadelphia, and within two years a Unitarian parish was gathering for worship in the city of brotherly love. Orthodox Christianity, however, viewed the new religious movement with alarm. Controversy waxed most violent toward the beginning of the nineteenth century. During these years of turmoil the Unitarian cause found an eloquent defender in the person of William Ellery Channing.[8]

[8] See Conrad Wright, *The Beginnings of Unitarianism in America* (Boston: Beacon Press, 1955); Conrad Wright, ed., *A Stream of Light: A Sesquicentennial History of American Unitarianism* (Boston: Unitarian Universalist Association, 1975); Conrad Wright, *The Liberal Christians: Essays on American Unitarian History* (Boston: Beacon Press, 1970); Conrad Wright, *The Unitarian Controversy: Essays on American Unitarian History* (Boston: Skinner House Books, 1994); Sydney E. Ahlstrom, "The Problem of the History of Religion in American Church History," *Church History* 39 (1970) 224–35; Sydney E. Ahlstrom and Jonathan S. Carey, *An American Reformation: A Documentary History of*

IV

William Ellery Channing first saw the light in Newport, Rhode Island, in April 1780. The gloom of predestinationist piety and the lugubrious preaching of Ezra Stiles and of Timothy Hopkins cast a religious pall over his childhood. As an adult, he recalled his shock on hearing his father after Sunday worship commend a sermon on judgment and damnation as "sound doctrine," but, to his relief, he realized that his father donned the vestment of theological orthodoxy only on Sunday. During the week, the elder Channing refused to let Calvinist orthodoxy intrude on the daily business of living. His father's only-on-Sunday piety began to undermine young William's ability to take orthodox faith too seriously.

In 1794 William attended Harvard College where fear that French revolutionary sentiment was undermining the very foundations of civilized living made a good Federalist of young Channing, as it did of many others. In 1798 Channing graduated at the head of his class. In the same year he accepted a post in Richmond, Virginia, as tutor to the family of David Randolph. There Channing discovered Jeffersonian republicanism, but his Puritan stiffness and his self-imposed penury excluded him for active participation in the gaiety of Richmond society. He read David Hume, succumbed to reverie, and in the late 1790s underwent a Calvinist religious conversion whose effects lingered until 1809.

In 1800 Channing returned to New England weakened in health, partly from his own penny-pinching. He enrolled in Harvard Divinity School. In 1802 he received approbation to preach and in the following year, the year of Ralph Waldo Emerson's birth, he accepted a pulpit in the Federal Street Church where he ministered to the Brahmins of Boston.[9] Sensitive to the debate developing between orthodox and Unitarian ministers, he himself did not take a clear Unitarian stand until 1819. After that he emerged as a chief spokesman for the Unitarian cause.[10]

In 1820 he published his "Moral Argument Against Calvinism." In the same year he received an honorary doctorate in divinity from Harvard University. In 1821 the university invited him to deliver the Dudleian Lecture. His admiring auditors included the young Ralph Waldo Emerson.

Unitarian Christianity (Middleton, Conn.: Wesleyan University Press, 1985); George Edward Ellis, *A Half-Century of the Unitarian Controversy: With Particular Reference to Its Origin, Its Course, and Its Prominent Subjects among Congregationalists of Massachusetts* (Boston: Crosby Nichols, 1857); Nathan O. Hatch, *The Democratization of American Christianity* (New Haven, Conn.: Yale University Press, 1989); Alan Ruston, "The Principles of Unitarian Christianity," *Faith and Freedom* 46 (1993) 95–9.

[9] See Madeleine Rice, *Federal Street Pastor* (New York: Bookman Associates, 1961).

[10] See Joseph A. Bassett, "In What Sense Unitarian?" *Unitarian Universalist Christian* 49 (1994) 49–57.

That same year Channing's health collapsed and he journeyed to England where he met William Wordsworth and Samuel Taylor Coleridge. On his return he helped organize the American Unitarian Association in 1825. He befriended the Boston Transcendentalists, who affectionately called him their "bishop," but Channing never embraced the Transcendentalist cause wholeheartedly. He made his closest approach to a Transcendentalist creed in his sermon "Likeness to God." In 1830 he gathered a number of his sermons and other writings into a single volume entitled *Discourses, Reviews, and Miscellanies.*

In the same year his wife's declining health prompted a trip to the West Indies. Thereafter, his sermons exhibited a growing preoccupation with slavery and other social issues. His queasiness at the radicalism of Boston abolitionists, however, kept him from identifying with their cause until he found himself publicly challenged to do so in 1836.[11] Thereafter he published a series of anti-slavery tracts. In 1838 Channing supported Emerson in the theological row provoked by the latter's "Divinity School Address." In 1842, on returning to Boston after a lecture engagement, he contracted typhoid fever and died on October 2.[12]

Channing viewed Calvinism and Catholicism with equal repugnance. He viewed Catholicism as a religion of external formalism and autocratic intolerance. It withheld the Bible from the faithful and forbade the election of bishops. The age of revolution and the spread of "just, natural, ennobling views of religion" spelled, Channing felt confident, Catholicism's eventual demise.[13]

[11] See T. F. Harwood, "Prejudice and Antislavery: The Colloquy between William Ellery Channing and Edwards Strutt Abdy," *American Quarterly* 18 (1966) 697–700; J. E. Reinhardt, "The Evolution of William Ellery Channing's Socio-Political Ideas," *American Literature* 26 (1954) 154–65; M. H. Rice, "William Ellery Channing: The Making of a Social Gospel," *Proceedings of the American Philosophical Society* 97 (1953) 31–43.

[12] See Len Gougeon, "The Anti-Slavery Background of Emerson's 'Ode Inscribed to W. H. Channing,'" *Studies in the American Renaissance* 9 (1985) 63–77. For general biographies of Channing see Octavius Brooks Frothingham, *Memoir of William Ellery Channing* (Boston: Houghton Mifflin, 1886); Paul Frothingham, *William Ellery Channing: His Messages from the Spirit* (Boston: Houghton Mifflin, 1903); Arthur Brown, *William Ellery Channing* (New York: Twayne, 1961); Jack Mendelsohn, *Channing: The Reluctant Rebel* (Boston: Little, Brown and Co., 1971); John White Chadwick, *William Ellery Channing: Minister of Religion* (Boston: Houghton Mifflin, 1903); Arthur W. Brown, *Always Young for Liberty: A Biography of William Ellery Channing* (Syracuse, N.Y.: Syracuse University Press, 1956); Frederick T. McGill, *Channing of Concord: A Life of William Ellery Channing* (New Brunswick, N.J.: Rutgers, 1967); Robert N. Hudspeth, *Ellery Channing* (New York: Twayne, 1973); Andrew Delbaco, *William Ellery Channing: An Essay on the Liberal Spirit in America* (Cambridge, Mass.: Harvard University Press, 1981); Conrad Wright, "The Channing We Don't Know," *Unitarian Universality Christian* 35 (1980–81) 35–47.

[13] William Ellery Channing, *Works* (Boston: American Unitarian Association, 1882) 468.

In Channing's eyes Calvinism posed a much more serious religious threat. It grounded religious faith in a paralyzing fear of a deity whose vindictive moral character degraded him beneath the standards of ordinary human benevolence. Channing viewed the Calvinist doctrine of human depravity as a manifest theological ploy to discourage critical reflection on the speculative inadequacies of the Calvinist evangelical scheme. Channing rejected the doctrine of natural human depravity, believed divine revelation proportioned to human reason, repudiated divine predestining election, affirmed God's universal saving benevolence, and rejected belief in both the incarnation and the Trinity.[14]

Channing probably made his most significant contribution to the cause of liberal religion in his attack on Calvinist belief in the total otherness of God. The Calvinist portrait of God as wholly other than human nature only lent fallacious plausibility, he argued, to the even more appalling belief in divine wrath and vengeance. Calvinist belief in the otherness of God placed the deity beyond the pale of ordinary human morality and allowed God to act with an injustice and vindictiveness which human ethics rightly condemns. Covenant theology had attempted to remedy this defect in classical Calvinism by maintaining that God freely bound himself to act according to the terms of his covenant with humans even though nothing in God's nature required him to do so. Not surprisingly, Channing found this solution artificial.

Channing conceded to traditional Calvinist piety the infinity of God, although his speculative reasons for doing so remained vague. He also conceded that infinity made God different from finite humans. In moral matters, however, Channing refused to concede any difference between God and his rational creatures. The moral principles which sanction divine activity must, he insisted, coincide with the principles of human morality. He concluded, therefore, that God and humanity share one and the same moral essence.[15] Channing viewed this doctrine of essential sameness as the mainspring of Unitarian faith and piety. Enlightenment religion reduced religious practice to the patient cultivation of virtue. Channing's doctrine of essential sameness gave pious Unitarians the assurance that the natural cultivation of virtue made one like God.[16]

In a sense, the Protestant reformation sought to purify Christian faith and practice by recovering its original biblical essence. American Deism, as we have seen, tended to see itself as the heir and fulfillment of Protestant religious reform. The American Deists sought to reduce Protestantism

[14] Ibid., 459–62.
[15] Ibid., 462–3.
[16] Ibid., 291.

to its pure philosophical essence. Militant Deists like Paine, Allen, and Palmer despaired of effecting the philosophical purification of religion within the established churches. In this sense, they represented the separatist wing of Enlightenment religion. Channing's Unitarianism, by contrast, sought with the sweet light of a genteel, socially respectable reason to purify institutional Protestantism from within. That quest gave distinctive color to his defense of Unitarian religion. In fending off attacks against Unitarianism, Channing typically responded by arguing that one could just as easily invoke philosophy as theology in order to ground traditional Calvinist heart worship.

Edwards had argued that religious conversion gives one new eyes to perceive the divine beauty manifest in the universe.[17] Channing argued that natural, moral assimilation to God through the free cultivation of virtue has the same effect. Channing wrote:

> It is plain, too, that likeness to God is the true and only preparation for the enjoyment of the universe. In proportion as we approach and resemble the mind of God, we are brought into harmony with creation; for in that proportion we possess the principles from which the universe sprung; we carry within ourselves the perfections of which its beauty, magnificence, order, benevolent adaptations, and boundless purposes are the results and manifestations. God unfolds himself in his works to a kindred mind. It is possible that the brevity of these hints may expose to the charge of mysticism what seems to me the calmest and clearest truth. I think, however, that every reflecting man will feel that likeness to God must be a principle of sympathy or accordance with his creation; for the creation is a birth and shining forth of the Divine Mind, a work through which his spirit breathes. In proportion as we receive this spirit, we possess within ourselves the explanation of what we see. We discern more and more of God in every thing, from the frail flower to the everlasting stars.[18]

Edwardsean piety had focused upon the person of Jesus as the key to religious enlightenment. Channing assured his congregation that the Unitarian does no less. The Unitarian, he insisted, finds in Jesus the supreme embodiment of those divine and moral traits which every person perfects in human nature by the patient cultivation of natural virtue. By the nobility of his character, Jesus confronts the believing Unitarian as the most beautiful of humans.[19] Indeed, Channing insisted, the Unitarian may even look to Jesus as the supreme natural revelation of God's moral essence.

---

[17] Jonathan Edwards, *Religious Affections,* ed. John E. Smith (New Haven, Conn.: Yale University Press, 1959); Roland Delattre, *Beauty and Sensibility in the Thought of Jonathan Edwards* (New Haven, Conn.: Yale University Press, 1968).

[18] Channing, *Works,* 292.

[19] Ibid., 307, 316–7.

Every virtuous person, of course, reveals the same divine moral essence; but the singular perfection of Jesus' character transforms him into a special manifestation of the moral essence of God. Unitarian veneration of Jesus rests, then, not upon sectarian conversion to belief in his divinity but upon the virtuous beauty of his human nature as a special revelation of the essential nature of God.[20] Rational reflection, not supernatural faith, transforms Jesus into a revelation of God. Reason must first acknowledge Channing's doctrine of essential sameness: namely, that God and humans have the same moral essence. The rational believer must then contemplate the moral perfection in Jesus' natural human character, raise that perfection to an infinite degree, and project it into the Deity.[21]

Channing went even further. If one grants a unique perfection to Jesus' human character and ethical doctrine, in a sense, the devout Unitarian can even look upon him as a "redeemer." Because the doctrine of essential sameness precludes attributing vindictive anger and vengeance into the deity, redemption for the Unitarian cannot consist in an act of infinite atonement. It consists instead in Jesus' clear revelation by doctrine and example of the divine moral perfection in which all humans naturally participate. Jesus' moral excellence challenges others to cultivate in themselves the same divine traits which he exemplifies in an outstanding manner.[22]

The doctrine of essential sameness also helped Channing ground belief in human immortality. Because the human soul has the capacity through natural virtuous action to assimilate itself to the infinite divine being, it participates, despite its essential finitude, in the very infinity of God. The soul's alleged "infinity" consists in its capacity for endless progress in knowledge and in virtue.[23] In 1834 Channing proclaimed Jesus' resurrection as only a divine aid to belief in human personal immortality.[24]

Finally, Channing insisted that Unitarian Christianity, like traditional Calvinist piety, challenged people to selfless living. For the devout Unitarian, the willingness to suffer dutifully in the cause of what reason affirms as right and true provides the ultimate test of virtue.[25]

---

[20] Ibid., 226–30, 318–9.

[21] Ibid., 294–7.

[22] Ibid., 300, 322–5, 401–3; H. L. Smith, "Nature and Grace: Their Significance for William Ellery Channing," *Religion in Life* 30 (1964) 395–406; S. E. Ahlstrom, "Interpretation of Channing," *New England Quarterly* 30 (1957) 99–105; Robert Patterson, *The Philosophy of William Ellery Channing* (New York: Bookman Associates, 1952); Bruce M. Stephens, "From the Nature to the Character of Christ: Channing's Critique of Classical Christology," *Unitarian Universalist Christian* 44 (1989) 37–45.

[23] Channing, *Works*, 354–9.

[24] Ibid., 314, 359–66.

[25] Ibid., 336–47.

Contemporary readers often find it hard to imagine Channing as the spokesperson for a religious revolution. When juxtaposed with the fiery rhetoric of Paine and Palmer, Channing's staid Unitarian tracts sound bland and platitudinous in contemporary ears. His conciliatory stance toward established religion becomes more intelligible, however, when one reads it against the background of militant secular Deism. The militant infidelity of Deists like Allen and Palmer allowed Channing to claim the middle ground as the great conciliator between evangelical and philosophical religion. Channing's Unitarianism took its stand midway between "the cavils and scoffs of infidelity" and the excesses of revivalistic, evangelical emotionalism. It respected traditional forms of Protestant worship and it invoked both miracles and the Bible in confirmation of the chief tenets of Enlightened, philosophical religion. Unitarians continued to call God Father. They perpetuated Sabbath observance, Sunday school, and fast days. At the beginning of the nineteenth century they continued to use many of the traditional Calvinist hymns. Unitarianism blended with these traditional Christian practices Deistic insistence on civic duty and public philanthropy. Channing's social gospel remained, however, colored by his Federalism. He regarded the preservation of national union as a matter of primary importance.[26]

Channing's Federalism also tinged his attitude toward the unwashed masses with a measure of condescension. His exhortations to the laboring classes to improve their lot through personal initiative and self-culture betray a bourgeois insensitivity to the harsh economic realities of impoverished urban living. Channing's praise of the virtues inculcated by hard manual labor would have sounded less hollow on the lips of a laboring man. Moreover, like a true Federalist, Channing feared any political agitation which originated in the lower classes. He deplored their excessive use of alcohol, but he actively supported the ministry among the lower classes undertaken by the Benevolent Fraternity of Churches.[27] His known Federalist tendencies eventually lent a measure of respectability to the abolitionist cause, and his somewhat belabored vindication of the inalienable rights of slaves helped win over conservative sentiment to the movement.[28]

Channing also enjoyed a reputation as a man of letters and of culture. He wrote poetry[29] and published a number of historical and critical articles and reviews. These worldly interests in a man of the cloth contrasted with a dour Calvinism which tended to cast a jaundiced eye on such secular pur-

---

[26] Ibid., 629–42.

[27] Ibid., 12–116.

[28] Ibid., 688–742.

[29] William Ellery Channing, *The Collected Poems of William Ellery Channing,* ed. Walter Harding (Gainesville, Fla.: Scholars' Facsimiles and Reprints, 1967).

suits. In Channing's case, his urbanity helped endow Unitarianism with both social respectability and gentility. Cast off the gloom of Calvinist depravity and predestinationism, Channing's example seemed to say, and one can recognize religious significance in every natural human achievement.[30]

The Unitarian compromise, its willingness to claim the middle ground between Calvinism and militant Deism, brought Enlightenment religion into the mainstream of culture in the United States. Unitarian ministers like Channing continued to use Christian language but redefined its meaning by reducing "Christian" faith to the fundamental tenets of Enlightenment religion: a religion based in natural reason, not in supernatural, justifying faith; the equation of religion and natural morality; the reduction of religion to the cultivation of natural virtue; rational faith in God and in a divine system of rewards and punishments for virtue and for vice; faith in personal immortality. While the first American Deists, like Franklin and Jefferson, tolerated the mainline Protestant churches, and while militant deists like Paine, Allen, and Palmer denounced their hypocrisy, Unitarianism played out a different religious gambit: it sought to bring the mainline churches into line with Enlightenment religion. At the same time, Unitarian congregations at the beginning of the nineteenth century continued to use Calvinist hymns and to celebrate Calvinist rituals. The inertia of religious ritual helps explain this pastoral anomaly, but ritual conservatism and a conciliatory pulpit rhetoric also eased the transition from Protestant orthodoxy to an "Enlightened" rational approach to "Christianity." The perpetuation of earlier ritual practices and of Christian-sounding language gave the illusion that nothing had really changed even though everything really had, for in the end one can no more reconcile the rational religion of the Enlightenment with Christian faith than one can equate kangaroos and cockatoos. Moreover, as we shall see in the following section, unresolved tensions within Unitarianism helped launch Transcendentalism as a movement and with it the incremental Transcendental critique of Enlightenment modernism.

[30] See David Edgell, *William Ellery Channing: An Intellectual Portrait* (Boston: Beacon Press, 1955); David M. Robinson, "The Legacy of Channing: Culture as a Religious Category in New England," *Harvard Theological Review* 74 (1981) 221–39; Andrew Delbanco, *William Ellery Channing: An Essay on the Liberal Spirit in America* (Cambridge, Mass.: Harvard University Press, 1981); Kevin P. Van Anglen, "William Ellery Channing and the Unitarian Milton," *Studies in the American Renaissance* 7 (1983) 101–27; Carl Scovel, "Channing's Troublesome Legacy: An Anti-Sectarian Christianity," *Unitarian Universality Christian* 35 (1980) 13–16; Victor H. Carpenter, "Let the Full Heart Pour Itself Forth: Channing's Struggle Against the Evil Effects of Class Privilege," *Unitarian Universalist Christian* 35 (1980) 17–23; Edward H. Madden, "William Ellery Channing: Philosopher, Critic of Orthodoxy, and Cautious Reformer," *Transactions of the Charles S. Peirce Society* 33 (1997) 558–88.

Chapter 5

RELIGION, ENLIGHTENMENT, AND MODERNISM IN YOUNG AMERICA

The short of the matter is this,
that without reason we could not have faith,
and without the eye or eyes we could not see.
But once admitting that we are rational,
faith follows of course,
naturally resulting from the dictates of reason.

—Ethan Allen

I

In the current debate over modernity and postmodernity, one can begin to clarify the meaning of both of these weasel words if one equates "modernity" with the presuppositions of Enlightenment thinking. A phrase like "the presuppositions of Enlightenment thinking" itself labors under considerable vagueness, however, until one begins to endow it with historical concreteness. One must distinguish the English, the French, and the German Enlightenment from the American and then deal with each on its own terms. This study focuses on the American Enlightenment, but the latter derived in part from the English Enlightenment.

The Enlightenment built on three intellectual pillars: the logic of Francis Bacon (1561–1626), the scientific theories of Isaac Newton (1632–1704), and the epistemology and political philosophy of John Locke (1642–1727). Bacon's *The Great Instauration* (1603) and *Novum Organon* (1620) broke with the Aristotelian model of deductive, syllogistic reasoning which had characterized medieval scholasticism. Scholastic logic tended to base its arguments on first deductive principles whose truth rested on a priori assumptions. Bacon called for a logic which rested instead on facts and which bore fruit in the rational control of nature.[1] Isaac Newton put Bacon's new empirical logic to the test in his *Philosophiae Naturalis Principia Mathematica* (1687) and *Optics* (1704). In the *Principia* Newton undertook to explain the movement of material bodies by the laws of inertia, change of motion, and reaction. He concluded that nature operates with mathematical, even mechanical regularity. While Newton provided Enlightenment thinkers with a mechanistic understanding of physical nature, John Locke articulated a nominalistic interpretation of how the scientific mind works. Locke reduced the objects of thought to the "simple ideas" provided by human sensory experience. The mind generates complex ideas from the simple ideas of sense and, through a process of abstraction, transforms them into the universal principles of reason.

Locke's epistemology exemplifies what Charles Sanders Peirce and Francis Ellingwood Abbot would later call "conceptual nominalism." Classical nominalism denied categorically any reality to universals by reducing them to concrete words applied repetitiously to the same concrete object. Conceptual nominalism allowed that universals exist, but it confined their existence to human subjectivity and denied them real existence apart from the mind.[2] The subjectivism which characterized Locke's account of universals calls attention to another questionable presupposition of his theory of knowledge, namely, that in Lockean epistemology all knowing takes place between one's ears. In Lockean epistemology, the human mind grasps not sensible things but subjective ideas about sensible things. The mind then applies to ideas of sense abstract, conceptual ideas derived from them.

In other words, Locke articulated the nominalistic, di-polar construct of human experience which Hume, Kant, James, Bergson, and Whitehead subsequently popularized. A nominalistic, di-polar construct of experience characterizes human experience as the subjective interrelation of concrete, sensible percepts and abstract, universal concepts. In other words, in a di-polar nominalism concrete percepts and abstract concepts constitute the two poles of experience. Moreover, since di-polar nominalism finds no universal intelligibility in reality, it tends to understand knowing as the correlation of percepts and concepts within human subjectivity.[3]

---

[1] Francis Bacon, *The Works of Francis Bacon,* ed. James Spedding, R. L. Ellis, and D. D. Heath (Boston: Houghton Mifflin, n.d.) 1:40–1.

[2] Charles Sanders Peirce, *Collected Papers,* ed. Charles Hartshorne and Paul Weiss, 8 vols. (Cambridge, Mass.: Harvard University Press, 1931–) 1:26–7; Francis Ellingwood Abbot, *Scientific Philosophy: A Theory of Human Knowledge* (London: 1882) 475.

[3] See Donald L. Gelpi, *The Turn to Experience in Contemporary Theology* (Mahwah, N.J.: Paulist Press, 1994).

Roberto Mangabeira Unger has correctly called attention to the analogy between the theory of knowledge which Locke first formulated and the liberal political theory which he defended. In either theory, its basic units—the building blocks either of knowledge or of society—consist of unrelated atomic units. In the case of knowledge, Locke constructed all theoretical knowing from otherwise unrelated, concrete ideas of sense. In the same way, Lockean politics constructed human society from atomic individuals who lack all social relationship until they freely enter into a social contract for mutual benefit. Unger's *Knowledge and Politics* examines the multiple legal impasses to which such a political theory leads.[4] Robert Bellah's *Habits of the Heart* examines some of its moral impasses.[5]

Conceptual nominalism, subjectivism, epistemological atomism, and social atomism exemplify, then, fundamental presuppositions of English Enlightenment modernity. Moreover, despite the Enlightenment critique of scholastic logic, it tended to derive from scholastic thinking another questionable philosophical presupposition: essentialism. Scholasticism built on the foundations of classical Greek philosophy, especially on Plato and Aristotle. Every metaphysical hypothesis generalizes some metaphor for reality into a theory of the whole. Both Plato and Aristotle equated reality metaphorically with an idea. Plato located those ideas in an eternal, transcendent realm of spirit; Aristotle transformed those same ideas into metaphysical principles of sensible realities, into the forms of things which endow them with essential stability and intelligibility. The belief that finite reality enjoys the essential fixity of an idea generated philosophical belief in the great chain of being: in the hierarchical ordering of natural essences according to their degree of natural perfection. While English Enlightenment thinking despised Aristotelian logic, it assumed that the laws of nature and of morality enjoy the same fixity as an Aristotelian essence. In like manner, American Enlightenment thinkers tended to assume the fixity and uniformity of all natural laws, including the moral laws which govern human interaction. In dealing with physical nature, that assumption left Enlightenment thought ill equipped to deal with historical and biological evolution. In dealing with human morality, that same assumption left Enlightenment *philosophes* poorly prepared to deal with the personal and cultural diversity of human ethical perceptions.

After the seventeenth century, the case of Galileo came to symbolize conflict between empirical investigations of nature and religious authority. Such conflicts inclined most Enlightenment thinkers to assume with

---

[4] Roberto Mangabeira Unger, *Knowledge and Politics* (New York: Free Press, 1975).
[5] Robert Bellah et al., *Habits of the Heart: Individualism and Commitment in America* (Berkeley and Los Angeles: University of California Press, 1985).

precipitate haste an irreconcilable hostility between scientific reason and institutionalized religion. That hostility also induced Enlightenment *philosophes* to exalt the revelation of God in nature over the historical revelation of God enshrined in sacred books. As a consequence, Enlightenment rationalism tended to acknowledge no authority as absolute save the authority of empirical scientific reason. Eventually, this line of thinking would lead more skeptical Enlightenment philosophers like David Hume to relegate religion and morality to the realm of irrational subjective human preferences.

As we have seen, however, the American Enlightenment moved initially in a different direction. While the American Enlightenment tended to dismiss revealed religion as irrational superstition, American Deists tended to assume that the individual conscience has natural access within subjectivity to the essentially fixed and immutable principles of human morality. Moreover, those principles allegedly enjoy the same givenness as scientifically demonstrable natural laws. This assertion was built less on Locke and more on the Platonism which inspired the Augustinian bias of classical Protestantism.

Initial successes resulting from the application of empirical logic to scientific problems generated the inflated hope among Enlightenment philosophers that empirical science could one day unravel all of nature's secrets and would enable humanity to exercise perfect, rational control of all natural processes. Moreover, the Enlightenment extended this inflated, overweening belief in human rational potential into the political order as well. The improvement of human life which would result from the scientific conquest of nature would find a parallel in the progressive reform of human social institutions according to the principles of moral reason. Unbridled optimism about the human prospect tended, therefore, to endow the American Enlightenment with an often seriously inflated confidence and enthusiasm.

II

Intellectual movements like the Enlightenment exemplify major cultural shifts. Cultures differ from one another, but, like history, culture too tends to rhyme. The rhyming character of both history and culture endows each with an analogous structure. All human cultures devise elaborate symbolic structures designed to meet fundamental human needs for survival, growth, and humane living, but different cultures devise different symbolic and practical strategies for meeting those needs. Common human needs endow cultures with an element of sameness; the contrasting symbol systems and practical strategies which different societies devise for fulfilling those needs make cultures differ analogously. The systematic study of cultures can raise to consciousness significant likenesses and significant differences among them. Moreover, in an age of worldwide technological communication, cultures do not exhibit the same geographical rootedness as they once enjoyed. We live in an era of the international blending of cultures. That blending blurs without obliterating differences among geographically rooted cultures.

The analogy of culture provides an important principle of interpretation in assessing the issues raised by a cultural movement like the Enlightenment. In the eighteenth century, Enlightenment thinking arrived on the shores of the British colonies as a foreign export from the mother country, but, as the seeds of Enlightenment thinking took root in Yankee soil, the cultural climate in the British colonies gave its own coloring to their fruit. As a consequence, while the American Enlightenment bore an analogous resemblance to its European counterpart, it also developed distinctive cultural traits of its own. In other words, if modernity derives its presuppositions from the Enlightenment, then modernity comes in more than one form because so does the Enlightenment. The American Enlightenment exemplifies a particular kind of modernity, at the same time that it bears an analogous resemblance to Enlightenment thinking in other parts of the western world.

What made the American Enlightenment different? The preceding reflections suggest that both the class structure and the religious climate of the British colonies colored Enlightenment thinking in the new world. Moreover, class and religion interacted in ways which rendered Enlightenment Deism especially appealing to a significant number of middle-class Americans.

Enlightenment rationalism appealed especially to liberal elements in the colonial middle class. Until the Unitarian compromise, effected largely toward the end of the eighteenth century, laymen spearheaded Enlightenment thinking in the new world. Moreover, those laymen exhibited considerable dissatisfaction with the Protestant religious establishment as they knew it. The Reformation had divided Christianity into bickering religious sects. The religious fragmentation of Christendom found a parallel in its political fragmentation into warring nation states and conflicting national interests politicized both the Protestant Reformation and the Catholic Counter-Reformation. The principle *cujus regio ejus religio* sanctioned the political establishment of religion, and religious establishment institutionalized religious intolerance and persecution. The so-called wars of religion, which never sprang exclusively from religious motives, also served to put religious sectarianism into popular disrepute.

The disintegration of the late medieval cultural synthesis, the corruption of the medieval and renaissance Church, and the ruthlessness and violence of late medieval and renaissance secular culture all combined in order to lend plausibility to a classical Protestant rhetoric of human depravity. A well-fed and increasingly prosperous colonial bourgeoisie saw the world through rosier and often naively optimistic glasses, but the American Deists never got beyond the dualistic opposition which a rhetoric of depravity posed between nature and grace. They tended to assume without question that they had to choose one or the other. Having chosen nature and reason, they assumed that they had to reject supernatural, divine grace. Among American Transcendentalists it would take the genius of Orestes Brownson to see that one could affirm both nature and grace without rational contradiction. Deists in the new world remained mired in the multiple dualisms of a classical Protestant, Augustinian, dialectical imagination.[6]

Persistent confusions and abuses within Protestant Christianity initially allowed Enlightenment thinkers in the British colonies to claim the high moral ground in the name of the God of Reason. Sectarian bickering, religious persecution, and wars fought nominally in the name of religion dramatized for the first American Deists the irrational character of revealed religion. The universal love and forgiveness which authentic Christianity demands also condemned sectarianism, religious intolerance, and holy wars as sinful and unacceptable, but bitter animosity among Christians and aggressive clerical attacks on Enlightenment rationalism as the latest form of religious heresy gave the American Deists considerable rhetorical advantage over their Calvinist adversaries. If Calvinist Christians believed in universal love, the rhetoric of their clergy did not exemplify it. That fact allowed the American Deists to claim a greater universality and humane tolerance for purely rational religion than one seemed to find in organized, revealed religion. Anyone had access to the self-revelation of God in nature. As a result, American Deists found themselves rhetorically well placed to claim for a religion of reason a universalism which Christianity claimed but too seldom lived. In contrast to the Calvinist doctrine of predestination, Deism excluded no one in principle from entering into a life-giving relationship with God through the conscientious cultivation of natural virtue. At the same time, naive Deistic optimism about the essential innocence and integrity of human nature made living universal benevolence seem possible for anyone.

However, the condescending moral tone of American Deistic rhetoric concealed deeply felt animosities. While early Deists like Franklin and Jefferson refrained, on the whole, from public criticism of the Protestant establishment, both men displayed a deeply felt anti-clericalism. Those

[6] See Lee Hudson, "Deism: The Minimal Religion of Social Utility," *Dialog* 16 (1977) 205–10.

feelings did not lack for a realistic motive. Deistic anti-clericalism fed upon the high-handed clericalism, dogmatism, and authoritarianism of some Christian clerics. Not all ministers, of course, fitted anti clerical stereotypes, but enough of them did to confirm their Deistic adversaries in their suspicion and hostility toward the clerical establishment.

Needless to say, Deists both in Europe and in young America ran afoul of both the Protestant and the Catholic churches for other reasons than their open criticism of clerical abuses in the Christian denominations. Deism provoked the unrelenting antipathy of both Catholic and Protestant alike because it denied and often enough ridiculed fundamental Christian beliefs with cavalier condescension. Faith in the incarnation and in the Trinity which it reveals gives fundamental shape to the Christian creed. The Deists denied and derided both doctrines.

The American Deists differed from their European counterparts in that they antagonized a predominantly Protestant religious establishment whose proclamation of the Christian faith tended to endorse the main lines of the Calvinist evangelical scheme. Catholicism constituted a negligible presence in the British colonies. Even if Catholicism had enjoyed greater influence in colonial culture, at the turn of the eighteenth century Protestant anti-Catholic prejudice would have almost certainly blinded the American Deists to the philosophical and theological subtleties of the Catholic tradition. The American Deists simply took it for granted that Catholicism incarnated manifest religious error and authoritarian abuse and therefore deserved no serious consideration, but the colonial *philosophes* took the Calvinist evangelical scheme with more seriousness, both because it shaped their own religious heritage and because it informed popular American religiosity.

When George Whitefield brought Wesleyan revivalism to the American colonies, he found that the colonials, in contrast to English Christians, had little use for John Wesley's Arminianism. Whitefield concluded that popular religion in the colonies had a decidedly Calvinistic caste, and confronting the Calvinist evangelical scheme gave American Deism much of its distinctive cultural flavor.

In that confrontation the Deists once again often claimed condescendingly the higher rhetorical ground. Calvinist theology drew much of its inspiration from the theology of St. Augustine of Hippo. Like Lutheranism, Calvinism endorsed the principle of *sola scriptura*. In other words, Calvinism regarded the Bible as the only valid norm for interpreting Christian revelation.

Augustine of Hippo lived in the fourth and fifth centuries and his theology abounded in ideas which in fact have no clear biblical foundation.

Augustine's pessimistic belief that sin had so corrupted human nature that it could perform no virtuous acts without the help of divine grace rooted itself in the Manicheism which Augustine the Christian convert had renounced but never fully exorcized from his thought. Augustinian belief in divine predestination rooted itself in significant ways in the bishop of Hippo's Neo-Platonic understanding of the divine intelligence. Calvinist atonement christology blended elements from Anselm of Canterbury's *Cur Deus Homo* and an Augustinian doctrine of natural human depravity. In a Calvinist account of Jesus' saving death, the total vitiation of human nature through original sin transformed humanity into God's unreconciled enemy, until divine vindictive wrath against human sinfulness vented itself on a surrogate victim, namely, on God's own incarnate Son.[7] Paradoxically, a Calvinist sense of the total otherness of God seemed to sanction God doing whatever God pleased, even act with an all too human viciousness. If the doctrine of total human depravity combined with Anselmian christological motifs in order to render a Calvinist understanding of atonement both rationally and theologically problematic, Calvin's endorsement of an Augustinian theology of predestination rendered it at least potentially elitist by teaching the converted to regard themselves, at least in their less secular moments, as members of the limited number of the elect chosen arbitrarily by God for eternal salvation.

Despite its glorification of Reason and Reason's God, Deistic rhetoric in young America blended rationality and irrationality. In its critique of the Calvinist evangelical scheme, the American Deists frequently displayed a sure sense of which Calvinist doctrines collapsed most easily under rational critique. Franklin zeroed in on the Calvinist doctrines of predestination, election, and divine reprobation. Other Deists correctly questioned the idea of total human depravity and vindicated the capacity of natural reason to grasp the truth and of the natural conscience to foster natural virtue. They rightly decried the moral determinism which a Calvinist doctrine of predestination inculcated. They correctly deplored the moral vindictiveness of a God who could find personal satisfaction in the innocent suffering of his own Son. At the same time, the American Deists did not always practice the detached and tolerant rationality which they preached. Like the first Protestants, American Deists found negative critique easier than coming up with a viable moral and religious alternative to the realities they attacked.

The Council of Trent had taken exception to the same Calvinist doctrines as the American Deists, but none of them thought of turning to the

---

[7] John Calvin, *Institutes of the Christian Religion,* trans. John Allen, 3 vols. (Philadelphia: Presbyterian Board of Christian Education, 1936) I, i, 1–9; ii, 1–24; iv, 1–8; viii, 1–3; x, 1–23; xi, 1–15.

Catholic tradition for intellectual support. The American Deists shared the same anti-Catholic prejudices as their Calvinist adversaries. Like the Protestants whom they attacked, the American Deists decried the monarchical abuse of papal authority and the excesses of the Roman Inquisition, but a more promiscuous anti-Catholic bigotry prevented them from discovering anything of genuine religious value in what they regarded as an irredeemably corrupt Catholic tradition even though Catholic theology had taken public exception to many of the same Calvinist doctrines as the Deists.[8]

The anti-Catholic prejudices of the American Deists dramatize another paradoxical dimension of their movement: despite its assault on the Protestant religious establishment, especially in its Calvinist expressions, American Deism remained in many of its religious attitudes and orientations profoundly Protestant. Many of the American Deists wore their Protestantism proudly, like a badge. In proclaiming himself a "true Christian," Jefferson meant a "true Protestant Christian." Moreover, the American Deists tended routinely to see the rational reform of Protestant Christianity as the completion of the program of religious reform which the Protestant Reformation had begun.

As the American Enlightenment turned increasingly political, propagandists like Tom Paine did not hesitate to use Calvinist themes of predestination, of election, and of holy war in order to endow the American revolution with the aura of a Christian crusade. In the early days of colonial resistance to the British, John Adams struck a chord which echoed in subsequent revolutionary rhetoric: the purgation of American soil of a feudal monarchy only completed the work which the Protestant reformation had inaugurated. Deists like Paine and Palmer played unabashedly on millenarian religious aspirations engendered among British colonials during the Great Awakening. Both men painted glowing pictures of the American Eden which the Deistic reform of Protestantism would effect. When it suited their purposes, the Federalists used analogous rhetoric in order to endow the national Constitution with a predestined, quasi-religious aura.

The Deists exploited flaws in the Calvinist evangelical scheme in other ways as well. They tended to dismiss rhetorically all theological thinking as sterile logic-chopping and as the needless obfuscation of religion. Instead, they contrasted the simplicity and intelligibility of a Deistic creed with the theological obscurity and unintelligibility of Calvinist Christianity. The rational clarity and simplicity of Deistic religious faith appealed to an emerging bourgeois laity increasingly disgruntled and dissatisfied with the obscure theological points scored by one Christian sect against another. In its worst expressions, this rhetorical strain in American

---

[8] *DS* 1554–7, 1567.

Deism ended in stereotyping the positions of theological adversaries and in the slaughter of theological straw men.

The American Deists displayed their Protestant bias in yet another way. The dualisms which characterized the Augustinian tradition shaped in decisive ways the typically dialectical character of the Protestant imagination. The dialectical imagination displays a uniform preference for disjunctive, either-or thinking. The dialectical imagination contrasts with the analogical imagination which invokes similarity-in-difference in the cause of inclusive thinking and which tends, therefore, to prefer, with proper qualification, both-and thinking to dualistic either-or thinking.[9]

The child of philosophical and theological dualisms, the dialectical imagination displays considerable vulnerability to dualistic patters of thought. Dualistic thinking conceives of two interrelated realities in such a way as to render their relationship to one another subsequently unintelligible. Augustinian theology abounded in dualisms. It demanded a clear and sharp choice between a totally corrupt human nature and the absolute victory of divine grace. Jefferson correctly saw that the least tenable aspects of Calvinism sprang from its Platonic presuppositions, and Platonism inculcated an epistemological dualism by teaching the human mind to find intelligibility only within human subjectivity and not within material sensible reality. That same epistemological dualism fueled Protestant diatribes against the formalism of all merely external sacramental worship. Platonic epistemology also encouraged the subjectivism of Protestant inner-light piety. Protestantism helped to popularize a Platonic spirit-matter dualism, which had cosmic, substantial, and psychological ramifications. With the Platonists, Calvinism divided the universe into the essentially different realms of eternal, intelligible spirit, on the one hand, and ephemeral, opaque matter, on the other. It divided the human person into a spiritual soul essentially distinct from its physical body. It encouraged an operational dualism which distinguished essentially between human spiritual powers and human organic powers of operation.

The American Deists tended to approach religious questions with the dialectical imagination which they had imbibed from their Protestant upbringing. While the medieval scholastics had regarded both nature and supernatural revelation as legitimate sources of religious insight, the American Deists demanded a sharp choice between the God of reason revealed in nature and the God of revelation revealed in the Bible. They extolled the reasonableness of natural religion and derided revealed religion as irrational, obscurantist double-talk. While the medieval scholastics had found a middle

[9] See David Tracy, *The Analogical Imagination: Christian Theology and the Culture of Pluralism* (New York: Crossroad, 1981).

ground between total human depravity and total human innocence, the American Deists demanded an uncompromising choice between the two. Deistic belief in the natural innocence and integrity of human nature fueled in turn naive, unrealistic belief in the United States' national innocence and in the unlimited rational and technological perfectibility of human nature in general and of American society in particular.

In their defense of natural religion, American Deists also showed a spontaneous affinity for Protestant inner-light piety. In authoring the Declaration of Independence, Jefferson popularized his naive Deistic belief that the unchanging principles of moral reason manifest themselves with a priori self-evidence to each educated, individual conscience. Paine secularized the Quaker inner light when he denied that any human or institutional intermediaries can in any way mediate between the individual conscience and its God. Ethan Allen deplored the abuses of irrational religious fanaticism, but his own "rational" account of a religion of morality rooted itself in an individualistic, subjectivistic construct of the human conscience with deep Calvinistic roots.

The dualistic distinction between subjectivity and objectivity also fueled the American Deists' belief in human and national innocence. That distinction justified objectifying human history and human institutions as both external and corrupt. American Deism externalized moral evil by objectifying it in errors and vices of the past and in corrupt social institutions allegedly alien to the individual human conscience. Classical Protestantism had spoken analogously of Catholic institutions. The dualistic objectification of evil lent initial rhetorical plausibility to a Deistic projection of a prelapsarian innocence into the subjective workings of the human conscience. In other words, subject-object dualism gave illusory philosophical warranty to Deistic belief in the untrammeled moral integrity of the natural, individual conscience provided the conscience could in fact keep itself free of historical and institutional influences. Ironically, the American Deists all failed miserably in the attempt to avoid the contagion of history and of Protestant religious institutions. Naive belief in both individual and national innocence also gave Enlightenment optimism its chief speculative warranty. While the piety of the Great Awakening rooted millenarian hopes in the manifest workings of divine saving grace, Enlightenment religion regrounded those same hopes in belief in the American Adam: in the natural innocence of individual subjectivity and in a corporate national innocence rooted in a futile American declaration of independence from history and from its corrupting social institutions.

Two centuries later, contemporary Americans find it easy to discredit the naivete of Deistic optimism. Today's politically correct Americans smile superiorly at the fact that the subjectively self-evident moral truths which the Deists proclaimed confidently in the eighteenth and early nineteenth centuries remained embarrassingly vulnerable to sexist, racist, and religious bigotry. However, as we shall see in the following section, Deism displayed a remarkable resilience in absorbing and incorporating both feminism and abolitionism into its moral code, although it never fully relearned the religious tolerance of Franklin. The endorsement of abolitionism did not make one invulnerable to racism, as the case of Ralph Waldo Emerson will illustrate, but as Deism evolved, a religion of pure reason could argue on the dualistic presuppositions which American Deists defended that sexism and racism express not the innocent workings of the natural conscience, but its corruption by external, historical social institutions.[10]

The following section begins to examine the Transcendental critique of American Deism. That criticism initially sprang from dissatisfaction with the Unitarian compromise. It also sprang from the realization that David Hume's religious skepticism rooted itself directly in the nominalistic presuppositions of Enlightenment religion. Both Jefferson and Palmer saw that Locke's reduction of the real objects of knowledge to sensible realities led logically to materialism. Convinced materialists, both men believed that they could reconcile materialism and theism. Ralph Waldo Emerson greeted any such suggestion with derision. Moreover, his dissatisfaction both with Hume's skepticism and with the "corpse-cold" condition to which a religion of reason had reduced American Unitarianism led him to revise the epistemological presuppositions on which natural religion built. That revision inspired his Transcendental "saturnalia of faith."

[10] See Robert W. Jensen, "The Kingdom of America's God," *Dialog* 15 (1976) 12–20.

PART TWO:
THE TRANSCENDENTAL CRITIQUE OF AMERICAN MODERNITY

Chapter 6

THE TRANSCENDENTAL REVOLT:
THE THREE FACES OF
RALPH WALDO EMERSON

*The whole object of the moral and material creation . . . is the
formation of your character.*

—Ralph Waldo Emerson, 1828

Ecstasy is the law and cause of nature.

—Ralph Waldo Emerson, 1841

Fate. There is a thick skull that is Fate.

—Ralph Waldo Emerson, 1851

I

Ralph Waldo Emerson first opened his eyes to the light on May 25, 1803, only two days after Thomas Jefferson annexed the Louisiana Territory to the fledgling United States. Baby Waldo's father, the Rev. William Emerson, served as pastor of First Church in Boston. Theologically ecletic, William felt well disposed toward Unitarianism. Unfortunately, William died prematurely in 1811. Emerson's mother, Ruth Haskins Emerson, moved with her brood of eight children to Concord, Massachusetts. A woman of simple biblical faith, Ruth struggled to care for her children. In Concord, young Ralph's maiden aunt, Mary Moody Emerson, took a shine to the lad and exercised considerable influence over his formative years. A woman of formidable intellect, idiosyncratic religious piety, and philosophical mysticism, Aunt Mary shared her enthusiasms with the maturing Emerson. They remained close until Emerson's renunciation of his Unitarian pulpit left the two estranged.[1]

Emerson entered Harvard College in 1817, where he studied the common sense philosophy of Dugald Steward, Thomas Reid, and William Paley. Four years after his graduation from Harvard and toward the end of an undistinguished career as a schoolteacher to young women, Emerson began theological studies at Harvard Divinity School. There he met Sampson Reed, a devout Swedenborgian who would later devote his fortune to spreading the Swedenborgian gospel in America. As a divinity student, Emerson began reading Samuel Taylor Coleridge. Emerson received approbation to preach in 1826.[2]

A month later he nearly went blind. Part of his convalescence included a trip to Florida, where he encountered Catholic worship and piety for the first time. On his return voyage to New England, Emerson made the acquaintance of the young French prince Achille Murat. Emerson, after endless theological discussions with the Frenchman, pronounced him the first "consistent atheist" he had ever encountered.

On March 11, 1829, Emerson received ordination as the Unitarian pastor of Second Church in Boston. Six months later he married Ellen Tucker, a woman of frail health whom young Emerson loved passionately. Her death in two short years left the young widower shaken and bereft. He found himself increasingly ill at ease with the Unitarian compromise which William Ellery Channing was in process of consolidating. The emotionally reserved Emerson also found himself ill-suited for pastoral ministry. He deemed the Unitarian perpetuation of Calvinist hymns and rituals religiously contradictory and hypocritical. He finally pronounced Boston Unitarianism "corpse cold" and resigned the ministry in October 1832. In his last sermon he protested against the Unitarian celebration of the Lord's Supper.[3]

[1] See Nancy Barcus, "Emerson, Calvinism, and Aunt Mary Moody Emerson: An Irrepressible Defender of New England Orthodoxy," *Christian Scholar's Review* 7 (1977) 146–52; Phyllis Blum Cole, "The Divinity School Address of Mary Moody Emerson: Women's Silence and Speech in American Literature," *Harvard Divinity Bulletin* 16 (1986) 4–6.

[2] See Albert J. Von Frank, "Emerson's Boyhood and Collegiate Verse: Unpublished New Texts," *Studies in the American Renaissance* 7 (1983) 1–56.

[3] See Roger Lundin, "Emerson and the Spirit of Theory," *Religion and Literature* 21 (1989) 17–42; Wesley T. Mott, "From Natural Religion to Transcendentalism: An Edition of Emerson's Sermon Number 43," *Studies in the American Renaissance* 9 (1985) 1–27; Peter Schneller, "Emerson and Contemporary Religious Attitudes," *Journal of Religious Thought* 26 (1969) 61–9; Frank J. Schulman, "Emerson's Struggle with Ministry," *Religious Humanism* 2 (1988) 65–79; Ivy Schweitzer, "Transcendental Sacramentals: 'The Lord's Supper' and Emerson's Doctrine of Form," *New England Quarterly* 61 (1988) 398–418.

On Christmas of the same year he sailed for Europe. In the Vatican museums he found himself religiously transported by the master works of European art. He underwent an analogous experience in touring an exhibition of natural science in the Jardin des Plantes in Paris. In England he visited with three of the idols of his youth: Samuel Taylor Coleridge, William Wordsworth, and Thomas Carlyle. The last became a life-long friend and faithful correspondent.[4] On the return voyage, Emerson began drafting his first book; he called it *Nature*.[5]

On returning to New England Emerson began a career as a popular lecturer. He looked upon the lecture podium as a secular pulpit for proclaiming a national religion of culture and creativity which gave meat and substance to his Transcendental vision. In September 1835 he was married again, this time to an intellectual young woman named Lydia Jackson. Emerson, who abhorred the tendency of Bostonians to add the letter "r" to words ending in a vowel, forestalled the mutilation of his wife's name by nicknaming her Lidian.

Emerson published *Nature* in 1836. It sold only one hundred copies in its first year, but it would emerge with time as the charter of the Transcendental revolt stirring in Unitarian circles. In 1836 Emerson also befriended Henry David Thoreau. In a little more than a decade they became estranged.[6]

In 1838 Emerson accepted an invitation to address the graduating class of the Harvard Divinity School. He used the address as an occasion to invite the graduates to abandon their Unitarian pulpits for a ministry dedicated to proclaiming Emersonian Transcendentalism. He found himself roundly denounced by more conservative Unitarians for fomenting the

[4] See Len Gougeon, "Emerson, Carlyle, and the Civil War," *New England Quarterly* 62 (1989) 403–23.

[5] See Evelyn Barish, *Emerson: The Roots of Prophecy* (Princeton, N.J.: Princeton University Press, 1989); Kenneth Walter Cameron, *Emerson's Philosophic Path to a Vocation* (Hartford, Conn.: Transcendental Books, 1996); David Robinson, "Emerson's Natural Theology and the Paris Naturalists," *Journal of the History of Ideas* 41 (1980) 69–88.

[6] See Robert Sattelmeyer, "When He Became My Enemy: Emerson and Thoreau, 1848–49," *New England Quarterly* 63 (1989) 187–204.

[7] See John W. Barons-Johnson, "Emerson and the Language of Faith," *Religious Humanism* 24 (1990) 63–73; Robert E. Burkholder, "Emerson, Kneeland, and the Divinity School Address," *American Literature* 58 (March 1986) 1–14; Jonathan Sinclair Carey, "'For God or Against Him': Princeton, Orthodoxy and Transcendentalists," *Journal of Presbyterian History* 64 (1986) 243–58; Carol Johnston, "The Underlying Structure of the Divinity School Address: Emerson as Jeremiah," *Studies in the American Renaissance* 9 (1985) 47–61; Frank G. Novak, "Divine Provocateur: Ralph Waldo Emerson's American Preacher," *Restoration Quarterly* 28 (1986) 87–96; David M. Robinson, "Poetry, Personality, and the Divinity School Address," *Harvard Theological Review* 82 (1989) 185–99; Priscilla J. Brewer, "Emerson, Lane, and the Shakers: A Case Study of Converging Ideologies," *New England*

"latest form of infidelity."[7] In 1841 he polished some of his lectures and published them as a first volume of essays.[8]

Emerson doted on his little boy Waldo. The child's death in 1842 left Emerson emotionally shattered. He also found himself increasingly disillusioned with the failure of his lectures to evoke the kind of creative religious response he had ambitioned. In 1844 a second series of essays muted the optimism of his early lectures and publications. A volume of poems followed in 1846.[9] In 1849, despite shifts in his own religious beliefs and attitudes, Emerson republished *Nature* together with a selection from his early lectures in a volume entitled *Nature, Addresses, and Lectures.*

In December of the same year he completed *Representative Men,* the most ambitious work he had attempted to date, and saw the volume into print. It expressed his muted Transcendental vision. Emerson's lecture tour in England and his subsequent travels on the European continent between October 1847 and July 1848 bore fruit in *English Traits,* a study of the creative genius of the "fair Anglo-Saxon man." The superficial reader might mistake *English Traits* for a travelogue, but read as an Emersonian exercise in Transcendental discernment this book, which appeared in 1856, completed the revision of Emerson's Transcendental metaphysics which *Representative Men* had begun.[10]

In 1860 Emerson published his most sustained reflection on an ethics of creativity. He called this work *The Conduct of Life.* In 1867 he edited an expanded collection of his poetry in *May-Day and Other Pieces.*[11] In 1870 a collection of essays entitled *Society and Solitude* expanded Emerson's post-Transcendental ethics to include questions of public morality. In the same year he delivered a series of lectures at Harvard University on "the natural history of intellect." He repeated the course the following year with minor variations.

In 1870 Emerson's lecturing took him to California where he met the naturalist John Muir in Yosemite Valley. Tempted by Muir's invitation to sleep beneath the giant sequoias, the aging Emerson, in response to the

---

Quarterly 55 (1982) 254–75; Robert D. Habich, "Emerson's Reluctant Foe: Andrews Norton and the Transcendental Controversy," *New England Quarterly* 65 (1992) 208–37.

[8] See Richard A. Grusin, *Transcendentalist Hermeneutics: Institutional Authority and the Higher Criticism of the Bible* (Durham, N.C.: Duke University Press, 1991).

[9] See Joseph M. Thomas, "'The Property of My Own Book': Emerson's Poems and the Literary Marketplace," *New England Quarterly* 69 (1996) 406–25.

[10] See E. D. Mackerness, "A Transcendentalist among Cutlers: Emerson in Sheffield, 1848," *Faith and Freedom* 41 (1988) 1–12.

[11] See James W. Armstrong, "'Common Sense Inspired': Bacon's Philosophy and Emerson's Poetic Vocation" (Ph.D. dissertation, Boston University, 1996).

alarmed protests of his companions, finally decided to decline the offer, to Muir's wry amusement. In 1872 a fire damaged the Emerson home in Concord. The emotional shock of the event seems to have accelerated Emerson's gradual drift into senility. By 1875 Emerson could no longer write without help. James Eliot Cabot assisted the old scholar in revising and editing a final book of essays: *Letters and Social Aims*. Cabot apparently did the lion's share of the work. Emerson died quietly in Concord in 1882.[12]

II

Emerson's speculative and religious development fell roughly into three periods. His pre-Transcendental period extended from 1817 to 1832. During it Emerson grounded Unitarian faith in a form of Neo-Platonism. In the decade between 1832 and 1842 Emerson formulated and popularized his Transcendental gospel of spontaneous cultural creativity. In the years following 1842 he revised his Transcendental religious vision in muted terms which took better into account human finitude.

In the course of his religious and intellectual development Emerson challenged basic presuppositions of Enlightenment religion and developed other presuppositions in influential ways. Emersonian Transcendentalism sought to transcend, or get beyond, two fundamental tenets of Enlightenment modernity: its nominalism and its obsession with scientific, empirical forms of thinking. Already in his early journals Emerson repudiated the nominalistic presuppositions on which Enlightenment religion rested and replaced them with a Neo-Platonic realism. His over-enthusiastic Transcendental vision which he formulated largely in the decade of the 1830s fused Neo-Platonic mysticism and Romanticism into a religious doctrine of ecstatic cultural creativity. Emersonian mysticism accorded to imaginative, intuitive forms of thought a privileged grasp of Being which transcended in its synthetic breadth of insight the analytic, "linear logic" of scientific reason. Finally, bereavement, middle age, and a disillusioned sense of his personal limitations caused Emerson to mute, during his mature period, the naive optimism which Enlightenment religion inculcated.

In other respects Emerson not only acquiesced in many of the questionable presuppositions of Enlightenment modernity but exacerbated them. His dualistic reading of the Platonic tradition placed the problem of dualism at the heart of his Transcendental religion. It would take the genius of Orestes Brownson to exorcize the dualistic demon. From the beginning,

---

[12] See Robert D. Richardson, *Emerson: The Mind on Fire* (Berkeley: University of California Press, 1995); Glen M. Johnson, "Emerson's Essay 'Immortality': The Problem of Authorship," *American Literature* 56 (1984) 313–30.

Brownson saw the futility of dualistic patterns of thinking. As we shall see, Brownson's vitalistic metaphysics, his epistemology, and his incarnational account of religious intuition all offered speculative alternatives to the dualisms which marred both Emersonian Transcendentalism and Enlightenment rationalism.

Emerson also endorsed and developed the individualism which Enlightenment modernity inculcated. Indeed, Emerson's mature philosophy of bias formulated and popularized the ideology of expressive individualism which continues to inform popular religious and cultural attitudes in the United States. Let us reflect in turn on each of these Emersonian responses to Enlightenment modernity.

III

Emerson grew up as a child of Enlightenment religion, which he imbibed in its most genteel form. He grew up Unitarian. Emerson found himself troubled by the religious skepticism of David Hume, but Emerson never wavered seriously in his early Unitarian beliefs. His Aunt Mary had introduced him early in his religious development to Platonic mysticism. The young Emerson gradually acquiesced in a Neo-Platonic vision of the universe, and that acquiescence gave him a platform from which to criticize the nominalistic presuppositions on which Enlightenment religion rested. Emerson never found David Hume's skepticism entirely persuasive because the Platonic tradition offered him an alternative realistic epistemology and metaphysics in which to ground the fundamental tenets of Enlightenment religion, namely, Platonic realism.[13]

Thomas Jefferson had censured Platonism as the *fons et origo* of Calvinist theological error, but Emerson found the dualistic world of Plato positively congenial. Platonism inculcates an epistemological subjectivism. It teaches one to seek for unchanging truth, not in the ever-changing world of sense, but in the subjective apprehension of eternal truth. Several influences in Emerson's religious and speculative formation predisposed him toward a Platonic view of reality. At Harvard, he learned from Dugald

---

[13] In *Endless Seeker: The Religious Quest of Ralph Waldo Emerson* (Lanham, Md.: University Press of America, 1991), I have included fairly extensive documentation of any secondary source criticism relevant to understanding Emerson's religious and intellectual progress available up to the date of publication. This essay summarizes much of the argument of that work while situating Emerson's thought with respect to Enlightenment religion. In this chapter, therefore, I refer the reader to those pages in *Endless Seeker* which discuss and document its content in greater detail. In the footnotes to this essay, I shall include references to relevant secondary source criticism which has appeared since 1991. For fuller discussion and documentation of the issues treated in this section see Gelpi, *Endless Seeker,* 3–31.

Stewart that the human mind grasps intuitively and subjectively both the eternity and immutability of the difference between right and wrong. Emerson's Unitarian upbringing had taught him to reduce the essence of Christianity to moral fidelity to duty. Emerson concluded that, if the human mind has access within individual subjectivity to the eternal principles of ethical conduct, then subjectivity also yields adequate cognitive access to the substance of divine revelation. Emerson's personal appropriation of Channing's doctrine of essential sameness only reinforced these Platonizing tendencies, for if the divine and the human moral essence coincide, then the intuitive grasp of the fundamental principles of human morality yields a grasp of the divine moral essence. Emerson's early self-immersion in Platonic mysticism under the tutelage of Mary Emerson predisposed him toward a kind of pantheism. On reading John Abernathy's *Discourse on the Being and Natural Perfections of God,* Emerson remarked in his journal: "Abernathy thinks the best way of conceiving of the divine attributes, is not to attempt to grasp an abstract idea of immensity or omnipotence, but to consider God as present and active in all parts of his works."[14] In 1825, while pondering the death of Henry Clay, Emerson mused: "That ancient doctrine that a human soul is but a larger or less emanation from the Infinite Soul is so agreeable to our imagination that something like this has always been a cherished part of popular belief."[15]

Moreover, very early Emerson's Platonism, derived in part from American Calvinism, acquired a deterministic caste. Classical Calvinism had held that either grace or the devil rides the human will. In other words, either the action of divine grace determines the human will to choose the virtuous good, or the total depravity of human nature determines the will to choose sin and vice. In *Freedom of the Will* Jonathan Edwards had sought to reconcile freedom and determinism. The young Emerson read Edwards's treatise as a student at Harvard and found Edwards's argument convincing. Thereafter, he regarded the principle that every effect has a cause as "the foundation of the doctrine of human necessity."[16] Emerson espoused the same deterministic belief until the end of his life. Within the context of his own Platonic vision, the "doctrine of human necessity" meant that human choices either follow the necessary determination of the transcendent laws of Spirit or they acquiesce in the physical determination of matter.

[14] Ralph Waldo Emerson, *The Journals and Miscellaneous Notebooks of Ralph Waldo Emerson,* ed. W. H. Gilman et al., 14 vols. (Cambridge, Mass.: Harvard University Press, 1960–) 2:46–50.

[15] Ibid., 2:46–50.

[16] Ibid., 1:87–8; 2:35, 51–3, 159, 161–2; 3:71. See also G. S. Amur, "The Beautiful and the Necessary: A Note on Emerson's Idea of Form," *Literary Criterion* 18 (1983) 63–74.

During his ministry as pastor of Second Street Church, Emerson devised a method for bringing his Platonic vision of reality to something approaching systematic statement. Emerson called his method "spiritual discernment." It advanced descriptively and intuitively rather than logically and experimentally. Emersonian spiritual discernment intended nothing less than a descriptive demonstration of the "good of evil."[17] The discerning process presupposed the reality of a Platonic division of the cosmos into eternal Spirit, on the one hand, and ephemeral matter, on the other. Moreover, Emersonian discernment also presupposed that one need only describe to people the metaphysical structure of the cosmos for them to perceive it self-evidently within their individual subjectivity. In this sense Emersonian discernment gave systematic expression to the subjectivism which tended to characterize both classical Protestantism and American Enlightenment modernity. Emersonian discernment presupposed that the divine essence unifies the cosmos and that the inner, subjective discovery of God unifies and sanctions human moral striving.

On July 17, 1831, Emerson preached for the first time a sermon which explained the method of spiritual discernment which he would invoke in one form or another for the rest of his life. During Emerson's Unitarian period, discernment endorsed a vaguely Calvinistic, dualistic understanding of human nature. The young Emerson saw humanity as capable either of transcendent openness to the divine reality or of the most debased and degenerate moral perversions. The sense-bound character of human knowing made human reason hopelessly fallible.[18] Accordingly, the method of spiritual discernment rested on belief in the dual nature of the human individual who lives "wonderfully placed in the possession of two worlds": the physical world of the body and the spiritual world of the soul. Vicious carnal behavior leaves the spiritual soul "imbedded in the senses," but ascetical discipline and the patient cultivation of virtuous duty gradually teach the spiritual soul to dwell habitually in the realm of the spiritual and the divine.[19]

Pastor Emerson's spiritual discernment of the good of evil promised his parishioners that genuine faith "in the gospel sense" consists not in "hope" but in "sight." By that he meant that religious faith consists in the self-evident grasp within subjectivity of the reality of spiritual things

[17] Emerson, *Journals and Miscellaneous Notebooks,* 2:65–6, 419–20; see also 1:92–3, 109; 2:56–7, 131; Zacharias Thundyil, "Emerson and the Problem of Evil: Paradox and Solution," *Harvard Theological Review* 18 (1969) 51–61.

[18] Emerson, *Journals and Miscellaneous Notebooks,* 1:5, 9, 79–80, 131, 193, 306, 335–6; 2:42; 3:4.

[19] Ralph Waldo Emerson, *Sermons,* Houghton (121), 3, 5–6; Emerson, *Journals and Miscellaneous Notebooks,* 3:274.

"wholly independent of time and place." That Emerson would equate this dubious philosophical understanding of religious experience with faith "in the gospel sense" illustrates well how early Unitarian rhetoric played fast and loose with Christian terminology. The subjective grasp of trans-historical reality enlarges the spiritual soul's appetite and capacity for "possession of the treasures of unbounded truth" and for both virtue and "fellowship and cooperation with all good minds in the works of love."[20] Spiritual discernment yields, then, a practical knowledge of transcendent, ahistorical realities through moral assimilation to the eternal realm of Spirit. As Emerson put it: "The whole secret is in one word, likeness. The way to see a body is to draw near it with the eye. The way to perceive a spirit is to become like it."[21]

Emerson's early discernment of "the good of evil" advanced in stages scattered over the sermons which he preached to his apparently apathetic, possibly puzzled Second Church congregation. The discerning process moved from the discernment of virtue to the discernment of truth, from the discernment of truth to the discernment of one's true spiritual self, and from the discernment of one's true spiritual self to the discernment of one's es-sential oneness with God. In each case, Emersonian discernment began with the description of an experience of material finitude and expanded to include the eternal, invisible spiritual laws which ground sensible reality.

The discernment of virtue begins as an argument with the experience of physical, sensible evil: frustration, disease, suffering, error, death. Physi-cal evil roots itself in the body, but it demands of the soul the cultivation of spiritual virtues which empower one to cope with and to transcend physical evil. Self-discipline bears fruit in self-direction and self-command and in the middle-class, Franklinsonian virtues of industry, enterprise, and prudent moderation. Virtuous living also yields an inner, subjective peace which el-evates one beyond bodily pain and the vicissitudes of life. Moral elevation breeds altruism and, eventually, the love of virtue for its own sake. The prac-tical cultivation of virtue assimilates the soul to the eternal realm of spirit, and that assimilation purges the mind of errors rooted in the fallible senses. Eventually the conscience seeks to rule all choices by the "naked purpose to do right" despite its physical, sensible consequences. Even death itself be-gins to lose its terror as one learns that "God has made us capable of an in-definite improvement which shall depend on ourselves."[22]

[20] Emerson, *Sermons,* Houghton (121), 13; Houghton (46), 7.

[21] Emerson, *Sermons,* Houghton (121), 6, 17–18; Emerson, *Journals and Miscella-neous Notebooks,* 3:275.

[22] Emerson, *Sermons,* Houghton (12), 5–7; Houghton (19), 7; Houghton (20), 2; Houghton (22), 13; Houghton (24), 4; Houghton (25), 3–9; Houghton (26), 9; Houghton

The discernment of truth begins, as an argument, with the experience of ignorance, error, and doubt. All three problems derive from the limitations of sensation and from physical and moral evil. The experience of ignorance, error, and doubt breeds spiritual discontent and the desire for genuine intellectual satisfaction. The discerning mind perceives that the transcendence of intellectual darkness requires the transcendence of sense knowledge and of the physicality in which it roots itself. Scientific knowledge, the analytic investigation of sense phenomena, leaves the religious soul dissatisfied, however, because ultimately the religious person seeks not analytic insight, but self-integration through synthetic insight. The pursuit of science demands, however, moral discipline, and moral discipline, as the discernment of virtue has shown, holds the key to ethical insight.

A comparison between scientific and ethical insight reveals the latter's superiority. Science rests content with speculative conclusions, but ethical insight has an inherently practical character which links it to the business of living. Moral insight grows through moral practice. Moreover, moral insight has a synthetic, rather than an analytic character, which elevates it above the certitudes of science. Finally, the ethical truths which the conscience grasps within human subjectivity enjoy self-evidence, while science can only produce fallible knowledge of sensible things. The discernment of truth discovers, then, three degrees of knowledge: sense knowledge of concrete, particular things; fallible, analytic knowledge of the laws which govern natural phenomena; and self-evident moral insights into the eternal unifying principles of human conduct.[23]

The discernment of Being provides a rapid corollary to the discernments of truth and of virtue. The discovery of eternal, ethical truth reveals the works of the self-indulgent sensualist as mere illusion. That discovery teaches the heart to desire virtue for its own sake as the only unchanging,

---

(35), 1; Houghton (45), 15–16; Houghton (47B), 2–3, 9–11; Houghton (54A), 5; Houghton (63), 1–18; Houghton (65), 1–3; Houghton (67), 32; Houghton (71), 2, 7, 9; Houghton (72), 14–15; Houghton (77A), 5; Houghton (79A), 6–7; Houghton (82), 3–4; Houghton (83), 4, 10; Houghton (93), 14; Houghton (117), 7, 11–22; Houghton (144), 7; Houghton (125), 5–31; Houghton (127), 17–18; Houghton (141A), 5–8; Emerson, *Journals and Miscellaneous Notebooks,* 3:140, 174–5, 211; Arthur McGiffert, ed., *Young Emerson Speaks* (Boston: Houghton, Mifflin & Co., 1938) 16, 106, 141, 165, 185.

[23] Emerson, Sermons, Houghton (11), 3–4; Houghton (16), 7–8; Houghton (22), 3; Houghton (125), 5–31; Houghton (22), 3; Houghton (30), 1–8; Houghton (36), 1–11; Houghton (43), 1–15; Houghton (45), 5–7; Houghton (56), 1–2; Houghton (63), 11–23; Houghton (66), 1–18; Houghton (83), 1–27; Houghton (93), 1–26; Houghton (95), 7–20; Houghton (98), 22–5; Houghton (124), 2–3, 10–20, 22; Houghton (127), 1; Houghton (154), 5–11; Houghton (159), 20; Emerson, *Journals and Miscellaneous Notebooks,* 3:220–3, 258–9; McGiffert, *Young Emerson Speaks,* 101, 112–3, 136, 152, 154–6.

stable reality. The seeming inexhaustibility of the intelligible world corresponds to the soul's spontaneous longing for the infinite. As it learns to dwell in the realm of the eternal and the spiritual, the soul spontaneously recognizes that realm as ultimately real, as Being therefore, where Being connotes that which satisfies the deepest longings of the human spirit.[24]

The discernment of the self marks step four in Emerson's discernment of "the good of evil." Reflecting the Augustinian roots of New England piety, Emerson regarded self-discovery as "the proper business" of religious living. Self-discovery begins in the common human experience of selfish, sensuous egotism. As the lure of Being educates proud, sensuous persons to the reality of truth and of virtue, they gradually learn to govern their conduct by "the naked purpose to do right." Assimilation to the eternal realm of Spirit teaches the sensualist first to discover, then to draw systematically upon inner, spiritual resources. In the process of learning moral living, selfish souls discover the egotistical pride which motivates the foolish, sensual counterfeit of authentic self-reliance.

True self-reliance results from a spiritualizing moral discipline which assimilates one practically to spiritual reality. Since the ethical reality of the divine and of the human coincide, the selfless moral self discovers its true self by acknowledging its moral identity with the divine self. Emerson's discernment of the self discloses, then, three levels within human selfhood: (1) the finite human self, which can either live enslaved to selfish passion and to corrupting social custom or learn to live for selfless moral values; (2) the individual moral self, which lives by transcendent, spiritual values and which expresses one's personal moral uniqueness; and (3) a universal, impersonal divine "Self," which grounds and unifies the spiritual diversity of individual moral selves.[25]

The young Emerson's discernment of "the good of evil" culminates in the discernment of God. It begins in skepticism and unbelief and builds to a synthetic insight which unifies all the preliminary stages in the discerning process. The conflicting religious claims of individuals and of churches tend to breed religious skepticism. So does the hypocrisy of self-styled

[24] Emerson, *Sermons,* Houghton (46), 10–12; Houghton (53), 7–16; Houghton (57), 2; Houghton (62A), 11–29; Houghton (66), 8; Houghton (67), 17–22; Houghton (114), 5–26; Houghton (121), 5–13; Houghton (145), 1–24; Houghton (158), 20.

[25] Emerson, *Sermons,* Houghton (4), 10; Houghton (16), 5–8, 11–13; Houghton (27), 3–5; Houghton (35A), 23; Houghton (45), 17–18; Houghton (47B), 2–10; Houghton (63), 19–21; Houghton (65), 9–14; Houghton (67), 31; Houghton (70), 11; Houghton (88), 4–5; Houghton (106), 1ff.; Houghton (127), 28–9; Houghton (134), 13–17; Houghton (141A), 22, 26; Houghton (144), 8; Houghton (145), 9–13; Houghton (146), 10–13; Houghton (149), 13–14; Houghton (153), 17; Emerson, *Journals and Miscellaneous Notebooks,* 4:67–8; McGiffert, *Young Emerson Speaks,* 1, 183.

believers whose conduct belies their creedal professions. As the soul ascends the scale of Being, however, it finds both atheism and religious skepticism increasingly dissatisfying. It gradually rises above "gross and sensuous" depictions of the deity well exemplified in Calvinist portraits of a vindictive God. Ethical assimilation to the realm of Being and of Spirit teaches the pilgrim soul to recognize that the deity eludes all sensory images. In the end, practical moral assimilation to the deity demonstrates God's existence immediately, intuitively, and self-evidently. In other words, the discernment of virtue, of truth, of Being, and of the self all culminate in an intuitive, self-evident grasp of the divine essence itself. The conscience experiences God as an immutable, irresistible, omnipresent, infinite reality. The moral soul experiences the judgments of this divine transcendent reality as prompt, unerring, unfaltering, and inescapable. The infinity of the divine "Self" makes it transpersonal, since in Emerson's mind personal existence implies individuality and finitude. Nevertheless, the realization that truth, goodness, and reality all coincide with the impersonal moral essence of God discloses to the discerning conscience the identity of the individual moral self with the divine essence. As Emerson put it:

> I feel that we have God to serve and please as well as ourselves, but shall
> come to perceive that in the soul he is most present (that right reason and
> pure love are the most we know of him), that his right worship consists in
> the constant acknowledgement that our individual life flows from him con-
> tinually as light from the sun.[26]

Emerson's discernment of "the good of evil" moved well within the presuppositions of Enlightenment religion; its originality consisted to a great extent in the fact that it pits one strain of American Enlightenment thinking against another. As we saw in the preceding section, the American Enlightenment tended to acknowledge two different ways of grasping

---

[26] Emerson, *Sermons,* Houghton (146), 20; for the discernment of God see *Sermons,* Houghton (2), 2–13; Houghton (6), 8–11; Houghton (7), 2; Houghton (12), 11–13; Houghton (13), 17–18; Houghton (21), 1–12; Houghton (22), 2; Houghton (23), 2–4; Houghton (35B), 8–9; Houghton (37B), 11; Houghton (40), 5; Houghton (46), 6–7, 12; Houghton (53), 13, 15; Houghton (54A), 15; Houghton (51), 1–13; Houghton (56), 1–16; Houghton (51), 3; Houghton (61), 16; Houghton (66), 1–3; Houghton (67), 17–21; Houghton (77B), 6–8; Houghton (85), 5; Houghton (85A), 2–19; Houghton (85B), 3–12; Houghton (97), 14–17; Houghton (98), 3–6; Houghton (102A), 18; Houghton (105), 3–19, Houghton (108), 5–13; Houghton (109A), 9, 19; Houghton (110), 1, 13–14; Houghton (127), 28–9; Houghton (153), 21; Houghton (170), 21, 28; Houghton (173), 7; Emerson, *Journals and Miscellaneous Notebooks,* 3:130, 134, 139, 182–3; McGiffert, *Young Emerson Speaks,* 104, 113–4, 151–3. See also Jane Ellen Mauldin, "Emerson's Mystical Response to Suffering," *Religious Humanism* 22 (1988) 120–34; Zacharias Thundyil, "Emerson on the Problem of Evil: Paradox and Solution," 51–61.

reality: one, empirically and scientifically; the other subjectively and self-evidently. Emersonian discernment in its first formulation clearly claimed the superiority of the latter form of knowing over the former.

Emerson's method of discernment also displayed originality, even if one legitimately questions the mind's ability to reach metaphysical conclusions through phenomenological description alone. The process of discernment which Emerson developed and articulated in his sermons provided him with a set of recurring and related operations which he would apply again and again in virtually everything he wrote. The method of discernment would, as we shall see, evolve as Emerson moved from his Unitarian period to his Transcendental "saturnalia of faith" and finally to the mature formulation of his personal Transcendental creed. The discerning process always began by describing sensible facts and then proceeded to a descriptive account of the eternal, transcendent laws which ground those facts. Emerson assumed that he could describe spiritual realities as easily as he could describe sensible ones. Moreover, he deemed the description of transcendent, spiritual realities sufficient to reveal them to others as self-evidently true. Despite the repeated failure of other minds to endorse the self-evidence of his metaphysical vision, to the end of his life Emerson never really abandoned this dubious metaphysical and epistemological presupposition.

Reflection on the process of discernment as Emerson practiced it in his sermons also clarifies what he meant by demonstrating "the good of evil." The evils of this life—suffering, moral viciousness, error and deception, selfish egotism, religious agnosticism, and atheism—motivate a spiritual discontent which gradually, through the patient, self-reliant cultivation of virtue, schools the soul to recognize the illusory character of physical sensible things and to dwell in the realm of genuine reality, truth, and goodness. That realm and the realm of the divine coincide. As a consequence, frank confrontation with the evils of this life teaches the individual soul to recognize its essential oneness with the eternal, impersonal moral essence of God.

In the end, however, Emerson's discernment of the good of evil in his early journals and in the Unitarian sermons he preached to his unresponsive congregation left him personally dissatisfied. The experience of pastoring an urban parish convinced him of his temperamental unsuitability for such work. Moreover, in his sermons the method of discernment advanced through the patient, life-long cultivation of "the naked purpose to do right." In the end he deemed plodding, life-long, virtuous assimilation to the divine boring. He found turn-of-the-century Boston Unitarianism devoid of emotional zest. While he deplored the lack of gentility in revivalist piety, he admired the spontaneous religious enthusiasm which revivalist preachers like Charles Gradison Finney generated, and he wondered what form a genteel religious revival might take.[27] Emerson resigned his pulpit ostensibly over his theological reservations about Unitarians celebrating the Lord's Supper, but his own personal restlessness provided the deeper motives for a change in the direction of his religious ministry. One suspects that he had begun to find his own Unitarian sermons boring.[28]

Nevertheless, one should not underestimate the importance of the religious synthesis which Emerson reached during his years as a Unitarian pastor. American Transcendentalists all sought to get beyond the limitations of rational, Enlightenment religion. Both Emerson and Parker would try in different ways to transform Enlightenment religion from within. In both cases, their criticism of the limitations of Enlightenment piety never extricated itself completely from the modernist presuppositions of Enlightenment thinking. Emerson's endorsement of the Platonic tradition had, however, convinced him of the absolute need to transcend one of the key philosophical presuppositions of modernist, Enlightenment thought: its nominalism. With prodding from David Hume, Emerson saw clearly and correctly that a philosophical religion which reduces the objects of knowledge to sense experiences can never do justice to the reality of religious experience. Emerson replaced Lockean and Humean nominalism with a metaphysical Platonic realism which he would defend in one form or another for the rest of his life.

III

A sobered Emerson would refer to the period of his religious development between 1832 and 1842 as a "saturnalia of faith." By "a saturnalia" he meant "an excess," and by excess he meant a naive and biased enthusiasm. From his college days Emerson had read extensively in English and German Romanticism, and he longed to suffuse a rational, genteel, Enlightenment religion with Romantic passion. His voyage to Europe at the end of 1832 and especially his experiences of religious ecstasy in the Vatican museums and in the Jardin des Plantes in Paris gave him a glimmer of how to Romanticize rational Enlightenment religious faith. He

---

[27] Emerson, *Sermons,* Houghton (111A), 7–10; Houghton (111B), 1–11; Houghton (147), 23; Emerson, *Journals and Miscellaneous Notebooks,* 3:207; 4:27, 33, 38; McGiffert, *Young Emerson Speaks,* 86–8.

[28] See Susan L. Robertson, *Emerson in His Sermons: A Man-Made Self* (Columbia: University of Missouri Press, 1995); Paul H. Beattie, "Unitarian Universalism's Greatest Exponent," *Religious Humanism* 22 (1988) 57–64; Elisabeth Hurth, "William and Ralph Waldo Emerson and the Problem of the Lord's Supper: The Influence of German 'Historical Speculators,'" *Church History* 62 (1993) 190–206.

gave voice to his revised Enlightenment creed in his early lectures and in his little book *Nature*.[29]

The term "spiritual discernment" does not appear in the text of *Nature*, but, by the beginning of Emerson's Transcendental period, this method of thinking had become co-natural to his mind. As a consequence, the same descriptive method which structured Emerson's Unitarian sermons also structured the argument of his early lectures and of the text of *Nature*. During the "saturnalia of faith," however, the goal of discernment shifted. During Emerson's Unitarian period it sought to inculcate the patient cultivation of selfless dedication to virtuous duty. During the "saturnalia of faith," Emersonian discernment sought to evoke from others a life of spontaneous, creative ecstasy.[30]

In Romanticizing his earlier religious vision, Emerson did not completely abandon it. He preserved his belief that religious insight has an essentially ethical dimension. He continued to affirm that knowledge has three degrees: sensation, analytic thought, and synthetic intuition. He still asserted three distinguishable levels in the self: (1) the illusory egotistical self; (2) the individual spiritual self; and (3) the impersonal, divine, universal ground of all finite, personal selves. He still identified Being with the universal, the impersonal, and the eternal. He continued to understand ultimate Being in relational terms, as that which ultimately satisfies the longing of the human spirit. He never abandoned his search for a felt, subjective conviction of one's essential oneness with God. He continued to use the method of discernment as a privileged means for leading people to a subjectively grasped religious insight.

Still, the transformation of Emerson's Platonic Unitarianism into a full-fledged Transcendentalism significantly modified his earlier, more pedestrian religious vision. The Transcendental Emerson realized that he had erred in placing the method of discernment at the service of sectarian, Unitarian religion. The Transcendental Emerson decided that henceforth the discerning process must serve non-sectarian, universal, philosophical truth. He also decided that Transcendental discernment must build on three fundamental postulates. It must take for granted (1) that the human mind can in fact answer every question, (2) that a non-sectarian, philosophical account of nature must have the capacity to explain "all phenomena," and

---

[29] For a fuller discussion and documentation of the issues treated in this section, see Gelpi, *Endless Seeker,* 33–66.

[30] For a rhetorical analysis of nature see Alan D. Hodder, *Emerson's Rhetoric of Revelation: Nature, the Reader, and the Apocalypse Within* (University Park: Pennsylvania State University Press, 1989); Irena S. M. Marnshka, *Religious Imagination and Language in Emerson and Nietzsche* (New York: St. Martin's Press, 1994); Carlos Baker, "Moralist and Hedonist: Emerson, Henry Adams, and the Dance," *New England Quarterly* 52 (1979) 27–37.

(3) that the deliverances of Transcendental insight must, like the principles of the Scottish common-sense conscience, appear self-evidently within subjectivity. The first and third postulates derived from Emerson's pre-Transcendental thought. As for the second postulate, the Transcendental Emerson expected to "explain all phenomena" by elaborating a causal theory of imaginative creativity.[31]

During his Unitarian period Emerson had resolved, at least to his own satisfaction, the problem of evil. He had come to believe that physical and moral evil form part of the scheme of things, because they school us to the love of eternal, transcendent, spiritual realities, but Emerson resigned his Unitarian ministry in part because he despaired of evoking from human hearts an enthusiastic religious response by ethical preachments alone. The Transcendental Emerson sought for a religious formula which would somehow unite mind and heart, reason and intuition, in a felt, creative response to divine Beauty. As a consequence, Emerson's transcendental discernment proceeded in three steps. It began with a revised discernment of the purpose of scientific insight, then advanced to a discernment of the subjective human experience of love, and synthesized these two preliminary exercises in a discernment of genius which Emerson expected to evoke from his audience a spontaneous response of ecstatic cultural creativity.[32]

The Transcendental discernment of science began with the human search for "commodity." By "commodity" Emerson meant the use of the analytic Understanding in order to supply physical human needs. Emerson derived the term "Understanding" from his reading in the English Romantics and equated it, more or less, with Baconian logic. Understanding yields progressive control of physical nature. One cannot, however, control natural phenomena without an insight into the laws which govern them. As the scientific mind develops, however, its love of the beauty revealed in nature motivates the scientist's willing submission to the moral constraints which the exact application of scientific logic requires. Moreover, as scientific thinking progresses it loses interest in mere commodity and experiences increasing fascination with the beauty and order of nature itself. The universal order of nature has an essentially ethical character, and its contemplation stirs the hearts of scientists as well as their minds.

---

[31] Ralph Waldo Emerson, *The Complete Works of Ralph Waldo Emerson,* Centenary Edition, 14 vols. (Boston: Houghton, Mifflin & Co., 1903–04) 1:3–4; Ralph Waldo Emerson, *The Early Lectures of Ralph Waldo Emerson,* ed. Stephen Wicher et al. (Cambridge, Mass.: Harvard University Press, 1960–) 1:23; Emerson, *Journals and Miscellaneous Notebooks,* 3:225–6; 4:80–1, 356–8, 365; 5:8–21, 34, 497–8; 6:110–1.

[32] See Clark W. Gilpin, "Scholarship: The Not Altogether Illusory Hope by Which It Lives," *Criterion* 29 (1990) 18–20.

At the same time, the scientist realizes that analytic forms of logical, mathematical thinking can never adequately express the cosmic, moral beauty which science contemplates.[33]

Emerson's Transcendental discernment of science marked an important advance over his pre-Transcendental discernment of truth. During his Unitarian period Emerson contrasted the fallible, analytical modes of scientific thinking with the self-evident, synthetic insights of the conscience in its grasp of the divine essence. The Transcendental Emerson still deemed scientific insight inferior to the highest forms of moral and religious insight, but now he located the inferiority of scientific thought in its drive toward emotionally detached, objective forms of expression. In other words, the Transcendental Emerson no longer regarded scientific thinking as purely analytic. Instead, he conceded that the scientific mind in its exploration of nature eventually glimpses a synthetic, cosmic beauty, but it knows it can never adequately express that beauty in the objectifying, analytic forms of scientific thinking.

If the scientist eventually learns the limits of objectification, the lover comes to discover the limitations of human subjectivity. Emerson's Transcendental discernment of love reveals that the human heart drives toward the same vision of cosmic beauty as the scientist but approaches it from a different angle of vision. The Transcendental discernment of love begins as an argument in a descriptive exploration of sensual, erotic, romantic love. Romantic love may begin by focusing on the physical endowments of one's beloved, but it inevitably deepens into an admiration of the beloved's character and personal moral traits. However, the beloved's failure to abide perfectly by the moral ideals he or she espouses alerts the lover to the fact that ultimately love seeks not the personal moral beauty of the beloved, but the impersonal, universal moral principles to which the beloved stands committed. In other words, the exploration of human subjectivity through a discernment of love reveals that in the end scientist and lover find themselves contemplating the same transcendent moral beauty, but from different angles of vision. The scientist views transcendent Beauty objectively; the lover, subjectively.[34]

[33] Emerson, *Complete Works,* 1:11–13, 33; 2:326–8, 334–5; Emerson, *The Early Lectures,* 1:11–12, 14–18, 23, 41–5, 71; Emerson, *Journals and Miscellaneous Notebooks,* 5:169. See also Robert Edward James, "'Bow to the Rising Sun': Emerson, Unitarianism, and the 1833–1834 Lectures on Science" (Ph.D. dissertation, University of California, 1995); Thomas D. Birch, "Toward a Better Order: The Economic Thought of Ralph Waldo Emerson," *New England Quarterly* 68 (1995) 383–401.

[34] Emerson, *Complete Works,* 2:170–1, 182–3, 188, 334–6; Emerson, *Journals and Miscellaneous Notebooks,* 5:217–76.

Emerson's Transcendental discernment of Beauty synthesized the insights of the scientist and of the lover in an experience of ecstatic, intuitive creativity. The discernment process began as an argument with the contemplation of the creative achievements of individual human geniuses. The beauty manifested in their life and work inspires the spontaneous human desire to imitate them, but the uniqueness of any great individual's genius prevents any would-be imitator from reduplicating the same career. The very attempt to imitate great geniuses awakens one, therefore, to the uniqueness of individual creativity. That discovery forces imitators to cultivate their own personal genius. The cultivation of personal genius centers human creativity where it belongs: in one's own individual, creative potential. The cultivation of personal genius sensitizes creative activity to the universal laws which ground and inspire all genuine human creativity. As this centering process deepens, it gives spontaneous rise to ecstatic creative activity.

Individual creative ecstasy grasps effectively and intuitively the universal, eternal, cosmic laws which ground all natural phenomena, laws which the discernment of science has already discovered. By immersing one's individual, personal genius in this impersonal, cosmic All, the individual discovers his or her true "Self," which in its universality transcends all individual, personal selfhood. The experience of ecstatic creativity thus reveals to each creative individual that all natural creativity draws on the same transcendent, impersonal Source. In the moment of creative ecstasy, one grasps transcendent·truth and cosmic law both self-evidently and actively. Authentic creativity derives ultimately, however, not from one's finite, individual, personal self but from the infinite, impersonal World-Soul in which the whole of nature participates. The experience of that transcendent source of creative inspiration yields an experience of what the Transcendental Emerson, with hints from English Romanticism, called "Reason." As he put the matter: "The Understanding, listening to Reason, on one side, which saith It is, and to the senses on the other side, which say, It is not, takes middle ground and declares It will be."[35] In other words,

---

[35] Emerson, *Complete Works,* 1:1–25, 140–1, 221–2; Emerson, *Journals and Miscellaneous Notebooks,* 5:334–5; see also Emerson, *The Early Lectures,* 1:101ff., 104–5, 110, 112–6, 291, 424–5; Ralph Waldo Emerson, *The Letters of Ralph Waldo Emerson,* ed. Ralph L. Rusk, 6 vols. (New York: Columbia University Press, 1939) 1:412–3; 4:174–5; 5:179–81. See Alan D. Hodder, "After a High Negative Way: Emerson's 'Self-Reliance' and the Rhetoric of Conversion," *Harvard Theological Review* 84 (1991) 423–46; Frank J. Schulman, "Emerson and Compensation," *Religious Humanism* 22 (1988) 99–103; Gayle L. Smith, "Emerson and the Luminist Painters: A Study of Their Styles," *American Quarterly* 37 (1985) 193–215; Thomas P. Joswick, "The Conversion Drama of 'Self-Reliance': A Logological Study," *American Literature* 53 (1983) 507–24.

creative insight occupies the middle ground between eternal truth and value, on the one hand, and surd, valueless, and illusory facts, on the other.

Emerson's Transcendental doctrine of creativity sought to effect the synthesis between religion and culture to which Channing had rather ineffectually aspired. That synthesis inspired in Emerson the lecturer a vision of history as the creative, symbolic expression of the eternal immutable laws which govern the cosmos. Every human achievement—science, art, literature, politics, religion, trade, manners—gave visible, temporal embodiment to the Beautiful Necessity which rules the universe. Moreover, during the excesses of his "saturnalia of faith," Emerson naively believed that each individual has the capacity to develop into a universal genius in the manner of a Renaissance genius like Michelangelo or Leonardo da Vinci.[36]

This vision of history as the progress of uninterrupted individual creative ecstasy revised Emerson's doctrine of moral necessitarianism. The Transcendental discernment of Beauty revealed every sensible fact as surd and valueless except in the moment when an influx of creative energy from the divine Over Soul endowed it with momentary, fleeting reality and value. As a consequence, for the Transcendental Emerson finite humans face two fundamental options: either to submit to the grinding sameness of the factual past or to transform it through creative insight. Creative insight, however, expresses the Beautiful Necessity which rules the cosmos. Either its spiritual laws determine the character of one's creative transformation of nature or one lives imprisoned in the brute fatality of the past. At first Emerson's naive expectation that everyone could live a life of uninterrupted personal creativity caused him to underestimate the fatalism of the past. Disillusionment would eventually force him to take the fated past much more seriously.

This same necessitarian vision of human creative activity also forced the Transcendental Emerson to revise his Unitarian discernment of Being. As a Unitarian pastor, Emerson had found Being, reality, only in universal, transcendent moral laws. His Transcendental creed taught, however, that in the moment of creativity itself, transcendent Beauty and Reality also achieve an all too fleeting embodiment in space and time. Emerson put the matter in these terms: "Let us acquiesce. Let us take our bloated nothingness out of the path of the divine circuits. Let us unlearn our wisdom of the world. Let us lie low in the Lord's power and learn that truth alone makes rich and great."[37]

---

[36] Emerson, *The Early Lectures,* 1:101–201; 2:80–110. See also Meili H. Steele, "Romantic Epistemology and Romantic Style: Emerson's Development from Nature to the Essay," *Studies in the American Renaissance* 7 (1983) 187–202; Eddy P. Wilson, "Emerson and Dewey on Natural Piety," *Journal of Religion* 75 (1995) 329–46.

[37] Emerson, *Complete Works,* 1:160. See also Lou A. Lange, *The Riddle of Liberty: Emerson on Alienation, Freedom, and Obedience* (Atlanta: Scholars Press, 1986).

Transcendental enthusiasm also caused Emerson to revise his earlier discernment of the self. The self continued to have three dimensions: a material, sensible, factual dimension; an individual personal dimension; and an impersonal, infinite dimension. The saturnalia of faith, however, transformed the second level of the self—the self which mediates between the infinite Over Soul and surd, finite, valueless facts—into an individually unique, personal, creative genius.[38]

Finally, the saturnalia of faith caused Emerson to revise his understanding of the discerning process itself. He gave expression to the dynamic shape of Transcendental discernment in his essay "The Method of Nature." Emerson wrote the essay in 1841 at the very end of his Transcendental period in the solitude of Nantasket Beach. In the essay he equated the method of nature with creative ecstasy and creative ecstasy with the inevitable outcome of the discernment and experience of transcendent, divine Beauty. Creative ecstasy teaches individual human experience to think "prospectively," away from the surd factual past and toward the transforming influx of divine creative life. The method of nature and the method of Genius coincide, and Genius advances endlessly, spontaneously, effortlessly.[39]

On April 11, 1838, Emerson summarized his new Transcendental credo in his journal:

> I believe, not only in Omnipresence, but in Eternity. And these are not words but things. I believe in the omnipresence; that is, that the All is in each particle; that entire nature reappears in every leaf and moss. I believe in Eternity: that is, I can find Greece and Palestine and Italy and England and the Islands,—the genius and creative principle of each and all eras, in my own mind.[40]

---

[38] Emerson, *The Early Lectures,* 1:100–201. See also Franciscus Henricus Albers, "Transatlantis: Utopian Self-Hood in Rousseau and Emerson" (Ph.D. dissertation, Harvard University, 1996).

[39] Emerson, *Complete Works,* 1:202–23.

[40] Emerson, *Journals and Miscellaneous Notebooks,* 5:183. See also Mary Kupiec Cayton, *Emerson's Emergence: Self and Society in the Transformation of New England, 1800–1845* (Chapel Hill: University of North Carolina Press, 1989). For a study of the nineteenth-century roots of twentieth-century New Age religion see Catherine L. Albanese, *Nature Religion in America: From the Algonkian Indians to the New Age* (Chicago: University of Chicago Press, 1990). See also Catherine L. Albanese, "Religion and the American Experience: A Century Later," *Church History* 3 (1988) 337–51; Evelyn Barish, *Emerson: The Roots of Prophecy* (Princeton, N.J.: Princeton University Press, 1989); William Bevis, "Emerson: Ecstasy and Aphorism," *Studia Mystica* 3 (1982) 44–59; David Ross Chandler, "Emerson and Transcendentalism," *Religious Humanism* 22 (1988) 135–43; Richard G. Geldard, *The Esoteric Emerson: The Spiritual Teachings of Ralph Waldo Emerson* (Hudson, N.Y.: Lindesfarne Press, 1993); Marion Montgomery, "Emerson and the

IV

Three circumstances conspired to force Emerson to acknowledge the naivete of his Transcendental "saturnalia of faith." In the first place, he seems to have expected his lectures during the 1830s and early 1840s to evoke from his audiences a spontaneous and continuous burst of cultural creativity. Instead, most people left his secular sermons scratching their heads.[41] Second, having located human salvation in continuous creative activity, he discovered in the repetitiousness of his own lectures evidence of his own finite fund of creative ideas. Third, the death of his "beloved boy" left the mature Emerson incapable of the naive optimism which characterized the second stage of his religious progress. With characteristic personal integrity, he decided that he had to revise yet again his personal religious creed.[42]

Many Emersonian critics give the impression that Emerson did his really creative thinking during the 1830s and that thereafter he kept repeating the same insights, even though they struck him as increasingly unbelievable. Certainly, the post-Transcendental Emerson saw the need to modify his original Transcendental faith, but those modifications show genuine originality. Moreover, Emerson's final restatement of his personal version of Transcendentalism displays a measure of horse-sense realism (as opposed to Platonic realism) which renders his final position somewhat more plausible, even if finally unconvincing.

The waning of Transcendental enthusiasm convinced Emerson that, during his "saturnalia of faith," he had failed to credit the irreducible finitude of every human experience. He came to believe that the finite character of personal genius prevented most lives from exemplifying uninterrupted creative

---

Emptying of Nature," *Center Journal* 1 (1981) 25–43; Merton M. Sealts Jr., "Mulberry Leaves and Satin: Emerson's Theory of the Creative Process," *Studies in the American Renaissance* 9 (1985) 79–94; Curtis Smith, "The Concept of Self-Identity in the Essays of Ralph Waldo Emerson," *Religious Humanism* 26 (1992) 123–32; Christopher Perricone, "Santayana's Criticism of American Idealism and the Grounds of Common Sense," *Transactions of the Charles S. Peirce Society* 24 (1988) 239–64; Arthur E. Murphy, "Emerson in Contemporary Thought," *Transactions of the Charles S. Peirce Society* 24 (1988) 309–16; Raymond Gardella, "The Tenets and Limits of Emerson's All-Conscious Man," *American Benedictine Review* 21 (1970) 375–88; Christopher W. Sten, "Bartelby the Transcendentalist: Melville's Dead Letter to Emerson," *Modern Language Quarterly* 35 (1974) 30–44; Brian M. Bailour, "Emerson's 'Poetic Prose,'" *Modern Language Quarterly* 35 (1974) 157–72.

[41] See Mary Kupiec Cayton, "The Making of an American Prophet: Emerson, His Audiences, and the Rise of the Culture Industry in Nineteenth-Century America," *American Historical Review* 92 (1987) 597–620.

[42] For a fuller discussion and documentation of the issues treated in this section see Gelpi, *Endless Seeker,* 71–129.

ecstasy. He still believed, however, that the genius assigned to each individual by an impersonal nature defined a specific task to accomplish, a special, personal contribution to make to the cosmic scheme of things. He also believed that nature endowed each individual genius with an excess of energy which sought to ensure that one would indeed complete the task which Nature intended one to accomplish, much as a pitcher on the mound imparts a different spin to each ball thrown over the plate. That excess of energy accounted, he now believed, for the universal fact of personal oddities and idiosyncracies. Having reduced personal genius to a blend of spiritual fate and personal eccentricity, Emerson called the result a "bias." Having faced his own bias and those of others head on, Emerson saw that the integration of the concept of bias into his Transcendental vision modified it in significant ways. The mature Emerson summed up the matter in the following way:

> We animate what we can, and we see only what we animate. Nature and books belong to the eyes that see them. It depends on the mood of the man whether he shall see the sunset, or the fine poem. There are always sunsets and there is always genius; but only a few hours so serene that we can relish nature or criticism. The more or less depends on structure or temperament. . . . Temperament puts all divinity to rout.[43]

The fact of universal bias forces each individual to marshal the limited creative energies allotted one by nature in order to expend them in the fulfillment of one's fated life work. Squandered vital energy leaves one trapped in the illusory world of sense and of surd, meaningless facts. The reward of such self-discipline comes in rare moments of "surprise" when the sensible veil which obscures day-to-day, humdrum living parts and discloses vistas of spiritual possibility.[44]

Doggedly Platonic in his philosophical convictions, Emerson even discovered in his new philosophy of bias a resolution of the perennial argument between nominalists and realists. The whole of nature includes both the universal and the concrete, even though the finitude of any individual bias prevents any person from grasping the whole. Still, every concrete sensible reality recapitulates the transcendent, universal law which its genus represents. The mature Emerson observed:

> All the universe over, there is but one thing, this old Two-Face, creator-creature, mind-matter, right-wrong, of which any proposition may be affirmed or denied. Very fitly therefore I assert that every man is a partialist;

---

[43] Emerson, *Complete Works,* 3:54; see also 50–1, 56.

[44] Emerson, *Complete Works,* 3:55–79; *The Journals of Ralph Waldo Emerson,* ed. Edward Emerson and Waldo Forbes, 10 vols. (Boston: Houghton, Mifflin & Co., 1909–14) 6:50. For Emerson's different formulations of the notion of bias see Emerson, *Complete Works,* 3:40–51, 56–60, 62, 64–79, 184–5; 6:12, 131–2, 267; 8:306–7.

that nature secures him as an instrument of self-conceit, preventing the tendencies to religion and science; and now further assert, that, each man's genius being nearly and affectionately explored, he is justified in his individuality, as his nature is found to be immense; and now I add that every man is a universalist also, and, as our earth, whilst it spins on its own axis, spins all the time around the sun through the celestial spaces, so the least of its rational children, the most dedicated to his private affair, works out, though as it were under a disguise, the universal problem. We fancy men are individuals; so are pumpkins; but every pumpkin in the field goes through every point of pumpkin history.[45]

Bias also came to explain for Emerson the distinction between materialists and idealists. Materialists experience an eccentric bias to the concrete and the sensible, while idealists experience an eccentric bias toward the universal and the spiritual. In the total scheme of things, idealists, who recognize the reality of transcendent universal laws, counterbalance the limitations inherent in every other human bias by luring humanity toward transcendent creativity.[46]

Emerson brought these insights to something like systematic expression in *Representative Men*. In *Representative Men*, the mature Emerson undertook to discern the universal teleologies operative in the biases of the great geniuses of human history. The goal of spiritual discernment remained the same, namely, through a descriptive process to lead the reader to a perception of the universal, transcendent laws which govern the universe. In *Representative Men*, however, the philosophy of bias began to endow the discerning process with something like a triadic, dialectical character, very vaguely reminiscent of German idealism.

As the argument of *Representative Men* unfolds, the descriptive exploration of each particular bias inevitably reveals its negative limits. When that occurs, a negation of the negation yields a discerning glimpse of the universal divine essence which every finite, creative bias expresses.[47] In *Representative Men*, Plato exemplifies the bias to speculation; Immanuel Swedenborg, the mystical (or moral) bias; Michel de Montaigne, the bias toward healthy skepticism; William Shakespeare, the bias to poetry; and Napoleon, the bias toward action.

Platonism provided *Representative Men* with its metaphysical scaffolding. The "Old Two-Face" to whom Emerson alluded in his second series

---

[45] Emerson, *Complete Works*, 3:245–6; see also Sandra Morris, "The Threshold Poem, Emerson, and 'The Sphinx,'" *American Literature* 69 (1997) 547–70.

[46] Emerson, *Complete Works*, 1:329–59.

[47] Emerson, *Complete Works*, 4:8–34; Emerson, *Journals and Miscellaneous Notebooks*, 8:301–2; 9:268–9; *The Journals of Ralph Waldo Emerson*, 8:35.

of essays designated the Platonic division of being into motion and rest. The elder Emerson observed:

> The uneasiness which the thought of our helplessness in the chain of causes occasions us, results from looking too much at one condition of nature, namely, Motion. But the drag is never taken from the wheel. Wherever the impulse exceeds, the Rest or identity insinuates its compensation. All over the wide fields of earth grows the prunella or self-heal.[48]

The discerning process in *Representative Men* situates each typical human bias in relationship to these two contrasting poles of reality, which Emerson found universally pervasive. Rest in Emersonian Platonism unifies, while motion diversifies:

> If speculation tends thus to a terrific unity, in which all things are absorbed, action tends directly to diversity. The first is the course of gravitation of mind; the second is the power of nature. Nature is manifold. The unity absorbs and melts or reduces. Nature opens and creates. These two principles reappear and interpenetrate all things, all thought; the one, the many. One is being; the other, intellect: one is necessity; the other freedom: one, rest; the other, pleasure: one, genius; the other, talent: one, earnestness; the other, knowledge: one, possession: the other, trade: one, caste; the other, culture: one, king; the other, democracy: and if we dare carry these generalizations a step higher, and name the last tendency of both, we might say, that the end of the one is escape from organization,—pure science; and the end of the other is the highest instrumentality, or use of means, or executive deity.[49]

In *Representative Men* Plato exemplifies the perennial philosophical effort to wrestle with the relationship of the one to the many. Plato also illustrates the strengths and the limitations of the speculative bias. The strength of the speculative bias lies in its ability to grasp the fundamental metaphysical structure of things. Its limitation consists in its inability to translate its intellectual insights into creative embodiment. Instead, persons with a speculative, metaphysical bias squander their energies on constructing systems which can never finally comprehend the cosmic order they contemplate. As a consequence, they remain ineffectual in dealing practically with the sense manifold.[50]

The Swedenborg of *Representative Men* represents the mystical or prophetic bias. The Emersonian mystic lives attuned to moral truth. Commentators on Representative Men have, not without warrant, suggested that Swedenborg the mystic bears a strong resemblance to Ralph Waldo

---

[48] Emerson, *Complete Works,* 4:194–5.
[49] Ibid., 4:52–53.
[50] Ibid., 4:39–89.

Emerson. Certainly, Emerson discovered in the writings of Swedenborg many of the key doctrines which he himself had articulated during his saturnalia of faith: the doctrine of transcendent forms, the doctrine of the hierarchical ordering of values, the doctrine of divine influx, and the doctrine of correspondence between the material and spiritual orders.[51] If the limitations of the speculative bias make it ineffectual, the limitations of the mystical bias make it insensitive to beauty. Swedenborg's penchant for tedious moralizing left him "entirely devoid of the whole apparatus of poetic expression, which that perception creates."[52]

Montaigne, the skeptic, represents a bias toward bias. Healthy skeptics like Montaigne refuse the temptation to which vicious skepticism yields. The vicious skeptic reduces all reality to matter and to sense; the healthy skeptic recognizes the limitations present in all human biases and therefore refuses to credit the ultimate truth of any particular human perception of the real. The healthy skeptic opposes all forms of human dogmatism and social extremism. The healthy skeptic even cheerfully acknowledges the limitations of his own skepticism:

> He labors to plant his feet, to be the beam of balance. He will not go beyond his card. He sees the one-sidedness of these men of the street; he will not be a Gibeonite; he stands for the intellectual faculties, a cool head and whatever serves to keep it cool; no unadvised industry, no unrewarded self-devotion, no loss of brains in toil.[53]

The moral earnestness of the prophetic mystic partially counterbalances the narrowly theoretical bent of the speculative intellectual. The healthy skeptic counterbalances the mystical visionary. The skeptical bias reveals its limitation, however, in the universal propensity of the skeptical mind to acquiesce in vicious skepticism, in a one-sided vision of reality which effectively denies the reality of the spiritual and of the transcendent.[54] The poetic bias, which Shakespeare preeminently represents, counteracts the limitations of the skeptical bias by sensitizing humanity to Beauty.

The poetic bias negates the speculative bias's lack of practicality by its spontaneous creativity. Of all the biases, then, the poetic exhibits the greatest centering in the di-polar essence of God and of humanity, because it participates simultaneously in both rest and motion. It grasps reality simultaneously as both true and good, and it does so in a synthetic insight which creates finite expressions of transcendent Beauty. The poetic bias, however, lacks the prophetic mystic's ability to penetrate deeply into the

[51] Ibid., 4:109–26.
[52] Ibid., 4:43.
[53] Ibid., 4:155.
[54] Ibid., 4:149–86.

moral essence of deity. As a consequence, its creations, however beautiful, never achieve the moral profundity and prophetic power of the mystic. As for Shakespeare himself:

> It must ever go into the world's history that the best poet led an obscure and profane life, using his genius for the public amusement. . . . The world still wants its poet-priest, a reconciler, who shall not trifle with Shakespeare the player, nor shall grope in the graves with Swedenborg the mourner, but who shall speak, and act, with equal inspiration.[55]

If the poet exemplifies the most centered of finite human biases, in Emerson's mature religious vision, Napoleon, the man of action, probably exemplifies human bias's most eccentric exaggerations. Napoleon exemplifies the human bias to action. If the speculative bias remains anchored too exclusively in rest, the bias toward action remains too exclusively anchored in motion. Among the human biases, the bias to action manifests spiritual obtuseness, monumental self-infatuation, and blatant immorality. In other words, the bias to action remains blind to the strengths of the speculative, the mystical, and the skeptical bias. Viewed as a representative of the bias to action, Napoleon's life teaches the lesson "which vigor always teaches:—that there is always room for it. To what heaps of cowardly doubts is not that man's life the answer."[56]

In a revealing entry in his diary dated October 1849, Emerson paralleled the human "big endians" whom he had described in *Representative Men* with "little endians" of his personal acquaintance. The passage makes it clear that Emerson thought that the heroic biases which "representative men" exemplify find less heroic expressions in the lives of smaller human lights, like himself and other New England Transcendentalists. In his diary he paired Plato with Bronson Alcott, Swedenborg with Jones Very, Shakespeare with Charles Newcomb, Montaigne with William Ellery Channing, and Napoleon with Thoreau.[57] He compared himself to Goethe. That last comparison also throws light on the final essay of *Representative Men,* which describes Goethe the writer. Emerson discovered writ large in the works of Goethe the same method as he had employed in writing *Representative Men.* As a consequence, the essay on Goethe yields some important insights into how the waning of naive enthusiasm had further modified the method of spiritual discernment.

The chastened discernment employed by Goethe/Emerson in describing the metaphysical structure of the universe abjured any claim to

---

[55] Ibid., 4:218–9. See also Charles W. Mignon, "Classic Art: Emerson's Pragmatic Criticism," *Studies in the American Renaissance* 7 (1983) 203–21.

[56] Emerson, *Complete Works*, 4:247.

[57] Emerson, *Journals and Miscellaneous Notebooks,* 8:62.

creative ecstasy. It merely disposed and arranged facts descriptively in a novel order, much as the memory does, with the result that "the facts do not lie inert; but some subside and others shine; so that soon we have a new picture, composed of eminent experiences."[58] The description of different typical human biases in *Representative Men* consciously played off the limitations of one bias against another until the reader began to glimpse "the universal, bi-polar essence of man" which lies beyond limited biases and grounds all of them. In other words, *Representative Men* sought through a process of description and negation to show the reader a glimpse of "old Two-Face," of the transcendent being which lies at the basis of the universe and which divides into motion and rest. Like Goethe, Emerson made no claim to having offered a final account of universal being, since the fact of bias puts any such account beyond the reach of any individual. Yet, like Goethe, Emerson believed that the discernment of bias in *Representative Men* did gravitate toward the truth.[59]

Emerson's journals illumine another interesting facet of *Representative Men:* the mature Emerson retained a fascination with the figure of Jesus. On hearing of Renan's publication of a life of Christ, Emerson confided to his journal:

> Renan writes *Vie de Jésus.* Many of his contemporaries have no doubt projected the same theme. When I wrote *Representative Men,* I felt that Jesus was the "Representative Man" whom I ought to sketch; but the task required great gifts,—steadfast insight and perfect temper; else, the consciousness of want of sympathy in the audience make one petulant or sore, in spite of himself.[60]

The mature Emerson continued to proclaim the Unitarian Christ from his secular pulpit. His Jesus still bore little resemblance to Christian orthodoxy. Not a divine person incarnate, Emerson's Jesus exemplified the least biased human being who ever lived, the one person who managed to bring together all the creative traits of the different human biases whose strengths and limitations he had meditated in *Representative Men.*

During his mature period, Emerson published a second work which employed the same descriptive techniques as structured the argument of *Representative Men.* Like the earlier work, this second exercise in mature discernment claimed to do no more than to gravitate fallibilistically toward the truth. He called this work *English Traits.* Much more than a travelogue or personal history, *English Traits* undertook an analysis of the national bias which lay at the basis of Anglo-Saxon culture in England and in the United States.

---

[58] Ibid., 4:262.
[59] Ibid., 4:270–3, 284–90.
[60] *The Journals of Ralph Waldo Emerson,* 9:59.

Emerson's description of the British landscape in *English Traits* teaches the reader to view it as "a miniature of Europe," i.e., as "representative" of the same geographical forces which produced European culture. Emerson next seeks to convince the reader that the Anglo-Saxon race blends "representative" traits of the different European racial strains. Celtic ancestry gives the Britons solid interest in material values. German blood gives them moral strength, courage, and unconquerability. The Nordic and Gallic strains in English ancestry account for British materialism and moral venality.[61] The racial blend, however, makes the English "not a final race . . . but a race with a future."[62]

In *English Traits* British national creativity and achievement results from the intersection of felicitous European racial strains with a representative European geography. In the Anglo-Saxon race the "great range and variety of character" manifests that, in creating "the fair Anglo-Saxon man," nature has conspired to produce the most "centered" race in history, a race whose total blend of biases best represents the universal, bi-polar essence of humanity and of God.[63]

As a social class, however, the Cockney symbolized for Emerson the fatal limits of the Anglo-Saxon bias. The same materialistic sensualism which Cockney culture "represents" reached philosophical expression in Lockean nominalism and empiricism. *English Traits* predicted the decline of English world domination in consequence of the British people's lack of moral stamina to resist the corrupting cultural influences of institutional conservatism, commercialism, sensualism, nominalistic skepticism, and empiricism. That dim prognosis, however, prepared the way in *English Traits* for a brighter future for British culture in the United States. The bracing moral strain which New England Puritanism infused into the American representatives of the "fair Anglo-Saxon man" promised to counterbalance corrupting materialistic influences endemic to the national bias. Where the British would fail, Americans would succeed. Despite cultural decline in the mother country, Anglo-Saxon creativity would come to a new and more vital corporate expression in the new world. In the United States, the Platonic tendencies of the British genius would overcome Lockean nominalism and empiricism. Emerson believed that Francis Bacon, the "centered" Platonic empiricist, represented this creative strain in British culture.[64]

Taken together, *Representative Men* and *English Traits* constitute Emerson's most sustained attempt to make a metaphysical statement about

---

[61] Emerson, *Complete Works,* 5:44–73.

[62] Ibid., 5:68.

[63] Ibid., 5:74–143.

[64] Ibid., 5:116–260.

the ultimate constitution of the world. He undertook this ambitious ontological discernment at the very moment in his life when he had come to believe that the finitude of each personal bias prevents it from reducing the cosmos to a verbal system. The discovery of finitude endowed the mature Emerson with a sense of personal fallibility. Like Goethe, he now settled for only an approximate formulation of the mystery of a sphinx-like universe.

Still, a contemporary reader cannot help but feel disappointment at the results of Emerson's mature experiment in discernment. In *English Traits* especially, Emerson concluded that the moral essence of deity and the white, Anglo-Saxon race more or less coincide. Despite his Yankee racism, Emerson publicly joined the abolitionist movement, though tardily, with the passage of the Fugitive Slave Act. His reluctance in publicly supporting abolition stemmed in part from the fact that he recognized that he had little taste or competence for political barnstorming. Moreover, while he disapproved of slavery, to the end of his life he remained mildly racist and regarded black-skinned people as racially inferior to whites. Contemporary readers find it hard to credit that the racist prejudices of a nineteenth-century New England intellectual and the metaphysical structure of the cosmos do in fact coincide, but the author of *English Traits* had no serious doubt on that point.[65]

On the other hand, Emerson's discovery of human bias endowed his Transcendental religious vision with a much needed modesty. During his saturnalia of faith Emerson had acquiesced in the overly optimistic prognosis of the human prospect which Enlightenment modernity popularized. The Transcendental Emerson believed that every American had access to an unlimited, spontaneous, creative potential which his Transcendental gospel of creativity would unleash. Bereavement and a conviction of personal limitation led him, however, to question in significant ways the rosy picture of the future which an inflated Enlightenment enthusiasm had tricked him into endorsing. The philosophy of bias taught Emerson that only rare geniuses achieve the creativity of a Michelangelo and that even the greatest genius views reality from a limited angle of vision. He continued to hope, however, that what the individual could not accomplish

---

[65] See Len Gougen, *Virtue's Hero: Emerson, Antislavery, and Reform* (Athens: University of Georgia Press, 1990). In my judgment, Gougen overstates the extent of Emerson's active commitment to abolitionism and underestimates the extent of his racism. It would also appear that Emerson harbored a degree of anti-Semitism; Robert J. Loewenberg, *An American Idol: Emerson and the Jewish Idea* (Lanham, Md.: University Press of America, 1984); Robert J. Loewenberg, "Emerson and the Genius of American Liberalism," *Center Journal* 2 (1983) 107–28; Robert J. Loewenberg, "Emerson and Abolition: The Silent Years, 1837–1844," *American Literature* 54 (1982) 560–75; Barbara Ryan, "Emerson's Domestic and Social Experiment," *American Literature* 66 (1994) 485–508.

personally the divinely centered, creative, Anglo-Saxon race could accomplish collectively. Emerson's revised Transcendental gospel of creativity held out a rosy future to the new American nation. He predicted a corporate outburst of cultural creativity which would transform the United States into the heir of British imperial domination of the planet.[66]

One cannot, however, understand fully the dark side of Emerson's genius until one ponders how the philosophy of bias modified his Transcendental ethics of creativity. He brought that ethics to its final mature formulation in *The Conduct of Life* and *Society and Solitude.* In the following section I turn to this final dimension of Emerson's thought.

V

Emerson probably found the figure of Napoleon morally troubling. He had come to believe that nature foreordained for each individual a specific life work by assigning to each genius, whether humble or heroic, a bias and an excess of energy which impelled it to accomplish that work. In *Representative Men,* however, his discernment of the bias toward action exemplified in Napoleon had forced him to recognize that a morally obtuse bias toward action could impel one, as it had Napoleon, to acts of gross immorality. Did that mean that nature, like some Calvinist Jehovah, could predestine some individuals to lives of immorality? In *The Conduct of Life* Emerson set about the task of reconciling his new philosophy of bias with his earlier Transcendental ethics of creativity.

The argument of *The Conduct of Life* presupposed the reality of personal finitude. In this work Emerson consistently portrayed human moral striving as a constant oscillation between finite, fatal limits, on the one hand, and conscious creativity, on the other. In *The Conduct of Life* the discerning process retained its descriptive character, and it continued to move from factual description to a description of the law which explains the fact. In Emerson's mature ethics, however, fact had taken on fatal limits which his saturnalia of faith had underrated. The challenge of moral living for the elder Emerson consisted in outwitting fate. *The Conduct of Life* argued that despite the fact of fatal finitude, human genius still retained the capacity to transcend those limits in order to act for universal, selfless ends. Emerson observed at the beginning of *The Conduct of Life:*

> The element running through entire nature, which we popularly call Fate, is
> known to us as limitation. Whatever limits us we call Fate. If we are brute and

[66] See Douglas R. Anderson, "An American Argument for Belief in the Reality of God," *International Journal for Philosophy and Religion* 26 (1989) 109–18.

barbarous, the fate takes a brute and dreadful shape. Our checks become finer. If we rise to spiritual culture, the antagonism takes a spiritual form.[67]

The universal prevalence of fate, whether it assumes a gross, material embodiment or a finer, spiritual form, transforms moral striving into something like a war of attrition. "We can," the mature Emerson mused, "afford to allow limitation, if we know it is the meter of the growing man. We stand against Fate, as children stand up against the wall in their father's house and notch their height from year to year."[68] Emerson's philosophical collision with bias and limitation caused him to espouse an ethical meliorism. "Fate involves the melioration."[69] The human spirit can never free itself totally from the limitations of fate, but it can experience amelioration, enhancement.

The qualified fatalism in Emerson's mature ethics only reinforced his earlier moral necessitarianism. Either the confining necessity of fate or the liberating necessity of functioning as a limited, creative channel of the transformative, spiritual laws of the universe rules the individual: "Let us build altars to the Beautiful Necessity. If we thought men were free in the sense that in a single exception one fantastical will could prevail over the law of things, it were all one as if a child's hand could pull down the sun."[70]

In *The Conduct of Life* the discerning process exhibits some of the dialectical quality of *Representative Men*. Emerson's ethical discernment begins with the description of some complex of fatal limits to human moral striving and then describes the negation of fate through thought. "Intellect annuls Fate."[71] The conquest of fate through thought elevates the conscience to a higher level of moral striving, but each level of moral activity contains its own kind of fatal limit. Thus as human life and striving improve, "the checks become finer."

In its crudest form fate takes physical shape in natural disasters, wars, the laws of physiology, heredity, violence, disease. Dissatisfaction with physical limitation gives rise to reflection on how to overcome it. The conquest of physical limitation through thought engenders power. Power in its crudest form coincides with natural bias, with the excess of energy imparted by Nature to each individual to accomplish his or her allotted task in life. Self-discipline, however, transforms the eccentricities of bias into self-transcending creative energy.[72]

[67] Emerson, *Complete Works,* 6:20.
[68] Ibid., 6:30.
[69] Ibid., 6:36.
[70] Ibid., 6:49.
[71] Ibid., 6:23.
[72] Ibid., 6:53–82.

As the analytic intellect tames and disciplines power, it generates wealth. The amassing of wealth, however, requires the cultivation of Franklinsonian virtues like industry, frugality, and submission to the laws and seasons of nature. The cultivation of virtue in turn schools the conscience to recognize ethical values. Unethical business practices inevitably take their toll of one's possessions and thus, paradoxically, also teach the businessman that virtue pays. As ethical awareness grows, it negates the mindless human tendency to amass wealth for its own sake. Gradually, the conscience learns that

> Wealth is mental; wealth is moral. The value of a dollar is, to buy just things; a dollar goes on increasing in value with all the genius and all the virtue in the world. A dollar in a university is worth more than a dollar in jail; in a temperate, schooled, law-abiding community than in some sink of crime where dice, knives and arsenic are in constant play.[73]

As the cultivation of intellect refines the pursuit of wealth, it gives rise to culture.[74] Culture schools the human spirit to appreciate and value things which transcend mere pragmatic efficiency. Personal bias, however, also endows culture with its fatal aspect. Even the greatest geniuses, as Emerson had argued in *Representative Men,* betray a cramping egotism.

> This goitre of egotism is so frequent among notable persons that we must infer some strong necessity in nature which it subserves; such as we see in the sexual attraction. The preservation of the species was a point of such necessity that Nature has secured it at all hazards by immensely overloading the passion, at the risk of perpetual crime and disorder. So egotism has its root in the cardinal necessity by which each individual persists to be what he is.
> This individuality is not only not inconsistent with culture but is the basis of it. Every valuable nature is there in its own right, and the student we speak to must have a motherwit invincible by his culture,—which uses all books, arts, facilities, and elegancies of intercourse, but is never subdued and lost in them. He only is a well-made man who has a good determination. And the end of culture is not to destroy this, God forbid! but to train away all impediment and mixture and leave nothing but pure power.[75]

The very realization that narrow egotism lies at the basis of culture challenges the developing conscience to transcend it. "Incapacity of melioration is the only mortal distemper."[76] The moral need to overcome egotism schools the conscience in the selfless cultivation of the imagination. At the beginning of *The Conduct of Life* Emerson had warned: "If we rise to spir-

---

[73] Ibid., 6:103.
[74] Ibid., 6:85–127.
[75] Ibid., 6:134.
[76] Ibid., 6:140; see also 131–59.

itual culture, the antagonism [of fate] takes a spiritual form." Manners embody the fatal form of culture. They embody imagination hardened into usage, but despite their fatal power over human behavior manners educate the conscience to civility. In the process, manners gradually teach personal bias to seek the social benefit of humanity as a whole.[77]

As the creative imagination universalizes its concerns, it enters into the realm of religion and of worship. Religion has its own fatal checks: "the peacock ritualism, the retrogression of Popery, the maundering of Mormons, the squalor of Mesmerism, the deliration of rappings, the rat and mouse revelation, thumps in table drawers, and black art."[78] Nevertheless, a melioristic ethics of imaginative creativity reveals that a religious impulse lies at the basis of all human culture. That impulse lapses into unbelief only when it fails to discipline personal bias through the selfless contemplation of impersonal, transcendent Beauty. If, then, one follows the melioristic trajectory at the basis of human moral striving it teaches one that love of eternal Beauty grounds all morality.

> The cure for false theology is mother-wit. Forget your books and traditions, and obey your moral perceptions at this hour. That which is signified by the words "moral" and "spiritual," is a lasting essence, and, will certainly bring back the words, age after age, to their ancient meaning. I know no words that mean so much. In our definitions we grope after the spiritual by describing it as invisible. The true meaning of spiritual is real; that law which executes itself, which works without means, and which cannot be conceived as not existing. . . . Let us replace sentimentalism by realism, and dare to uncover those simple and terrible laws which, be they seen or unseen, pervade and govern.[79]

The ethical quest of *The Conduct of Life* culminates, then, in the realization that the love of impersonal, transcendent Beauty ultimately motivates all of human moral striving, even in its lowest, crudest expressions. In the meditation on Beauty which brings the argument of *The Conduct of Life* to its rhetorical culmination, Emerson, quite consistently, refuses to define "the Beautiful." Instead, he contents himself with describing some of its experienced traits. Beauty lures love beyond sensuous delight. It coincides with spiritual law, with truth, with normative good. It finds its highest physical expression in the feminine physique and its highest spiritual expression in the heroism and creativity of great-souled individuals. Beauty fires the imagination and resists analytic definition because the

---

[77] Ibid., 6:169–97.
[78] Ibid., 6:209.
[79] Ibid., 6:214–5.

universal, cosmic scope of its relationship finds more adequate symbolic embodiment in the synthetic insights of the creative imagination.[80]

The ethical discovery of transcendent Beauty finally negates all fatal negation by revealing its illusory character. Appropriately, then, *The Conduct of Life* ends with a meditation on the illusions of fate, for if transcendent Beauty coincides with the real, then immanent, finite limitation—whatever fatal form it assumes—belongs to the realm of non-being, of illusion. A melioristic ascent from physical fate to the contemplation of transcendent Beauty reveals, then, that

> there is no chance and no anarchy in the universe. All is system and grada-
> tion. Every god is there sitting in his sphere. The young mortal enters the hall
> of the firmament; there is he alone with them alone, they pouring on him
> benedictions and gifts, and beckoning him up to their thrones. On the instant,
> and incessantly, fall snow-storms of illusions. . . . What is he that he should
> resist their will, and think or act for himself? Every moment new changes
> and new showers of deceptions to baffle and distract him. And when, by and
> by, for an instant, the air clears and the cloud lifts a little, there are the gods
> still sitting around him on their thrones,—they alone with him alone.[81]

The mature Emerson found the message of *The Conduct of Life* aptly summarized in an ancient Persian proverb: "Fooled thou must be, though wisest of the wise: / Then be the fool of virtue, not of vice."[82] He himself had decided to settle for playing the fool for virtue. With Plotinus he sought to be "alone with the alone." The older he grew the more the coyness of "the gods," the parsimoniousness with which they dispensed creative ecstasy, suffused his self-imposed solitude with poignant loneliness.[83]

A miscellany of essays, *Society and Solitude* lacks the coherence of argument which one finds in *The Conduct of Life*. Still, it extends the ethi-

---

[80] Ibid., 6:281–306.

[81] Ibid., 6:325.

[82] Ibid. See Marwan M. Obeidat, "Emerson and the Muslim Orient," *Muslim World* 78 (1988) 132–45; George K. Rishmawi, "Emerson and the Sufis," *Muslim World* 85 (1995) 147–55; Allen Leon Raikes, "Sufism, Taoism, and Ralph Waldo Emerson: A Cross-Cultural Perspective on the Rhetoric of Place Between" (Ph.D. dissertation, Michigan State University, 1995).

[83] See Stanley Cavell, *Conditions Handsome and Unhandsome: The Constitution of Emersonian Perfectionism* (Chicago: University of Chicago Lectures, 1990); David M. Robinson, *Emerson and the Conduct of Life: Pragmatism and Ethical Purpose in the Later Work* (Cambridge: Cambridge University Press, 1993); "Grace and Works: Emerson's Essays in Theological Perspective," *American Unitarianism, 1805–1865,* ed. Conrad Wright (Boston: Massachusetts Historical Society, 1989); Russell B. Goodman, "East-West Philosophy in Nineteenth-Century America: Emerson and Hinduism," *Journal of the History of Ideas* 51 (1990) 625–45.

cal meliorism of *The Conduct of Life* into the realm of social ethics. The book explores the mature Emerson's view of the paradoxical relationship of the individual to society. The elderly Emerson viewed the world of nineteenth-century America as the institutionalization of an aggressive, crudely pragmatic, bourgeois commercialism which rebuffs individual creative genius and drives it into social isolation, but a deeper purpose than getting and spending makes geniuses into hermits.

> But the necessity of solitude is deeper than we have said, and is organic. I have seen many a philosopher whose world is large enough for only one person. He affects to be a good companion; but we are still surprising his secret, that he means and needs to impose his system on the rest. The determination of each is from all others, like that of each tree up into free space.[84]

A cunning nature has seen to it that genius thrives on solitude. One needs isolation in order to discover and to cultivate one's individual genius. Social isolation also prepares a better way of relating socially than mere convention. It frees individuals to seek out others who share a bias similar to their own for the purpose of creative collaboration. The reordering of human relationships for the sake of cultivating one's personal, creative genius forces one to redefine the meaning of solitude. Solitude does not signify mere isolation but the ability to maintain one's creative self-identity in all circumstances.

> Solitude is impracticable, and society is fatal. We must keep our head in the one and our hands in the other. The conditions are met, if we keep our independence, yet do not lose our sympathy. These wonderful horses need to be driven by a fine hand. We require such a solitude as shall hold us to its revelations when we are in the street and in palaces. . . . Society and solitude are deceptive names. It is not the circumstance of seeing more or fewer people, but the readiness of sympathy, that imports; and a sound mind will derive its principles from insight, with ever purer ascent to the sufficient and absolute right, and will accept society as the natural element in which they are applied.[85]

In other words, by forcing the creative individual into solitude and isolation, a crudely commercialistic society unconsciously provokes the progressive conquest of fate which *The Conduct of Life* described.

The other essays in *Society and Solitude* suggest new directions for developing the "higher civility" to which *The Conduct of Life* had aspired. The mature Emerson believed that the nation could transcend petty, partisan politics only when true political genius inspired the kind of visionary

---

[84] Emerson, *Complete Works,* 7:8.
[85] Ibid., 7:15–16.

oratory which would galvanize the creative potential of each individual American. The drabness of domestic life must stimulate families to focus domesticity on the cultivation of beauty. Agrarian society must resist the blandishments of commercialism and stay close to the lessons of nature itself. The shallowness of a money-grubbing economy must teach Americans to cultivate deeper relationships than mere utilitarian collaboration. The formation of clubs which foster common interests should provide social stimulus to individual creativity.[86]

Emerson's mature ethics of cultural melioration continued to rest on creative, individual self-reliance, but on a self-reliance deprived of anything like mystical ecstasy. The mature Emerson believed that courage, not mysticism, holds the key to moral and cultural progress, that is, the courage to trust one's individual, creative bias and to discipline it to act on universal, impersonal principles of moral conduct. Those principles coincide with the "Beautiful Necessity" which rules the universe and which orders all things to its own universal, impersonal ends.[87]

The essay on courage in *Society and Solitude* ends with a bit of doggerel about a mountain man named George Nidiver and his devoted Native American servant. Attacked by two grizzly bears, Nidiver selflessly used his last bullet to kill the bear attacking the Indian boy. He then cowed the other grizzly into retreat by the sheer power in his courageous glance. During Emerson's saturnalia of faith he imagined that a social reformer would act like some nineteenth-century Michelangelo, advancing from one creative ecstasy to another. For the mature Emerson, the social reformer looked more like old George Nidiver staring down his grizzly bear.[88]

The philosophy of bias effected, then, something like a synthesis of the first two phases of Emerson's religious development. During his saturnalia of faith Emerson had replaced the patient cultivation of virtue with ecstatic, creative insight. The rediscovery of fate, finitude, and bias convinced him of the rarity of creative ecstasy. The melioristic ethics of

   [86] Ibid., 7:19–250. See also Paul Allen Colby, "The Doctrine of the Farm: Emerson and the Problem of Labor in Nineteenth-Century New England" (Ph.D. dissertation, Duke University, 1995); Robert D. Richardson, "The Social Imperatives of Transcendentalism," *Religious Humanism* 22 (1988) 82–8; Leonard N. Neufeldt, "The Science of Power: Emerson's Views of Science and Technology in America," *Journal of the History of Ideas* 38 (1971) 329–44.

   [87] Emerson, *Complete Works*, 7:253–67.

   [88] See Mary Kupiec Cayton, *Emerson's Emergence: Self and Society in the Transformation of New England, 1800–1845* (Chapel Hill: University of North Carolina Press, 1989); Frank J. Seibold, "The Armageddon-Narcissism Syndrome," *Religious Humanism* 20 (1986) 71–3; Peter A. Obuchowski, "Emerson, Evolution, and the Problem of Evil," *Harvard Theological Review* 72 (1992) 150–6.

creativity which his philosophy of bias inspired exhibited the same patient, plodding character as Emerson's Unitarian ethic, but in his post-Transcendental period he continued to orient the moral quest to the creation of beauty rather than to duty. In a sense, however, the post-Transcendental Emerson continued to adhere to "the naked purpose to do right." As a result of his saturnalia of faith, however, "the right" had come to signify for him "the Beautiful" rather than "the good."

In the development of ethical thought in the United States, Emerson's philosophy of bias created a moral watershed. It gave initial formulation to the ethics of expressive individualism which pervades popular American culture. Expressive individualism teaches people that they possess a core self which needs protection from other persons and from all forms of institutional encroachment. While Walt Whitman and others helped popularize this particular American ethos, Emerson first formulated it.

The ethics of expressive individualism matured with Emerson himself. Emerson laid the remote speculative foundations for his doctrine of expressive individualism in his pre-Transcendental discernment of the self. That discernment described three interrelated levels within the self: a sensuous, earth-bound self; a finite spiritual self; and an impersonal divine "Self" on which the finite, spiritual self must rely if it hopes to act with genuine self-reliance. In Emerson's simplified Neo-Platonism, the finite spiritual self mediates between the sensual self and the divine, transcendent "Self." In Emerson's universe, one applies the term "self" only with considerable qualification to an infinite, transcendent reality, because only finite selves finally qualify as persons. The infinite, divine "Self" remains eternally impersonal. In other words, while the Over Soul inspires individual, personal creativity, it remains itself trans-personal.

The saturnalia of faith transformed each finite spiritual self into one's personal genius, that is, into the source of one's spontaneous, personal creativity. Moreover, in his optimistic naivete the Transcendental Emerson believed that finite, personal genius had immediate access within subjectivity to the infinite creative power of the Over Soul. For that reason, Emerson the Transcendentalist saw no reason why each individual could not live a life of uninterrupted, creative ecstasy.

The post-Transcendental Emerson knew better. In his mature thought Emerson transformed personal genius into personal bias. He now recognized both the radical finitude and egocentric distortions which dog individual, personal genius. As a consequence, personal genius now assumed for him the form of a personal, spiritual fate. An impersonal nature assigns to each individual a specific creative task within the cosmic scheme of things. Moreover, in assigning individual biases, an impersonal nature seeks an impersonal, universal good, not individual, personal advantage. That implied that obedience to one's bias need not lead to personal fulfillment even if one successfully made one's fated contribution to the total good of the cosmos. As the mature Emerson wryly observed: "A subject and an object,—it takes so much to make the galvanic circuit complete, but magnitude adds nothing. What imports it whether it is Kepler and the sphere, Columbus and America, a reader and his book, or puss with her tail?"[89]

The conviction that an impersonal nature had fated one to accomplish a specific creative task and had assigned one only a limited amount of energy in order to accomplish that task grounded Emerson's mature ethics of expressive individualism. Squandered energy could leave one bereft of the power to accomplish one's fated cosmic chore. As a consequence, one must guard one's genius from all forms of external dissipation. Fidelity to one's individual bias expressed, therefore, one of the most fundamental moral imperatives in the conduct of life.

Society and Solitude, Emerson's final major work completed without Cabot's assistance, made this moral point most explicitly. The Emersonian imperative—"Cultivate thy own genius"—led the mature Emerson to idealize clubs as the best form of social intercourse. Clubs brought together persons sharing the same creative bias. They stimulated personal creativity through invigorating conversation. Still, one remained free to withdraw from a club as soon as it failed to stimulate one's personal genius,[90] for in the end true moral courage consists in fidelity to one's own bias. A similar moral non-engagement provided the new left of the 60s with its battle-cry: "Do your own thing." Emerson explained what cultivating one's own bias means in the following terms:

> If you accept your thoughts as inspirations from the Supreme Intelligence, obey them when they prescribe difficult duties, because they come only so long as they are used; or, if your scepticism reaches to the last verge, and you have no confidence in any foreign mind, then be brave, because there is one good opinion which must always be of consequence to you, namely, your own.[91]

Often people read the genial moral advice of the sage of Concord without probing its deeper, darker implications. Emerson, however, took his ethics of expressive individualism with deadly seriousness. Concern to preserve the integrity of his own fated genius kept him from joining Brook Farm. It made of him a tardy and reluctant abolitionist. In the end, that same fidelity seems to have left him frustrated and self-isolated. The frus-

---

[89] Emerson, *Complete Works*, 3:80.

[90] Ibid., 7:225–36.

[91] Ibid., 7:277.

tration and self-isolation resulted in his case from the coyness of the World Soul, who proved much less profligate with creative inspirations than the sage of Concord would have preferred.

The elusiveness of enthusiasm troubled Emerson throughout his life. Emerson the youth castigated himself in his journals with the complaint: "Ungenerous, selfish, cautious and cold, I yet wish to be romantic." Despite his religion of creative ecstasy, even the mature Emerson feared an excess of passion. The "rage of the passions" unleashed by puberty must, he feared, end in forcing creative Reason to submit to the domination of a sense-bound and pedestrian Understanding. Typically, after the death of little Waldo, the bereaved father grieved at his inability to grieve properly.[92]

The waning of creative enthusiasm during Emerson's post-Transcendental period transformed the coyness of the Over Soul into a major moral and religious problem. Having designated himself the prophet of a religion of spontaneous, uninterrupted creativity, Emerson felt his own inability to open himself to the creative influx of the divine as a vexing conundrum. He called the problem "the double consciousness." By "the double consciousness" he meant the rareness of moments of creative insight and the pervasiveness of humdrum drabness during the greater part of life. The universal presence of fatal limitation convinced him of the need to formulate a "philosophy of waiting," of waiting, that is, for the Over Soul to reveal itself.[93]

Waiting, however, left him extremely frustrated. "This vexes me," he confessed in his journal, "that I should be of that infirm temper as to owe my ebbs and flows of estimation to any thing extrinsic."[94] He began to dream of a direct intellectual assault on the vexing problem of the "double consciousness." As early as 1838 he asked his journal: "Could not the natural history of the Reason or universal Sentiment be written? One that would be that all that is alive and genial in thought must come of that?" A week later, he wrote:

> Write the Nat[ural]. His[tory]. of Reason. Recognize the inextinguishable dualism. Show that after the broadest assertions [proclamation] of the One nature we must yet admit always the co-presence of a superior influx, must pray, must hope (and what is hope but affirmation of two?), must doubt. But also show that to seek the Unity is a /law/necessity of the mind [,] that we do not choose to resist duality, complexity. Show that the Will is absurd in the matter."[95]

---

[92] Emerson, *Journals and Miscellaneous Notebooks,* 1:131–2; Ralph Waldo Emerson, *The Letters of Ralph Waldo Emerson,* ed. Ralph L. Rusk, 6 vols. (New York: Columbia University Press, 1939) 3:9–10.

[93] Emerson, *Journals and Miscellaneous Notebooks,* 2:123; 4:275–7, 368.

[94] Ibid., 5:217, 273, 435.

[95] Ibid., 5:481–2.

During Emerson's second voyage to England in 1847, this ambitious philosophical project began to take shape in his mind after he listened to two scientific lectures by Richard Owen and Michael Faraday. After the lectures he penned the following journal entry:

> I have used such opportunity as I have had, and lately in London and Paris, to attend scientific lectures; and in listening to Richard Owen's masterly enumeration of the parts and laws of the human body, or Michael Farady's explanation of magnetic powers, or the botanist's descriptions, one could not help admiring the irresponsible security and happiness of the attitude of the naturalist; sure of admiration for his facts, sure of their sufficiency. They ought to interest you; if they do not, the fault lies with you. Then I thought—could not similar enumeration be made of the laws and powers of intellect and possess the same claims on the student? Could we have, that is, the exhaustive accuracy of distribution which chemists use in their nomenclature and anatomists in their descriptions applied to a higher class of facts; to those laws, namely, which are common to chemistry, anatomy, astronomy, geometry, intellect, morals, and social life;—laws of the world?[96]

When Emerson's assault on the "double consciousness" came it took the form of a series of lectures: "The Natural History of Intellect" in 1848, "The Natural Method of Mental Philosophy" in 1858, "Philosophy of the People" in 1866, and the "Harvard Lectures" in 1870 and 1871. After the first series of Harvard lectures, Emerson confided to Carlyle on June 17, 1870:

> The oppressive engagement of writing and reading 18 lectures on Philosophy to a class of graduates in the college, and these in six successive weeks, was a task a little more formidable in prospect and nature than any foregoing one. . . . I doubt the experts in Philosophy will not praise my discourses; but the topics give me room for my guesses, criticisms, admirations and experiences with the accepted masters, and also the lessons I have learned from the hidden great. I have the fancy that a realist is a good corrector of formalism, no matter how incapable of syllogism or continuous linked statement. To great results of thought and morals the steps are not many, and it is not the masters who spin the ostentations of continuity.[97]

Emerson wrote out the full text of each of his sermons and stitched them together into little booklets. The later lectures, however, consist of

---

[96] Emerson, *Complete Works,* 9:3–4.

[97] Joseph Slater, ed., *The Correspondence of Emerson and Carlyle* (New York: Columbia University Press, 1965) 570. The phrase "ostentations of continuity" could refer to the German idealistic philosophers. In any event, the phrase alludes to the mature Emerson's belief that the finitude of personal bias prevents any thinker from comprehending the riddle of the universe in a rational system. See David L. Smith, "Emerson and Deconstruction: The End(s) of Scholarship," *Soundings* 4 (1984) 379–98; David L. Smith, "The Open Secret of Ralph Waldo Emerson," *Journal of Religion* 70 (1990) 19–35.

scraps of paper with ideas scribbled on them. As a consequence, reconstructing Emerson's "natural history of intellect" leaves any scholar who peruses these late manuscripts guessing at the sage of Concord's ultimate intent. The scholar finds, as Emerson acknowledged frankly to Carlyle, only guesses at the riddle of the "double consciousness," only tentative schematizations of the powers of the mind according to their varying degrees of creativity.[98] Perhaps Emerson came closest to a succinct description of how creativity happens in this dense passage from his late essay "Poetry and Imagination":

> The senses imprison us, and we help them with meters as limitary,—with a pair of scales and a footrule and a clock. How long it took to find out what a day was, or what this sun is, that makes a day! It cost thousands of years only to make the motion of the earth suspected. Slowly, by comparing thousands of observations, there dawned on some mind a theory of the sun,—and we found the astronomical fact. But the astronomy is in the mind: the senses affirm that the earth stands still and the sun moves. The senses collect the surface facts of matter. The intellect acts on these brute reports, and obtains from them results which are the essence of intellectual form of the experiences. It compares, distributes, generalizes and uplifts them into its own sphere. It knows that these transfigured results are not brute experiences, just as souls in heaven are not the real bodies they once animated. Many transfigurations have befallen them. The atoms of the body were once nebulae, then rock, then loam, then corn, then chyme, then chyle, then blood; and now the beholding and co-energizing mind sees the same refining and ascent to the third, the seventh, or the tenth power of the daily accidents which the senses report, and which make the material of knowledge. It was sensation; when memory came, it was experience; when mind acted it was knowledge; when mind acted on it as knowledge it was thought.[99]

In the end, however, Emerson confessed himself utterly baffled at the coyness of the Over Soul. He sensed that the key to creativity lay in what he called "perception," that is, in the transition from concrete sense data to a teleological insight into the laws which ground that data; but he found himself at a loss to make that insight happen. If it did happen, he found himself unable to translate insight into creative action. Instead he found that, as soon as the mind moves into the realm of generalization, it thereafter wanders aimlessly from one idea to another; but, except in the case of extraordinary genius, finite human minds apparently have no power to translate insight into original acts of creation. A chastened Emerson finally admitted to himself:

---

[98] For my own attempt to construct something like a system out of these random hints in Emerson's lecture notes and published writings see Gelpi, *Endless Seeker,* 124–35.

[99] Emerson, *Complete Works,* 12:23–4.

This slight discontinuity which perception effects between the mind and the object paralyzes the will. If you cut or break in two a block or stone and press the two parts closely together, you can indeed bring the particles very near, but never again so near that they shall attract each other so that you can take up the block as one. That indescribably small interval is as good as a thousand miles, and has forever severed the practical unity. Such is the immense deduction from power to discontinuity.

The intellect that sees the interval partakes of it, and the fact of intellectual perception severs once for all the man from the things with which he converses. Affection blends, intellect disjoins subject and object. For weal or woe we clear ourselves from the thing we contemplate.[100]

One should not underestimate the frustration to which the coyness of the Over Soul subjected the sage of Concord. Having proclaimed that spontaneous creativity endows life with its religious significance, the mature Emerson found the experience very hard to come by. Always reticent, Emerson only rarely confided to others his personal frustration with an impersonal Deity. In 1853, however, he included this confession of frustration in a letter to Carlyle:

But though rebuked by a daily reduction to an absurd solitude, and by a score of disappointments with intellectual people, and in the face of a special hell provided for me in the Swedenborg Universe,[101] I am yet confirmed in my madness by the scope and satisfaction I find in a conversation once or twice in five years,—if so often; and so we find or pick what we call our proper path, though it be only from stone to stone, or from island to island, in a very rude, stilted and violent fashion.[102]

Five years later Emerson confided an even starker assessment of his religious state to his diary after a frustrating encounter with Anna Barker Ward. A young woman of Boston Brahmin ancestry, Anna had horrified her family by announcing that she desired to convert to Catholicism. The family sent her to Emerson so that the sage of Concord could talk some sense into her head. The sage failed. Reflecting ruefully on his failure, he confided the following to his diary:

I said to her, do you not see that though I have no eloquence and no flow of thought, yet that I do not stoop to accept anything less than truth? that I sit here contented with my poverty, my mendacity, and deaf and dumb estate, from year to year, for youth to age, rather than adorn myself with any red rag of false church or false association? My low and lonely sitting here by the wayside is my homage to truth, which I see is sufficient without me; which

---

[100] Ibid., 12:44–45; *Lectures* 1866, Houghton (13), 3–6.

[101] Swedenborg in his visions described a descent into the nether regions.

[102] Slater, ed., *The Correspondence of Emerson and Carlyle,* 491.

is honored by my abstaining, not by super-serviceableness. I see how it burns up and will none of your shift patchwork of additions and ingenuities.[103]

The passage breathes with frustration, loneliness, and Stoic integrity. Moreover, Emerson's remark that "truth . . . is sufficient without me" hints at an even darker creed. Emerson's dualistic equation of ultimate truth, reality, goodness, and beauty with impersonal, transcendent, spiritual laws left him at a perennial loss to attribute ultimate value to persons. He seems to have sensed an inadequacy in his position but did not know how to avoid its logic. As he found himself more and more trammeled in the coils of finitude and fate, he came to relegate persons and personal relationships to the fleeting realm of finite illusion. In that context, he ruefully conceded that an impersonal nature uses persons for its own impersonal, universal ends irrespective of harm or benefit to them. If so, then Stoic acceptance of one's lot, however lonely, provides the incense one burns in homage on the altar of the Beautiful Necessity. Calvinist divines had challenged believers to stand ready to suffer damnation selflessly if the glory of God required it. In the end Emerson required the devotees of a capricious nature to suffer loneliness and frustration in this life and to accept a dubious personal future in the next.[104]

VI

In a sense, Emerson's repudiation of the Unitarian compromise created Transcendentalism as a religious and philosophical movement. Emerson found the Unitarianism of his day religiously two-faced. While claiming to profess a religious faith based on reason alone, early nineteenth-century Unitarianism clung inconsistently to the external forms of Calvinist worship. In exchanging his pulpit for the lecture podium, Emerson turned his back once and for all on sectarian religion and dedicated himself to the task of formulating a purely philosophical religion. His fidelity to that task transformed him into a popular American symbol of religious and intellectual integrity.

Emerson, however, found himself dissatisfied not only with Unitarian piety but also with fundamental philosophical presuppositions of eighteenth-century American Enlightenment religion. He repudiated its nominalism and

---

[103] Emerson, *Journals and Miscellaneous Notebooks,* 9:242–3; Richard D. Birdsall, "Emerson and the Church of Rome," *American Literature* 21 (1959) 273–81; Glen M. Johnson, "Ralph Waldo Emerson on Isaac Hecker: A Manuscript with Commentary," *Catholic Historical Review* 79 (1993) 54–64.

[104] See Khoren Arisian, "Daybreak: Emerson and the Quest for Wholeness," *Religious Humanism* 22 (1988) 107–19; Paul H. Beattie, "The Sphinx," *Religious Humanism* 22 (1988) 89–98; Donald L. Gelpi, "Emerson's Sense of Ultimate Meaning and Reality," *Ultimate Meaning and Reality* 15 (1992) 93–111; Peter A. Obuchowski, "Emerson, Evolution, and the Problem of Evil," *Harvard Theological Review* 72 (1979) 150–6.

replaced it with a modified Neo-Platonic realism, and he remained a philosophical realist to the end of his days.

Emerson also realized that a religion rooted in reason alone lacks the capacity to inspire genuine enthusiasm. He therefore relocated religious insight in the creative imagination and, during his saturnalia of faith, he endowed the creative imagination with intuitive self-evidence. For the Transcendental Emerson, both the self-evidence of imaginative insight and its synthetic scope elevated it above the "linear logic" employed by an objectifying, scientific reason. With the waning of Transcendental enthusiasm, however, Emerson spoke less of the self-evidence of imaginative insight. The finitude of human biases convinced him that the human mind rarely achieves the kind of mystical ecstasy to which he had aspired in the 1830s. Different biases converge on the truth from different angles of vision, but no bias grasps or comprehends the whole truth. Still, even during his post-Transcendental period a chastened Emerson continued to regard the synthetic character of imaginative insight as evidence of its superiority to logical, inferential modes of thought.

Emerson's appeal to intuition as a philosophical strategy for overcoming Enlightenment rationalism set the pattern for other Transcendental religious thinkers. Like Emerson, Transcendentalists such as Theodore Parker and Orestes Brownson sought to transcend, to get beyond, the limitations of eighteenth-century Enlightenment religion. Like Emerson, they believed that intuitive insight held the key to moving beyond the limits of purely rational thought. Both Parker and Brownson, however, offered a very different account of religious intuition from Emerson. Still, by asserting privileged cognitive claims for intuitive over analytic, inferential thinking, Emerson carved out the turf on which American Transcendentalism would do battle with Enlightenment modernism.

Before reflecting on the achievements and limitations of other Transcendental critiques of modern Enlightenment religion, one would, then, do well to understand the strengths and limitations of Emersonian Transcendentalism. As we have seen above, Enlightenment modernism rested on a number of questionable philosophical assumptions, among them conceptual nominalism, epistemological atomism, subjectivism, dualism, and social atomism. How did Emersonian Transcendentalism respond to each of these Enlightenment tenets?

As I have already indicated, Emerson repudiated the nominalism of Locke and of Hume and replaced it with a form of Neo-Platonic realism. He also discovered in Platonic realism an alternative to the atomistic account of human knowing propounded by Locke and endorsed by Hume. Emerson conceded to British Empiricism that knowing begins with sensory experience, but he believed that phenomenological description of sense data will inevitably lay bare the laws which ground human sensory awareness. Emerson also believed in the organic interconnectedness of all transcendental, spiritual laws, and he affirmed that imaginative, intuitive insight better expressed that organic interconnectedness than scientific reason.

Emerson's Platonism, however, taught him to endorse the subjectivism of Enlightenment philosophy at least in the sense that he believed that one discovers transcendent, organic truth by withdrawing from the senses and ascending within subjectivity to the eternal realm of Spirit. During his "saturnalia of faith," Emerson held that, in the moment of creativity itself, an influx of life and of insight from the divine Over Soul suffused surd, sensible reality with a fleeting reality, truth, goodness, and beauty. However, once the creative energy of the Over Soul had spent itself, the finite thing of beauty it had created reverted to a surd and valueless fact. As a consequence, with the waning of enthusiasm, the coyness of the Over Soul—the rarity with which Emerson himself experienced moments of liberating, creative insight—left him haunted by a sense of fatal entrapment in the finite, humdrum dimensions of ordinary, day-to-day experience.

Not only did Emerson fail finally to overcome the subjectivism of Enlightenment modernism, but the dualistic caste of his modified Platonism only compounded the problem of dualism which epistemological subjectivism exemplifies. Emerson endorsed a dualistic understanding of spirit and of matter, of time and of eternity. These dualisms combined with his expressive individualism in order to undermine his attempts to transcend the social atomism propounded by Enlightenment modernism.

Throughout his life Emerson looked upon historical institutions as tainted, corrupt, and unworthy of moral commitment, but the sage of Concord did not lack all civic virtue. The optimism of his Transcendental period inspired in him a rosy prognosis for the transformation of culture in the United States. Even the post-Transcendental Emerson continued to sound a muted trumpet of social reform in *Society and Solitude*. During his saturnalia of faith he expected each individual genius to function as a continuous conduit of divine creativity and social transformation. The philosophy of bias, as we have seen, severely dampened that expectation. Still, the mature Emerson trusted in the "centered," racial bias of Anglo-Saxon America to bring about the cultural renaissance for which he had hoped during his saturnalia of faith.

The mature Emerson imagined the United States as a kind of theocratic democracy in which the Over Soul assigns to each individual a specific creative task which advances the deity's impersonal, universal ends, but the need to protect one's genius from social encroachment by persons or institutions left social relations in Emersonian America conditioned and tenuous. One should foster social relations insofar as they foster one's creative bias, but one must withdraw from them as soon as they begin to sap one's finite reservoir of creative energies. As I have already indicated, Emerson insisted on the organic interconnectedness of all things, but, in the last analysis, stable relationships in Emerson's universe have an eternal, transcendent, and spiritual character. The Over Soul provides the metaphysical glue which binds Emerson's universe into an organic whole. In the world of space and time, social bonds among finite human persons have a much more tentative and tenuous character since social commitment remains strictly conditioned on its ability to foster one's individual genius.

Clearly, Emerson's insistence on the cosmic interrelatedness of all things suggests that he recognized the need to overcome the social atomism implicit in Enlightenment social-contract theory, but in the end his expressive individualism allowed only tenuous and conditioned historical bonds among the citizens of the American republic. Emerson's relegation of real interrelatedness to the realm of the Over Soul did little to build social bridges among individual persons living in space and time.[105]

The multiple dualisms in Emerson's Transcendentalism also reflected the fact that he had inherited the dialectical imagination of his Protestant forebears. Emersonian transcendentalism required one to choose between matter and spirit, time and eternity, fidelity to one's creative bias and social commitment. Those same dualisms left Emerson open to the charge of antinomianism, and, indeed, his Transcendental and post-Transcendental thought offers a secularized version of Quaker "inner light" piety. Emerson had no Quaker upbringing like Tom Paine, but Quakerism did influence his thinking.[106] His Platonism, however, offers the most obvious explanation for Emerson's fascination with the inner light. The Platonic mind can find no intelligibility as such in a surd, sensible universe. Instead, it must retire within itself, ascend to the realm of pure Spirit, and discover in the eternal mansion of the Over Soul the dwelling place of reality, truth, goodness, and beauty.

Emerson himself would, no doubt, have dismissed the charge of antinomianism with the observation that eternal, unchanging laws ruled his universe. He expected every individual who searches within subjectivity to discover the same eternal laws and to derive from them spontaneous, individual creativity. He believed those laws more real than any factual, spatio-temporal reality. He also presupposed that one need only describe the reality of spiritual laws for them to appear spontaneously in the subjectivity of other

---

[105] See H. G. Callaway, "Emerson and Romantic Individualism," *Journal of Humanism and Ethical Religion* 5 (1992) 66–74.

[106] See Gelpi, *Endless Seeker,* 30–1, n. 53.

persons. When he did that to audience after audience to no apparent avail, it left others suspecting that in grounding religion and morality in the transcendent realm of the Over Soul, Emerson was, in fact, building castles in the air. Since Emerson's moral critics doubted that individuals would, on turning inward, discover the eternal laws of the cosmos, his counsel to seek those laws within subjectivity sounded to them like "inner light" antinomianism.[107]

Emerson's philosophy of bias did, however, dampen somewhat the unbridled social optimism of eighteenth-century Enlightenment. The post-Transcendental Emerson rediscovered what he called human "fallenness," but he equated that fall with the Neo-Platonic fall into finitude. With the waning of his Transcendental enthusiasm, he continued to hope doggedly that the Anglo-Saxon race had the capacity to advance the universal ends of the Over Soul by effecting a sustained cultural revival in the United States which would transform it into the historical heir to imperial England's worldwide hegemony. The mature Emerson, however, could offer no assurance to individuals that, in achieving the impersonal ends of nature, they would experience personal satisfaction or fulfillment. In Emerson's philosophy of bias, a cunning nature could use individuals for its own impersonal purposes whether it left those individuals personally fulfilled or not. Individual persons had no choice but to follow the bias assigned them by the Beautiful Necessity and achieve their fate, even if that achievement left them isolated, alone, and frustrated, as it did in Emerson's case.

Did Emerson make any permanent contribution to the speculative critique of Enlightenment modernism? As we shall see in the final section of this study, C. S. Peirce in the course of dismantling the Enlightenment opted, like Emerson, for a kind of metaphysical realism. Peirce's realism, however, derived its inspiration not from Plato but from the great medieval scholastic philosopher and theologian John Duns Scotus. Moreover, as we shall also see, Peirce rejected out of hand the kinds of intuitionism which Emerson and Parker defended philosophically. In the end, however, Peirce's epistemology would vindicate a significant cognitive role for common sense, imaginative forms of thinking. Finally, in his theory of the normative sciences, Peirce would develop one of the central themes in Emerson's mature ethics. Peirce would discover the lure of the beautiful at the heart of human moral striving. In other words, Emerson's realism, his vindication of the cognitive claims of intuitive forms of thought, and his aesthetic approach to ethical thinking would all find a significant place in C. S. Peirce's constructive postmodernism.

---

[107] Wesley T. Mott, "Emerson and Antinomianism: The Legacy of the Sermons," *American Literature* 50 (1978) 369–97; Ellen Kappy Suckiel, "Emerson and the Virtues," *American Philosophy,* 135–52.

Chapter 7

ABSOLUTE RELIGION: THEODORE PARKER AND THE FOUNDATIONS OF ENLIGHTENMENT FUNDAMENTALISM

This absolute religion,
this worship in spirit and in truth,
at all times, in every place, and with each faculty,—
that is the only form of religion
and has nothing to hinder the most complete and
perfect human joy.

—Theodore Parker

In the 1840s two significant shifts occurred in New England Transcendentalism. First, Emerson began his patient muting of the excesses of his saturnalia of faith. Second, as Emerson's confidence in his original Transcendental message faltered, militant leadership of Transcendentalism as a religious and theological movement passed into the hands of Theodore Parker. Like Emerson, Parker sought to ground religion in a subjective intuition of divine truth. In Parker's writing and preaching, however, religious intuition came to mean something very different from what Emerson meant by the term. In Emerson's Transcendental and post-Transcendental thought, "intuition" connoted individual creativity. For the Transcendental Emerson the experience of creativity gave immediate access to the infinite creative energies of the Over Soul. For the post-Transcendental Emerson, creativity meant fidelity to one's individual, finite creative genius. Parker defended a more pedestrian understanding of intuition. He derived his understanding of intuition from a misreading of Kant and described it as the subjective intuition of objective moral and religious truths.

I

In Lexington, Massachusetts, on August 24, 1820, Hannah Parker, the wife of John Parker, gave birth to her eleventh and last child, a son. His parents called him Theodore, which means "gift of God." John Parker, as a child, had witnessed the first shots of the American Revolution in the skirmish on Lexington common. A voracious reader and congenital skeptic, John Parker bequeathed both habits to his son. As a child young Theodore began "a severe and silent struggle . . . with the ghastly doctrine of Eternal Damnation and a wrathful God." By the age of seven he had lost all fear of God.[1] Hannah Parker's sense of God as "an Omnipotent Father, filling every point of space with his beautiful and loving presence"[2] may have helped young Theodore slay the "Goliath" of Calvinist theology, as the mature Parker characterized belief in a wrathful, vengeful deity.[3]

Parker records another childhood incident which made a permanent impression on him. Tempted as a lad to kill a turtle, he refrained, feeling a check of conscience. On recounting the incident to his mother, she told him that the voice of God had spoken to him through his conscience and that his life depended on always heeding that voice. The mature Parker reflected: "I am sure no event in my life has made so deep and lasting an impression on me." Indeed, both of these early experiences shaped decisively Parker's Transcendental creed.[4]

Poor as church mice, the Parkers looked to their large brood to contribute to their family's support. Accordingly, at the age of nineteen Theodore began earning a modest wage as a teacher in Concord. The following year he registered as a part-time student at Harvard. Penury barred him from full residence. Not until 1840, the year Harvard granted him a master's degree, would the penurious Parker achieve full-time student status at his alma mater.

In 1831 young Theodore took a position as instructor in a private school in Boston. In the same year Lyman Beecher's virulent, anti-Catholic pulpit diatribes led to the burning of an Ursuline convent in Charlestown. Beecher's bigoted Calvinism confirmed the young Parker in his repudiation of trinitarian religion. In 1832 Parker moved to Watertown. There he met and became engaged to his future wife, Lydia Cabot. In Watertown Parker also befriended Convers Francis, destined to become one of the minor lights among the Boston Transcendentalists. Francis helped Parker

---

[1] John Weiss, ed., *The Life and Correspondence of Theodore Parker,* 2 vols. (New York: D. Appleton & Co., 1864) 2:452.

[2] Ibid., 1:23.

[3] Ibid., 2:452.

[4] Ibid., 1:26.

deepen his hold on the Greek and Roman classics, literature, theology, and German philosophy. In 1834 Parker enrolled in the Harvard Divinity School, where his extensive study of German exegesis reinforced his skepticism of biblical religion.

Parker completed his studies of divinity in 1836, the same year Emerson published *Nature*. The following year Parker accepted a call to a pulpit in West Roxbury. Convers Francis preached at his ordination and George Ripley, another member of the inner circle of Boston Transcendentalists, extended to him "the right hand of fellowship."[5]

Parker's preaching brought him increasing notoriety. In 1840 he addressed the Groton Convention, a convocation of religious dissidents sponsored by the Second Adventists and Come Outers. The following year his sermon at the ordination of Charles Schackford on "The Transient and Permanent in Christianity" outraged the attendant congregation, but their outrage paled to insignificance with the publication in 1841 of Parker's *Discourse of Matters Pertaining to Religion*. The book brought down a storm of controversy upon his head and transformed him into Emerson's successor as Transcendental critic of established religion. Eventually, the book led to Parker's trial before the Boston Ministerial Association on the charge of subverting traditional Christian religion. The half-hearted hearings began with both Parker and his inquisitors agreeing not to "catechize" one another. The association decided not to censure Parker, and he burst into tears of relief on hearing the verdict.[6]

Thereafter, Parker suffered his first physical collapse. During his convalescence he toured England, France, Italy, Germany, and Switzerland. In London he visited both Thomas Carlyle and John Sterling, the British Hegelian.

On returning to Boston in 1844, Parker preached at First Church on December 26, this time with a lack of orthodoxy so shocking to his hearers that he found all the pulpits of Boston subsequently closed to him. However, on January 22, 1845, a group of liberal Boston gentlemen hired out Melodeon Hall in order to allow Parker to air publicly his personal religious beliefs. His lecture pleased them well. In December they invited him to accept the post of permanent pastor to a group called "The Boston Society." Parker accepted. At his installation he received no charge from the society out of deference to his conscience.

[5] Joel Meyerson, "Convers Francis and Emerson," *American Literature* 50 (1978) 17–36.

[6] Henry Steele Commager, "Tempest in a Boston Teapot," *New England Quarterly* 6 (1933) 651–7; Perry Miller, "Theodore Parker: Apostasy from Liberalism," *Harvard Theological Review* 54 (1961) 275–95.

A voracious reader in several languages, Parker and James Eliot Cabot in 1845 together launched the *Massachusetts Quarterly Review*. In 1847 Parker moved to Boston, and three years later The Boston Society relocated its services in the Boston Music Hall. Parker's preaching showed a growing preoccupation with questions of social reform. He spoke out openly against slavery and for women's rights. His eloquence as a social activist attracted thunderbolts of wrath from the conservative Boston establishment. Their opposition only gave Parker more public notoriety. In 1850 a militant group of Boston abolitionists elected Parker as their leader. He also served on the executive board of The Vigilance Committee, a group organized to resist the Fugitive Slave Law. In this context, he participated in a bloody but futile skirmish to free Anthony Burns, a fugitive slave captured in Boston and returned to his southern owners by the federal authorities. Parker began to correspond with John Brown.[7]

Failing health put an end to Parker's social activism. Early in the 1850s it became clear that Parker was dying of consumption. He departed for a second convalescent cruise in the Caribbean. Then he traveled to England, France, and Rome. He died in Florence on May 10, 1860, at fifty years of age.[8]

II

Parker dedicated his pastoral and intellectual career to the defense of what he called "absolute religion." In 1859, not far from death, while laid up in Santa Cruz, he wrote to The Boston Society at their request a summary of his theological beliefs. His response gave a concise synopsis of his personal religious creed. That creed built on traditional pillars of Enlightenment religion: belief in an infinitely perfect God, confidence in the

---

[7] See W. H. Riback, "Theodore Parker of Boston: Social Reformer," *Social Service Review* 22 (1948) 451–60; Arthur I. Ladu, "Political Ideas of Theodore Parker," *Studies in Philology* 38 (1941) 106–23; Oscar Sherwin, "Of Martyr Build: Theodore Parker," *Phylon Quarterly* 20 (1959) 143–8. Despite his active abolitionism, Parker, like Emerson, espoused a form of racism. His concern to end slavery probably sought the betterment of the white race. See M. Fellman, "Theodore Parker and the Abolitionist Role in the 1850's," *Journal of American History* 61 (1974) 666–84.

[8] For further biographical information about Parker see Octavius Brooks Frothingham, *Theodore Parker: A Biography* (New York: Putnam, 1880); Henry Steel Commager, *Theodore Parker* (Boston: Little, Brown, & Co., 1936); Henry Steel, "The Dilemma of Theodore Parker," *New England Quarterly* 6 (1933) 257–77; Henry Steel, "Theodore Parker: Intellectual Gourmand," *American Scholar* 3 (1934) 257–65; William R. Hutchison, *The Transcendentalist Ministers* (New Haven, Conn.: Yale University Press, 1959); Robert E. Collins, *Theodore Parker: American Transcendentalist; A Critical Essay and a Collection of His Writings* (Metuchen, N.J.: Scarecrow Press, 1973).

adequacy of human nature to perform all the functions demanded of it, the availability to the human conscience of unchanging principles of morality, and the fact of personal immortality. Still, Parker's passion for "absolute religion" introduced novel emphases into these standard Enlightenment themes. John Locke had fathered the philosophical religion of the eighteenth-century Enlightenment. Parker claimed to found "absolute religion" on "Kantian" intuition. In fact, during his heresy trial Parker's appeal to Kant rather than to Locke persuaded his interrogators not to regard him as a Deist. In fact, Parker filtered Kant's epistemology through one of the familiar lenses of eighteenth-century American Deism.

Parker described the Kantian inspiration of "absolute religion" in the following terms:

> I found [in Kant] certain great primal intuitions of human nature, which depend on no logical process of demonstration, but are rather facts of consciousness given by the instinctive action of human nature itself. I will mention only the three most important which pertain to religion. 1. The instinctive intuition of the divine, the consciousness that there is a God. 2. The instinctive intuition of the just and the right, a consciousness that there is a moral law, independent of our will, which we ought to keep. 3. The instinctive intuition of the immortal, a consciousness that the essential element of man, the principle of individuality never dies.[9]

With hints from Friedreich Schleiermacher, Parker described the instinctive intuition of the divine as a spontaneous "sense of dependence," which, he believed, characterized all religious experience. In his *Discourse of Matters Pertaining to Religion* Parker put it this way:

> We feel an irresistible tendency to refer all outward things and ourselves with them, to a Power beyond us, sublime and mysterious, which we cannot measure, nor even comprehend. . . . Thus the existence of God is implied by the natural sense of dependence, implied by the religious element itself; it is expressed by the spontaneous intuition of reason.[10]

Parker discovered other intuitive faculties built into the human soul in addition to this innate faculty for intuiting the existence of God. He spoke of a "moral faculty" which teaches us our duties toward our fellow humans and of a "religious faculty" which teaches us duties to God. These ethical faculties endow religion with its practical side. They teach the conscience that authentic piety consists in *"voluntary obedience to the law of God, inward and outward obedience* to that law he has written on our nature,

---

[9] Theodore Parker, *The Collected Works of Theodore Parker*, ed. Frances Power Cobbe, 8 vols. (London: Truebner & Co., 1863) 1:6–7, 10.

[10] Ibid.

revealed in various ways, through instinct, reason, conscience, and the religious emotions."[11]

Finally, the human soul also grasps intuitively the truth of personal immortality with instinctive spontaneity. Belief in personal immortality precedes all rational arguments seeking to establish it, because that belief flows naturally and spontaneously from human nature itself. Still, Parker buttressed this primal intuition with supporting arguments. To begin with, Parker argued, the fact that all religions teach personal immortality testifies to the innate character of that belief. The universal human desire for immortality also reveals the instinctive character of belief in personal survival after death. In addition, Parker believed that instinctive belief in an infinite, unconditioned, absolute, all-powerful, all-wise, and all-good God entails belief in personal immortality, since such a God must both conceive and will this blessing for humans. The social nature of humans also makes it necessary that life after death have both a self-conscious and a social character. Moreover, trust in an all-loving God deprives faith in future life of all fear of divine retribution.[12]

At first glance, Emerson's and Parker's Transcendental accounts of intuition bear superficial resemblance to one another. Both theories rooted themselves in Enlightenment religion. Both attempted to ground the basic truths of Unitarian piety—belief in God, in morality, and in personal immortality—in self-evident, subjective intuitions. Emerson believed that through the creative influx of impersonal, transcendent, spiritual laws, one discovers one's identity with the creative essence of God. The discovery of that identity also grounded Emerson's belief in a kind of human immortality, although, in Emerson's world, an immortality rooted in one's essential identity with a universal, impersonal, divine reality left the personal character of human immortality in question.

A closer examination of their positions, however, reveals significant differences. Emerson grounded the possibility of intuitive knowing in his pantheistic Platonism. Parker rejected pantheism.[13] Instead, he grounded the self-evident givenness of basic religious truths in an infallible, cognitive connection between the religious "faculties" of the human soul and the realities which they know. He regarded religious truths as "given" within consciousness with a facticity analogous to the givenness of sensi-

[11] Ibid., 1:18–33.

[12] Ibid., 3:327–38; see also G. F. Newbrough, "Reason and Understanding in the Works of Theodore Parker," *South Atlantic Quarterly* 47 (1948) 64–75; Peter White, "Reason and Intuition in the Theology of Theodore Parker," *Journal of Religious History* 11 (1980) 111–20; Edward H. Madden, "Ralph Waldo Emerson," *Transactions of the Charles S. Peirce Society* 29 (1993) 179–209.

[13] Weiss, *The Life and Correspondence of Theodore Parker,* 2:166.

ble facts. Moreover, this "givenness" of religious truth within individual human subjectivity defined what Parker meant both by religious Transcendentalism and by "absolute religion."[14]

With eighteenth-century Deism, Parker asserted that, if authentic religious faith roots itself in the unchanging character of God and of human nature, then only philosophical, non-sectarian religion counts as authentic. He called his own philosophical faith "absolute religion" and rooted it in the unerring character of the innate faculty of Reason. The pluralism of sectarian religious creeds he attributed not to the faculty of Reason but to finite, fallible "a posteriori reasonings" about religion which falsify and distort the self-evident, a priori givenness of absolute religious truth. The product of finite, fallible minds, these sectarian reasonings about God necessarily fail to grasp and therefore falsify and distort the truth which the faculty of Reason grasps with a priori facticity. As Parker put it, "a belief in this relation between the feeling [of dependence] in us and its object independent of us [i.e., God], comes unavoidably from the laws of man's nature; there is nothing of which we can be more certain." And again: "The soul feels its direct dependence on God, as much as the body sees its own direct dependence on matter."[15]

This distinction between the a priori certitude of religious Reason and the fallibility of a posteriori religious reasonings allowed Parker to develop his own myth of the historical origins of different religious creeds. His myth traced the evolution of human religions from fetishism through polytheism to monotheism.

Parker characterized fetishism as a worship of sensible, physical objects which springs from gross ignorance of the laws of nature. This crude form of religion roots itself in the lowest of the human faculties, namely, in the sensate powers. Fetishism also generates the priestly caste. Its plurality of tribal gods rationalizes the inter-tribal wars which abound in barbaric societies. Parker also believed that fetishism survived in the superstitious practices of monotheistic piety.[16] Still, the pastor of the Boston Society strove to avoid Beecher's bigoted attitude toward other religions. He discovered some traces of "absolute religion" in every sectarian, historical religious tradition, even in a religion as primitive as fetishism. In Parker's mind, fetishism correctly recognized two fundamental truths of "absolute religion": that God is present in matter and that spiritual power outranks all other forces. Fetishism errs in equating God with matter.[17]

---

[14] Parker, *The Collected Works of Theodore Parker,* 6:22–38.
[15] Ibid., 1:9–11, 170.
[16] Ibid., 1:39–50.
[17] Ibid., 1:92.

If fetishism functioned largely at the level of sensate awareness, in Parker's myth of religious history polytheism rendered religion more intellectually reflective. Polytheism deified not physical, sensible objects, but human persons and human social relationships. In other words, in polytheistic religions anthropomorphic conceptions of deity replaced the deification of physical nature. The polytheistic priestly caste promoted, in a primitive form, science, art, patriotism, and, in a fashion, love of others, but the priests also began to manipulate the thoughts of others by claiming the divine right to prescribe actions and to prohibit ideas of which they disapproved. Polytheism continued to provide religious rationalizations for war and it also sanctioned the enslavement of enemies. In polytheistic religions ritual evolved with an initial robustness, but it remained doomed one day to degenerate into "weakish cant" and "sniveling sentimentality."[18] Like fetishism, polytheism too expressed in garbled form a truth proclaimed by "absolute religion": the divine omnipresence and activity throughout the universe, including the world of human social relationships. Polytheism erred chiefly in multiplying deities.[19]

Pantheism mediated between polytheism and the emergence of monotheism. In its crude expressions pantheism equated the reality of God with the material universe. The more religiously elevated forms of pantheism proclaimed the reality of God and the illusory character of everything else. Presumably, Parker would have located Emersonian Transcendentalism among the higher expressions of pantheistic religion.[20]

With monotheism, religion entered into a period of maturity. Monotheism negated any distinction among nations and tribes. It therefore ceased to provide religious justification for tribal and national wars. In asserting the one God's omnipresence, monotheism restored divine inspiration democratically to all. It therefore undercut priestly hegemonic control of religious truth. Only natural ability limited religious inspiration. "Inspiration, then, is the consequence of a faithful use of our faculties." Monotheism distinguished between God and creation, but it viewed created reality as "a symbol of God."[21]

Parker distinguished three elements within monotheistic religion: the sentiment of God, the idea of God, and the conception of God.[22] He found the sentiment of God vague, mysterious, more or less strong, more or less corrupted by spurious conceptions of God. The idea of God corresponded

---

[18] Ibid., 1:51–72.
[19] Ibid., 1:92–3.
[20] Ibid., 1:75–9.
[21] Ibid., 1:80–95, 194.
[22] Ibid., 1:82, 219.

in his mind to Reason's intuitive perception of the reality of God,[23] while the conception of God corresponded to fallible "reasonings" about God.[24] In Parker's mind the "clarity and distinctness" of the idea of God prevented one from confounding it with mere conceptions about the deity.[25]

The sentiment of God explained for Parker abuses in monotheistic religion. That sentiment often expressed ignorance and fear and therefore served as the seed bed of superstition, religious hatred, and malignant fanaticism. Parker felt none of Emerson's sympathy for the popular enthusiasm generated by nineteenth-century revivalism. Instead, the pastor of The Boston Society feared both revivalism's unbridled emotionalism and its Calvinistic fundamentalism. On the whole, he judged that in the United States religious revivalism had done more harm than good, that it had popularized a false Calvinistic theology, and that it could only end by corrupting natural human morality. Parker equated genuine religious revival with political and social reform and with the just vindication of women's rights.[26]

Not unlike the American Deists, Parker believed that his proclamation of "absolute religion" carried to its ultimate conclusion the Protestant project of purifying religion of historical accretions and abuse. In the preface to his *Discourse of Matters Pertaining to Religion,* Parker declared that in publishing this work he intended "to remove the rubbish of human invention from the fair temple of divine truth."[27] Parker's account of "absolute religion" also reflected the subjectivistic bias of Protestant piety and its roots in the Augustinian tradition, for Parker grounded authentic religious piety in subjective intuitions of unchanging, objective, spiritual truths. He therefore largely relegated the history of religion to the realm of fallible, garbled "reasonings" about ahistorical, transcendent realities, although he did seek to discover distorted hints of "absolute religion" in every religious tradition.[28] At the same time, from the privileged, olympian, ahistorical standpoint afforded him by his subjective intuition of unchanging, objective religious truth, Parker also felt free to pass personal judgment on the limited reasonings of the historical religions.

As for Jesus, Parker deplored his erroneous belief in demons and in demon possession, his false interpretations of the Hebrew Scriptures, and his tendency toward religious enthusiasm. On the positive side of the ledger, Parker found Jesus justly indignant about religious abuses, not

---

[23] Ibid., 1:9–10.
[24] Ibid., 1:11, 141–50.
[25] Ibid., 1:142.
[26] Ibid., 1:118–27; 4:381–400.
[27] Ibid., 1:ix.
[28] Ibid., 1:367.

without charity, and possessed of an excellent character despite the decadence of his age. Parker doubted that Jesus ever performed miracles,[29] and, in the end, the apostle of "absolute religion" dismissed miracles as "of no religious significance." Parker acknowledged that Jesus preached a religion of love. Parker's Jesus discovered divine life in every action performed in obedience to the human soul and in perfect harmony with God's will. Parker's Jesus also commanded others to love one another as they loved themselves. On the whole, Parker's Jesus lived a manly piety, despite manifest defects in his religious scheme. Moreover, Parker believed that the excellence of Jesus' teachings consisted principally in the fact that they allow one to advance indefinitely beyond them until, presumably, one arrives at "absolute religion" itself.[30]

Parker acknowledged the antiquity and power of Catholic Christianity. Initially, the Catholic tradition separated spiritual from temporal power, exerted a civilizing influence on barbarous peoples, raised and elevated the poor and downtrodden, and in principle at least acted in a kindly and humane manner. It established convents and monasteries in order to protect "delicate" spirits from the barbarity of the world and it exhibited a self-diffusive impulse. Unfortunately, however, the formation of organized Church institutions pandered to the needs of "sensual people." In addition, the Catholic priesthood in their pride assumed temporal power, and the pope arrogated to himself the power to act as the vicar of Christ. From the fourteenth century on, the Catholic tradition fell into a decadence which provoked the Protestant reformation. Parker sanctioned the Catholic Church for claiming divine authorization for doctrines which neither "reason" nor "revelation" can justify. While, in Parker's mind, Catholics claimed to discover religious truth in the Bible, in unscriptural written and oral traditions, and in a divinely inspired official magisterium, in the end Church authority passed judgment on religious doctrine and practice and assumed mastery over the souls of individuals. The "peculiar merit" of the Catholic tradition, in Parker's estimate, lay in the fact that it recognized that God continues to inspire humans in every age.

Parker regarded Protestantism as a courageous step forward in humanity's progress toward absolute religion. Protestantism recognized only the Bible as the infallible word of God and vindicated the right of each individual to interpret its meaning. In Parker's judgment, Protestantism correctly denounced the Catholic Church as no longer fit to speak with religious authority, correctly denounced its religious abuses and the Church's

[29] See Robert Bruce Mullin, "Horace Bushnell and the Question of Miracles," *Church History* 58 (1989) 460–73.

[30] Parker, *The Collected Works of Theodore Parker,* 1:225–67.

temporal authority, correctly rejected the apocryphal books of the Bible, and correctly vindicated the right of individual conscience. Protestantism erred, however, in restricting the private judgment of religious truth to the Bible, in denying God's immanence in the Church, and in flouting any contemporary claim to divine inspiration.[31]

In Parker's reading of Church history, Protestantism split into two parties: those who proclaimed the sovereignty of God and those who, like Parker's mother, announced the benevolent paternity of God. By the "party of Sovereignty" Parker meant the Calvinist tradition, which he portrayed as preaching a vision of God as "an awful king" who wreaks "awful vengeance" on his enemies. Parker also linked this Protestant party to belief in the need for redemption, in a substitutionist doctrine of satisfaction, and in a trinitarian conception of God. Parker commended Calvinism for its hatred of sin and for its austere morality, but he faulted it for its degradation of human nature, for its denial of human freedom, for its deification of Jesus, for its narrow biblicism, and for its emotional frigidity. The Protestant party of divine paternity, in Parker's estimate, grasped imperfectly a mighty truth—the total goodness of God and the ultimate triumph of goodness—but liberal Protestantism blended this belief with other confusing elements from the Protestant tradition. Parker's "liberal Protestants" continued to rely on religious authority and to make humans dependent on Christ.[32]

Unitarianism, in Parker's vision of the Christian tradition, took yet another half-hearted step in the direction of absolute religion, but its conservative wing remained mired in a poor and sensual (empiricist) philosophy and in the trappings of the Christian tradition.[33] Parker regarded his own doctrine of "absolute religion" as the ultimate purification of religion from the distortions of historical reasonings about God. Absolute religion relied on no church, on no tradition, and on no Scripture. Instead, it relied on "the divine presence in the nature of man; the eternal word of God which is TRUTH, as it speaks through the faculties [God] has given."

---

[31] Ibid., 1:393–402. See Gary Collison, "Every Man a Scholar: Unitarians, Transcendentalists, and Biblical Criticism," *Religion and Philosophy in the United States of America,* ed. Peter Freese, 2 vols. (Essen: Verlag die Balu Eule, 1987) 1:111–24; Suzanne Spencer, "Grounding the Prophetic Imperative: The Bible in Unitarian Thought," *Unitarian Universalist Christian* 42 (1987) 5–42; Louis Weeks, "God's Judgment, Christ's Command: Use of the Bible in Nineteenth-Century American Political Life," *The Bible in American Law: Law, Politics and Political Rhetoric,* ed. J. Johnson (Philadelphia: Fortress Press, 1985) 61–77.

[32] Parker, *The Collected Works of Theodore Parker,* 1:415–9. For the influence of Auguste Comte on Parker's thought see Charles D. Cashdollar, "European Positivism and the American Unitarians," *Church History* 45 (1976) 490–506.

[33] Parker, *The Collected Works of Theodore Parker,* 1:420–8.

Absolute religion denied any distinction between Reason and revelation, affirmed the presence of God in all of creation, and acknowledged both the maternity and the paternity of God.[34]

At a doctrinal level, Parker, as we have seen, relegated Emersonian Transcendentalism to an advanced pantheistic stage in the historical evolution of religious "reasonings," but the contrast between his and Emerson's versions of Transcendental religion appears perhaps most dramatically in each man's account of religious practice. Emersonian Transcendentalism at least aspired to ecstatic religious mysticism. Parker's Transcendentalism sniffed suspiciously at all forms of ecstatic religion. Parker's absolute religion required the balancing of four different natural powers of the soul: intellect, morality, affectivity, and religious sentiment.[35]

Of these four faculties of the soul, Parker believed that the religious sentiment exhibited the greatest power, for it tended to tyrannize over the other human faculties. Therefore, the religious sentiment needed tempering by the other powers of the soul. The moral faculty must teach religion strength of character and practical dedication to the reform of human society. The intellectual faculty must teach religious sentiment the rational discipline required by absolute religion. The affective power must teach religious sentiment benevolence toward other people and emotional moderation. Disciplined control rather than ecstatic surrender characterized Parker's approach to religion.[36]

Parker did not entirely lack Emerson's sense of the sacramentality of nature. Parker acknowledged the presence of God in all things,[37] but in the end he found the greatest natural sacramental significance in the balanced living of life.[38]

Parker never wrote a religious ethic, but he did attempt to give his Boston congregation moral instruction through example. He had experienced poverty personally and concerned himself with the care of the poor, especially with their housing, employment, and education. He actively supported women's suffrage. He called for prison and penal reform. He ministered to delinquent girls and placed disadvantaged children in foster homes. A militant abolitionist, he also protested against capitalistic exploitation of the poor and he actively supported government provision of adequate public recreational and camping facilities.

[34] Ibid., 1:429–51.

[35] Ibid., 3:1–111.

[36] Ibid., 3:113–239. See Carl E. Wennerstrom, "Channing, Parker, and People," *Pastoral Care in the Liberal Churches* (Nashville: Abingdon Press, 1970) 46–63.

[37] Parker, *The Collected Works of Theodore Parker,* 1:429.

[38] Ibid., 3:275. For a scholarly study of Parker's thought see John Edward Dirks, *The Critical Theology of Theodore Parker* (New York: Columbia University Press, 1948).

Parker's moral and political radicalism probably sprang in part from his pleasure in provoking Boston Brahmin society. He resented their condescending treatment of him as an outsider and an upstart, but he believed passionately in the public causes which he espoused. He also deemed those causes justified by the self-evident moral intuitions of his ethical faculty.

All the Transcendentalists wrestled with the destiny of the young American republic. Parker's *Historic Americans,* published in 1870, celebrated the virtue and moral character of significant figures in U.S. history: Benjamin Franklin, George Washington, John Adams, Thomas Jefferson, John Quincy Adams, Daniel Webster. Emerson saw representative, metaphysical significance in the lives of great heroes and geniuses. Emerson's *English Traits* discerned and probed the cultural destiny of the American republic. Parker took the nation's leaders at face value and found national instruction in the personal virtues which each individual exemplified. Brownson, as we shall see, would undertake to rethink the philosophical and theological foundations of government in the United States. Parker showed no such speculative ambition. Instead, Parker contented himself with writing idealized, edifying lives of America's secular saints. Parker, however, precisely because of his unquestioning certitude about the objective truth of the deliverances of his subjective cognitive powers, did finally deal with the fate of the republic, but he did so more through politics than through print. He sought through political activism and prophetic preaching to redirect the course of the nation's history. Indeed, his case illustrates well the potentially close kinship between moral fundamentalism and political radicalism.[39]

III

Parker seems to have trusted his own religious instincts. Even as a child he rebelled spontaneously against the idea of a vengeful Jehovah who predestined sinners to eternal damnation. By his own testimony, he learned from his mother to obey instinctively the spontaneous promptings of his own conscience. His instinctive revulsion at the religious bigotry of Lyman Beecher seems to have turned him decisively against all expressions of trinitarian faith.

Parker's highly personalized appropriation of Kant and of Schleiermacher provided him with a rationalization of that spontaneous trust. With Emerson, Parker realized that Enlightenment religion needed to transcend its roots in British empiricism if it hoped to give an adequate account of human

---

[39] See Kendyl Gibbons, "Implicit Models for a Local Congregation in Liberal History and Tradition," *Religious Humanism* 24 (1990) 74–88.

religious experience. Moreover, like Emerson, Parker played one strain of Enlightenment religion off against another. Both men invoked the belief which the American Enlightenment had popularized that the human mind has the capacity to grasp with self-evident certitude elemental moral and religious beliefs within subjective, individual experience. Emerson Platonized this American Enlightenment prejudice. Parker used it as his hermeneutical key for misreading Kantian philosophy.

Parker invoked the Kantian inspiration of his philosophical religion in order to defend himself against the charge of Deism, but Parker apparently failed to realize that Kant, along with both Locke and Hume, espoused a version of conceptual nominalism. Moreover, Parker endowed Kant's ideals of Reason with realistic claims that would have appalled Kant himself. Kant regarded the ideals of pure reason as empty concepts, devoid of any sensible, empirical correlate, and therefore as incapable of making any metaphysical claims upon the human mind. Parker mistakenly took Kant to mean that the spiritual faculties of the soul not only perceive religious realities within individual subjectivity but do so with a givenness analogous to the givenness of physical sensations.

While Emerson appealed to Platonic realism in order to justify the intuition of religious truths, Parker invoked a modified version of faculty psychology for the same intellectual end. Parker asserted, without ever proving his assertion, that an "infallible" correlation between the spiritual powers of the soul and their religious and moral objects allows one to assert with a priori certitude the reality of those objects. Certain forms of contemporary Transcendental Thomism make analogous claims, but their arguments no more conclude than Parker's did.

Parker invoked Schleiermacher's "sense of dependence" in order to provide the a priori intuition of the reality of God with its objective content. Moreover, since the alleged "clarity and distinctness" of the Reason's intuition of God set it apart from fallible reasonings about God, Parker seems to have believed fallaciously, as Schleiermacher did, that the intuition of a sense of dependence on the deity precedes any human act of interpretation.[40] Indeed, Parker endowed the intuition of spiritual realities with quasi-sensate givenness.

However, one lesson Parker did learn well from Kant was a priori argumentation. Having assumed the existence of fixed powers of the soul each oriented a priori to its proper object, Parker used this panoply of human faculties in order to schematize a priori his facile reading of the historical development of religion. The powers of sense twist Reason's

---

[40] See Wayne Proudfood, *Religious Experience* (Berkeley: University of California Press, 1985) 1–40.

perceptions of divine realities into fetishism. The intellectual power refines those distortions, without fully correcting them, in anthropomorphic religion. With the emergence of monotheism Reason takes center stage and prepares for the emergence of "absolute religion," but only after rational reflection has dispelled the distortions with which an unbridled sentimentality encumbers monotheistic belief.

Emerson's Transcendentalism expressed a mind biased toward poetic and imaginative forms of thought and expression. The mature Emerson's Platonism combined with his extensive reading of Asian mysticism in order to reduce history to a fatal illusion. Parker had the mind of a scholar. As a result, Parker recognized with greater clarity than Emerson did that Enlightenment religion had to deal with the results of scholarly investigations into the history of religion. In the end, however, the a priori character of Parker's reading of history left him as incapable as Emerson to deal with historical reality on its own terms and with an insensitivity to its nuance and complexity.

An implicit essentialism blinded Parker to dealing with history on its own terms. Parker believed that the fixed, essential orientation of the faculties of the human soul toward their essentially fixed and unchanging objects defined the reality and content of "absolute religion." Parker also equated his understanding of "absolute religion" with ultimate reality. Moreover, since he believed like a good Enlightenment thinker in the forward progress of history, he read the history of religion as the progressive elimination of the distortions with which the lower faculties of the soul encrust the self-evident deliverances of the higher power of Reason.

In the end, Parker's Transcendentalism remained even more thoroughly enmeshed in the trammels of the Enlightenment than Emerson's. While Emerson saw clearly the need to replace the philosophical nominalism of the British empiricist tradition with some form of defensible philosophical realism, Parker acquiesced in the conceptual nominalism of Kantian philosophy. While Parker recognized that intuitive thinking makes a significant contribution to human religious experience, he failed finally to endow intuitive insight with the metaphysical claims which Emerson made for the creative imagination. In Parker's Transcendentalism, reason and conscience must together purify imagination of its illusions and render it realistic. It also comes as no surprise, therefore, that Parker failed to endorse Emerson's regrounding of ethical thinking in aesthetics.

Parker's Transcendentalism also endorsed the individualism and subjectivism of Enlightenment thinking. Parker located human contact with ultimate reality solidly in the a priori structure of individual human subjectivity. Like Emerson, Parker looked upon the historical and social dimensions of human experience as peripheral and extrinsic to authentic human knowing. They expressed fallible reasonings about realities which the spiritual powers of the soul grasped with infallible certitude.

When the constraints of the Unitarian compromise encroached on Emerson's conscience and on his sense of his own genius, he bade the Unitarian ministry goodbye without any apparent qualm. Emerson seems to have felt sufficiently sure of himself as a social insider that he neither needed nor sought the endorsement of the Unitarian religious establishment. His resignation from the Unitarian ministry and his Divinity School Address give ample evidence of Emerson's religious independence of mind. Parker, the penurious poor boy and social outsider, battled in order to legitimate the orthodoxy of his "absolute religion" within American Unitarianism. Despite his individualistic diatribes against institutional corruption, Parker both needed and sought ecclesiastical approval for his own idiosyncratic theology. During his lifetime Parker found that approval fleeting and elusive. With the passage of years, however, the Unitarian Church abandoned its early attachment to the trappings of Calvinist Christianity, an attraction which disconcerted both Emerson and Parker. Today Unitarianism owns Parker as one of its brighter lights. Still, despite Parker's search for official ecclesiastical legitimation, in the end the conscience and religious experience of each atomic individual held pride of place in his "absolute religion."

In fact, Parker's religious thought remained so thoroughly rooted in the presuppositions of the American Enlightenment that some scholars have questioned the legitimacy of including him in the inner circle of American Transcendentalists.[41] In my judgment, Parker does finally qualify as a Transcendentalist. Like Emerson, he sought to get beyond—to transcend, if you will—the speculative limitations of British empiricism. Moreover, like Emerson, Parker believed that intuitive thinking held the key to effecting that Transcendental leap.

One also finds a suggestive analogy between Emerson and Parker in their understanding of the complexity of religious experience. The mature Emerson dealt with the complexity of human experience largely in terms of his philosophy of bias. He assumed that some individuals receive a fatal bias from nature toward thought, others toward conscience, others toward poetic creativity, others toward action, others toward a skeptical sensitivity to the limitations of bias. However, on this issue Parker saw more deeply into human experience than Emerson. Both Parker's suspicion of religious enthusiasm and his penchant for reasonable control of the unruly

[41] See H. S. Smith, "Was Theodore Parker a Transcendentalist?" *New England Quarterly* 23 (1950) 351–64.

"religious faculty" led him to seek harmony and balance in human religious growth. Like Jonathan Edwards he found exaggeration in religion suspect. Parker recognized four realms of human experience in need of harmonious balancing: affectivity, rational thought, the moral conscience, and religious transcendence. In the course of religious growth Parker expected each of these powers to temper one another like pebbles in a rock polisher. In my judgment, on this one issue Parker showed greater sensitivity to the complexity of experience than Emerson. In the end, however, Parker lacked Emerson's originality of mind.[42] Nevertheless, by endowing the religious assumptions of the Enlightenment with self-evident, objective truth and by grounding that truth in the a priori, subjective structure of the mind, Parker brought the fundamentalistic assumptions of Enlightenment religion to systematic formulation, and, in its own way, his Enlightenment fundamentalism foreshadowed that of many a contemporary secular academic.

[42] See Joel Myerson, *Theodore Parker: A Descriptive Bibliography* (New York: Garland, 1981).

Chapter 8

ORESTES AUGUSTUS BROWNSON: SYNTHETIC FAITH

It is the actuality of God that renders creation possible,
and it is only in the intuition of that actuality,
that possible creatures or perfections are conceivable.

—Orestes Augustus Brownson

I

On September 16, 1803, approximately four months after Emerson's birth, in Stockbridge, Vermont, Relief Brownson, the wife of Sylvester Brownson, gave birth to twins: a girl and a boy. The proud parents gave classical names to both children: they named the girl Daphne and the boy Orestes Augustus. Neither child knew Sylvester, who died shortly after their birth. Relief Brownson struggled to keep her family together; but in 1809 she bowed to the inevitable. A kindly Calvinist couple agreed to take Orestes in and raise him. The pious pair knew not what they did. Precocious and pugnacious, young Orestes at the age of seven had already espoused Arminianism and he stoutly defended his heretical beliefs against the theological objections of his foster parents.

In 1817 the fourteen-year-old Brownson rejoined his mother in Ballston Spa in upstate New York. He fed his theological liberalism by reading Universalist tracts, but he found religious rationalism thin spiritual broth. In 1822 he converted to Presbyterianism. Two years later he accepted a teaching post in Detroit, where he contracted and almost died of malaria. In the meantime he began to find the contradictory interpretations of the Bible which he heard on the lips of Presbyterians frustrating and confusing; and he gradually drifted back into the Universalist fold, the only form of rational religion which he had known firsthand. In 1825 he received ordination as a Universalist minister. He accepted a pastorate in Elbridge, New York, where in 1827 he wooed and wed Sally Healy.

Pastor Brownson soon moved to New York City, but Universalist religion never really satisfied him and by 1829 his official ties with that Church had all but dissolved. He despaired of finding religious satisfaction within organized religion and decided to take his conscience as his religious guide. He published "My Creed," a personal profession of religious faith which equivalently reduced religion to the practical service of one's fellow humans. At this point in his religious pilgrimage Brownson met Fanny Wright, a Scotswoman, feminist, and social radical. She introduced him to the social communism of Robert Owen and she helped him found the Owenite Workingman's Party. By 1830 Brownson's life-long passion for truth forced him to recognize that social activism alone left him religiously disconsolate.

In the same year Channing's sermon "Likeness to God" fell into Brownson's hands. Channing's doctrine of the "essential sameness" of God and humanity fired his imagination as it had initially fired Emerson's. Brownson accepted a Unitarian pulpit in Walpole, New Hampshire, and began publishing in Unitarian periodicals. In 1834 Brownson named his third son after Channing. A voracious and omnivorous reader, he immersed himself in the writings of Benjamin Constant, Victor Cousin, and Claude Henri de Rouvroy, Comte de Saint-Simon.

In 1836 Brownson moved to Mount Bellingham in Chelsea. He began attending the meetings of the Transcendental Club in Boston and developed a warm friendship with both George Ripley and Theodore Parker. Life-long outsiders both, Parker and Brownson orbited the inner circle of the Transcendental Club like satellites. Brownson's social and political radicalism rubbed off on Parker and sowed the seeds of the latter's political activism.

The year 1836 marked the *"annus mirabilis"* of New England Transcendentalism. It saw the publication of six religious and philosophical manifestos by members of the Transcendental Club: Convers Francis's *Christianity as a Purely Internal Principle,* George Ripley's *Discourse on the Philosophy of Religion,* Bronson Alcott's *Conversations with Children on the Gospels,* W. H. Furniss's *Remarks on the Four Gospels,* and, of course, Ralph Waldo Emerson's *Nature.* In the same year Brownson added fuel to the fires of public religious debate with his *New Views of Christianity.* Only in the process of converting to Catholicism in 1844 would Brownson develop his own Transcendental doctrine of intuition. By his own testimony, in the late 1830s he espoused an optimistic version of Jeffersonian democratic liberalism.

In July 1836 Brownson began editing *The Boston Reformer.* In politics the young Brownson supported the Jacksonian Democrats, and he gave enthusiastic public support to Martin Van Buren. In December of the following year he founded *The Boston Quarterly Review,* which he viewed as an instrument for stimulating public discussion of important intellectual and topical issues. Brownson's Transcendental affiliations combined with his outspoken political radicalism in order to transform him into a social pariah in conservative Boston. Nevertheless, the financial panic of 1837 and the depression which followed it only intensified Brownson's political and economic radicalism. His essay "The Laboring Classes" published during the national elections of 1840 caused a public furor. In it Brownson argued passionately that only by transferring political power into the hands of the poor and oppressed could the United States guarantee equal constitutional rights for all citizens. Brownson's political extremism evoked horrified protest from William Ellery Channing. It also drew cries of dismay from the political supporters of Martin Van Buren's presidency. They deemed that the radical Brownson's active support for Van Buren helped ensure his defeat through a combination of "hard cider" and "Tippecanoe and Tyler Too."

Brownson gloried in a good fight. He publicly supported Emerson during the furor which followed the latter's "Divinity School Address," and in 1841 Brownson defended Parker against the storm of protest evoked by the publication of his "The Transient and Permanent in Christianity." Nevertheless, Brownson's liberal pugnaciousness at the beginning of the 1840s masked a deeper personal transformation in his own heart and conscience. The "hard cider" campaign of 1840 permanently marked Brownson. Prior to Van Buren's defeat he had accepted without question the Enlightenment doctrine of human innocence. The ease with which the Whigs had used shallow sloganism in order to bamboozle the American voters into voting against their own best interests shook profoundly Brownson's naive endorsement of Enlightenment optimism. In the same year which saw Van Buren's defeat and the election of William Henry Harrison to the American presidency, Brownson gave voice to his latest religious gropings in a highly philosophical "novel" entitled *Charles Elwood, or the Infidel Converted.* The political debacle of 1840 had forced Brownson to face experientially the fact of human folly and fallenness. In 1842 in an open letter to Channing, Brownson, with help from the writings of the French political philosopher Pierre Leroux, published his second thoughts about Jesus' redemptive role in the history of salvation. He called the essay "The Mediatorial Life of Jesus."

Brownson publicly supported George Ripley's experiment in utopianism at Brook Farm even to the extent of sending his son Orestes to join

Ripley's commune. Although Brownson himself never lived at Brook Farm, he visited the place regularly and both dazzled and intimidated his auditors with the argumentative brilliance of his mind. At Brook Farm Brownson also befriended Isaac Hecker, who would also convert to Catholicism and would eventually found a religious congregation known as the Paulists.[1]

In 1842 *The Boston Quarterly Review* died of economic anemia, but two years later it rose again, like the phoenix from its ashes, as *Brownson's Quarterly Review*. In attaching his own name to the review rather than that of a city, Brownson was making an editorial statement. By 1844 he had begun to consolidate a personal philosophical vision, and he intended to use *Brownson's Quarterly Review* as a vehicle for developing and disseminating that vision. In 1843 the review published a seminal essay by Brownson called "Synthetic Philosophy." It offered his initial formulation of a Transcendental doctrine of intuition.

As Brownson's enthusiasm for Jefferson's naively optimistic democratic idealism waned, he began to recognize the need for authority in the regulation of religious belief. In the course of reflecting on "The Mediatorial Life of Jesus," Brownson had discovered the double role of community and of sacramentality within religious worship. Both shifts in perception brought him closer to the Catholic Church. In 1844 Brownson made inquiries with Bishop Fenwick of Boston about receiving instruction in the Catholic faith. He found the bishop's response warm and sympathetic and after a second interview he began catechetical instructions with Bishop John Fitzpatrick. Brownson found Fitzpatrick a high-handed Irishman and grew to dislike him heartily, but, having tried virtually every other available religious option, Brownson had come to look upon Catholicism as a last religious resort. His baptism into Roman Catholicism on October 20, 1844, coming as it did at the height of a highly controversial public career, only sealed his final ostracism from waspish social circles in Boston society.

After his conversion Brownson dedicated the rhetorical power of his formidable polemic to the defense of Catholicism. He delved into scholastic philosophy, proclaimed the Catholic Church the only source of salvation, and attacked Protestantism, Nativism, and Know-Nothingism with an aggressiveness which eventually gave even Catholics pause. He alienated

---

[1] See Joseph F. Gower and Richard M. Leliaert, eds., *The Brownson-Hecker Correspondence* (Notre Dame, Ind.: University of Notre Dame Press, 1979); John Farina, *An American Experience of God: The Spirituality of Isaac Hecker* (New York: Paulist Press, 1981); Edward J. Langois, "Isaac Hecker's Political Thought," *Hecker Studies,* ed. John Farina (New York: Paulist Press, 1983).

former friends with broadsides against Transcendentalism and "Parkerism." In 1854 he published a second philosophical novel entitled *The Spirit-Rapper.* The book assailed popular fascination with the occult and defended the reality of the devil.[2]

In 1849 Archbishop John Hughes of New York, impressed by Brownson's forthright Catholicism, invited him to bring *Brownson's Quarterly Review* to New York City. Periodic conflicts with the narrow and autocratic Bishop Fitzpatrick over religious censorship gave the invitation special allure, and in 1855 Brownson accepted Hughes's invitation.

In the same year, however, Brownson found himself embroiled in a public debate with Archbishop Hughes over the issue of Catholic education. Brownson regarded with alarm the formation of a Catholic school system and feared that it would eventuate in a withdrawal of Catholics from the mainstream of life and culture in the United States. His public advocacy of Catholic attendance of public schools set him at odds with Archbishop Hughes, a vocal advocate of the formation of a Catholic school system.[3] Brownson's open criticism of the Democratic Party also irritated many Catholics, who gravitated by preference toward the political left. Brownson's growing dissatisfaction with medieval scholasticism also led him to rethink his role as a lay intellectual within the Catholic Church. In 1858 he published *The Convert.* In this autobiographical work he commented on most of the religious movements which had flourished in nineteenth-century America, defended the intellectual integrity of his conversion to Catholicism, and declared his intellectual independence as a lay Catholic philosopher and theologian. As his philosophy and theology matured, his anti-Protestant rhetoric mellowed somewhat. At the same time he began to fear that his independence of thought might be leading him into troubled waters. He greeted Pius IX's Syllabus of Errors with very mixed feelings. In the ensuing Catholic witch-hunt, his old adversary Archbishop Hughes defended him from Roman censure.[4]

[2] See Donald Capps, "Orestes Brownson: The Psychology of Religious Affiliation," *Journal for the Scientific Study of Religion* 7 (1968) 197–209; William J. Gilmore, "Comments on Donald Capps's Interpretations of Orestes Brownson," *Journal for the Scientific Study of Religion* 8 (1969) 324.

[3] See James M. McDonnell, *Orestes A. Brownson and Nineteenth-Century Catholic Education* (New York: Garland, 1988); James M. McDonnell, "Orestes A. Brownson: Catholic School, Public Schools, and Education," *An American Church: Essays on the Americanization of the Catholic Church* (Moraga: St. Mary's College of California, 1979); Edward J. Power, *Religion and the Public Schools in Nineteenth-Century America: The Contribution of Orestes A. Brownson* (Mahwah, N.J.: Paulist Press, 1996).

[4] T. T. McAvoy, "Orestes Brownson and Archbishop John Hughes in 1860," *Review of Politics* 24 (1962) 19–47.

Although Brownson opposed slavery, he sniffed suspiciously at abolitionist radicalism, and, prior to the Civil War, he supported John C. Calhoun's defense of states' rights. After Fort Sumter, however, he rallied to the Union cause. The tragedy of the war, which also caused the death of two of Brownson's sons, forced him to rethink the foundations of American political institutions, and in 1865 he published his revised political creed as *The American Republic.*

After 1860 Brownson experienced periodic blindness. The deterioration of his vision led him to discontinue *Brownson's Quarterly Review.* It comes as no surprise that a man as contentious as Brownson refused to "go gentle into that good night." He fumed against the frustrations of old age. In 1873, at the request of his dying wife, he revived the *Quarterly Review.* In 1874 in pages of the review he fired a philosophical and theological broadside against atheism.[5] He died in Detroit on April 17, 1876. His remains were subsequently translated to Sacred Heart Church on the campus of the University of Notre Dame.[6]

II

Brownson's passion for truth motivated his intellectual restlessness. He could not bring himself to defend positions which no longer made sense to him, even if he had once espoused them personally. As a result, the young Brownson's personal religious pilgrimage recapitulated in rapid order most of the major options in early nineteenth-century American religious thought. The young Orestes passed from Arminianism, to Calvinism, to Universalism, to secular Deistic humanism, to Unitarianism, and eventually to a Catholic version of Transcendentalism. His intellectual ca-

[5] See Richard M. Leliaert, "Brownson's Approach to God: The Catholic Period," *Thomist* 40 (1976) 571–607.

[6] For biographical studies of Brownson's life see Henry F. Brownson, *Orestes A. Brownson's Early, Middle, and Latter Life,* 3 vols. (Detroit: Thorndike Nourse, 1898–1900); Theodore Maynard, *Orestes Brownson: Yankee, Radical Catholic* (New York: Macmillan, 1943); Arthur Schlesinger, *Orestes A. Brownson: A Pilgrim's Progress* (Boston: Little, Brown & Co., 1939); Rufus Griswold, *Prose Writers of America* (Philadelphia: Carey & Hart, 1849) 422–5; Americo D. Lapiti, *Orestes A. Brownson* (New York: Twayne, 1965); Thomas R. Ryan, *Orestes A. Brownson: A Definitive Biography* (Huntington, Ind.: Our Sunday Visitor, 1976); Per Svino, *Orestes A. Brownson's Road to Catholicism* (New York: Humanities Press, 1970); D. R. Le Breton, "Orestes Brownson's Visit to New Orleans in 1855," *American Literature* 16 (1944) 110–4; Virgil Michael, "Orestes Brownson," *The Catholic World* 125 (1927) 499–505; Daniel Sargent, *Four Independents* (New York: Sheed & Ward, 1935) 187–243; J. Barcus, "Structuring the Rage Within: The Spiritual Autobiographies of Newman and Orestes Brownson," *Cithara* 15 (1975) 45–57; Patricia O'Connell Killen, "Social Concerns and Religious Commitment: Orestes Brownson and Contemporary American Catholicism," *New Theology Review* 5 (1991) 52–75.

reer exemplified philosophical fallibilism before Charles Peirce popularized the term.

The boy Orestes found himself moved by the Bible, and he read
Jonathan Edwards's *History of Redemption,* which told the story of salvation history as a series of religious revivals. Even as a lad, however,
Brownson found Calvinist piety both puzzling and frightening. He resented it when true believers told him either to "get religion" and "be re-
born" or "go to hell." He noted that, as his fear of hell waxed, his love of
God waned. Eventually, he came to view his resistance to Calvinist orthodoxy as intellectual pride. He converted to Presbyterianism in order to
"abnegate" his reason, but he soon found himself unable to make sense of
a Church which defended private interpretation of the Bible and then ex-
communicated its members for exercising that right. "I regarded that as
unfair treatment."

At the age of twenty-one he decided that he had made a mistake in
becoming a Presbyterian—an honest mistake, but a mistake nonetheless.
In the end he could not force himself to swallow Calvinist belief in total
human depravity. He decided that abandoning reason would cause him "to
sink myself to the level of brute creation." He therefore decided that a fallible human reason afforded him the only light by which he could see anything, and he preferred it to blind assent to a religious book about whose
meaning no two persons seemed able to agree. If God had in fact revealed
himself in human history, the youthful Brownson reasoned, then someone
ought to have the power to speak authoritatively about the character of that
revelation, but he could find within Presbyterianism no religious authority
which commanded his assent.[7]

Brownson drifted into Universalism as the only form of "reasonable"
Christianity which he had experienced personally. A Universalist aunt had
introduced him at the age of fourteen or fifteen to the theological writings
of the Universalist pastor Dr. Elhanan Winchester. These and similar treatises persuaded Brownson to approach religion relying on reason alone. To
his dismay he found himself expected as a Universalist minister to defend
Universalism "as a scriptural doctrine." He tried to think of the Bible as
inspired but not authoritative. He failed. In the end, he concluded: "I cannot, if I try, believe what appears to me unreasonable on the authority of
reason alone." With characteristic integrity he decided that he could no
longer present himself to others truthfully as a Christian minister.

Brownson abandoned the Universalist ministry for reasons analogous
to those which persuaded Emerson to resign his Unitarian pulpit. Emerson

---

[7] Orestes A. Brownson, *The Works of Orestes A. Brownson,* 18 vols., ed. Henry F.
Brownson (Detroit: H. F. Brownson, 1902) 5:1–20.

found the Unitarian compromise of blending Deism with the trappings of Calvinist worship inconsistent and unacceptable. Brownson found the Universalist demand that he regard Deism as biblical faith equally unacceptable.

The "creed" which Brownson published after abandoning his Universalist pulpit summed up in four articles what he could at that point in his pilgrimage honestly affirm as religiously true:

> Art. I. I believe that every individual of the human family should be honest.
> Art. II. I believe that every one should be benevolent and kind to all.
> Art. III. I believe that every one should use his best endeavors to procure food, clothing, and shelter for himself, and labor to enable all others to procure the same for themselves to the full extent of his ability.
> Art. IV. I believe that, if all mankind act on these principles, they serve God all they can serve him; that he who has this faith and conforms the nearest unto what it enjoins is the most acceptable unto God.[8]

Brownson the Catholic would look back on this personal manifesto with mixed feelings. He concluded that this honest avowal of personal unbelief brought him closer to gospel truth than any of his earlier religious experiments. Here at least he had the rudimentary beginnings of a foundation on which to build. Certainly, he never abandoned the passion for honesty, truth, and justice for the poor to which his personal manifesto testified.

However, Brownson had a long way to go before he could begin constructing a religious superstructure atop his creed. He summed up the religious attitudes which his creed expressed in the following terms: "My end was man's earthly happiness, and my creed was progress."[9] The mature Brownson even deemed his espousal of socialism a partial move in the right direction. In retrospect he found within socialism echoes of the Christian gospel. He also found that his flirtation with communism began to wean him away from an individualistic ethos.[10] The maturing Brownson began to sense that the self-sacrifice which passionate commitment to the cause of social justice demanded required of him a measure of religious commitment which his creed lacked. In order to effect progress, he concluded, one needed to believe in more than progress.[11]

In this context he discovered Channing's doctrine of "essential sameness." Perhaps faith in a moral sentiment common to God and humans would fill the gap in his personal creed. He joined the Transcendental circle. Parker's vision of the historical development of religion seems to

[8] Ibid., 5:44–5.
[9] Ibid., 5:49.
[10] Ibid., 5:51.
[11] Ibid., 5:66–7.

have convinced Brownson that all religion inevitably finds embodiment in institutions, and he longed for a Church which would embody the most advanced sentiments of the human race. That longing found verbal expression in his first major work: *New Views of Christianity, Society, and the Church.* The book reflected his growing suspicion that the churches probably asserted the truth in what they affirmed and erred principally in what they denied. He began a reexamination of the positive religious assertions of both Catholicism and Protestantism.[12]

Brownson's essay on "The Laboring Classes" extended his growing passion for institutional justice to politics and economics. In it he argued that unless political equality rested on social equality, the poor lacked the power to claim the rights which in fact the Declaration of Independence and the Constitution guaranteed them. In other words, it booted nothing to talk of human "rights" unless one guaranteed human "mights," or the power to claim one's rights. The universal chorus of denunciation which his essay provoked took Brownson by surprise: "I had drawn from the premises furnished me by my non-Catholic and democratic countrymen, their strictly logical conclusions, and these same countrymen had recoiled from me with horror. Either they are wrong in doing so, or their premises are false."[13]

The overwhelming defeat of Van Buren in the election of 1840 left Brownson disgusted. His study of the politics of Aristotle finally reconciled him to the need for institutional authority as a guarantee to personal liberty. He decided that: "Liberty is not in the absence of authority but in being held to obey only just and legitimate authority."[14] At the same time he began to doubt that a humanity as flawed in its perceptions as the American electorate lacked the wherewithal to save itself. "Man only equals man."[15]

Until this point in his career Brownson had settled for a philosophical and theological eclecticism. His study of Pierre Leroux convinced him of the need to move beyond eclecticism toward a synthetic vision of reality. In Leroux he found a theory of knowledge which overcame the subject-object dualism at the heart of Enlightenment thinking. He also found there

---

[12] Ibid., 5:72–90. See also William J. Gilmore, "Orestes Brownson and New England Religious Culture," *Church History* 42 (1973) 120.

[13] Brownson, *The Works of Orestes A. Brownson,* 5:121; see also Arthur M. Schlesinger, "Orestes Brownson: An American Marxist before Marx," *Sewanee Review* 47 (1939) 317–23; Judith Kent Green, "Conservative Voices in the Western Messenger: William Greenleaf Elliot and Harm Jan Huidkoper," *Harvard Theological Review* 77 (1984) 331–52.

[14] Brownson, *The Works of Orestes A. Brownson,* 5:122.

[15] Ibid., 5:124.

a social theory of life which freed him definitively of Enlightenment individualism. With kindling excitement Brownson realized that "man lives and can live only by communion with what is not himself. In himself alone cut off from all that is not himself, he is neither a progressive nor a living being."[16] Having despaired of discovering in human nature the capacity to endow life with any kind of ultimate meaning, Brownson went further still. He realized that

> man cannot think without an object, and, being finite, he can never be his own object. Only God can be the object of his own intelligence, or be intelligent without other than himself; man, whatever else he is, is a dependent being, and is in no instance, in no respect, alone sufficient for himself. . . . He cannot lift himself, but must be lifted, by placing him in communion with a higher elevating object. . . . I was obliged, then, to give up all my hopes of progress, or abandon my doctrine of no God but the God in man, or the identity of the human and the divine.[17]

Brownson had begun to see through some of the false promises of Enlightenment modernism. The Enlightenment's assurance of endless human perfectibility rested on a false and naive belief in humanity's innocence and complete self-sufficiency. That same fallacious self-sufficiency fueled Enlightenment individualism and subjectivism. It taught people to trust spontaneously in the insights of their fallible individual intellects. The repudiation of individualism and subjectivism entailed by reverse logic commitment to a social, communal understanding of human nature. Commitment to community meant institutional commitment, and institutional commitment entailed respect for legitimate authority. Commitment to community immersed one in history, and belief in human fallenness meant that it would take more than human effort to guarantee human progress.

As we have seen, New England Congregationalism began its drift into Unitarianism by denying the doctrine of total human depravity and by replacing it with an Enlightenment faith in the complete integrity of human nature. Belief in human innocence eliminated the need for a redeemer. The elimination of a redeemer entailed the denial of the incarnation, and the denial of the incarnation entailed the denial of the Trinity. The denial of the Trinity entailed Unitarianism.

Brownson now made the same inferential journey in reverse. He could not believe in the total depravity of human nature, but his personal confrontation with the spontaneous refusal of the human heart to embrace those means which guarantee a just social order had forced him to concede

---

[16] Ibid., 5:131.
[17] Ibid., 5:130.

the fact of human fallenness. A fallen humanity, he now realized, needs redemption by a reality greater than itself. He found that he could accept the
idea of supernatural grace as long as it did not annihilate humanity but corresponded relationally to its legitimate natural needs. The eruption of the
supernatural into history, however, entailed belief both in divine providence
and in graced illumination. The Calvinist doctrine of natural depravity,
Brownson now saw, had forced him into a needless choice between nature
and supernature, between revelation and reason. Brownson had long since
abandoned belief in a predestining God, but he now found that he could relate to a God who relates to humanity with dialogic and benevolent freedom. "I shall never forget the ecstasy of that moment," he wrote in *The
Convert,* "when I first realized to myself that God is free."[18]

Having acknowledged the fallacy of a forced option between nature
and supernature, having affirmed the social, communal character of human
nature, and having conceded the need to bend to legitimate authority,
Brownson began to suspect that a graced providence was leading him to
seek in Catholicism for an authoritative, historical revelation of God in
which divine grace effects the kind of human progress which a fallen humanity, left to its own resources, can never effect. Brownson distilled the
fruits of these insights into his open letter to Channing on the subject of
"The Mediatorial Life of Jesus." In the letter he argued that only an incarnate God, a God who also freely took human nature into the deity, offered
the requisite means for effecting the free communion of all persons in God
for which a fallen humanity longs and which it desperately needs.[19]

In an essay on the thought of Pierre Leroux also published in 1842
Brownson wrote:

> The metaphysical principle, which becomes, as it were, a universal solvent
> of whatever pertains to life, is simply that the me can never manifest itself,
> that is, live, save in communion with the not-me. This is the principle on
> which is based our new system of philosophy; but as important as we have
> found this principle in the region of metaphysics, we had not suspected half
> its importance in the region of politics and theology, till reading this work
> by Leroux. We see now the literal truth of what has been asserted of Christ
> as the mediator between God and men; we see how he can be both literally
> and truly and indissolubly God-man, and therefore strictly a mediator be-
> tween God and men; how his mediation does and can hold in God's provi-
> dential plan for the salvation of men, the place commonly assigned to it, and
> how he can communicate his life to the world, and by so doing become lit-
> erally, really, not by way of example, representation, or imputation, the life

---

[18] Ibid., 5:144.
[19] Ibid., 5:122–44.

and salvation of the world. These great doctrines, which have been asserted and held on to by the church, as if life and death depended on them, which have been great and painful mysteries, and which in these days have driven so many from the church and from Christianity, if we do not greatly deceive ourselves, we can clear up, make philosophically plain and certain, in the most simple and literal sense, and on as high a degree of evidence, as that which we have for our own existence. A glorious discovery, for which we thank God, and which restores us without any subtlety, without refining of terms, to the great household of believers.[20]

Brownson, like all creative thinkers, borrowed insights from other thinkers but integrated them into his own personal synthesis. His reading of Leroux had finally enabled him to make the transition from a Protestant, dialectical imagination, with its artificial either-or options, to a Catholic analogical imagination, which seeks as much as possible to think in both-and rather than in either-or terms. The analogical imagination seeks for a synthetic insight into reality, an insight which grasps the unifying relationships which gather diverse beings into a unity. Leroux taught Brownson to shift from a dyadic, dualistic frame of reference to a triadic, synthetic frame of reference. The following section begins to trace Brownson's intellectual progress from dyad to triad, from dualism to synthesis.[21]

III

In *The Convert* Brownson defended the consistency of his progress toward Catholicism. The book also declared his right to think his own thoughts as a lay Catholic intellectual. A careful reading of Brownson's works reveals, moreover, coherence in the incremental development of his own brand of Transcendentalism despite the fact that Brownson chose to think things through publicly and not always consistently in the published pages of *Brownson's Quarterly Review.* Brownson would no doubt have resisted the label "Transcendentalist," since he regarded the Transcendentalism which he had encountered in the Transcendental Club as the logical dead end of Protestant individualism.[22] Still, Brownson the convert did elaborate his own theory of intuition, and he presented that theory as a way of getting beyond, or transcending, the limitations of Enlightenment Deism. If by a Transcendentalist one means someone who invokes an intuitive epistemology as a strategy for getting beyond Enlightenment nomi-

---

[20] Ibid., 4:139. See also Donald Capps, "Orestes Brownson: The Psychology of Religious Affiliation," *Journal for the Scientific Study of Religion* 7 (1968) 197–209.

[21] See Arie J. Briffion, "Brownson's Early Christology," *American Benedictine Review* 44 (1993) 58–75.

[22] Brownson, *The Works of Orestes A. Brownson,* 6:116–33.

nalism, then Brownson qualifies as a Transcendentalist, even though he did not formulate his theory of intuition until he had severed connection with his former friends in the Transcendental Club by converting to Catholicism.

In his *New Views* Brownson, prior to embracing Catholicism, had called for a Church purified of the dualistic modes of thinking which had fragmented Christian perceptions in the past. The elder Brownson conceded the superficiality of his argument in *New Views,* but this early work nevertheless foreshadowed the direction in which his mature thought would evolve. In *New Views* Brownson still viewed religion in naturalistic terms: "Religion is natural to man and he ceases to be man the moment he ceases to be religious."[23] Still, even at this early date Brownson conceded that religion inevitably takes institutional shape. Moreover, he expected religious institutions to express the faith they embody.[24]

In *New Views* Brownson developed his personal myth of Church origins, a myth which in the end touched history only tangentially. The young Brownson believed that both Catholicism and Protestantism had distorted Jesus and his message by their acquiescence in a spirit-matter dualism. The Catholic tradition, Brownson argued, had opted for spirit rather than for matter. The lopsided spiritualism of the Catholic tradition condemned it to proclaim religious "exclusivity." This exclusivity Brownson interpreted cavalierly in Gnostic terms. In the young Brownson's eyes, religious "exclusivism" views the physical as inherently corrupt and it postpones salvation until the next life. In *New Views* Brownson also depicted Calvinism as the offspring of medieval spiritualism.[25] Catholic exclusivism, he alleged, views the Church as a privileged embodiment of sacred spirit which governs the thoughts and consciences of its members through the decisions of the pope. Throughout its history, the pre-Catholic Brownson charged, the Catholic Church vilified matter. It condemned materialism in Pelagius and defeated matter through the cult of celibacy.[26]

Within the Catholic tradition, those who embraced matter over spirit fostered immoral self-indulgence. A spirit of immorality bred licentiousness in the monasteries. The Catholic hierarchy corrupted itself through its abuse of wealth and power, all the while claiming hypocritically to stand for purely spiritual values. In Brownson's myth of Christian development, the Protestant reform focused Christianity on material values instead of on spiritual ones. Protestantism "brought up the state, civil liberty, human reason, philosophy, industry, all temporal interests."[27] Improbably, Brownson saw

[23] Ibid., 4:3.
[24] Ibid., 4:3–4.
[25] Ibid., 4:35–7.
[26] Ibid., 4:5–15.
[27] Ibid., 4:17.

Protestantism, which he seems to have equated with the liberal Protestantism of his own day, as having opted for reason rather than for submission to the spiritual authority of the Church. The pre-Catholic Brownson also blamed Protestantism for the rise of philosophical materialism.[28]

Since human religious aspirations inevitably take institutional form, Brownson in *New Views* argued that in the future Christianity had to find a way of reconciling the legitimate concerns of Catholic spiritualism and Protestant materialism. The spiritualists needed to embrace human nature; the materialists needed to recognize the sanctification of matter. The reconciliation of Catholic and Protestant, of spiritualist and materialist, in the church of the future would bring about the end of Christian sectarianism and effect the sacralization of both Church and state.[29] "And when this all takes place the glory of the Lord will be manifested unto the ends of the earth, and all flesh will see it and rejoice together"[30] in a world in which religion fosters unlimited natural human progress.[31]

In *The Convert* Brownson expressed himself embarrassed at the superficiality of his youthful reading of Christian history in *New Views*.[32] Nevertheless, this early work gave voice to speculative commitments which Brownson would never retract. In *New Views* Brownson endorsed Jefferson's insight that dualistic forms of thinking had seriously distorted the Christian message. Already in the mid-1830s Brownson longed for a synthetic philosophical vision which would transcend the distorting dualisms of the past. Pierre Leroux would teach Brownson to avoid philosophical dualism by thinking of reality as inherently relational.

From Leroux, Brownson learned to reconcile spirit and matter by subsuming them under the integrating category of "life." In 1842, with help from Leroux, he argued that the terms "spirit" and "matter" designate the same reality under different aspects. We find matter embodied in living substances endowed with force and perception. Life simultaneously synthesizes and actualizes both matter and spirit.[33] By the same token, Brownson reasoned, "life" synthesizes and integrates both the knowing subject and the reality known.[34] It also integrates and reconciles the individual and the community, since life consists fundamentally and essentially in communion.[35]

[28] Ibid., 4:17–23.
[29] Ibid., 4:28–55.
[30] Ibid., 4:50.
[31] Ibid., 4:52–5.
[32] Ibid., 5:84–8.
[33] Ibid., 4:70–1.
[34] Ibid., 4:138–9.
[35] Ibid., 4:144.

Brownson subsequently developed these key insights in articles published in the *Quarterly Review.* He called his resulting philosophical vision "synthetic." Brownson's synthetic philosophy viewed life, living, as the proper object of philosophical reflection. Philosophy enlarged and enlightened human understanding of the reality of life.[36] Of necessity, then, philosophical thinking expanded and enhanced human consciousness, human self-awareness. Consciousness did not flow from a special faculty or exemplify a distinct kind of activity. Instead, consciousness heightened and enhanced ordinary perceptions of reality. The human mind came to self-awareness precisely by grasping its distinction in relationship from some reality other than itself. Brownson put it this way:

> The true point of departure of philosophy is never in *being,* in the *esse, das reine seyn* of the Hegelians, whether of the subject or of the object; but in *life,* which is the manifestation of Being. And in *life,* according to what we have established, *the subject and object, me and not me, are one and indissoluble. . . .* The manifestation of being, that is, being putting itself forth in the phenomenon, is what I term *life;* and when this life is so intense that the subject recognizes itself as well as that which is not itself, I term the phenomenon, *thought,* or apperception.[37]

As the simultaneous product of subject and object, life has an inherently relational, synthetic character. Philosophy, then, has the task of exploring the network of vital relationships.[38]

Brownson's vitalism also acknowledged a certain givenness to facticity. He argued for the absurdity of the belief that one should regard only the conclusion of scientific argument as certain. With his customary blending of insight and pugnaciousness, Brownson asserted: *"every fact is incapable of proof just in proportion to its certainty."*[39]

Brownson's triadic account of vital cognition distinguishes the subject of cognition, the object of cognition, and the form of cognition. The form of cognition results from the dynamic interaction of subject and object. Consciousness emerges in the subject's taking account of the fact that it knows an object distinct from itself. Consciousness endows perception with a dimension of self-awareness. "In every act of consciousness I perceive, though I am not conscious in every fact of perception."[40]

Brownson's relational account of cognition considered and rejected the Enlightenment belief that cognition terminates at subjective ideas of

[36] Ibid., 1:58–9.
[37] Ibid., 1:65.
[38] Ibid., 1:65–6.
[39] Ibid., 1:67.
[40] Ibid., 1:29.

reality. While the form of cognition defines the way in which a subject knows an object, the subject's mind grasps the object itself and not just a mode of perceiving the object.[41] A theory of truth, therefore, must deal with how the mind knows reality, not whether it does so.

Brownson's synthetic philosophy undertook two complementary analyses: the formula of the subject explored psychology, while the formula of the object developed a metaphysics. The formula of the subject anatomized self-consciousness descriptively. On examination, self-consciousness reveals the subject to itself as an acting cause and therefore as a unified, substantive reality. The conscious self on reflection discovers within itself three vitally related, causal capacities: action, cognition, and sentiment.

Brownson's analysis of cognition began with *perception.* A sound understanding of perception rejected Locke's portrait of the mind as a tabula rasa which receives sensations passively. In all perception, the mind acts upon and in response to an impinging object.[42]

Memory makes perception historical, but it never discloses either one's personal past or history in an exhaustive manner. As a consequence, the mind's access to history remains partial. Memory makes past fact present in some way to consciousness, but memory lacks the sharp facticity of physical sensations. The remembered past functions as an object of thought, but it never results from the acting subject alone. Present experience evokes past remembrance. As a consequence, the memory of past events enhances present perceptions of environing realities. The recall of the past endows consciousness with an initial temporality by yielding a felt sense of the difference between present perceptions and remembered ones. The conscious subject has a vague presentiment, or *apperception,* of order and stability in nature, just as it experiences a vague presentiment of its own identity and persistence. The subject also experiences a similar vague presentiment, or apperception, of an unfolding future.[43]

As the analysis of perception unfolds it includes *imagination* among the principal modes of perception. Imagination engages all the powers of the soul, but it principally yields a perception of reality. Imagination enhances and clarifies vague apperceptions of the real. Imagination, therefore, always includes an imagined object, something *not me* to attain or create. Acts of imagination differ in the intensity with which they represent their object ideally to the subject. Still, Brownson regarded every stonecutter as an incipient Phidias. The creativity of the imagination both exemplifies and enhances the creativity ingredient in all activity. Brownson

[41] Ibid., 1:69–71.
[42] Ibid., 1:77–80.
[43] Ibid., 1:80–95.

also found a continuum linking the products of the creative imagination. In Brownson's view, the creative imagination deals largely but not exclusively with ideal objects. Still, all creative images drive the subject into interaction with the *not me*. Ecstasy or trance exemplify high intensity imaginative experiences.[44]

Brownson's formula of the subject discloses, then, a continuum of gradually expanding evaluative responses. Specific perceptions excite relevant memories. Perception always occurs within the context of a more vague apperception of the perceiving self and its world. Heightened apperception evolves into creative imagination, which in its more intense forms includes ecstasy and trance.

The acting subject, however, includes more than cognition. It also wills to act. An analysis of *willing,* then, completes the formula of the subject. Brownson's synthetic philosophy refuses to divide the activities of the subject into neatly defined and essentially distinct powers of the soul, in the manner of the medieval scholastics and, to a certain extent, of Enlightenment *philosophes.* Brownson rejected the idea of "pure, unmixed volitions." Instead, he viewed volitions as elements in a unified subjective response to reality. He discovered an element of volition in all activity, including cognitive activity. Willing in the strict sense, however, occurs when the subject has decided upon a specific way of responding to reality. In Brownson's formula of the subject, willing, like knowing, encompasses a spectrum of activities which merge and blend: attention, reflection, desire, passion, emotion, affection.[45]

The *conscience* elects one willed response rather than another. In the end, however, Brownson relegated conscience, somewhat hastily in my judgment, to the realm of memory.[46]

Brownson's early metaphysical analysis of the object of cognition focused on the contents of what he called "Reason." Here Brownson's Platonic tendencies began to manifest themselves. "Reason," he wrote, "properly defined is the world of necessary relations, abstract and universal truths, or the world of absolute and necessary *ideas,* using the word *Idea* in its original Platonic sense."[47] The objects of human knowing initially divide, then, into ideal objects and actual objects. The mind perceives ideal objects as abstract, universal, necessary, permanent, immutable, absolute, and infinite. The mind experiences actual objects as concrete, particular, contingent, transient, variable, relative, and finite. These two kinds

[44] Ibid., 1:95–106.
[45] Ibid., 1:107–12, 116.
[46] Ibid., 1:114.
[47] Ibid., 1:116.

of objects fuse, however, in the act of cognition itself, for one grasps the ideal in the actual. Said Brownson: "Ideas, absolute, necessary and universal truths, are perceived *by* the Subject, but not *in* itself." Brownson called the cognitive grasp of the ideal in the actual "intuition."[48]

Brownson's initial analysis of the object revealed, then, that the human subject relates simultaneously to three worlds: the world of time, the world of space,[49] and the world of eternity. One experiences the ideal objects which populate the world of eternity as real but not as factual, not as events. However, because "the Ideal is seen and known, but only in the Actual," one never experiences the ideal apart from the Actual. That necessity of human cognition endows authentic religious perceptions with an irreducibly incarnational character:

> Hence, it is that no man sees God, or can see him, save through a mediator, as manifested in the face of his Son; and hence, too, the reason why we cannot even see the Son through whom the Father is revealed, till incarnated, and only in so far as made flesh and dwelling among us.[50]

Brownson compressed his incarnational understanding of intuition into the following dense passage:

> Reason is the Transcendental World, the world of Ideas, kinds, genera, Universals, what I call the Ideal.—Only let it be kept in mind that the Ideal, if not Actual, is still real, and exists not in the Subject, but out of it, and is truly objective, and therefore not-me. It is as much and as truly an object of perception as a tree, a house, or a man. If it be asked how we know that we perceive it? the answer is, the perception *is* the *knowing* that it is perceived. The perception is not the medium of knowing, but the *knowing itself.* Reasoning is simply detecting and bringing forth in a clear and distinct light, in the various concrete objects of the actual world, the Ideal. It is to generalize.[51]

No Enlightenment nominalism for Brownson. Besides concrete, sensible actuality, the human mind knows real generality, universality, but it grasps the universal ideal only in the concrete, in the sensible, in the actual. Ontology and realism in the end coincide.[52] As we shall see in the final section of this study, Abbot, Peirce, and the mature Royce, like Brownson, endorsed a form of realistic ontology. Of the three, Peirce

---

[48] Ibid., 1:119. See also Armand Maurer, "Orestes Brownson and St. Augustine," *Modern Schoolman* 69 (1992) 463–74.

[49] Brownson had no conception of the space-time defended by relativity theory.

[50] Brownson, *The Works of Orestes A. Brownson,* 1:126. See also Luke Mancuso, "A Consideration of the Brownson–Virgil Michel Connections," *American Benedictine Review* 40 (1989) 274–90.

[51] Brownson, *The Works of Orestes A. Brownson,* 1:127.

[52] Ibid., 1:127–9.

would offer the most precise account of the relationship between logic, semiotics, and ontological realism.[53]

On the basis of his synthetic philosophy, Brownson mounted critiques of both Emerson and Parker. Brownson judged that Emerson had seen through the sham in Protestantism, but that he had dismissed Catholicism without giving it a proper hearing. Brownson professed himself struck "with the depth and breadth of his thought, as well as with the singular force and beauty of his expression." Still Brownson, the incarnational Platonist, faulted Emerson, the dualistic, naturalistic Platonist, on two major counts: Emerson's failure to distinguish adequately between the human soul and God and his reduction of finite reality to mere phenomenal appearance.[54]

Parker gave the lectures which he eventually published as his *Discourse* at the time when Brownson found himself increasingly attracted to Catholicism. Brownson attended the lectures and realized sadly that he and his old friend were moving in contradictory religious directions. Brownson reviewed Parker's *Discourse* when it appeared and pronounced it "sheer naturalism." By "sheer naturalism" Brownson meant an approach to religion which fails to acknowledge the gratuity of the divine gift mediated through the incarnation as well as the incarnation's transcendence of anything which created nature, left to its own resources, could effect. Brownson reduced Parker's position to three key theses: "I. Man is the measure of truth and goodness. II. Religion is a fact or principle of human nature. III. All religious institutions which have been or are, have their principle and cause in human nature."[55] Brownson disagreed with all three theses. The first proposition, Brownson argued, assumed fallaciously that purely subjective, human religious intuitions enjoy infallibility. Brownson questioned whether Parker's sense of dependence had the capacity to explain or ground all religious experience. Finally, he argued that in conceding the existence of God, Parker had logically to concede the possibility of a supernatural order and with it supernatural religion.[56]

In the end, Brownson summed up the substance of Parker's "absolute religion" in the following terms: "Be good and do good, and you will—be good and do good. Vary the phrase and mystify the subject as you please, this is the whole sum and substance of what Mr. Parker means by absolute

[53] See Thomas J. Joyce, "Orestes A. Brownson: His Theory of Intuition" (master's thesis, Boston College, 1959).

[54] Brownson, *The Works of Orestes A. Brownson,* 3:424–38. See also Russell Kirk, "Two Facets of the New England Mind: Emerson and Brownson," *Month* 8 (1952) 208–17; Alvan S. Ryan, "American Classic Reconsidered," *American Classics Revisited,* ed. H. C. Gardiner (New York: Scribner's, 1958) 98–120.

[55] Brownson, *The Works of Orestes A. Brownson,* 6:2.

[56] Ibid., 6:1–108.

religion."[57] In reflecting on Parker's portrait of Jesus as the prophet of absolute religion, Brownson exhorted his old friend in print: "O, go and study at the foot of the cross, and you will soon be sick of venturing these pretty sentimentalisms and rhetorical inanities."[58] If Parker ever read the exhortation, it fell on deaf ears.

Both Emerson and Parker paid lip service to Kant without really understanding Kantian philosophy. Not only did Brownson study Kant, but he grasped with remarkable insight the fallacies of Kant's transcendental analysis of human subjectivity. Brownson saw that a Kantian theory of human knowledge acquiesced in the nominalism which British empiricism had popularized. He also recognized the ultimate indefensibility of a nominalistic epistemology and metaphysics. Brownson faulted Kant primarily for espousing what he called a "sensist" position. By that Brownson meant that Kant reduced all the objects of knowledge to concrete sensibles.[59] Brownson never used Peirce's term "conceptual nominalism" in describing Kantian philosophy, but, like Peirce, Brownson recognized that Kantian nominalism differs from classical nominalism. Classical nominalism, Brownson argued, correctly asserted the existence of concrete individuals, but it erred in reducing genera and species only to empty words.[60] Brownson also believed that his incarnational Platonism corrected the errors in both positions. As for Kant, Brownson observed:

> A true doctrine of life, or ontology, will show us that the *noumenon* is in the phenomenon, the cause in the effect, the general in the particular, the necessary in the contingent; and therefore we see or detect, more or less obscurely, no doubt, the first category in the second.[61]

Brownson, like Emerson, believed that Platonic realism ultimately refutes all forms of nominalism and sensism. By objectifying Reason as a reality given to imaginative intuition Brownson reformulated Emerson's belief that the creative imagination gives the mind cognitive access to real generality. While Emerson was writing *Nature,* Brownson was wrestling with the problem of dualism and had diagnosed it as the ultimate intellectual bane of Christian theology. His dynamic vitalism gave him the relational categories he needed in order to transcend the dualisms which bedeviled Emerson's Transcendental aesthetic and metaphysics. Moreover, in overcoming dualism with a dynamic vitalism Brownson also learned to think analogically and incarnationally rather than dialectically and dualistically. As a conse-

---

[57] Ibid., 6:209.
[58] Ibid., 6:218.
[59] Ibid., 1:208.
[60] Ibid., 1:372–3.
[61] Ibid., 1:211.

quence, Brownson saw in a way which finally eluded Emerson that the human mind grasps real generality not by ascending to some pure and eternal realm of Spirit, but in the concrete, sensible individual.[62]

Having transcended the limitations of Platonic dualism, Brownson nevertheless remained a Platonist. He affirmed as fervently as Emerson that the mind encounters eternal verities as objects of thought. Brownson, however, played a muted Aristotle to Emerson's Plato. He saw that one grasps real generality in the concrete, the sensible, and only there. In fact, Brownson's epistemology and metaphysics fell somewhere between Platonism and Aristotelianism. With Plato Brownson asserted the transcendent reality of eternal verities, but with Aristotle he asserted that one grasps such verities in the concrete and the sensible. The Aristotelian bent of Brownson's mind enabled him to avoid strict ontologism. The human mind, Brownson insisted, has no direct or immediate access to ideas in the mind of God. It grasps real generality only in the cognitive encounter with concrete actualities by acknowledging the real generality which they embody.

Brownson lacked C. S. Peirce's mastery of logic, but Brownson's incarnational intuitionism advanced Transcendental thinking to the threshold of Peircean metaphysical realism. Both men espoused a form of epistemological and metaphysical realism. Both endorsed a triadic construct of knowledge and of reality. Of the two, however, Peirce would develop the more nuanced and defensible position.

IV

The synthetic philosophical insight which mediated Brownson's conversion to Catholicism had from the first theological implications. Brownson found assistance in developing a "synthetic theology" in the writings of Vincenzo Gioberti. Brownson discovered in Gioberti's thought three serious blunders: (1) Gioberti, Brownson felt, confounded the natural and the supernatural orders of reality; (2) he fallaciously identified the second person of the Trinity with God's creative act; (3) Gioberti misrepresented the incarnation as the completion of the act of creation.[63] Nevertheless, Gioberti confirmed Brownson in his belief that the mind cannot exist apart from an intuitive grasp of the first principles on which thinking rests. Brownson's theory of intuition identified "first principles" with the reality of God.

---

[62] See A. R. Caponigri, "Brownson and Emerson: Nature and History," *New England Quarterly* 28 (1945) 369–90; Chester A. Soleta, "Literary Criticism of Orestes A. Brownson," *Review of Politics* 16 (1954) 334–51.

[63] Brownson, *The Works of Orestes A. Brownson,* 2:187.

"All intuition," Brownson wrote, "is, then, intuition of real, independent, self-existing, and self-acting being, and such being is in all theologies termed God."[64] Brownson distanced himself from Gioberti by distinguishing principles which one discovers naturally from principles which God reveals supernaturally.[65] Nevertheless, Brownson found Gioberti's maxim *"ens creat existentias"* (being creates existences) both philosophically and theologically suggestive when interpreted in the light of his synthetic philosophy, for if in grasping the first principles of knowledge one grasps intuitively a divine reality, might not a philosophical analysis of the conditions for the possibility of intuitive knowledge reveal that the Being and reality of God functions as the creative ground for the very existence of conscious minds? The success of such a philosophical argument could, he hoped, break down the gulf between the natural and supernatural orders which Augustinian anthropology and the Protestant dialectical imagination had dug. Brownson put it this way:

> As existences proceed from the supernatural, *mediante* the creative act of God, it follows that the assumption of unbelievers and modern infidel scientists is inadmissible, namely, that the natural and supernatural are two distinct, separate, and unrelated orders, and that the supernatural is not necessary to complete the science of the natural.[66]

The mature Brownson brought the philosophical presuppositions which grounded this insight to their clearest expression in his philosophical refutation of atheism in 1873. In this essay he further embellished his metaphysics by developing in greater detail the analysis of the metaphysical object of cognition which he had sketched in 1843.

Brownson recognized that, if one acquiesces in the nominalistic reduction of the objects of knowledge to concrete sensible facts, one rules out in principle the possibility of human religious experience. Brownson also dismissed epistemological relativism as self-refuting, for if one relativizes all knowledge, then one deprives oneself of the means of proving relativism.[67] Brownson also saw that the denial of real generality renders all scientific understanding impossible, because it makes causal knowing impossible. One explains something scientifically by grasping the general law which renders it intelligible. Peirce would give logical precision to insights

---

[64] Ibid., 2:261.

[65] Ibid., 2:217–72.

[66] Ibid., 2:277; see also A. Robert Caponigri, "European Influences on the Thought of Orestes Brownson: Pierre Leroux and Vincenzo Gioberti," *No Other Allegiance: Essays in Brownson's Thought,* ed. Leonard Gilhooley (New York: Fordham University Press, 1980) 100–24; Bertin Farrell, *Orestes Brownson's Approach to the Problem of God* (Washington, D.C.: Catholic University Press, 1950).

[67] Brownson, *The Works of Orestes A. Brownson,* 2:12–13.

such as these. Because Brownson the incarnational Platonist discovered real generality ultimately in God, he also believed that his realistic epistemology held the germ of a proof of the existence of God. In the end, he would espouse a position not that far removed from the metaphysical epistemology of Joseph Maréchal,[68] and he would argue on grounds not unlike those defended by Maréchal. While Maréchal's argument would rest on the presuppositions of Thomistic faculty psychology, Brownson's argument rested on his analysis of the object of intuitive knowing.[69]

Still, like Maréchal, Brownson looked to the very structure of cognition for a demonstration of the reality of the divine. Brownson stated the fundamental presupposition of his argument in the following terms:

> Being must be intuitively presented or we cannot have the notion of being, and the intuitive presentation of being to the subject gives the subject simultaneously the consciousness of itself as the subject of the intuition. Being can be presented in thought, only under the relation of object, and in every thought is given simultaneously with the other two inseparable elements, subject and relation.[70]

In other words, a sound analysis of every act of cognition reveals three inseparably interrelated elements: a knowing subject, the object of knowledge, and the relationship which unites the two.

The elder Brownson turned to a more detailed analysis of the object as the foundation for his proof of the reality of God. An analysis of the object of knowledge reveals another triad: an empirical reality, an ideal reality, and the relationship between them. Brownson believed fallaciously with Kant that the ideal element in the object of cognition enjoys an a priori and apodictic character, but unlike Kant he gave both of these traits a metaphysical interpretation. The empirical element in the object of cognition exhibits only contingent existence. Nevertheless, the intuitive grasp of the contingent, sensible reality contains an ideal and apodictic element. One also grasps the two as both cognitively and really related, since the ideal element—the real general which the concrete, sensible actuality exemplifies—explains the latter. Brownson, moreover, regarded all three as given to intuitive perception. He wrote: "Intuition of the ideal is solely the act of the object and in relation to it the intellect is passive. It corresponds to the intelligible species of the peripatetics, or rather to what they call *species impressa.*"[71] Because Brownson denied ontologism, he also denied

[68] See Joseph Maréchal, *Le point de départ de la metaphysique*, 5 vols. (Louvain: Editions du Museum Lessianum, 1926–47); see especially volume 5.
[69] Brownson, *The Works of Orestes A. Brownson,* 2:15–23.
[70] Ibid., 2:45.
[71] Ibid., 2:53.

that the intuition of the ideal grasped an idea in the mind of God; instead, he assimilated it to the Thomistic intuition of first principles.[72]

Having isolated a realistic, ideal component in every act of cognition, Brownson's argument next advanced to an analysis of the ideal component itself. That analysis yielded another triad. The ideal upon analysis breaks down into the following three components: the necessary, the contingent, and the relationship between them.[73] These three categories, Brownson argued, exhaust the meaning of reality. Any existing thing must exemplify one of them. Real, necessary being, however, exists of itself. Any inference from contingent being yields only contingency, no necessity. Necessity becomes both real and knowable only when exemplified in a concrete, contingent reality. Traditionally, philosophers call the necessary "Being" *(ens)* and contingent being "existences" *(existentias)*.

Since the act of cognition discovers within the object of cognition a relationship between the necessary and the contingent, between Being and existences, the third step of Brownson's analysis of the object focused on the nature of that relationship. Since the mind grasps the relationship of the necessary to the contingent only in its knowledge of the object, it can analyze the relations of necessary Being to contingent being only as they really relate to one another. Because contingent reality depends on necessary reality, the relationship of the empirical to the necessary, of contingent beings to Being, exemplifies the relationship of effect to cause, because the necessary causes and explains the contingent, not vice versa. The ideal, therefore, causes the empirical. Without the cognitive grasp of that causal relationship, thought cannot happen. The realm of contingent being as a whole relates, therefore, to necessary Being as effect to cause, even though contingent beings cause their own contingent acts. Brownson therefore concluded: "The being given in ideal intuition is real and necessary being, self-existent, complete in itself, wanting nothing, and incapable of receiving any thing in addition to what it is, and is eternally."[74]

In grasping necessary Being as the cause of contingent beings, one grasps the fact of continuous divine creation. The divine creative act mediates God's immanent presence within all of creation. The reality of a God distinct from creation necessarily implies the reality of the supernatural. While not necessitated either to create or to reveal himself, such a God has the capacity to do so freely, if God so chooses.[75]

Moreover, a God who functions as the unique source of creation must

[72] Ibid., 2:54–6.
[73] Ibid., 2:56.
[74] Ibid., 2:77.
[75] Ibid., 2:76–81.

also function as its goal or end, since in creating something other than himself an infinitely good God must also create them for himself. Brownson put it this way:

> Being cannot act freely without will, and no one can will without willing an end; and no good being without willing a good end. No really good end is possible but God himself; we may, therefore, safely and certainly conclude God is our last cause as well as our first cause, at once the beginning and the end, the Alpha and the Omega of all existences, the original and end of all things.[76]

Brownson regarded this conclusion as more than logical. He believed it intuitively given in every act of cognition in a manner analogous to the intuitive perception of God as first cause which his proof for the existence of God had rendered thematic and explicit.[77]

If one concedes a God who creates, Brownson further argued, then one also concedes the possibility of a God who can a :t in and on his creation in any way he chooses. In other words, the creation of the natural world implies the possibility of God's intervening in the progress of affairs in the created universe in order to ensure that creation achieve the end for which God created it in the first place, namely union with himself. Hear Brownson himself:

> If revelation and supernatural grace are necessary to enable us to enter the teleological order, to persevere in it and attain to the full complement of perfection of our existence, we may reasonably conclude that the infinite love or unbounded and overflowing goodness which prompted him, so to speak, to create us will provide them. Hence, revelation, miracles, the whole order of grace, are as provable, if facts, as any other class of facts and are in their principle included in the ideal judgment.[78]

While Brownson carefully and correctly distinguished the order of creation from the order of salvation, he saw them as intimately related. God's supernatural intervention in human history ensures the original purpose of creation when human decisions deviate from that purpose and block the union of creature with God which originally motivated the divine creative act. Brownson brought these insights to their clearest expression in 1873, but already in the 1840s they had to some extent motivated his conversion to Catholicism. As we shall see, Peircean logic would call into question fundamental presuppositions of Brownson's argument.

In opposition to Emerson's doctrine of representative men, Brownson proposed his own doctrine of providential men. When in the course of

[76] Ibid., 2:86.
[77] Ibid., 2:85.
[78] Ibid., 2:88.

history the salvation of the human race requires it, God can and does send providential individuals "who come at long intervals of time and space, and by their superhuman virtue, intelligence, wisdom, love and power of sacrifice, found systems and eras, redeem and advance the race."[79]

In Jesus, Brownson found the ultimate "providential man," God incarnate, the savior who undoes the effects of human sinfulness and reorients humanity to God. Moreover, Brownson affirmed the close connection between God's will to create and God's will to become incarnate. Indeed, like Scotus, he found the will to become incarnate implicit in God's very decision to create, since humanity requires supernatural means to achieve perfect union with God. In an essay on the philosophy of the supernatural written in 1876, he asserted:

> The point we make here is that the act which creates the natural is the identical act which creates the Hypostatic Union, and founds the supernatural. The Hypostatic Union or Incarnation, is itself the initial order, in the first cycle, or the order of the procession of existences by act of creation from God as first cause. It completes that order of carrying the creative act to its highest pitch, and initiates or founds the teleological order, or the order of the return of existences without absorption in him to God, as final cause, or their last end.
>
> Hence, it follows that the entire creation, whether in the natural or supernatural, the initial or the teleological order, exists for the Incarnation, and finds in its relation to the Word made flesh its significance, its purpose, its unity, and its integrity.[80]

Brownson called the teleological order of grace "palingensis,"[81] the creative reorientation of sinful creation back to its creator through the action of supernatural grace. The grace of the incarnation creates "theandric[82] life," the initial, supernatural union of the divine and human which culminates in perfect union with God in the next life. The gift of the Spirit communicates theandric life to the redeemed. In his use of the term "theandric," Brownson remained well within the pale of Catholic orthodoxy. Neither in the incarnation nor in the gracing of humanity do the divine and human blend into some fictive monophysitic reality. The orders of nature and of grace remain distinct but intimately related, since grace enables nature to achieve supernaturally the end for which God created it in the first place.

---

[79] Ibid., 4:399. For an earlier formulation of Brownson's proof of God's existence see ibid., 1:253–74.

[80] Ibid., 2:281–2. See also Thomas R. Ryan, "Orestes Brownson on the Reading of Scripture," *Homiletic and Pastoral Review* 81 (1981) 31–42.

[81] Brownson, *The Works of Orestes A. Brownson*, 12:523, 573.

[82] Ibid., 12:484.

Moreover, Brownson insisted on the communal character of theandric life. The shared living of theandric life gives the Church its concrete, sensible, sacramental configuration, its shared appropriation of the graced reality made visible in the incarnate Word. The teaching authority of the Church functions constructively in the mediation of shared theandric life by ensuring the Church's corporate fidelity to the revelation it has received. Religious authority does this by instructing supernatural faith about the reality, the object, which it grasps. Brownson believed that only authoritative handing on of a historical revelation had the capacity to provide contemporary faith with an object. Moreover, since Brownson believed that the human mind can only grasp transcendent reality in an embodied object, he also believed that only the authoritative handing on of Christian revelation made faith possible. Additionally, the intensive living of the gospel grounds the Church's missionary expansion, its communication both of divine revelation and of the effects of redemptive grace, to the rest of humanity.[83]

Brownson the convert had harsh things to say about the Protestant tradition on which he had turned his back by becoming a Catholic.[84] His polemics ordinarily lacked the irenic, conciliatory tone of the Second Vatican Council. However, his criticism of Protestantism had speculative motives. As we have seen, American Enlightenment thinkers tended to portray themselves as carrying to its logical conclusion the religious reforms begun in the Protestant Reformation. At the beginning of the nineteenth century, both Unitarianism and Universalism saw themselves as expressions of Protestant Christianity. Brownson took both groups at their word and found a logic in their claims. He believed that the Protestant principle of private interpretation of the Bible, and therefore of Christian revelation, led logically to Protestant "inner light" piety. He also believed that the attempt to found Christian faith on such an individualistic, subjectivistic basis could only result in the fragmentation of the Church into the warring sects whose existence and scandal had in part motivated Enlightenment religion. The relational character of reality gave to the graced order of palingenesis an inherently social, communal, ecclesial character. Consent to grace required therefore consent to a community of grace which mediates salvation historically. Since communities require a social

---

[83] Ibid., 3:4–16, 51–115, 129–46, 304–19, 396–405, 442–57, 510–8, 529–31; 5:180–205; 10:545–8.

[84] In 1873 Brownson wrote: "We know nothing more reprehensible than the namby-pambyism babbled by sentimental Catholics about the good faith of 'our separated brethren'" (*Works*, 8:455). See Thomas Ryan, "Brownson's Technique in Apologetics," *American Ecclesiastical Review* 117 (1948) 12–22; Thomas Ryan, "Brownson on Salvation and the Church," *American Ecclesiastical Review* 117 (1947) 117–24.

principle of order, authentic Christian faith requires consent to legitimate ecclesiastical authority.[85]

V

The American Enlightenment, as we have seen, both absorbed and manipulated the millenarian hopes of the American people which the first Great Awakening had helped generate. The leaders of the American revolution taught the citizens of the emerging new republic to believe that the scouring of monarchy from the new world not only completed the work of the Protestant reformation but that the purgation of the land would usher in an era of unparalleled peace and prosperity. Enlightenment belief in the essential innocence of human nature inspired hope in unlimited human perfectibility. An Enlightenment pundit like Elihu Palmer saw in the future of the United States the ultimate triumph of Reason and technology.

Prior to his conversion, Brownson had resonated to such secular millenarianism. He believed in human innocence and in unlimited human perfectibility. He professed himself a Jeffersonian humanitarian.

But the "hard cider" campaign of 1840 had brought all these naive hopes for the nation crashing to the ground. The rediscovery of human fallenness set Brownson's feet on a path which led him into Roman Catholicism. Brownson the convert did not, however, abandon altogether his millenarian hopes for the United States; but after his conversion he eventually grounded those hopes not in the self-sufficiency of human nature, but in the working of divine grace. As the mature Brownson pondered the destiny of the American republic, his belief in palingenesis, in the graced return of humanity to God, expanded to include the United States within the sweep of salvation history. Brownson broadened his theory of providential men to embrace the providential destinies of nations. The rise and fall of nations, he now believed, reflected God's saving, providential wisdom. One needed, then, to discern the contribution which a providential God had called the United States to make to the graced return of humanity to God.

Brownson's mature account of the destiny of the American republic also responded to momentous historical events. Prior to the Civil War Brownson had supported the cause of states' rights. The war itself had convinced him of the error of his ways. Indeed the war, which took the life of two of his sons, caused him to believe that the survival of the American political experiment required a rethinking of the individualistic specula-

[85] Brownson, *The Works of Orestes A. Brownson*, 6:116–42, 192–218, 230–4; 7:260–97, 575, 589–97.

tive foundations of republican government in the United States. He sought to lay those foundations in *The American Republic.*[86]

In the opening pages of *The American Republic,* Brownson voiced his muted millenarian hopes for the American nation. "The United States, or the American people, has," he wrote, "a mission, and is chosen of God for the realization of a great idea."[87] Brownson believed that the destiny which God had assigned providentially to the United States surpassed in its importance the destiny of both Greece and Rome. The Greeks excelled in art, science, and philosophy; the Romans in the state, law, and jurisprudence. God, however, had called the United States to embody "the sovereignty of the people without social despotism, and individual freedom without anarchy."[88]

Properly understood, Brownson's *The American Republic* translated into a Catholic idiom Cotton Mather's *Magnalia Christi Americana.* Both books pondered the role which God has providentially assigned to the American people. Mather celebrated the triumph of the Protestant errand into the wilderness. Brownson integrated the history of the United States into his eschatological vision of palingenesis.

The universal scope of divine providence exorcized any stridently chauvinistic tendencies from Brownson's vision of the nation's future. In Brownson's view of salvation history, God calls every nation providentially to accomplish some task, to make some contribution to the evolution of the human race. Moreover, because each nation derives its own unique providential constitution historically from God, the social institutions and forms of government of one nation might not apply to the historical situation and destiny of another nation.[89]

Still, Brownson argued that the providential origin and constitution of the United States embodied a unique kind of call. A providential God had summoned the United States into being so that it could embody in the history of the race "the dialectic union of authority and liberty, of the natural rights of man and those of society." Greece and Rome had exalted the rights of the state over the rights of the individual; other modern republics exalt the rights of the individual to the detriment of the state. "The American republic has been instituted by Providence to realize the freedom of each with advantage to the other."[90]

[86] See Leonard Gilhooley, "Brownson, the American Idea, and the Early Civil War," *No Other Allegiance,* 125–41; Maurice A. Fitzmaurice, "Brownson's Search for the Kingdom of God: The Social Thought of an American Radical," *Review of Politics* 16 (1954) 22–36; Stanley J. Parry, "Premises of Brownson's Political Theory," *Review of Politics* 16 (1954) 194–211.

[87] Brownson, *The Works of Orestes A. Brownson,* 18:8.

[88] Ibid.

[89] Ibid., 18:74–113.

[90] Ibid., 18:8.

From the beginning, Brownson situated his treatise on government in the United States in a theological and historical context. Brownson endorsed a biblical theology of salvation history as the only adequate context for understanding the historical evolution of human institutions. A divine providence presides over the rise and fall of nations. Within that providence, each nation makes a unique contribution to the collective wisdom of the race. Moreover, because God functions as the ultimate ground of all authority, one must read the history of every nation, including that of the United States, through a theological lens.

Brownson also recognized the philosophical flimsiness of the social contract theory which had inspired the nation's founding fathers. In addition, the Civil War had dramatized for him the contradictions latent in a Federalist interpretation of the national constitution. In *The Federalist* Alexander Hamilton had presented the creation of the national government as the act of a single, sovereign people; James Madison had portrayed it as a contract among sovereign states. Prior to the Civil War Brownson had favored Madison over Hamilton, but the tragedy of secession and of bloody civil strife had convinced him of the error of his ways. *The American Republic* argued equivalently that Hamilton, not Madison, had correctly interpreted the providential constitution of the United States and had therefore correctly interpreted its written constitution.

Brownson insisted that social contract theory offered a woefully inadequate account of the nature and origin of government. It portrayed the origin of government as the work of atomic individuals acting in their own individual self-interest. Brownson replaced the atomic individualism of social contract theory with his own philosophy and theology of communion. *Ens creat existentias.* Humanity and indeed all of creation exists only by communion with God's creative act. Communion with God and with other persons defines, then, the providential destiny of the human race. The inherently social character of human nature makes government necessary.

Hobbes, therefore, erred when he attributed the origins of government to human corruption and fallenness. The organic interdependence of humans upon one another and upon God would have made government inevitable even if humanity had never sinned. Human governments imitate God's own providential governance of the universe. Human governments, which in the end derive their authority ultimately from God, must seek the same ends as does a providential deity: both the protection of individual liberty and its dedication to the achievement of the common good of all citizens. The punitive acts of government must seek the same positive ends.[91]

---

[91] Ibid., 18:13–14.

The individualism at the basis of social contract theory teaches one to suspect government as a necessary evil. In fact, a government which achieves its providential purpose exemplifies a great good. Good government inculcates the corporate virtue of loyalty. Americans, schooled on the individualistic fallacies of social contract theory, tend to view government with hostility and suspicion. The loyalty which good government inculcates, however, endows a people with moral nobility and with a goodness and generosity which make any corporate task possible. Indeed, Brownson regarded the corporate loyalty which good government commands as the natural, human raw material which supernatural grace transforms into charity.[92]

A sound political theory must justify the right of government to govern, that is, to direct the will of the governed to ends which simultaneously protect personal liberty and ensure the common good. Governments which violate personal liberty or which sacrifice the common good to individual or corporate vested interests thereby forfeit their right to govern.[93]

Brownson began his justification of government's right to govern by refuting inadequate theories of government. He believed that patriarchal government exemplified the most ancient form of government. In *patriarchal societies* authority has a personal, not a territorial, character. Territorial authority arises with the emergence of nation states. Barbaric states mistake territorial for personal authority and inevitably end in despotism.[94] Theories of the divine right of kings commit a similar blunder by failing to recognize that only a sovereign people exercises the corporate right under God to create and to depose governments.[95]

Social contract theory errs in a different direction. It opposes dualistically the state of nature to society. In the process, it makes social structures purely artificial and deprives them of their real foundation in the inherently social nature of the human. Social contract theory propagates the false idea that government can only bind those who freely enter into the contract which creates a government. As a consequence, what one generation does has no power to bind succeeding generations, and under such individualistic presuppositions society dissolves unless its members constantly renew the contract which alone creates their social communion. In fact, Brownson saw that human society has more organic foundations than the arbitrary decisions of atomic individuals.[96]

---

[92] Ibid., 18:16–17.
[93] Ibid., 18:17–18.
[94] Ibid., 18:18–26.
[95] Ibid., 18:54–61.
[96] Ibid., 18:27–39.

Brownson also rejected the notion that nature alone gives rise spontaneously to government. While Brownson rejected the Augustinian doctrine of natural depravity, he argued that human nature left to itself generates both good and evil impulses. However, if one invokes reason in order to curb human evil impulses, then, by the principle *"ens creat existentias,"* one invokes more than just reason. Reason emerges within nature as a subjective reality, but as soon as reason grasps the universal principles of natural law it loses both its purely natural status as well as its subjective character through its objective grasp of ideal, eternal, divine verities.[97]

A people can, then, function as the author of government only insofar as they derive the moral right to govern from God, the ultimate ground of all morality. National consensus alone has no ethical binding force, for nations can and do consent to moral evil. Nor can territory alone explain the origins of government, because the people define the territory, not the territory the people. Government grounded in ethical good also excludes both despotism and individualism, since both institutions violate fundamental personal rights.

Humanity experiences three kinds of communion: religious, social, and physical. Each form of communion gives rise to a different kind of institution. Human communion with God creates religious institutions. Social communion with other persons creates the state. Physical communion creates property. Moreover, since each person derives life directly from God *(ens creat existentias)*, personal rights have a more fundamental character than social rights. As a consequence, both society and government must hold all personal rights inviolable.[98]

Brownson summed up his argument in the following terms:

> The right of government to govern, or political authority, is derived by the collective people of society from God through the law of nature. Rulers hold from God through the people or nation, and the people or nation hold from God through the natural law. . . . Those who assert the origin of government in nature are right, so far as they derive it from God through the law of nature, and are wrong only when they understand by the law of nature the physical force or forces of nature, which are not laws in the primary and proper sense of the term. The law of nature is not the order or rule of the divine action in nature which is rightfully called providence, but is, as has been said, law in its proper and primary sense, ordained by the Author of nature, as its sovereign and supreme Lawgiver, and binds all of his creatures who are endowed with reason and free-will, and is called natural, because promulgated through reason common to all men. . . . The knowledge of natural

---

[97] Ibid., 18:53–9.
[98] Ibid., 18:41–7.

law has been transmitted from Adam to us through two channels—reason, which is in every man and in immediate relations with the Creator, and the traditions of the primitive instruction embodied in language and what the Romans call *jus gentium,* or law common to all civilized nations.[99]

Moreover, political sovereignty, or the right to govern, belongs to a people collectively, not personally or individually. As a consequence, the right to property, which exemplifies a natural, personal right, confers no right to govern. "The rich have in their riches advantages enough over the poor, without receiving from the state any additional advantage."[100]

Brownson's mature political theory distinguished, then, between the historical constitution of a state or nation, on the one hand, and of its government, on the other. God first constitutes the nation providentially, then the nation constitutes its government legally in a way which reflects its providential constitution by God. Moreover, as a nation develops under the providence of God it can alter its legal constitution by deliberate, corporate choices which reflect that providential development. The sovereign power of a nation to act presupposes its prior political and legal self-organization, but legal self-constitution cannot occur authoritatively until God constitutes the nation providentially.

Brownson recognized seven principal ways in which God has in fact providentially constituted a nation or people: (1) by the union of families into a tribe; (2) by the union of tribes into a nation; (3) by the migration of families, tribes, or nations; (4) by colonization; (5) by war and conquest; (6) by revolution; and (7) by the intermingling of conquerors and conquered.[101] The tribe exemplifies an inadequately developed state.

The natural, providential constitution of a state creates the state really, ontologically, historically, and naturally. "The providential constitution is, in fact, that with which the nation is born, and is, as long as the nation exists, the real living and efficient constitution of the state."[102] In other words, divinely guided historical events endow a people with the moral right under God to create the legal structures of government. The attempt of Europeans to found a state on political theories alone rather than on providential events accounted in Brownson's mind for political instability in nations like nineteenth-century France.[103]

Moreover, Brownson distinguished the natural, providential constitution of states from the graced, "palingenesiac" character of Christian social

[99] Ibid., 18:72.
[100] Ibid.
[101] Ibid., 18:74–80.
[102] Ibid.
[103] Ibid., 18:80–7.

order. "In the Christian order, nothing is by hereditary descent, but every thing is by election of grace."[104] Christian social order roots itself in the incarnation of the Son of God, which occurred in the fullness of time.

The events which found a nation define its fundamental corporate identity. "All the possibilities of the national constitution are given organically in the birth of the nation as all the possibilities of mankind are given in the first man."[105] Although the nation as sovereign has the freedom to constitute any government it chooses, it cannot adopt an essentially immoral form of government, like despotism. All moral forms of government in Brownson's view have a republican character. Still, specific legal constitutions must correspond to the providential events which sanction them. As a consequence, one cannot assume that one can export to any other nation the specific republican system adopted by the United States.[106]

In the case of the United States, Brownson argued that from the beginning the American people existed as a single people, not as several independent states. If the nation had existed as a confederation of sovereign states then the secession of the southern states belonged to them by incontestable right, even if one contested the wisdom of secession. In the political order the providential constitution of the nation under God precedes and grounds any legal constitution. From the beginning, however, the colonies acted in union. The English colonies did not declare their independence from England separately and one by one. Instead, they severed ties with the mother country by a single corporate declaration of independence. In addition, prior to their declaration of independence, the colonies, while inchoate states, never enjoyed the full powers of national sovereignty. They belonged to England and obeyed English common law. While the old Articles of Confederation did assume the sovereignty of the individual states, the Constitutional Convention correctly rejected the Articles of Confederation because they did not correspond to the providential constitution of the nation.[107]

The providential constitution of the United States requires, then, that sovereignty belongs to the people as a whole, not to the individual states. If the states in fact went into the Constitutional Convention as sovereign states, as John Calhoun had argued, then they left the convention as sovereign states. In fact, providence constituted the American people one sovereign people, existing in different colonial communities. The Constitutional Convention made the corporate will of that people con-

[104] Ibid., 18:80.
[105] Ibid., 18:88.
[106] Ibid., 18:88–97.
[107] Ibid., 18:100–13.

crete. Charles Sumner had the right of it, then, when he had proclaimed state secession state suicide.

The system of the division of powers distinguishes government in the United States from all preceding national constitutions. The federal constitution deliberately set out to preserve national unity and consciously avoided pitting regions of the country against one another. It also coordinated federal and state authority within a single national governmental system.[108] As we shall see, Brownson would argue for the compatibility of the United States Constitution with fundamental Catholic "principles."

Brownson concluded that the southern states had in fact not seceded but rebelled. None of the states had ceded their national sovereignty by joining the national union. Quite the contrary, the creation of the national union endowed the states with corporate national sovereignty and identity. By seceding, then, the Confederate states each committed political suicide. After the war, the former southern states enjoyed the legal status of territories capable of readmission into the federal union. These vanquished territories ought to have had the opportunity to re-enter the union and remain there without rancor or vengeance.

As Brownson saw it, the Civil War pitted a federal, territorial democracy against an individualistic, Jeffersonian democracy. The defeat of democratic individualism faced the nation as a whole with the need for national reconstruction. True reconstruction in the secessionist south must result from the collaborative work of the American people as a whole.[109]

In Brownson's eyes the work of reconstruction posed both political and religious challenges. The American political system blended elements from an individualistic British system of government and a federal, Roman system of government. Individualism had inspired both the southern slave holder and the northern abolitionist. The slave holders espoused an individualistic understanding of states' rights as a justification for secession. Brownson supported the abolition of slavery, but he deplored the principles on which the abolitionists demanded its abolition. The abolitionists, whom Brownson denounced as barbarians, refused to recognize the territorial rights of the southern states, individual rights, and both state and civil authority. As a consequence, the northern victory had undone the political presuppositions of both abolitionist and slave holder. The war had secured a victory for national union and in the process had vindicated Hamiltonian federalism.[110]

[108] Ibid., 18:125–42.

[109] Ibid., 18:161–92; Leonard Gilhooley, "Brownson, The American Idea, and the Early Civil War," *No Other Allegiance*, 125–41.

[110] Brownson, *The Works of Orestes A. Brownson,* 18:177–88.

In the wake of national civil strife, Brownson believed that the American people faced the challenge of reconciling individualism and federalism within their legal system. He urged the nation in dealing with this political challenge

> to eliminate the barbarous elements retained by the Roman constitution, and specially to realize that philosophical division of the powers of government which distinguishes it from both imperial and democratic centrism, on the one hand, and, on the other, from the checks and balances or organized antagonisms which seek to preserve liberty by obstructing the exercise of power.[111]

In other words, the American system of checks and balances defanged the despotism inherent in a tyrannical Roman federalism. At the same time, the providential and legal constitution of the United States as a nation both vindicated federal authority and countered individualistic efforts to subvert that authority.

However, the fact that God alone ultimately sanctions the exercise of political authority means that national reconstruction would also have a religious dimension to it. Moreover, within the work of national reconstruction Brownson discerned special possibilities and responsibilities for the Catholic Church. During the years prior to the Civil War, Brownson had wrestled with Enlightenment faith in America's predestined progress. He realized that this faith, which he had naively endorsed prior to his conversion, rested on false presuppositions, for it sprang from belief in human innocence while in fact humanity had fallen from divine grace and languished in a state of corporate and personal sinfulness. Brownson's rediscovery of the doctrine of original sin in its Catholic formulation caused him, for a time, to despair of human progress. By the 1850s, however, he had begun to hope that what human nature could never accomplish by itself, especially not in its fallen, sinful state, divine grace could accomplish. In other words, despite original sin one could continue to hope in human progress as long as one grounded that hope in a supernaturally graced palingenesis.[112]

As Brownson pondered God's providential purpose in guiding the history of the United States, he viewed the presence of a significant Catholic population in post–Civil War America as clearly providential. Brownson's epistemology and metaphysics required him to regard religion and politics

---

[111] Ibid., 1:207; see also 199–207.
[112] See Leonard Gilhooley, *Contradiction and Dilemma: Orestes Brownson and the American Idea* (New York: Fordham University Press, 1972); Peter J. Stanlis, "Orestes Brownson's *The American Republic* Today," *No Other Allegiance,* 142–62.

as inseparable. If the cosmos proceeds by God through creation and if all persons derive their self-awareness from God *(ens creat existentias)*, then created dependence on God unifies the entire creation. "The created universe is a dialectic whole distinct but inseparable from its Creator, and all its parts cohere and are essential to one another."[113] Conformity to the divine creator's will measures, then, the morality of all natural human institutions, including human political institutions. Moreover, divine creativity culminates in the incarnation, in the creation of the divine Word's humanity, and the incarnation begins the new creation, the graced process of palingenesis. Palingenesis, however, seeks to draw the entire human race into the orbit of God's saving plan.[114]

In Brownson's reading of the United States' salvation history, God had providentially chosen the United States in order to reveal to the world the true foundations of all government. The structures of government result not from some abstract political theory, but from God's providential constitution of a people as a nation. Legal constitutions have validity to the extent that they grasp and codify that providential, historical constitution. The Church too derives its structures from God's providential constitution. Grace begins objectively as a historical event and becomes subjective only when one recognizes the saving, supernatural character of the events which found the Church. Together, then, the incarnation and the sending of the Spirit create the Church and endow it with its essential, immutable structure. The state and the Church each result, then, from two different kinds of divine activity in history. The state results from God's creative providence, the Church from God's saving intervention in the history of a fallen race. The creation of a state gives a people its natural, national identity. The graced creation of the Church through the incarnation and Pentecost defines its supernatural, religious identity.[115]

The essential difference between the natural state and the supernatural Church justifies their institutional separation through the legal disestablishment of religion. The state has no authority over the Church and its dogmas, nor has the government of the United States the right to create a new church. While the Church may relate differently to different kinds of government, its own essential nature remains unaltered and unalterable. The separation of Church and state in the new world conforms, then, to "Catholic principles" because it implicitly recognizes the different constitution and purpose of the political order, on the one hand, and of the saving

[113] Brownson, *The Works of Orestes A. Brownson,* 18:208.
[114] Ibid.
[115] Ibid., 18:208–9. See William Peter, "Perceptions of Time in American Catholicism," *Journal of Religious Studies* 11 (1983) 1–13.

order of divine grace, on the other. Only in the new world, then, can the Church and the state relate to one another constructively and amicably.[116]

Sectarian forms of religion, Brownson believed, rest on individualistic principles which doom them to fragmentation and eventual disappearance, but a symbiotic relationship obtains between the United States' constitution and Catholicism. That relationship ensured that Catholicism would flourish in the political soil of the new world, and the saving presence of Catholicism within the United States' political system also provided graced grounds for hope in national "progress." The survival of the American political system depended, in Brownson's view, on the willingness of its citizens to respect legitimate authority, for without that respect society crumbles into chaos. The fact, then, that Catholics freely submitted to the moral and religious catechesis of Church authority made them better prepared than other citizens to participate in the processes of American republican government. Moral individualism had already made the American economy predatory, and it had generated huge corporations whose economic power could all too easily corrupt the democratic process and imperil the survival of republican democracy itself. However, if the national constitution successfully preserved the Catholic Church's freedom to fulfill its saving destiny, as indeed the constitution promised to do, then the Church would in turn begin through the normal processes of democracy to guide the United States to achieve the saving purposes for which God had providentially created it.[117]

---

[116] Brownson, *The Works of Orestes A. Brownson,* 18:210–6; 3:351–67. See also Richard M. Leliaert, "The Religious Significance of Democracy in the Thought of Orestes Brownson," *Review of Politics* 38 (1976) 3–26; Hugh Marshall, "Orestes Brownson: The Role of Catholics in America," *Catholics in America,* ed. Robert Trisco (Washington, D.C.: National Conference of Catholic Bishops, 1976); Thomas R. Ryan, "Orestes A. Brownson: Championship of the Church," *Homiletic and Pastoral Review* 82 (1982) 60–8; Thomas R. Ryan, "Orestes A. Brownson's Lectures in St. Louis, Missouri, 1852–1854," *American Catholic Historical Society of Philadelphia Record* 89 (1978) 45–59; Elwyn A. Smith, "The Fundamental Church-State Tradition in the Catholic Church in the United States," *Church History* 38 (1969) 486–505; Frederick E. McMahon, "Orestes Brownson on Church and State," *Theological Studies* 15 (1954) 175–228; Thomas McAvoy, "Orestes Brownson and American History," *Catholic Historical Review* 40 (1954) 257–68; Carl F. Krummel, "Catholicism, Americanism, Democracy, and Orestes Brownson," *American Quarterly* 5 (1953) 19–31.

[117] Brownson, *The Works of Orestes A. Brownson,* 18:212–43; see also 3:442–57, 509–18; 10:115–30; 11:120–33, 553–84; 12:2–101, 409–18, 465–95. See M. A. Fitzsimons, "Brownson's Search for the Kingdom of God: The Social Thought of an American Radical," *Review of Politics* 16 (1954) 22–36; S. J. Parry, "Premises of Brownson's Political Theory," *Review of Politics* 16 (1954) 194–211; A. I. Ladu, "Political Ideas of Orestes A. Brownson, Transcendentalist," *Philological Quarterly* 12 (1933) 280–9; Alvan S. Ryan, "Brownson's Significance for American Democracy," *No Other Allegiance,* 175–93; Hugh

VI

An old proverb has it that the third wave washes highest on the beach. Brownson rode the third wave of Transcendental thought, and without a doubt he carried the Transcendental critique of Enlightenment modernism much further than either Emerson or Parker. Moreover, Brownson succeeded in formulating a remarkably coherent philosophical and theological alternative to Enlightenment perceptions of reality. Indeed, Brownson's intellectual achievement so towers above that of any of his contemporaries that a contemporary student of his work must ask: How did he do it? What enabled him to see deeper and further than any of his peers?

Native genius certainly accounts for much of Brownson's intellectual accomplishment. Largely an autodidact like Franklin and Parker, Brownson possessed the dialectician's feeling for key issues in any given debate. His mind moved quickly to the heart of every argument and grasped both its strengths and limitations.

Still, native genius alone does not account for the extent of Brownson's achievement. As we have already seen, the American Enlightenment tended to see itself as a logical extension of the Protestant Reformation. Instead of criticizing the fundamental presuppositions of Protestant thought, Enlightenment thinkers in the new world preferred to turn the least tenable aspects of the Calvinist synthesis upon itself. Emerson and especially Parker both exemplified this tendency, and by mounting their critique of the Enlightenment largely on presuppositions compatible with the Enlightenment, both remained mired within the limits of a modernist problematic.

Emerson saw through Enlightenment nominalism, but he largely endorsed Enlightenment subjectivism. He not only acquiesced in Enlightenment individualism but even embellished it by giving classical expression to an American ethos of expressive individualism. Emerson's Platonic realism also led him to exacerbate the dualisms which mar Enlightenment modernism. Emersonian Transcendentalism inculcated a dualism of spirit and matter together with a corresponding operational and cosmic dualism. Emerson countered Enlightenment rationalism by claiming for imaginative, intuitive thinking a better, synthetic capacity to grasp the real than the linear, analytic logic of the sciences. In the end, however, Emerson failed to overcome the naturalism which Enlightenment Deism implicitly inculcated,

---

Marshall, *Orestes Brownson and the American Republic: An Historical Perspective* (Washington, D.C.: Catholic University of America Press, 1971); Gregory S. Butler, *In Search of the American Spirit: The Political Thought of Orestes Brownson* (Carbondale: Southern Illinois University Press, 1992).

with its distant God and all self-sufficient natural world. In Emersonian Transcendentalism, the Over Soul provided the ultimate, impersonal ground of natural creativity, but the frustrating coyness of Emerson's Over Soul invited skeptical disbelief.

Parker showed even less inclination to criticize the presuppositions of Enlightenment modernism than Emerson did. In fact, Parker's Transcendental doctrine of intuition transformed Enlightenment modernism into fundamentalism by endowing it with an allegedly objective self-evidence grounded entirely within human subjectivity.

Brownson saw through the Enlightenment with greater clarity and depth than either Emerson or Parker in part because his formulation of a Transcendental theory of intuition coincided with his conversion to Catholicism. More than one Brownson critic has tended to portray Brownson the convert as an intellectual conformist; but the book *The Convert* gives the lie to that interpretation. In *The Convert* Brownson declared his intellectual independence as a Catholic lay intellectual. Moreover, his writings during and after his conversion bear ample testimony to his intellectual independence and creativity.

Brownson found in Catholicism a coherent way of viewing reality which offered him a credible alternative to Enlightenment modernism, but Brownson's Catholicism alone does not account for his critique of Enlightenment thinking. Brownson lived for ideas, and throughout his life clung passionately to the truth as he perceived it. His very willingness to adopt and then discard positions testifies eloquently to the fact that he valued truth more than his own thoughts. It seems unlikely, then, that Brownson would have converted to Catholicism unless he could have made sense of Catholic perceptions of the real. As we have already seen, Brownson's study of Pierre Leroux showed him initially how to replace a Protestant, dialectical imagination with a Catholic, analogical imagination. Aristotle helped reconcile him to civil and ecclesiastical authority, and his subsequent critical appropriation of the thought of Vincenzo Gioberti allowed him to develop further the theological implications of the dynamic vitalism which he derived from Leroux. In other words, the unique, original, philosophical, and theological synthesis with which Brownson interpreted the message of Catholicism combined with his native genius in order to allow him to name with remarkable clarity most of the contradictions propounded by Enlightenment modernism. That synthesis also enabled him to formulate an impressive philosophical and theological alternative to modernist thinking.

To the nominalism of Enlightenment modernism, Brownson opposed an incarnational Platonic realism which found cognitive grasp of divine, eternal verities mediated by concrete, historical realities. Enlightenment nominalism endorsed a di-polar construct of human experience which reduces knowing to the subjective interrelation of concrete percepts and abstract concepts. To this di-polar version of cognition Brownson opposed a triadic account both of human knowing and of the object of knowledge. Enlightenment epistemology rooted itself in British empiricism and therefore espoused a cognitive atomism, for in British empiricism the building blocks of cognition consist of atomic ideas unrelated to one another until the mind creates those relationships. Brownson replaced conceptual atomism with a thoroughly relational account of human knowing.

Brownson also repudiated other forms of Enlightenment dualism. Brownson's metaphysical vitalism, which he derived in part from Leroux, taught him to replace a spirit-matter dualism with the integrating, synthetic category of life. His vitalism led him to affirm the organic interconnectedness of things, and, as a consequence, he replaced the social dualism which subtends Enlightenment contract theory with a philosophy of social communion. By invoking Gioberti's formula *ens creat existentias,* Brownson extended the concept of communion theologically to include the relationship between creatures and their creator. In Brownson's communal, incarnational Transcendentalism, all finite reality exists through communion with its creator. Finally, Brownson's formula of the subject replaced operational dualism with a descriptive analysis of human cognition which roots itself initially in sensation but expands in a continuum of feeling to include other forms of knowing.

Not only did Brownson's thoroughly relational vitalism enable him to overcome the multiple dualisms inherent in modernist thinking, but it also mediated his appropriation of the Catholic analogical imagination. As we have seen, the dualistic patterns of thought which classical Protestantism imbibed from a systematizing Augustinianism endowed it with a strong affinity for imagining reality in dialectical, either-or terms. The analogical imagination, by contrast, perceives reality relationally and synthetically. It seeks for the inclusive vision which overcomes indefensible dualisms. Leroux and Gioberti helped Brownson to understand what it means to imagine both experience and reality in analogical rather than in dialectical terms, but Brownson put their lessons to creative use in his theology of the incarnation. In Brownson's universe, the new creation that the incarnation begins grounds palingenesis, or the graced re-creation of the natural world which reorients it to the end for which God created it in the first place: union with the deity.

Brownson's relational incarnationalism also enabled him to overcome the false option which both classical Calvinism and Enlightenment rationalism posed between nature and grace, faith and reason. The Catholic Brownson saw that grace does not compete with nature but crowns and perfects it by elevating it to a new level of operation. Brownson the convert rediscovered original sin, but in its Catholic, Tridentine formulation, which eschewed the Calvinist doctrine of total human depravity. That rediscovery led him to faith in an incarnate redeemer and in Catholic sacramentalism. His epistemological conviction that one grasps eternal, divine truth only in the concrete and sensible gave a philosophical rationale to his newfound sacramental faith in God made flesh. In an analogous manner, his relational vitalism accorded well with the continuities which as a convert he discovered between natural and supernatural life. After his conversion Brownson's anti-Protestant rhetoric sometimes ran to extremes, but it targeted primarily the dualistic contradictions which he had discovered at the basis both of his own Protestant faith and of his early Enlightenment rationalism. In my judgment, those dualisms deserve rejection.

As impressive as Brownson's intellectual achievement remains, it nevertheless labored under some serious philosophical deficiencies. Brownson's epistemology failed to give an adequate account of either rational or deliberative thinking. By "Reason" Brownson meant the object of imaginative intuition, not logical inferential thinking. Brownson's formula of the subject also reduced the deliberations of the conscience hastily to a dimension of memory.

Brownson's thought took the critical use of history more seriously than any of the other American Transcendentalists. The idea of providence informed his understanding of historical development; and the providential development of history undergirded his political philosophy. His theology of palingenesis enabled him to re-incorporate into his understanding of history a supernaturally qualified endorsement of the idea of progress. Nevertheless, Brownson's static, Platonic essentialism prevented him finally from dealing adequately with the reality of historical development.

Brownson's debate with John Henry Newman over the development of doctrine perhaps best illustrates this deficiency in Brownson's thought. Brownson perceived Newman's theory of doctrinal development as "anti-Christian." He denounced it as a novelty which no Catholic theologian had ever held. In fact, Brownson argued, both divine revelation and the nature of the Church remain essentially fixed and unchangeable. Brownson put it this way:

> The church of God never varies, and the only variation a Catholic can concede in Christian doctrine is the greater clearness and distinctness as to what it is not, which results from presenting it so as explicitly to condemn novel errors as they arise; which is no variation in the substance or in the form of the

doctrine, and at most only a variation in the expression or mode of presenting it as the contradictory of error. The variation is apparent, not real. . . .[118]

So heterodox did Brownson judge Newman's notion of the historical development of doctrine that he urged the exclusion of his essay from every Catholic library.[119] Brownson faulted Newman for confusing doctrine with theology and with discipline. He accused him of confusing a divine revelation mediated by events and by authoritative Church teaching with a mere idea. In the end, Brownson ruled out categorically any possibility of development in the content of divine revelation.[120]

Even Homer nods. The fact, then, that Brownson failed finally to overcome adequately all the questionable aspects of Enlightenment modernism should not obscure the scope of what he actually achieved. As we have seen, Brownson's synthetic philosophy and theology brought American thought to the threshold of philosophical pragmatism. Like C. S. Peirce, Brownson repudiated nominalism and endorsed a triadic construct of both experience and reality. He advanced the Transcendental critique of Enlightenment thinking further than any of his contemporary Transcendentalists. His dynamic vitalism offered a relational construct of knowledge and its object which overcame the dualism, individualism, rationalism, and subjectivism of modernist thinking.

As for Brownson himself, he remained an intellectual outsider throughout his life. Both he and Parker never really belonged to the inner circle of the Transcendentalist movement. Brownson's early political radicalism alienated conservative Boston society.[121] His conversion to Catholicism rendered him a *persona non grata* in waspish America. His intellectual independence as a Catholic left him intellectually marginalized in an immigrant Church. Contentious and argumentative, his rhetoric rarely took a conciliatory tone. However, if during his own day Brownson

[118] Brownson, *The Works of Orestes A. Brownson,* 14:71. See also Thomas R. Ryan, "Orestes Brownson: Champion of Unmutilated Orthodoxy," *Homiletic and Pastoral Review* 77 (1976) 24–31; Allen Guttman, "From Brownson to Eliot: The Conservative Theory of Church and State," *American Quarterly* 17 (1965) 483–500.

[119] Brownson, *The Works of Orestes A. Brownson,* 14:73. See also Thomas R. Ryan, "Orestes Brownson and the Church of England," *Homiletic and Pastoral Review* 80 (1980) 57–63; Thomas R. Ryan, "Newman's Invitation to Orestes A. Brownson to Be Lecturer Extraordinary at the Catholic University of Ireland," *American Catholic Historical Society of Philadelphia Records* 85 (1974) 29–47.

[120] Brownson, *The Works of Orestes A. Brownson,* 14:3–139; see also Edwin Ryan, "Brownson and Newman," *The Catholic World* 52 (1915) 406.

[121] See C. C. Hollis, "Brownson on Native New England," *New England Quarterly* 40 (1967) 212–26; Gregory S. Butler, "Orestes Brownson and American Nativism," *Crisis* 14 (1966) 131–3.

produced no school of disciples, the fact that for a lifetime he managed to keep his many adversaries at bay speaks eloquently about the scope and power of his intellectual achievement.[122]

[122] For an assessment of Brownson's importance in the American Catholic tradition see John A. Coleman, "Vision and Praxis in American Theology," *No Other Allegiance,* 9–50; Thomas R. Ryan, *The Sailor's Snug Harbor: Studies in Brownson's Thought* (Westminster, Md.: Newman Book Shop, 1952); Mary Rose Gertrude Whalen, *Some Aspects of the Influence of Orestes A. Brownson on His Contemporaries* (Notre Dame, Ind.: University of Notre Dame Press, 1933); John P. Reidy, "Orestes Augustus Brownson: Conservative Mentor to Dissent," *American Benedictine Review* 21 (1970) 224–39.

PART THREE:
FROM TRANSCENDENTALISM TO PRAGMATISM

Chapter 9

FRANCIS ELLINGWOOD ABBOT: SCIENTIFIC THEISM

For to apprehend "a thing,"
or to understand "a relation,"
or to comprehend "a condition,"
necessarily involves and connotes the universals
in which these are units.

—Francis Ellingwood Abbot

F. E. Abbot, one of the strongest thinkers I ever encountered,
first showed me that there are just three [worlds];
the outer, the inner, and the logical.

—Charles Sanders Peirce

The Transcendentalist critique of Enlightenment modernism bore mixed results. Emersonian Transcendentalism repudiated the nominalism and rationalism of the Enlightenment. Emerson replaced Enlightenment nominalism with an idiosyncratic form of Neo-Platonic realism. The sage of Concord exalted the synthetic intuitions of the creative imagination over the plodding linear logic and objective discourse of positive science. The reluctant founder of Transcendentalism also sought to replace an Enlightenment morality of duty with one grounded in aesthetic experience. Theodore Parker developed a Transcendental theory of intuition which revised and systematized the subjectivistic claims of Enlightenment religion, but by claiming objectivity for the subjective intuition of the major tenets of Enlightenment religion Parker in the end reduced eighteenth-century Deism to a kind of religious fundamentalism. Brownson advanced the Transcendental attack on Enlightenment modernism further than either Parker or Emerson. He repudiated its dualism, its subjectivism, its nominalism, its insensitivity to history and tradition, its naive belief in human innocence and in the triumph of natural, technological reason, its social contract theory, and the social atomism on which that theory rested.

While they disagreed profoundly in their philosophical and religious beliefs, Emerson, Parker, and Brownson all agreed on one point: all three men looked to some form of intuitive thinking to provide the Ariadne's thread which would lead one out of the maze of Enlightenment rationalism. In the end, however, none of them provided a convincing philosophical justification for the claims which each made for intuitive cognition. Emerson's theory of intuition presupposed the self-evident givenness of an extremely questionable dualistic metaphysics without ever proving it, and his own philosophy of bias rendered personal accessibility to creative intuition thoroughly problematic. Parker claimed that the human mind possesses special faculties which exhibit the innate power of grasping within subjectivity the objective truth of religious and moral belief. Finally, however, Parker's claim left both religion and morality foundering on an epistemological contradiction: for how can pure subjectivity guarantee objective validity to anything? Parker appealed to the a priori structure of the mind in order to justify his epistemological claims, but he gave no convincing argument for taking those claims seriously. Brownson's theory of intuition rendered Platonic metaphysics incarnational by locating rational intuition of universals in the cognitive grasp of the physical and the concrete, but, like Emerson, he asserted dogmatically rather than proved the objective givenness of the eternal truths of reason. Moreover, as we have seen, the Platonic elements in his thought prevented him finally from dealing adequately with the historical development of human thought and insight.

Still, the Transcendentalists, especially Emerson and Brownson, correctly recognized the need not only to move philosophically beyond Enlightenment modernism but also to articulate a viable metaphysical, epistemological, ethical, and religious alternative to Enlightenment thinking. As a movement Transcendentalism succeeded only partially in both tasks, but two thinkers in the next generation of American intellectuals eventually picked up the fallen Transcendentalist banner. Both submitted the presuppositions of Enlightenment modernism to careful criticism. I refer, of course, to Francis Ellingwood Abbot and Charles Sanders Peirce.

Like the Transcendentalists, both men began their intellectual career by participating in a philosophical "club" similar to the Transcendental Club which gave birth to Romantic thinking in the United States during the first half of the nineteenth century. Peirce and Abbot both participated in the Metaphysical Club, which also included among its members William James and Chauncey Wright.

Among the participants in the Metaphysical Club, Wright, who defended a species of religiously agnostic, philosophical positivism, represented the refurbished voice of Enlightenment nominalism. Wright seems, moreover, to have functioned as the Metaphysical Club's speculative gadfly. His vigorous defense of a positivistic agnosticism helped inspire William James's doctrine of "the will to believe." It also convinced Peirce, for a time at least, to separate religious and scientific speculation. It prodded Abbot, who began and ended his career as a kind of Emersonian Transcendentalist, to reconcile his pantheistic religious creed with the claims of positive science.[1]

I

Francis Ellingwood Abbot dated his birth from 1836, the so-called *annus mirabilis* of New England Transcendentalism. His mother, Fanny Ellingwood Abbot, who bore him on November 6 of that memorable year, traced her lineage to Roger Conant, the founding father of Salem, Massachusetts. She inspired her son with a love of literature. His father, Joseph Hale Abbot, taught school in Boston. Sickly in his youth and the product of a stern family discipline, Francis developed a stammer as a child which plagued him until his college years.

[1] See Chauncey Wright, *Philosophical Discussions,* ed. Charles Eliot Norton (New York: H. Holt, 1877); *Philosophical Writings: Representative Selections,* ed. E. H. Madden (New York: Liberal Arts Press, 1958); *Letters of Chauncey Wright with Some Account of His Life,* ed. James Bradley Thayer (Cambridge, Mass.: J. Wilson, 1877); Edward Madden, *Chauncey Wright and the Foundations of Pragmatism* (Seattle: University of Washington Press, 1963); Edward Madden, "Chauncey Wright's Life and Work: Some New Material," *Journal of the History of Ideas* 15 (1954) 445–55; Edward Madden, "Chance and Counterfacts in Wright and Peirce," *Review of Metaphysics* 9 (1956) 420–32; "Wright, James, and Radical Empiricism," *Journal of Philosophy* 51 (1954) 868–74; E. H. Madden and M. C. Madden, "Chauncey Wright and the Logic of Pragmatism," *Philosophy of Science* 19 (1952) 325–32; D. W. Marcell, "John Fiske, Chauncey Wright and William James: A Dialogue in Progress," *Journal of American History* 56 (1970) 802–18; Gail Kennedy, "The Pragmatic Naturalism of Chauncey Wright," *Studies in the History of Ideas* (New York: Columbia University Press, 1935) 3:447–503; J. L. Blau, "Chauncey Wright: Radical Empiricist," *New England Quarterly* 19 (1946) 495–517; Borden Parke Bowne, "Chauncey Wright as a Philosopher," *New Englander* 37 (1878) 585–603; J. J. Chambliss, "Natural Selection and Utilitarian Ethics in Chauncey Wright," *American Quarterly* 12 (1960) 144–59; Robert Guiffrida Jr., "The Philosophical Thought of Chauncey Wright: Edward Madden's Contribution to Wright Scholarship," *Transactions of the Charles S. Peirce Society* 24 (1988) 33–64; "Chauncey Wright's Theory of Meaning," *Journal of the History of Philosophy* 14 (1978) 313–24.

At the Boston Latin School, young Francis produced academic work of high excellence. He studied as well with his brother Edwin, a baptized Swedenborgian. Under the tutelage of John Randall, a minor New England poet who befriended the lad, young Abbot discovered both poetry and philosophy. From Randall too he may have imbibed some of his theological skepticism.

Between 1855 and 1859 Abbot attended Harvard College, where he counted Charles Peirce among his fellow students. The year after his matriculation he accepted a teaching post in Concord. There he met his future wife, Katherine Fearing Loring. They married secretly in Nashua, New Hampshire, on August 3, 1859.

That same year Abbot entered Harvard Divinity School, where he enjoyed the reputation of a pious conservative. He left the Divinity School after only a year of studies for a teaching post in Meadville, Pennsylvania. There he began to develop an interest in science and in scientific method. He continued his study of theology at the Meadville Theological School. After graduating in 1863, he went for a short time to Detroit, and subsequently settled for a time in Dover, New Hampshire.

In 1864 he published two articles in the *North American Review:* "The Philosophy of Space and Time" and "The Conditioned and the Unconditioned." In the same year, as a result of these publications, he began corresponding with Chauncey Wright.

Once in the ministry, Abbot began to shed his earlier theological conservatism. As a divinity student he had held Parker suspect, but now Abbot found Parker's Transcendentalism more congenial. In his sermons Abbot began to challenge the need for Unitarian devotion either to the Bible or to the person of Jesus. In 1865 he tried unsuccessfully to liberalize the Unitarian Creed at the national Unitarian Conference in Syracuse, New York. He subsequently referred wryly to the incident as "The Battle of Syracuse," but his failure only confirmed him in his new theological radicalism.

In the following year he experienced a second defeat, this time an academic one: Harvard University turned down his application to their philosophy department. In 1867 Cornell University declined to include him on its faculty, despite enthusiastic letters of recommendation from Emerson, Wright, and others. In the same year he helped organize the Free Religious Association. Emerson graciously lent the association social respectability by accepting a lifetime honorary vice-presidency in the organization.

In 1868 Abbot's disgruntlement with organized Unitarianism reached a climax. He resigned his pastorate in Dover. At the urging of his liberal supporters in the parish, Abbot filed in court for the legal right to continue to use the parish facilities for his ministry. His case failed.

In 1869 he accepted a call to a parish in Toledo, Ohio, whose members assured him that his liberal views would serve him well among them. There he edited *The Index,* a progressive theological journal in which he published numerous tracts.[2]

In 1873 the Abbots moved to Shepherd Street in Cambridge, Massachusetts, where Abbot continued to edit *The Index.* Abbot's health began to deteriorate. He suffered from splitting headaches, nosebleeds, and dizzy spells.

In 1874 Abbot joined a "theology club" composed of Cambridge ministers. William James also invited him to join the Metaphysical Club, but initially Abbot attended the meetings only sporadically.

By the late 1870s Katherine's health showed a marked decline, and Abbot himself showed symptoms of overwork and nervous collapse. In 1880 a combination of deteriorating health and a growing passion for philosophy persuaded him to resign as editor of *The Index.* In 1882 he published an extended article in the London *Mind* entitled "Scientific Philosophy: A Theory of the Human Mind." It undertook a vigorous defense of philosophical realism against the prevailing nominalism of modern philosophical thinking.

In 1883 the Abbots built themselves a little cottage on Nonquitt Beach, where Abbot did much of his reflection and writing. In 1885 Abbot published his most influential work: *Scientific Theism.* It went into several editions, including a German one. Peirce read it with a considerable degree of approbation.[3]

In 1888 Abbot temporarily replaced Josiah Royce on the Harvard philosophical faculty. The following year Abbot published the substance of his Harvard lectures under the title *The Way Out of Agnosticism, or the Philosophy of Free Religion.* Royce panned Abbot's thought in print. In response, Abbot accused Royce of a libelous misrepresentation of his views.[4] Abbot's broadsides against Royce occasioned Mrs. Jack Gardner's wry epigram: "One should be sure of his own manners before attacking another man's morals."

Kate Abbot died in 1893. As in the case of Abbot's parents, the relationship between him and his wife had been marked by unhappiness and

[2] See Gardner Williams, "Francis Ellingwood Abbot: Free Religionist: The Toledo Episode, 1869–1873," *Northwest Ohio Quarterly* 20 (1948) 128–43.

[3] See D. D. O'Connor, "Peirce's Debt to F. E. Abbot," *Journal of the History of Ideas* 25 (1964) 543–64.

[4] Francis Ellingwood Abbot, *Professor Royce's Libel* (Boston: G. H. Ellis, 1891); Francis Ellingwood Abbot, *Is Not Harvard Responsible for the Conduct of Her Professors* (Boston: n.p., 1892); Creighton Peden, "The Abbot-Royce Controversy," *Religious Humanism* 24 (1990) 17–23.

some bitterness. Especially after Kate's death, Abbot experienced remorse at what he perceived as the failure of their marriage. The following year he resigned from the Free Religious Association, which he had helped organize. In the year his wife died Abbot had also begun work on a final systematic restatement of his philosophy. He called it *The Syllogistic Philosophy*. The dedication to the work read: "To the memory of my wife, in whose divine beauty of character, life, and soul I found the God I sought. Oct. 18, 1839: Oct. 23, 1893. She made home happy, and was all the world to her own." In 1903, his book finished, he wrote a simple suicide note and poisoned himself on his wife's grave on the anniversary of her death. *The Syllogistic Philosophy* appeared posthumously in 1906.[5]

II

As a Harvard Divinity student Abbot had quickly earned a reputation for pious conservatism, but once in the ministry he drifted into a wholly personal blend of "Parkerism" and "Emersonianism." He imitated Parker's flare for social activism and the "free religion" which he preached bore many of the traits of Parker's "absolute religion."[6] His theological liberalism also earned him the same kind of social ostracism in conservative Boston as had bedeviled both Parker and Brownson.

Emerson, however, exercised the deeper influence on Parker's early thought. In *The Index* he rhapsodized: "Ralph Waldo Emerson is the greatest legacy that God has yet bestowed on America . . . and this shall become more and more patent as our generations pass."[7] Indeed, Abbot looked upon Emerson as a prophetic figure in American history[8] and himself as the fulfillment of what Emerson foreshadowed. At the end of *Scientific Theism* he informed the reader that the scientific pantheism that his book argued and which he called "Free Religion" brought to its fulfillment the religious aspirations of the New England soul that Emerson had discerned and announced. Emerson had vainly sought to ground those religious aspirations in ecstatic intuition, but Abbot believed that *Scientific*

---

[5] Sydney E. Ahlstrom and Robert Bruce Mullin, *The Scientific Theist: A Life of Francis Ellingwood Abbot* (Macon, Ga.: Mercer University Press, 1987); Creighton Peden, *The Philosophy of Free Religion: Francis Ellingwood Abbot, 1896–1903* (New York: Peter Lang, 1992).

[6] See Stow Persons, *Free Religion: An American Faith* (New Haven, Conn.: Yale University Press, 1948).

[7] See Sydney Eckman Ahlstrom, "Francis Ellingwood Abbot: His Education and Active Career," 2 vols. (Ph.D. dissertation, Harvard University, 1952) 2:158.

[8] Francis Ellingwood Abbot, *The Way Out of Agnosticism or the Philosophy of Free Religion* (Boston: Little, Brown, & Co. 1890) 75.

Theism had demonstrated their compatibility with modern science.[9] Abbot's last public lecture, delivered on July 21, 1903, bore the celebratory title "Emerson, the Anti-Imperialist." Moreover, Abbot's *magnum opus, The Syllogistic Philosophy,* claimed to have demonstrated Emerson's belief that "moral law lies at the centre of nature, and mediates to the circumference." He hailed this pronouncement of Emerson's Delphic oracle as "scientifically true and ethically sublime."[10]

In his introduction to *The Syllogistic Philosophy* Abbot informed the reader that the book represented a lifetime of intellectual growth and reflection.[11] In fact, the basic tenets of his religious creed appeared in embryonic form in one of his *Index* tracts. The tract "Truths for the Times" reduced the substance of "liberal Christianity" to fifty basic affirmations which conflated Enlightenment religion with New England Transcendentalism. Like Parker and the American Deists, Abbot regarded religion as the product of natural human activity and of the human attempt to improve oneself and one's earthly lot.[12] With both Parker and Franklin, Abbot argued that since religion expresses the same humanity common to all persons on the earth, all religions share the same causal essence despite the different forms in which they express themselves historically. The elements common to all religions allegedly express the universal essence of religion.[13]

Abbot's Free Religion, like Parker's Absolute Religion, proclaimed itself the product of humanity's forward religious progress. Abbot viewed Christianity as a natural refinement of Judaism, Protestantism as a further historical refinement of Christianity, and "Free Religion" as the crown and glory of Protestantism.[14] The fifty theses in "Truths for the Times" included the following: "39. The great law of Free Religion is the still, small voice of the private soul. 40. The great peace of Free Religion is spiritual oneness with the infinite One." Proposition thirty-nine reproduced Parker; proposition forty, Emerson.[15]

The youthful Abbot also endorsed uncritically the religious prejudices of Transcendental religion, prejudices inherited from his Protestant and Enlightenment heritage. Abbot cavalierly equated "Christianity" with

[9] Francis Ellingwood Abbot, *Scientific Theism* (Boston: Little, Brown, & Co., 1885) 211–3.

[10] Francis Ellingwood Abbot, *The Syllogistic Philosophy, or Prolegomena to Science,* 2 vols. (Boston: Little, Brown & Co., 1906) 2:267.

[11] Ibid., 1:x–xi.

[12] Francis Ellingwood Abbot, "Truths for the Times," *Index Tract #1* (Toledo: Index Association, 1872) 1.

[13] Ibid.

[14] Ibid., 2–6.

[15] Ibid., 6.

Calvinistic belief in total human depravity and therefore dismissed it as dehumanizing. He viewed Christianity as fundamentally sectarian in its creed and therefore as insufficiently universal in its scope. Christianity had as a pre-philosophical religion, he announced, with historical inevitability to give way to rational religion. Abbot also deemed the Christian appeal to religious authority irreconcilable with reasonable religion. In other words, in contrast to Brownson the convert, Abbot began his theological career (as opposed to his philosophical career) by endorsing enthusiastically the dichotomizing world of the dialectical imagination from which he would only partially emancipate himself. Moreover, like other American Enlightenment thinkers, Abbot regarded the Free Religion which he proclaimed in the name of reason the authentic expression of Protestant Christianity.[16]

Abbot's Free Religion claimed the power to teach humanity to appreciate their natural freedom through the cultivation of a creative, Emersonian self-reliance. Like Emerson, Abbot believed in the organic interrelatedness of all things, but from the beginning he seems to have avoided the dualisms which bedeviled Emerson's religious vision. Free Religion teaches humans to regard nature as an organic whole which binds together all things and from whose all-comprehensive laws no one can escape. Immersion in nature gives one access to a share in the vital energy which inspires all human activity and creativity. Free Religion fosters the integration of all the powers of the human soul: conscience, affectivity, will, imagination, intellect. It promotes human solidarity and seeks to overcome all social divisions and barriers. It exhorts humanity to found a "Republic of Republics" with a common purpose and a common faith rooted in the universality of human nature. Abbot chose as the motto for his universal republic the American slogan *"E pluribus unum."*[17]

Abbot differed from Emerson principally in his unequivocal endorsement of the methods of positive science. Emerson, as we have seen, regarded imaginative intuition as a form of knowing superior to positive science in its scope and in its privileged, synthetic access to the truth. Abbot's Free Religion sought consciously to reconcile Emersonian Transcendentalism with scientific method. Abbot's conversion to the method of science coincided with the vogue of Spencerian evolutionary theory among the New England intelligentsia. He concluded that Transcendental religion must come to terms with evolutionary theory if it hoped to main-

---

[16] Ibid., 4–9. See also the following tracts by Abbot: "Christian Propagandism," "Impeachment of Christianity," "The God of Science," "Is Romanism Real Christianity?" and "A Study of Religion" (Toledo: Index Association, 1871–73); "The Catholic Peril in America," *Fortnightly Review* 19 (1876) 385–405.

[17] Abbot, "Truths for the Times," 5–15.

tain rational respectability. Moreover, before he met Chauncey Wright personally, Abbot engaged in a philosophical correspondence with New England's leading positivist beginning in 1864.[18] Abbot therefore set out to defend a form of Emersonian Transcendentalism from a double intellectual challenge: from the agnostic positivism defended by Wright and by others, on the one hand, and from the materialistic mechanism which he discovered at the basis of Spencerian evolutionary theory, on the other. These fundamental speculative concerns found a voice in two of his early articles.

In those articles, Abbot not only proclaimed scientific positivism compatible with religious belief, but he also insisted that any theology which fails to adopt a strictly positivistic, scientific methodology must abandon all claims to intellectual respectability. "Scientific methodology," he wrote, "must obtain in theology, if theology is to rank among real sciences."[19] If the physical sciences use scientific method to explain humanity's physical environment, then theology must use the same method in order to explain humanity's spiritual environment.[20] As for Spencer's mechanistic theory of evolution, Abbot faulted it for failing to recognize that not all natural laws function mechanistically. Organisms do not. The fact of organic evolution, therefore, forced Abbot's scientific religion to adopt a systematic philosophy of organism.[21]

III

In contrast to earlier Transcendentalists, who each defended an intuitionist theory of knowledge, Abbot's scientific theism began with a frontal attack on a Kantian doctrine of intuition. Abbot pronounced Kant a nominalist and rejected nominalism as indefensible. Peirce probably exerted some influence on Abbot on this point. Peirce boasted that he had espoused philosophical realism before he formulated his pragmatic maxim, and in 1909 Peirce also claimed to have led a discussion of scholastic realism at a meeting of the Metaphysical Club which Abbot attended. Peirce claimed that Abbot had profited from the presentation.

As we have seen above, in 1882 Abbot published an article in the London *Mind* entitled "Scientific Philosophy: A Theory of Human Knowl-

---

[18] Wright censured Abbot for defending "the position of a distinct faculty of supersensuous reason" in his article "The Philosophy of Space and Time." See James Bradley Thayer, ed., *Letters of Chauncey Wright,* 55–6.

[19] Francis Ellingwood Abbot, "Positivism in Theology," *Christian Examiner* 80 (1866) 259.

[20] Ibid., 248–51, 263–5.

[21] Francis Ellingwood Abbot, "Philosophical Biology," *North American Review* 107 (1868) 377–422.

edge." In it he rejected Kantian intuitionism as the inevitable logical outcome of a decadent medieval nominalism. Abbot also argued that only a modernized restatement of realistic philosophy could provide an adequate philosophical justification for the claims of scientific method. Abbot regarded the article significant enough to reprint it as an introduction to his book *Scientific Theism.*

In constructing his argument, Abbot defined "nominalism" as "the doctrine that universals, or terms denoting genera and species, correspond to nothing outside the mind." He distinguished two species of nominalism: the extreme nominalism of Roscellinus and the moderate nominalism of William of Occam. Extreme nominalism reduced the "universal" to a mere word and denied existence to universals either in things or in the mind. Moderate, or conceptual, nominalism allowed for the existence of universal concepts in the mind but denied that they have any substantive correlate in reality.[22]

Abbot censured Kantian epistemology as a species of conceptual nominalism because it derived universality exclusively from within human subjectivity and denied its presence in things-in-themselves. In Abbot's view, Kantianism refuted itself in its logical consequences, for Kant's denial of knowledge of the thing-in-itself led logically to idealism, that is, to the belief that in the end one knows only one's own ideas. Idealism in turn entailed solipsism. Solipsism, however, reduced nominalism to an absurdity.[23]

In its attempt to ground scientific knowledge, Kantianism ended by defending a position which contradicts the claims of science, which, in contrast to Kant, professes to offer an objective account of reality. The scientist does not investigate states of consciousness to which phenomena must conform but the laws of nature to which the human mind must conform. Abbot put the matter this way: "Nominalism teaches that things conform to cognition, not cognition to things; Scientific Realism teaches that cognition conforms to things, not things to cognition."[24]

With the medieval schoolmen, Abbot distinguished three kinds of universals: thoughts in the mind of God *(universalia ante rem)*, the essences of things *(universalia in re)*, and concepts in the human mind *(universalia post rem)*. Abbot's doctrine of relationism defended yet another position, that of *"universalia inter res* (universals among things)." Relationism taught that: "universals, or genera and species, are, *first,* objective relations of resemblance among objectively existing things; *sec-*

---

[22] Francis Ellingwood Abbot, *Scientific Philosophy: A Theory of Human Knowledge* (London: n.p., 1882) 461–2.

[23] Ibid., 463–6.

[24] Ibid., 466–7.

ondly, subjective concepts of these relations, determined in the mind by the relations themselves; and *thirdly,* names representative both of the relations and the concepts, and applicable alike to both."[25]

More specifically, relationism defends the following five "self-evident propositions":

> (1) Relations are absolutely inseparable from their terms. (2) The relations of things are absolutely inseparable from the things themselves. (3) The relations of things must exist where the things themselves are, whether objectively in the Cosmos or subjectively in the mind. (4) If things exist objectively, their relations must exist objectively; but if their relations are merely subjective, the things themselves must be merely subjective. (5) There is no logical alternative between affirming the objectivity of relations in and with that of things, and denying the objectivity of things in and with that of relations."

Abbot claimed, therefore, that his doctrine of relationism corrected the excesses both of nominalism and of scholastic realism. Relationism argued that:

> (1) . . . Extreme Realism was right in upholding the objectivity of universals, but wrong in classing them as independent and separable substances or things. (2) It shows that Moderate Realism was right in upholding the objectivity of universals, but wrong in making them inherent in individuals AS INDIVIDUALS *(in re)* rather than in individuals AS GROUPS *(inter res)*. Relations do not inhere in either of the related terms taken singly, but do inhere in all the terms taken collectively. (3) It shows that Extreme Nominalism was right in denying the objectivity of universals as substances or things (the great error of its opponent), and right in affirming the existence of universals as names; but wrong in denying their objectivity as relations and their subjectivity as concepts. (4) It shows that Moderate Nominalism or Conceptualism was right in denying the objectivity of universals as substances, and also right in affirming their subjectivity as concepts; but wrong in denying their objectivity as relations.[26]

In its broad outlines, Abbot's relationism converged with Brownson's "synthetic philosophy." For both men universals exist independently of thought; but for Abbot universals do not exemplify essences in individual things so much as the bond uniting classes of individual things. Moreover, Abbot made very different use of this doctrine of relations from Brownson. The latter used it as the foundation for his account of intuitive knowledge; Abbot invoked relationism as philosophical grounding for scientific method.

[25] Ibid., 476.
[26] Ibid., 477–8.

Abbot insisted that any theory of knowledge based on the method of science must defend the following doctrines. (1) Knowledge correlates in a dynamic way subject and object. (2) Knowledge has two sources of origin: the cosmos and the human mind. (3) These two sources of origin unite inseparably but distinguishably in cognitive experience. (4) Experience has, therefore, both an objective and a subjective side. (5) Both sides of experience depend on one another and both make a necessary contribution to knowing. (6) The objective side of experience requires the real existence of a known universe. (7) The subjective side of experience requires the real existence of a knowing mind. (8) Experience, whether sensitive or cognitive, exemplifies the mutual interaction of these two sources of knowledge. (9) Such an understanding of experience disproves the Kantian distinction between phenomenon and noumenon. (10) The human mind experiences "things in themselves" as partly known and partly unknown. (11) The mind knows things in their relations both phenomenally and noumenally. (11) The possibility of verifying discovered relationships in things offers a practical proof of the known, noumenal cosmos. In other words, Abbot concluded, all scientific thinking takes its stand, whether consciously or unconsciously, on the doctrine of relationism.[27]

Emersonian Transcendentalism had proclaimed the organic unity of nature, although the dualistic caste of Emerson's thought prevented him from giving a plausible account of that unity. Emerson had, however, grounded nature's organic unity in the existence of an infinite creative power at the heart of the cosmos. In *Scientific Theism* Abbot sought to shore up philosophically both of these fundamental Emersonian theses, as the aspiration which closes the book suggests: "May the hard-won thought of my little book be so clearly *truth* to your minds, that it may bring you renewed peace, serenity, and repose in the Infinite Soul of the All!"[28]

The method of science, Abbot argued in *Scientific Theism,* moves from observation to hypothesis and finally to positive verification. As he had argued in "Scientific Philosophy," the method presupposes real relations as the ground for the intelligibility of the cosmos. As Abbot put it, the pursuit of scientific method rests on the philosophical defense of *"objectively real relations among objectively real things."* In other words, the relation obtains in the universe independently of any conception of the human mind, but the mind knows of the relation's real existence only after having proved true the assertion of its reality.[29]

---

[27] Ibid., 484–90.
[28] Abbot, *Scientific Theism,* xiii.
[29] Ibid., 59–64.

Scientific thinking, therefore, has nothing to do with philosophical "phenomenism," which reduces the object of scientific investigation to a mere mental conception. This Kantian doctrine presupposes an indefensible nominalism. Any specific reality which science investigates exemplifies "a unitary system of closely correlated internal forces, and manifests itself by specific qualities, actions, or motions." The qualities, actions, and motions have a phenomenal, or describable, dimension to them, but they function as constitutive elements of the total, real, relational complex, or "thing," which science seeks to explain. The relational character of the "things" which science studies entails that these "things" constitute a complex set of cosmic relationships which we call "the Universe."

As the totality of cosmic relationships, the Universe exemplifies "the All-Thing." Only inclusive relational systems enjoy intelligibility. We experience disorder only with respect to an ordered set of relationships. As a consequence pure chaos cannot exist, since the experience of disorder presupposes some measure of order. Accordingly, nothing can enjoy intelligibility without existing, nothing can enjoy existence unless it also enjoys intelligibility, and nothing can enjoy both intelligibility and existence unless it possesses an immanent relational constitution. Finally, Abbot also argued that scientific relationism requires that "the infinite intelligibility of the universe, as the infinite, eternal, and self-existent All-Thing, lies in its possession of an infinite and immanent relational constitution." By metaphysical fiat, Abbot, following Emerson, called the "All-Thing" "Nature." In the process, he also presupposed the infinity of nature.[30]

Abbot's scientific theism next set out to prove that the infinite "All-Thing" must enjoy not only intelligibility but intelligence. Abbot argued that when one subjects intelligence to reflective analysis, it too reveals itself to consist of a system of relations. Abbot discovered three relational functions within intelligence: perceptive, conceptive, and creative. The mind *perceives* reality when things act upon the mind and thus force the mind to react upon itself as affected by things. Perception begins in sensuous intuitions, but sensed data acquire intelligibility only when the mind integrates them into a larger, more complex, causal relational structure. Perception culminates, therefore, in the identification of the particular "thing," or relational complex, under investigation. The perceptive function of the mind, therefore, entails its *conceptive* use. Conceptive thought grasps the dynamic, unified, relational structure which makes sense out of perceptual data. The conceptual grasp of the "thing" engages both imagination and intellectual thinking. Conceptual thinking endows the perceptual identification of the thing under investigation with explanatory clarity.

[30] Ibid., 119–33.

212 *From Transcendentalism to Pragmatism*

It reproduces in thought the relational complex which perception grasps more vaguely. The *creative* use of intelligence exhibits a teleological structure. Teleological thinking deals with ends and means. On analysis, however, an end exemplifies an ideal system of relations seeking realization at some future date, while a means exemplifies a complex relational system existing in the present and conducive to realizing an end.[31]

Abbot recognized two kinds of ends: egoistic and altruistic. Egoistic ends seek the expedient realization of the satisfaction of the one acting. Altruistic ends seek the ideal ends of truth, beauty, and goodness for their own sake. Altruistic creative action seeks justice or fidelity to the relational structure of the universe. Egoistic ends conflict with altruistic ends only when they seek to usurp the place of higher ends instead of seeking their place within the universal order of things. Understanding, not will, grounds the exercise of freedom through the perception of a variety of ends. We experience, therefore, different kinds of freedom. Intellectual freedom deals with a menu of possible true accounts of reality. Aesthetic freedom deals with a menu of beautiful ends. Moral freedom deals with a menu of ends which promise to foster growth in virtue.[32]

Creative understanding originates all novel systems of relations by combining percepts and concepts in free, new, and purely ideal relational complexes. Perceptive understanding discovers, conceptive understanding reproduces, but creative understanding gives rise to new subjective systems of relationships. Creative understanding exemplifies the highest form of teleology.[33]

Abbot's epistemology also distinguished judgment, reasoning, and intelligence. *Judgment* exemplified the essential act of understanding in which the mind either affirms or denies the objective existence of a possible complex of conceptual relationships or else declares their fitness to exist. *Reasoning* exemplified the continuous activity of understanding. Reasoning consists of the "strictly teleological combination of judgments of objective existence to produce a final judgment of precisely the same character." By originating systems of relations in being and thought which correspond to one another, reasoning masters the forces in one's surrounding environment. By "intelligence" Abbot meant "that which either discovers or creates relational systems of constitutions."

Intelligence occurs in nature in different forms and degrees, but it remains the same in all of them. Feeding organisms enjoy perceptive understanding and can discover objectively real relational systems. In other

[31] Ibid., 134–43.
[32] Ibid., 143–4.
[33] Ibid., 144–5.

words, feeding organisms perceive reality through biological assimilation and elimination. Organisms which act purposively, however, enjoy in addition conceptive and creative understanding, but a continuum of development unites the lower and higher forms of life.[34]

Abbot also argued for a continuity between finite and infinite understanding. Infinite understanding exhibits the two cognitive functions of perception and creation, but it would not need conceptive intelligence, which characterizes finite understanding as finite. A finite mind needs to formulate a conceptual idea of actualities outside of itself; an infinite mind encompasses everything within itself. Similarly, while a finite mind deals originally with given relational systems, an infinite mind originates both the matter and intelligible form of all relational systems. Both the continuity uniting all forms of understanding and the presumed infinity of nature together grounded Abbot's inference from finite minds to an all-encompassing infinite mind. If understanding organizes both finite and infinite intelligence, it would seem to follow that, as the totality of all Being, an infinite universe must also exemplify infinite intelligence. "Nature," therefore, exemplifies an infinite intelligence infinitely intelligible to itself. An infinite All-Thing can know no cause outside of itself. It must therefore exist as the absolute author of its own immanent relational constitution. Abbot therefore concluded that the Universe, or "Nature," exemplifies, as Emerson had suggested on different philosophical grounds, an infinite self-consciousness.[35]

The final step in Abbot's argument in *Scientific Theism* asserted the organic character of cosmic reality. An evolving, self-existent, infinitely intelligible, absolutely perfect cosmic system exhibits an organic, not a mechanical, structure. Because the Universe considered as the plentitude of being has no environment outside of itself to master, it experiences only immanent, vital operations. A developing system of systems forms an organism because it lives and grows. A finite human intelligence can create only machines, but an infinite self-consciousness creates an infinite organism which Abbot, following Emerson, dubbed "Nature." In a mechanistic view of nature, the cosmos cannot exemplify a perfect system because it lacks intelligent teleology. In an organic view of the cosmos, Abbot argued, nature exemplifies a perfect system within the limits of possibility. Evil, therefore, exists in an organic universe as an unavoidable condition for the possibility of finite existences. In a mechanistic view of the cosmos, nature cannot live and grow. In an organic cosmos, Nature does live and grow. In such a cosmos, then, one finds (1) non-living

[34] Ibid., 145–8.
[35] Ibid., 147–55.

organisms (called "machines") which can act only for ends external to themselves; (2) living finite organisms which act both for internal and external ends; and (3) the "All Thing" which acts only for internal ends. Finite organisms seek both self-fulfillment and altruistic ends. They seek the former through growth and self-reparation; they seek the latter through reproduction and cooperation.[36]

The God of science which *Scientific Theism* proclaims functions finally as the absolute ground of the identity of Being and Thought. Abbot put it this way:

> The absolute end of Being-in-itself, therefore, is the absolute "full-filling" of Thought-in-itself,—that is, creation of the Real out of the Ideal; and the absolute realization of this end is the *Eternal Teleological Process of the Self-Evolution of Nature in Space and Time,*—in a word, the *Infinite Creative Life of God.*[37]

Unlike Emerson's impersonal Over Soul, however, Abbot's All-Thing enjoyed a personal character. *Scientific Theism* defended a philosophical pantheism but not an impersonal theism.

Abbot, who has yet to emerge from intellectual obscurity, optimistically hailed belief in the God of Science as "the Faith of the Future" which promised to reconcile religion and science. Abbot's scientific theism summoned all humans to "kneel in worship side by side at the same altar, dedicated, not to the 'Unknown God,' still less to the 'Unknowable God,' but to the KNOWN GOD whose revealing prophet is SCIENCE."[38]

Moreover, Abbot pronounced *Scientific Theism* his most detailed explanation to date of the meaning of what he called Free Religion. *Scientific Theism* closed with the pronouncement: "For Scientific Theism is the PHILOSOPHY OF FREE RELIGION and the RELIGION OF FREE PHILOSOPHY."[39] One cannot avoid the impression that Abbot deemed his formulation of Free Religion the brightest jewel yet in the crown of Enlightenment religion, a creative blend of an eighteenth-century religion of scientific reason and of nineteenth-century Transcendentalism.

In 1888 Abbot replaced Josiah Royce for a year on the faculty of the Harvard philosophy department while Royce journeyed to Australia and New Zealand. In 1890 Abbot published his Harvard lectures under the title *The Way Out of Agnosticism, or the Philosophy of Free Religion.* In this

---

[36] Ibid., 157–93.
[37] Ibid., 202.
[38] Ibid., 202–18.
[39] Ibid., 218.

work Abbot summarized the conclusions of *Scientific Theism* and developed in an initial way their metaphysical implications.

The Way Out of Agnosticism argued the following three theses:

> I. The universal results of the special sciences, including the method common to them all, is the only possible data of philosophy or universal science.
> II. The universe is known as at once infinite machine, infinite organism, and infinite person—as mechanical in its apparent form and action, organic in its essential constitution, and personal in its innermost being: it is the eternally self-evolving and self-involving unity of the Absolute Real and the Absolute Ideal in GOD.
> III. The universe itself, as eternally self-evolving and self-involving unity of the Absolute Real and the Absolute Ideal in God, is the Ethical Realization of the INFINITE DIVINE IDEAL, as the sun reflects itself in the dew-drop; and the splendor of its reflection is proportioned to the intelligent, free, loyal, and loving obedience of the human soul to it, as at once the supreme law of Human Nature and the supreme known law of Universal Nature.[40]

In the course of his argument, Abbot contrasted the Greek and the German theory of universals with what he called "the American or Scientific Theory of Universals." By "the American or Scientific Theory" he meant, of course, the position which he himself had developed in *Scientific Theism*. By the "Greek theory," Abbot apparently meant some form of Aristotelianism. In the "Greek theory," only individuals counted as real and universals exist but only in each individual thing. By the "German theory," Abbot probably intended Kant. The German theory reified the universal concept or word. In the process, the German theory ended in an idealism which made the individual as such unknowable, and the unknowability of the individual led to agnosticism. The American or Scientific Theory, Abbot argued, avoided the fallacies of both the Greek and the German theories. The American Theory regarded the universal as equally real in word, concept, and genus, and it recognized as the sole object of knowledge a synthesis of the universal and the individual necessarily correlated in what Abbot here called "the Real Genus-in-itself." In *The Syllogistic Philosophy,* he would call the Real Genus-in-itself the "unit-universal."[41]

Abbot's Real Genus-in-itself clarified what he meant in *Scientific Theism* by *"universalia inter res"* (universals among things). Universals exist as generic laws which find exemplification in individual realities. When the human mind grasps those laws conceptually or expresses them verbally, it grasps and expresses a real, generic reality. A genus, therefore, consists of many individual things reciprocally related in one universal

[40] Abbot, *The Way Out of Agnosticism,* 5–6.
[41] Ibid., 8–29.

kind, or essence, or law. The scientific mind studies real genera-in-themselves, not just concrete realities which individualize a universal genus and certainly not universals which exist only in the mind. The method of science begins with the *observation* of many individual facts; it then advances to the *formulation of a hypothesis* which explains those facts; it concludes with the *verification* of a hypothesis. That verification grounds the observed facts in a real genus-in-itself and in the process explains them.[42] Abbot, then, recognized two fundamental kinds of scientific reasoning.[43] Scientific induction reasons from the individual to the universal, while scientific deduction reasons from the universal to the individual.[44]

In a sense, Abbot's theory of the Real Genus-in-itself developed the three theses concerning language which Emerson enunciated in the fourth chapter of *Nature*. Emerson had written: "1. Words are signs of natural facts. 2. Particular natural facts are symbols of particular spiritual facts. 3. Nature is the symbol of spirit."[45] In Emerson's Transcendental vision of the cosmos, concrete, individual natural facts exist in and exemplify universal laws, and in the moment of imaginative creativity fact and law fuse in a way which enables words to express their synthetic unity. Abbot endorsed a pantheism analogous to Emerson's, but he argued that one need not restrict the synthetic grasp of the individual in the universal to moments of ecstatic, imaginative creativity. Rather the kind of synthetic insight of which Emerson spoke occurs every time the scientific mind formulates and verifies a hypothesis.

Abbot's relationism also negated the multiple dualisms in Emersonian Transcendentalism and replaced them with an organic relationism. The final lectures in *The Way Out of Agnosticism* appealed to the organic structure of the cosmos in order to subsume the mechanistic universe of eighteenth-century science into an updated vision of an evolving, organic, Darwinian universe. Summarizing insights from *Scientific Theism,* Abbot divided "real Being" into three verifiable categories: the machine, the organism, and the person. Machines, which always seek ends outside of themselves, when viewed within the cosmic scheme of things, function within organisms and serve the purposes of organic growth and development. Machines exemplify in their operation the principle of causality; organisms, the principle of final-

---

[42] Ibid., 36–40.

[43] Peirce would correct Abbot on this point by arguing for three irreducible kinds of rational inference.

[44] Abbot, *The Way Out of Agnosticism,* 41.

[45] Ralph Waldo Emerson, *The Complete Works of Ralph Waldo Emerson,* Centenary Edition, 14 vols. (Boston: Houghton, Mifflin & Co., 1903–04) 1:25. See also Abbot, *The Way Out of Agnosticism,* 75.

ity. Persons, or organisms which act with conscious self-determination, follow the laws of morality. Finite persons reveal the personal character of the cosmos as a whole, conceived as an organic reality which seeks only its own internal ends of growth and development; and the personal character of the cosmos reveals that moral law, as Emerson had prophetically proclaimed, lies at the heart of the cosmos. For Abbot, then, the way out of agnosticism lay in the confession of an absolute monism in which God exemplifies at one and the same time infinite machine, infinite organism, and infinite person, with the mechanical aspects of the universe subsumed under the organic and the organic processes of the cosmos serving the development of an infinite divine Person.[46]

IV

In his *Syllogistic Philosophy,* Abbot attempted to reduce the cosmic vision which he had articulated in his two earlier books to a final systematic statement. In this final summary work Abbot would argue that the cosmos has a syllogistic structure and that every syllogism interrelates three realities. As we shall see, the syllogism of Being interrelates specimens, species, and genera. The syllogism of Being grounds metaphysics. The syllogism of knowing interrelates percepts, concepts, and ideas. The syllogism of knowing grounds epistemology. The syllogism of doing interrelates deeds, purposes, and ideals. The syllogism of doing grounds ethics. The syllogism of philosophy, which Abbot also called "the syllogism of syllogisms," combines in a synthetic unity the syllogisms of being, knowing, and doing. The syllogism of philosophy grounds Free Religion.

Like René Descartes, Abbot began his syllogistic philosophy with a search for a self-grounding philosophical axiom. Here, as we shall see, Abbot's scientific theism parts company with Peircean logic. Descartes had grounded all philosophical thinking in his *"Cogito ergo sum."* In formulating an analogous starting point for his system, Abbot recognized that he must avoid the individualistic solipsism of the Cartesian *Cogito.* Accordingly, Abbot founded his syllogistic philosophy on the broader social affirmation that "human knowledge exists."[47]

In formulating his *Syllogistic Philosophy,* Abbot probably had an eye upon Hegelian idealism as well. Like Hegel, he sought to offer a metaphysics grounded in a logic, but Abbot in contrast to Hegel refused to equate history with the evolution of the Concept. Still, his syllogistic philosophy claimed to exemplify an absolute logic. The fundamental principle

[46] Abbot, *The Way Out of Agnosticism,* 47–75.
[47] Francis Ellingwood Abbot, *The Syllogistic Philosophy,* 1:8, 64–92.

of that logic asserted: "Whatever is evolved as consequent must be involved as antecedent."[48]

In the proposition "human knowledge exists" Abbot claimed to have found a unique starting point for all philosophical thinking. He regarded the affirmation as self-grounding in a double sense: (1) The affirmation "human knowledge exists" roots itself in an experience of human knowing. (2) By the fundamental principle of absolute logic, the proposition "human knowledge exists" must derive its grounding from something rationally prior to it. The speculative ground of human knowledge, however, lies within the ambit of human knowing. As a consequence, the proposition "human knowledge exists" exemplifies a self-grounding proposition.

Indeed, Abbot argued, the proposition "human knowledge exists" exemplifies the only self-grounding proposition and therefore provides a unique starting place for all human thinking. Even though human knowledge, as a contingent reality, need not exist, still if the human mind asserts such a proposition it must do so necessarily. Moreover, Abbot's human mind, unlike the Cartesian *Cogito,* transcends individual human consciousness. "Human knowledge exists" asserts the shared human experience of knowing. One asserts both the personal experience of knowing and its objective universality. The human mind can neither doubt nor deny the proposition "human knowledge exists" without contradiction. Moreover, since the proposition "human knowledge exists" includes both an experienced reality and its ground, one can only assert it, not demonstrate it. In a sense, the rest of Abbot's syllogistic philosophy explored the ground of "this axiom of philosophy," his alleged ultimate starting point for all human thought.[49]

The Syllogistic Philosophy justified its self-grounding proposition through an argumentative regress. A regressive argument, Abbot argued, must accomplish two interrelated tasks: it must ground the particular content of the proposition and it must show the identity of that content with its universal ground. A regressive argument, however, elaborates "concentric, necessary principles of increasing universality." Moreover, since, the meaning and context of the axiom of philosophy coincide, as its meaning expands, so too must the ground which explains that meaning. The method of regress summarized Abbot's argumentative strategy in *The Syllogistic Philosophy* for regrounding Emersonian pantheism. The method expanded its ground in ever-widening metaphysical circles until it embraced the infinite, divine ground of all reality, the all-embracing divine I.[50]

[48] Ibid., 1:vii.
[49] Ibid., 1:1–33.
[50] Ibid., 1:45–63.

Abbot's axiom of philosophy also claimed to overcome the extreme, concrete individualism of the Cartesian *Cogito* as well as the extreme abstract rationality of Kant's account of the ego.[51] The axiom of philosophy asserted the knower as a unit separate from other knowers but inseparably related to them. The knowing "I" who asserts the axiom of philosophy accounts for its unitary character, for its affirmation of an individual, concrete knower. The human knower, however, comes to self-awareness as the member of a human community, that is, of a universal reality which grounds each individual human consciousness. The human community, the universal ground of the individual I, also endows human knowing with a hereditary, racial character. Abbot summed the matter up this way:

> Race-consciousness is the I's knowledge of itself as a unit in its own universal, and self-consciousness is the I's knowledge of itself as a universal in all its own units; but neither race-consciousness nor self-consciousness is possible in any real I, except in one personal consciousness of the I in the We, as a universal unit in its own unitary universal.[52]

By a "community," then, Abbot meant the universal element common to all the members of that community but abstracted from all their personal individual traits.[53]

In the past, philosophers tended to ground the origins of consciousness in the contrast between the me and the not-me. Abbot's axiom of philosophy claimed to expand a philosophical account of the origins of knowledge in order to include the "we," the genetic community which makes knowing possible. The inner world of the I, therefore, includes the individual self in each and all of its conscious states as part of a larger, universal We. The not-I, which embraces everything else, includes all other selves besides myself and all things which do not qualify as selves, and the Universe coincides with the sum total of the me and the not-me. The We, the community, embraces both the sum total of other conscious humans like myself plus my own self-consciousness. The community, therefore, exists in all its individual units, or conscious selves. The not-Me, the human community's outer world, includes everything which does not have consciousness, and the sum total of the community and its world equals the Universe. Abbot called

---

[51] Ibid., 1:64–114.

[52] Ibid., 1:118.

[53] Ibid., 1:115–27. In *The Problem of Christianity*, Josiah Royce, building on Peirce, would offer a more detailed, and in my judgment a more plausible, account of community, although Abbot insisted more explicitly than Royce on the organic roots of community. See Josiah Royce, *The Problem of Christianity*, 2 vols. (Chicago: University of Chicago Press, 1968).

the law which asserts the existence of individuals as members of a universal, grounding reality "the law of unit-universals."[54]

The law of unit-universals asserts the irreducibly triadic character of all knowing. It equates the unknowable with the non-existent. It defines Being as something of some kind. It includes the knowledge of Being within reality and defines knowledge as either a percept or a concept of something of some kind. Finally, the law of unit-universals asserts that every act of knowledge which relates a percept or concept to some known reality, however partially or erroneously, expresses the act of a mind which has the capacity to function simultaneously as both percept and concept, both sensibility and understanding, both experience and reason. That mind exemplifies a knowing I within a knowing We. Knowing, in other words, always engages a reality known, a way of knowing it, and a mind which exists as an individual consciousness within a larger, organically evolving social consciousness.[55]

Abbot's law of unit-universals grounded in turn his syllogistic philosophy. Indeed, Abbot claimed that "the law of unit-universals . . . constitutes the *immanent reason of reason itself.*" Abbot also regarded the syllogism as the fundamental act of the human mind. Abbot described a syllogism in the following manner: "Every valid syllogism is an existent cognition as a given fact in consciousness, and its own content as *unconditioned dependence of the conditioned on its condition* is at once a *fact of existence* and the ultimate, absolute, unconditioned *reason of that fact.*"[56] Abbot characterized his syllogistic philosophy as a critical realism which overcomes the empirical reduction of reality to actuality and the rationalist reduction of reality to subjective necessity. Critical realism affirms an objective necessity which includes both "to be" and "to be thought."[57]

Although Abbot distinguished hypothetical reasoning from verification, he tacitly equated the syllogism with deduction. His syllogism takes the following logical form:

$$A = B$$
$$C = A$$
$$\text{hence, } C = B.$$

Abbot therefore equated all reasoning with the deductive subsumption of a species under a genus. That subsumption, however, has to grasp a reality, otherwise the syllogism proves nothing. Said Abbot: "Inference is sim-

[54] Abbot, *The Syllogistic Philosophy*, 1:128–208.
[55] Ibid., 1:143–317.
[56] Ibid., 2:8–9.
[57] Ibid., 2:9–15.

ply a connecting of relating comprehension of necessary inherences as objective relations. The syllogism proves because Being syllogizes." In other words, because reality itself synthesizes a genus, a species, and a specimen (or individual member of a species), when the mind reasons, it grasps the fact that reality itself organizes individual existents into species through their exemplification of a more universal generic reality. The logical syllogism, then, grasps the syllogistic structure of reality itself.[58]

Reasoning, then, does not exemplify cognitive spontaneity but the "orderly movement of mind from the involved necessities of Being to the involved necessities of thought."[59] In other words, when the mind interprets reality correctly, it grasps correctly how real consequences relate to the real, universal conditions which generate them. The real, developmental grounding of the consequence in its universal condition, the syllogism of Being, therefore grounds the syllogism of knowledge, or the mind's grasp of that complex of organic relationships. We observe evolutionary processes in nature. We experience but do not observe the involutionary processes of thought which grasp the processes of evolution.[60]

Humans, however, not only know but they act in consequence and in the light of what they know. As thought becomes action, the syllogism of knowing gives rise to the syllogism of acting. Action engages energy; energy exemplifies activity; but thought, or reason, gives energy its personality, its character. The syllogism of acting affirms that "every species is evolved from and inheres in its own genus." Human sexuality illustrates this process of evolution. Male and female both evolve from and inhere in their own species. Male and female then evolve new specimens which both evolve from and inhere in their own species and genus. "Reason thinks it [the specimen] in the premises, Energy makes it in the conclusion." In Abbot's syllogistic universe, the syllogism of knowing synthesizes percepts and concepts in general ideas; the syllogism of doing synthesizes the real right with and ideal right in order to effect the right deed.[61]

Abbot argued that the syllogisms of Being, of thought, and of action structure the cosmic process. These three syllogisms taken together disclose the fundamental relational structure of the universe, which consists of ontological, epistemological, and ethical relationships. The syllogism of Being, not unlike the transcendental Emerson's act of intuitive creativity, synthesizes invariable, eternal, unconditioned, necessary relationships of reason with conditioned, originated, spatio-temporal relationships of

---

[58] Ibid., 2:26–58.
[59] Ibid., 2:58.
[60] Ibid., 2:59–160.
[61] Ibid., 2:121–63.

experience. The syllogism of knowledge recognizes the unconditioned, eternal relations disclosed in the syllogism of Being as the a priori of Reason and conditioned, spatio-temporal relations as the a posteriori of experience. The syllogism of action recognizes the unconditioned, eternal relations as the a priori of duty and justice and conditioned, variable, spatio-temporal relations as the a posteriori of purpose. The synthetic unification of Being, thought, and action, Abbot called the syllogism of philosophy.[62]

Abbot also called the syllogism of philosophy the "syllogism of syllogisms." This culminating syllogism also implies the "Absolute syllogism." The syllogism of syllogisms summarizes the syllogism of philosophy by interrelating synthetically Being, knowing, and doing. It asserts: (1) Knowing is Being (or true judgments are real specimens); (2) Doing is Knowing (ethical deeds are true judgments); hence, (3) Doing is Being (ethical deeds are real specimens). The syllogism of philosophy grounds the finite and the contingent in eternal, necessary reality, and the Absolute syllogism explicates the ultimate metaphysical implications of the syllogism of philosophy. The Absolute syllogism asserts:

> WE ARE in I AM.
> I AM in WE ARE.
> hence, I AM in I AM.

In other words, the individual human I derives its being from the We, the community, from which it originates, but every community derives its reality ultimately from the great I AM, who synthesizes the totality of eternal, unconditioned, necessary relationships. The Absolute I and the finite I resemble one another generically but have a different "reific essence," namely, each I's free, unique, self-born individual character. Moreover, both the personal consciousness of each finite I and the shared consciousness of each community roots itself ultimately in the personal consciousness of the Absolute I.[63]

V

In the development of classical philosophy in the United States, Abbot links transcendentalism and pragmatism. His lifelong reverence for Emerson as the religious prophet of American rational religion and his single-minded dedication to regrounding Emersonian pantheism in an updated philosophy of science anchors one pole of his thought solidly in the Transcendental tradition. So do the similarities between Abbot's Free Religion and Parker's Absolute religion. Both Parker and Abbot remained

[62] Ibid.
[63] Ibid., 2:283–90.

solidly rooted in the presuppositions of eighteenth-century Enlightenment religion. Both endorsed a form of Enlightenment rationalism as the logical outcome and fulfillment of the Protestant reformation.

At the same time, Abbot's repudiation of Transcendental intuition and his dedication to finding some way of wedding religion and scientific method locate Abbot solidly in the generation of William James and Charles Peirce. In addition, the fact that Abbot not only earned Peirce's intellectual respect but even influenced the development of Peirce's own philosophy links Abbot's thought in a significant way to the emergence of American pragmatism.

The transitional character of Abbot's thought helps account for some of the ambivalence which characterized his philosophical and religious achievement. Abbot's sound and devastating philosophical critique of Enlightenment nominalism deservedly earned Peirce's admiration. Abbot also saw clearly the need to advance beyond Enlightenment individualism. Abbot's relational, communitarian, organic account of reality struck at the heart of the atomic individualism which grounded Lockean social contract theory. Abbot's relational depiction of human cognition did away with the atomism which mars Locke's epistemology. While Emerson and Parker had endorsed the subjectivism of Enlightenment religion and morality, Abbot developed a robust epistemological and metaphysical realism. He correctly insisted on the social, developmental character of human self-awareness and of human knowing. Evolutionary theory rendered Abbot's philosophy overtly historical by teaching it to acknowledge and to come to terms with the developing character of both reality and thought.

When dealing with strictly philosophical issues Abbot's mind gravitated to analogical thinking, but when he confronted strictly theological questions his imagination retained the dialectical character which he inherited from his Protestant heritage. Echoing Parker, Abbot assumed with naive optimism that his Free Religion marked the culmination of human religious thought. His rationalistic dismissal of all forms of historical religion betrayed him into approaching theological questions with the shallowest kind of stereotypes. His more virulent attacks on Catholicism dramatize eloquently that he had acquiesced uncritically in the religious bigotry of militant Deists like Ethan Allen and Elihu Palmer. With militant Enlightenment Deism Abbot refused to allow any continuity between reason and revelation, between nature and the supernatural.

In endorsing Emersonian pantheism, Abbot transformed it. Abbot's doctrine of relationism negated all the dualisms of matter and spirit, of time and eternity, of individual and society, which marred Emerson's thought. It also transformed Abbot's understanding of what Emerson called the Over Soul. The Emersonian Over Soul and Abbot's Absolute I bore a significant resemblance to one another. Both exemplified the universal laws of the cosmos, but, while Emerson's sundering of time from eternity relegated the laws of the universe to an unchanging, transcendent, metaphysical realm dubiously related to the fatal realm of matter and of sense, Abbot's relationism caused him to transform the Over Soul into something like an Under Soul. In Abbot's universe, laws which constitute the Absolute I constitute the matrix in which all finite reality exists and evolves. Moreover, in Abbot's thought the Absolute I itself would seem to evolve in the finite, created, internal relationships which constitute and manifest its organic, cosmic life.

The dialectical character of Abbot's imagination also appeared in his acquiescence in Emerson the prophet's demand that one choose between intuitive and scientific thinking. While Emerson exalted imaginative, creative intuition over the linear logic of scientific thinking, Abbot repudiated intuitionism and awarded the epistemological crown to scientific logic. As we shall see, Peirce, who probed more deeply into questions of logic and epistemology than Abbot, eventually came to recognize that both rational, inferential thinking and imaginative, non-rational thinking make legitimate cognitive claims, claims which in his mature thought he cheerfully accorded to both.

One can also clarify the relationship between Abbot, on the one hand, and both Transcendentalism and the Enlightenment, on the other, by a dialectical comparison of Abbot and Brownson. Both espoused a kind of Platonic realism. That realism rooted the grasp of concrete sensible realities in eternal and unchanging verities which functioned as the laws of the universe. Both espoused a philosophical vitalism. Abbot acknowledged more explicitly than Brownson that nature exhibits some mechanical properties, but he subsumed them into the higher organic processes of individual living things and of the Absolute I. The organic interrelatedness of all things also played a more important role in Abbot's thought than in Brownson's. Abbot's philosophy of organism purified of dualism Emerson's belief in organic, cosmic relationships, and, in the process, Abbot anticipated the philosophy of organism developed both by John Dewey and by Alfred North Whitehead. Both Abbot and Brownson replaced a di-polar, nominalistic understanding of cognition with a triadic construct which foreshadowed some of Peirce's best metaphysical and epistemological insights. In philosophy, both Abbot and Brownson thought analogically, although, as I have already indicated, Abbot failed to approach theological questions with an analogical imagination while Brownson the incarnationalist did. Both Abbot and Brownson rejected Enlightenment subjectivism and endorsed an epistemological and metaphysical realism. Both men accommodated themselves imperfectly to the historical character of thought and reality. Brownson's Platonism, however, prevented him from developing a thorough going historicism which could accommodate the development of doctrine, while Abbot's historicism exhibited a priori traits similar to Parker's naive reading of human religious history. Abbot's thought acquired a historical flavor chiefly through his endorsement of evolutionary theory and through his attempt to incorporate evolution into his pantheistic creed.

Abbot and Brownson also disagreed. Brownson would have found Abbot's philosophical naturalism experientially and theologically naive. Abbot inherited none of the darker side of the mature Emerson's religious creed. One finds no hint in Abbot of the fact of human fallenness which Brownson, like Jonathan Edwards, regarded as experientially given. Brownson, as we have seen, came to view the eschatological future with a qualified optimism, but he rooted that optimism in the action of supernatural grace not in fallen humanity. Moreover, Brownson would have deplored Abbot's failure to extend his doctrine of relationism to an understanding of divine grace. Brownson the convert recognized that one need not oppose the two dualistically to one another, but that one can legitimately understand grace with the medieval scholastics as healing, perfecting, and elevating human nature. While Brownson defended an epistemological intuitionism, Abbot rejected it. Brownson reified "Reason" as the object of intuitive knowing, while Abbot correctly viewed reason as a form of human thinking.

Both Abbot and Brownson in different ways brought the Transcendental critique of Enlightenment modernism to the threshold of pragmatism. As we shall see, Charles Peirce finally brought that critique to philosophical completion. Moreover, as we shall also see, in Peirce's philosophy Transcendentalism died only to rise in transmuted form from its own speculative ashes.

Chapter 10

CHARLES SANDERS PEIRCE: PRAGMATIC THEISM

I may mention, for the benefit of those studying
mental biographies,
that I was born and reared in the neighborhood of Concord—
I mean Cambridge—
at the time when Emerson, Hedge, and their friends were
disseminating
the ideas that they had caught from Schelling,
and Schelling from Plotinus,
from Boehm, or from God knows what minds,
stricken with the monstrous mysticism of the East.
But the atmosphere of Cambridge held many an antiseptic
against Concord Transcendentalism,
and I am not conscious of having contracted any of that virus.
Nevertheless, it is probable that some cultured bacilli,
some benignant form of the disease was implanted in my soul,
unawares,
and that now, after long incubation, it comes to the surface,
modified by mathematical conceptions and by training in
physical investigations.

—Charles Sanders Peirce

I

On September 10, 1839, in Cambridge, Massachusetts, Sarah Mills Peirce, the niece of Senator Elijah Hunt Mills, presented her newborn son,

Charles, to his father, Benjamin Peirce, the distinguished professor of mathematics and astronomy at Harvard University. Benjamin Peirce had a reputation for eccentricity and he bequeathed that characteristic to Charles, whom he would prefer to his other three sons because of the young man's precociousness. We know little of Charlie's first ten years; but he seems to have passed a normal childhood. He loved books and displayed both an infectious laugh and a ready wit which he never lost. Young Charlie developed very early another life-long passion: an almost religious fascination with the scientific study of nature.

The Benjamin Peirce household functioned as a meeting place for New England's intellectual and cultural elite. Ralph Waldo Emerson, Oliver Wendell Holmes, Margaret Fuller, Theodore Parker, Daniel Webster, Cyrus Bartol, Louis Agassiz, William Story, and Henry Wadsworth Longfellow numbered among the frequent distinguished visitors.

As he matured, Charles showed special aptitude for mathematics and for contentious argumentation. Benjamin Peirce, a Unitarian in religious matters who in politics supported the institution of slavery, took the brilliant young Charlie under his wing for special tutoring. In order to improve the boy's concentration, father and son would play games of double dummy from ten in the evening until sunrise, with the father sharply and relentlessly criticizing every blunder his son made.

Charlie went through several disciplinary scrapes in high school, but he graduated in 1851 with honors and entered Harvard College. While at Harvard he developed a passionate, life-long commitment to the study of logic. As a young student Charles idolized his father, treasured his own privileged tutelage by one of the nation's leading mathematicians, and thought little of his classroom instruction. Charles did, however, distance himself somewhat from his father in religious matters. He converted to the Episcopal Church out of an attraction for "the general essence and spirit of it." In 1859 Peirce graduated from Harvard College, an undistinguished sixty-first in a class of ninety-three.

In Charles's senior year at Harvard he developed trigeminal neuralgia, which regularly caused him excruciating facial pain. The disease had no cure at the time and helped account for the mature Peirce's erratic behavior. Those who suffer from trigeminal neuralgia tend to act with coldness and aloofness during bouts with agonizing pain. They battle depression, exhibit symptoms of paranoia, and explode in violent outbursts. Peirce suffered from this disease throughout his life and dulled the pain with cocaine and morphine to which he almost certainly became addicted. His dependence on drugs probably exacerbated his social eccentricities.

In 1862 Peirce received a master's degree in science from Harvard, and in the same year he married Harriet Melusina Fay, whom he called Zina. Raised a dedicated feminist, Zina remained committed throughout her life to the cause of women's rights. In the beginning the newlyweds got on well together. Around the time of the marriage, Peirce also began a lifelong friendship with William James.

Peirce pursued advanced studies in science under the renowned Louis Agassiz. During the 1864–65 academic year he lectured at Harvard on the philosophy of science; two years later he delivered the Lowell Lectures on the topic "The Logic of Science and Induction." James dutifully attended but understood very little.

In 1868 Peirce published three articles of critical importance in the development of philosophy in the United States: "Questions Concerning Certain Faculties Claimed for Man," "Some Consequences of Four Incapacities," and "Grounds of Validity: Further Consequence of Four Incapacities." In 1869 Peirce once again delivered the Harvard lectures in philosophy, and in the same year he took a temporary post at the Harvard Observatory. Peirce ached passionately for a faculty appointment at Harvard, but its conservative president Charles W. Eliot, whom Peirce despised in intellectual matters, regarded the young genius as too eccentric and as of questionable character. Accordingly, the priggish Eliot saw to it that Peirce never succeeded his father on the Harvard faculty.

In 1870 Benjamin Mills Peirce, Charles's hard-living, mercurial younger brother, died prematurely. The young Benjamin had practiced mining engineering and died out west. James Peirce, another brother and an extremely discreet practicing homosexual, did advance through the ranks of academia and eventually presided as dean of the Harvard Graduate School. It would appear that only the remaining brother lived a relatively normal and obscure life.

In the year of Benjamin's death, Charles and Zina traveled to Sicily with a group of scientists in order to observe an eclipse of the sun; on their return journey Charles dazzled the best logicians in England with his brilliance of insight. On returning from Europe Peirce participated in the Metaphysical Club. He later claimed to have formulated the pragmatic maxim in the course of the club's debates. In 1871 he joined the Coastal Survey and took responsibility for pendulum experiments in gravity, geodesy, and gravimetrics.[1]

---

[1] See P. P. Wiener, "Peirce's Metaphysical Club and the Genesis of Pragmatism," *Journal of the History of Ideas* 7 (1946) 218–33; C. Eisele, "Scientist-Philosopher: C. S. Peirce at the Smithsonian," *Journal of the History of Ideas* 18 (1957) 537–47; Max H. Fisch, "Was There a Metaphysical Club in Cambridge?" *Studies in the Philosophy of Charles Sanders Peirce, Second Series,* ed. Edward C. Moore and Richard S. Robin (Amherst: University of Massachusetts Press, 1964) 3–32 (hereafter this volume will be abbreviated as *Studies, II*); Victor F. Lenzen, "Charles S. Peirce as Astronomer," *Studies, II,* 34–50.

By the 1870s Peirce's marriage with Zina had begun to unravel. Charles seems to have psychologically abused both Zina and his second wife, Juliette, and during his explosions of anger he may also have abused them physically. Zina recognized Charles's extraordinary brilliance and intellectual promise, but she came to regard him as spoiled, self-indulgent, and self-defeating. Juliette would with time reach a similar verdict. In 1875 the Peirces attended the International Geodetic Conference in Paris. While in Europe Charles also intended to study European gravimetric techniques. There, Peirce's marriage for all practical purposes came to an end. Zina left him, although she did not formally divorce Charles until five years later. In 1876 Charles, who always found it hard to cope with emotional pressure, suffered a serious nervous collapse diagnosed as conversion hysteria, or dissociative reaction, a seizure which rendered him temporarily but completely paralyzed.

In 1877, after his return to the United States, Peirce published "The Fixation of Belief" in the *Popular Science Monthly*. In the same year he returned to Europe for another geodetic conference, and in the smoking room of the vessel taking him to Plymouth, England, he wrote "How to Make Our Ideas Clear." The essay appeared in 1878, once again in *Popular Science Monthly*. In this article he enunciated the pragmatic maxim. In the same year, in the midst of complaints about his treatment at the Harvard Observatory, Peirce published his only full-length book, *Photometric Researches,* the result of his work at the observatory.

Johns Hopkins University opened its doors in 1876, and in 1879 Peirce accepted a part-time lectureship in logic there, which he held for five years while continuing his work with the Coastal Survey.[2] An effective teacher, in 1883 Peirce edited and wrote the lead essay in a volume entitled *Studies in Logic,* with his students contributing the other pieces. The book broke significant new ground in logic and exemplified the kind of shared systematic inquiry which Peirce promoted in his philosophical writings. On April 23 of the same year Peirce married a French woman several years younger than himself, who sometimes called herself Juliette Portelai, and other times Juliette Froissy. The marriage took place only two days after Charles's divorce from Zina. Genteel America neither forgot nor forgave this social indiscretion. The following year Johns Hopkins failed to renew Peirce's lectureship. Peirce protested the action bitterly in a letter, but he never learned the reason for his dismissal. It would appear

---

[2] See Max H. Fisch, "Peirce at Johns Hopkins University," *Studies in the Philosophy of Charles Sanders Peirce, First Series,* ed. Philip P. Wiener and Frederic H. Young (Cambridge, Mass.: Harvard University Press, 1952) 277–311 (hereafter this volume shall be abbreviated as *Studies, I*).

that, in addition to his eyebrow-raising divorce and remarriage, he had alienated at least one other member of the faculty by his high-handed ways and intellectual brilliance.

The year 1883 began Peirce's tragic decline into poverty. In 1887 he and the chronically ill Juliette moved to Milford, Pennsylvania. They seemed to love and need one another in a doomed sort of way. In 1888 they bought Arisbe, a two-thousand-acre estate and farm which they could neither afford nor support. As Peirce's financial situation worsened, both he and his wife continued to live in the extravagant manner to which they had become accustomed. Throughout his life Peirce dreamed of striking it rich through some novel, scientific invention. Now he dreamed in vain of discovering a rich benefactor who would support him and his wife while he completed the logic, semiotic, and metaphysics on which he never ceased to labor. No financial bonanza materialized. In 1891 the Coastal Survey fired Peirce and charged him with neglect of his duties. Thereafter, the Peirces eked out a living on the slender revenue which Charles earned by writing articles and reviewing books supplemented by doles from family and friends. Brother James offered some financial assistance and vainly sought to persuade an unrelenting Harvard University to hire Peirce. William James's faithful financial care for his ruined friend led Charles to adopt Santiago (Saint James) as a middle name. For almost a year impending legal suits against Peirce for physically assaulting a woman servant and for non-payment of debts made him a temporary fugitive from the law. Charles threatened suicide several times toward the end of the 1890s.

With remarkable prescience, at the turn of the century Peirce anticipated that he had about thirteen years left to complete the philosophical project to which he had devoted his life and to which he felt that God had called and dedicated him. In 1903 James arranged for him to lecture before the Lowell Institute in Boston on the subject of "Pragmatism." Once again James faithfully attended the lectures but summarized what he derived from them as "flashes of brilliance in the midst of a Cimmerian darkness." As death began to stalk Peirce, another pain, probably of cancer, compounded the pain of neuralgia. Charles Sanders Peirce died in Milford, Pennsylvania, on April 19, 1914.[3]

As I ponder the tragic unraveling of Peirce's life in the light of the simplicity, the scope, and the occasional sublimity of his philosophical vision, I discern a spirit compounded paradoxically of arrogance and of self-mocking humility, of towering intellectual strength and of enormous brokenness and fragility, of religious passion and secular interests, who by

[3] See Joseph Brent, *Charles Sanders Peirce: A Life* (Bloomington: Indiana University Press, 1993).

passing through the alembic of agonizing physical pain, academic ostracism, poverty, personal humiliation, and failure distilled from it all a profound wisdom. He never to his own satisfaction completed the intellectual project to which he felt divinely called, but what he did complete worked a revolution. I shall argue in what follows that his achievement ushered in the era of constructive postmodern philosophy.

II

Charles Peirce believed devoutly in the fallibility of all human minds, including his own. As a consequence, his thought evolved constantly. One can, however, discern identifiable stages of progress in his speculative development. Until 1862 Peirce wrestled with Kantian philosophy. Between 1862 and 1869 his studies of the syllogism and of medieval logic led him to abandon Kant. His analysis of syllogistic reasoning convinced him that one can reduce all inference to one of three kinds: abductive, or hypothetical inference; deductive, or predictive inference; and inductive, or verifying inference. Scholars often refer to the period between 1869 and 1883 as Peirce's middle period. During these years Peirce formulated and published the pragmatic maxim and brought his philosophy to an initial systematic formulation. Between 1883 and 1914 Peirce subjected the insights of his middle period to critical revision, labored on the formulation of a scientific metaphysics, and pondered the wedding of religion and science.[4]

Anyone familiar with the development and complexity of Peirce's thought will easily recognize the futility of attempting to summarize his intellectual achievement in a short chapter like this one. Accordingly, this chapter ambitions no such folly. It only summarizes selected themes from Peirce's work, themes relevant to the topic of this book and to issues raised in the preceding chapters. As we shall see, Peirce not only revised in radical ways many key presuppositions of the Enlightenment, but he criticized, absorbed, and transformed a number of Transcendental themes. This chapter deals with three major strains in Peirce's thought: (1) his initial rejection of intuitionist thinking and formulation of the pragmatic maxim, (2) the development of Peirce's pragmatism and its relationship to his metaphysical realism, and (3) the "wedding of religion and science" which Peirce attempted to effect during the final stage of his thought.

As we have seen, first-generation Transcendentalists looked to some form of intuitive knowledge in order to deliver both religion and human

---

[4] See Murray G. Murphy, *The Development of Peirce's Philosophy* (Cambridge, Mass.: Harvard University Press, 1961); Roderick M. Chisholm, "Fallibilism and Belief," *Studies, I,* 93–110; A. J. Ayer, *The Origins of Pragmatism: Studies in the Philosophy of Charles Sanders Peirce and William James* (London: Macmillan, 1968).

cognition from the nominalism inculcated by British empiricism. Emerson, Parker, and Brownson each meant something very different by the term "intuition," but all three agreed that intuitive thinking could emancipate one from Enlightenment nominalism and from the religious skepticism which nominalism engendered. The young Peirce, by contrast, began his published philosophical career with a refutation of the thesis that intuitive thinking grasps a "transcendental object" within subjectivity alone.

Peirce defined "intuition" as "a cognition not determined by a previous cognition of the same object, and therefore so determined by something out of consciousness." By cognition which came "out of consciousness" Peirce meant sensibly and symbolically unmediated knowing.[5] In other words, his definition of intuition opposed intuitive thinking both to sensibly derived knowledge and to temporally and symbolically conditioned knowledge. That meant that either the "transcendental object" of which he spoke would have to arise in consciousness without any prior sensory experience, or else it would have to escape the limits and mediation of historically conditioned, discursive thinking. The intuitive knowing of which Peirce spoke need not take the form of a judgment, since he applied the term "intuition" to any cognition whatever. However, if an intuitive judgment occurred, then by his definition of "intuition" it would have to exemplify a "premiss not itself a conclusion," for every conclusion results from some form of symbolic mediation.[6]

Peirce also distinguished between experiencing an intuition and justifying its intuitive character intuitively. Clearly, in order to justify intuitively calling an intuition intuitive, one would have to show that it grasps its transcendental object without the mediation either of sensation or of reasoning with symbols.

One might, Peirce suggested, try to validate intuitive knowing by appealing to "feeling." One just feels that the intuition grasps its object immediately and without the mediation of other forms of knowing. The appeal to feeling, however, carries no probative value, for even those who make such an appeal disagree about which cognitions count as intuitions. An appeal to external authorities suffers the same fate, for those authorities also disagree about the way intuition works. Finally, the factual evidence we possess tends to support the mediated character of cognition. Peirce therefore concluded that the claim to have experienced an intuition in the sense in which he defined the term lacks proof.[7]

[5] Charles Sanders Peirce, *The Collected Papers of Charles Sanders Peirce,* ed. Charles Hartshorne and Paul Weiss, 8 vols. (Cambridge, Mass.: Harvard University Press, 1931–) 5:213, n. 1.

[6] Ibid., 5:213.

[7] Ibid., 5:214–24.

Peirce also questioned the intuitive character of self-awareness, since self-awareness engages more than personal subjectivity. Initial self-awareness enables one to distinguish between one's own body and environmental stimuli. The experience of erroneous judgment further enhances self-awareness, for the discovery that what one assumed would happen differs from the actual event dramatizes the difference between the self viewed as a complex of personal expectations and the world which defeats those expectations.[8]

Finally, one cannot validate intuitive knowledge by "introspection," by an inner look into one's own subjectivity, for in order to establish the subjective character of feelings, beliefs, and attitudes one must show that they fail to correspond to events which exist independently of one's subjective expectations. Similarly, any argument which would conclude to the intuitive character of any cognition by definition requires more than intuition in order to establish its truth.[9]

Peirce's rejection of unmediated intuitions whose objects derived from within subjectivity alone implied a reverse affirmation, namely, that human knowing has a sensuous origin and engages symbolic mediation. In other words, without using signs the human mind can know nothing. Moreover, the very concept of "being" includes "cognizability," or a mediated symbolic relationship to mind, for knowledge exists and constitutes part of the realm of "being." As a consequence, no sign can signify the uncognizable, despite nominalistic claims to the contrary. Moreover, the mediated, symbolic character of all human knowing requires that the cognition of any cognition result from a previous, symbolically mediated cognition.[10]

Peirce summed up the preceding conclusions in four theses:

> 1. We have no power of Introspection, but all knowledge of the internal world is derived by hypothetical reasoning from knowledge of external facts.
> 2. We have no power of Intuition, but every cognition is determined logically by previous cognitions.
> 3. We have no power of thinking without signs.
> 4. We have no conception of the absolutely incognizable.[11]

In his logical assault on intuition, Peirce addressed himself to a philosophical tradition which stretched its roots deep into the Middle Ages and beyond. That tradition claimed for the human mind a faculty which grasps the first principles of deductive reasoning as self-evident truths.

---

[8] Ibid., 5:225–38.
[9] Ibid., 5:244–9.
[10] Ibid., 5:250–63.
[11] Ibid., 5:265.

As I have already suggested, nothing in Peirce's early essays suggests that, in repudiating intuitionism, he targeted in a special way the theories of the American Transcendentalists. Still, one may ask whether, in defining intuition as he did, Peirce spread his logical net wide enough to refute the Transcendental theories of Parker and of Emerson. Peirce's argument certainly ruled out Parker's claim that intuitive knowing because of its grounding in privileged faculties of the mind yields the subjective grasp of objective philosophical truths. Peirce's argument also ruled out any philosophical claim to grasp immediately within subjectivity transcendental realities independent of space and time, as Emersonian Platonism and virtually every other form of Platonic metaphysics does.

In his assault on intuitionism, however, Peirce angled for much larger philosophical fish than either Emerson or Parker. In his early articles in the *Journal of Speculative Philosophy,* the young Peirce attacked what he called "the spirit of Cartesianism." The spirit of Cartesianism holds that philosophical thinking must begin with universal doubt, and it locates the test of certainty within consciousness. The spirit of Cartesianism also equates inferential reasoning with deduction.

Peirce, by contrast, questioned that the mind can force itself to doubt artificially, as Cartesian method requires. Moreover, universal doubt refutes itself because it exempts the method of universal doubt from doubt. In addition, through his studies of the syllogism and of medieval logic, Peirce had proved to his own satisfaction that inference involves more than deduction. Finally, one must validate deductive reasoning, not in consciousness alone, but through practical interaction with the realities one investigates.[12]

To intuitionism and "the spirit of Cartesianism" Peirce opposed his own logic of inference. According to Peirce, inferential knowing advances in three stages. It begins abductively by formulating a hypothesis. It then predicts deductively the operational consequences of that hypothesis. Finally, inferential knowing verifies or falsifies the original hypothesis through some form of inductive reasoning, or one verifies it statistically, that is, within a range of probability.[13]

In Peircean logic, propositions often function as linguistic shorthand for an inference, and every inference interrelates a rule, a case, and a result. A rule offers an account of some law assumed to obtain in reality. A result identifies factual data in need of explanation. A case characterizes the relevant data.

---

[12] Ibid., 5:264.
[13] See Robert G. Meyers, "Peirce on Cartesian Doubt," *Transactions of the Charles S. Peirce Society* 1 (1967) 13–23.

Moreover, the three forms of inference all interrelate a rule, a case, and a result differently. An *abduction* concludes to a *case*. On the basis of a rule which it assumes to obtain in reality, it categorizes in a preliminary way data in need of explanation. A *deduction* concludes to a *result*. It argues that if a given abduction has categorized the data correctly, then the rule which grounds that categorization will also justify the prediction that other facts *(results)* not currently in evidence will appear under specifiable conditions. An *induction* concludes to a *rule*. Inductive reasoning argues that the appearance of the deductively predicted facts justifies concluding that the rule which one's abduction assumed to obtain in reality actually does so. The non-appearance of the predicted facts would call the reality of the same rule into question. The appearance of the predicted facts in only some cases would suggest that the rule applies only within a range of probability. In questions of any complexity, inductions usually apply within a range of probability.[14]

All this sounds terribly abstract, but the following homely example makes Peirce's theory of inference intelligible to most people. Imagine the young Columbus sitting on a dock and gazing out to the ocean. As a vessel approaches, he sees first the top of a mast, then the whole mast, then the entire ship growing larger and larger as it nears the harbor. Columbus reasons that if the laws of nature had made the earth flat, not round, as most of his contemporaries assumed, then he would not see the ship piecemeal, as in fact he does. On his first sighting of the ship, he would see the entire vessel, at first tiny in the distance, then growing larger and larger. The fact, then, that the ship does appear piecemeal, beginning with the highest part of the mast, suggests that the ship is sailing on a curved as opposed to a flat surface. If the ocean surface curves, then it probably covers a curved ocean floor. The curvature of the ocean floor suggests the curvature of the earth. Columbus, therefore, reasons abductively: "The earth is round, not flat." In Peirce's logic, the proposition, "the earth is round, not flat," expresses in linguistic short-hand the preceding complex abductive ratiocination. The inference qualifies as abductive because it concludes to a case by categorizing the world as round.[15]

[14] Ibid., 5:266–82. See also Francis E. Reilly, *Charles Peirce's Theory of Scientific Method* (New York: Fordham University Press, 1970); H. G. Frankfurt, "Peirce's Notion of Abduction," *Journal of Philosophy* 55 (1958) 593–7; H. G. Frankfurt, "Peirce's Account of Inquiry," *Journal of Philosophy* 55 (1958) 588–92; Idus Murphee, "Peirce's Theory of Inquiry," *Journal of Philosophy* 56 (1959) 667–78; Len O'Neill, "Peirce and the Nature of Evidence," *Transactions of the Charles S. Peirce Society* 29 (1993) 211–37.

[15] See A. W. Burks, "Peirce's Theory of Abduction," *Philosophy of Science* 13 (1946) 301–6; W. L. Reese, "Peirce on Abstraction," *Review of Metaphysics* 14 (1961) 704–13; R. Michael Sabre, "Peirce's Abductive Argument and the Enthememe," *Transactions of the Charles S. Peirce Society* 24 (1990) 363–72.

Having decided abductively to affirm the roundness of the earth, Columbus next reasons deductively: If the laws of nature have in fact made the earth round, not flat, then, contrary to popular expectation, I can reach Asia, "the Orient," the "Far East," by sailing west. This second inference counts as a deduction because it concludes to a result, not to a case, not to a rule. It concludes to a *result* because it predicts that facts not yet in evidence (namely, reaching the Orient) will in fact appear under specified conditions (namely, by sailing west instead of east).

Columbus put his deductively clarified theory to the test when he secured the Niña, the Pinta, and the Santa Maria and sailed west across the Atlantic Ocean. The American continent blocked his passage to Asia, but, years later, when the crew of Magellan successfully circumnavigated the globe by sailing west, their feat justified the inductive inference that the laws of nature had in fact made the earth round rather than flat. This final inference qualifies as an induction because it concludes to a *rule,* not to a result, not to a case.[16]

Peirce next argued that, if one can reduce the cognitive actions of the rational mind to some example of abduction, deduction, or induction, then inferential thinking has an irreducibly triadic structure. By that he meant that every inference exhibits a *quality,* a *relation,* and a *representation.* The way the mind perceives the realities it seeks to understand endows every "thought-sign" with a qualitative character. By a *quality,* Peirce meant an instance of "particular suchness." The quality of a sign corresponds logically to a case. The mind's inferential use of qualitative predicates exhibits a *relational* character since it connects one thought with another. Finally, every thought-sign has a *representative* character, since it signifies some reality. Representation exemplifies a logical relationship. Indeed, Peirce characterized his logic as a logic of relations.

Inferential thought-signs always think about something. Moreover, a successful induction results in a habitual way of perceiving reality. The human mind consists, then, in a complex of acquired interpretative habits which represent reality to itself and to other minds. The inherently representative character of the mind reveals, moreover, the inherently symbolic character of human nature.

Because inductive inference grasps a generalized way of behaving in nature and does so under specifiable conditions, Peirce's theory of inference

---

[16] See J. S. Ullian, "Peirce, Gambling, and Insurance," *Philosophy of Science* 29 (1962) 79–80; Edward H. Madden, "Peirce on Probability," *Studies, II,* 122–40; Arthur W. Burks, "Peirce's Two Theories of Probability," *Studies, II,* 141–50; John W. Lenz, "Induction as Self-Corrective," *Studies, II,* 151–62; G. H. Merrill, "Peirce on Probability," *Transactions of the Charles S. Peirce Society* 11 (1975) 90–109.

requires the assertion of real generality in objects of inferential knowing. In other words, a sound inferential logic grounds a metaphysical realism.[17] Peirce put the matter this way:

> No cognition of ours is absolutely determinate, generals must have a real existence. . . . Such being the nature of reality in general, in what does the reality of mind consist? We have seen that the content of consciousness, the entire phenomenal manifestation of mind, is a sign resulting from inference. Upon our principle, therefore, that the absolutely incognizable does not exist, so that the phenomenal manifestation of the substance is the substance, we must conclude that the mind is a sign developing according to the laws of inference.[18]

In other words, the human mind exemplifies a developing habit of thinking, and the human organism serves as an instrument of thought.

The symbolic character of human existence also renders it inherently *social and communal,* for a sign signifies something about reality to another mind. Because sign-making presupposes and creates a community of inquiring minds, inferential judgment about the true case of things also has an inherently social and communal character. The decision of a community of inquirers must determine the ultimate truth of any given question:

> In this way, the existence of thought now depends on what is to be hereafter; so that it has only a potential existence, dependent on the future thought of the community.
>
> The individual man, since his separate existence is manifested only by ignorance and error, so far as he is anything apart from his fellows, and from what he and they are to be, is only a negation. This is man,
>
> ". . . proud man,
> Most ignorant of what he's most assured,
> His glassy essence."[19]

In his essay "The Fixation of Belief," Peirce developed practical implications of the social theory of logic which he had proposed. At the beginning of this essay Peirce insisted that reasoning does not come naturally to humans. They must master the art over time and must do so with some difficulty. The history of science narrates the story of the human

---

[17] Peirce, *Collected Papers,* 5:283–313.

[18] Ibid., 5:311–3.

[19] Ibid., 5:316–7. See also Joseph P. De Marco, "Peirce's Concept of Community: Its Development and Character," *Transactions of the Charles S. Peirce Society* 7 (1971) 24–36; Mary B. Mahowald, "Peirce's Concept of Community: Another Interpretation," *Transactions of the Charles S. Peirce Society* 9 (1973) 175–86; Jacob Liszka, "Community in C. S. Peirce: Science as a Means and as an End," *Transactions of the Charles S. Peirce Society* 14 (1978) 305–21.

attempt to master the art of reasoning. The same history also dramatizes human fallacies.[20]

The reasoning mind seeks to pass from settled knowledge to the grasp of something it does not understand. The achievement of understanding creates a belief, a habit of judgment. Specific inferences yield particular beliefs. However, the fact that one can reduce all inferential arguments logically to one of three types of inference—abduction, deduction, or induction—points to a more generalized habit of reasoning which grounds each generic type of inference. Peirce called the logical formulation of the generic mental procedures which govern a particular kind of inference a "guiding principle." The proposition "every abduction concludes to a case" exemplifies a guiding principle.[21]

Inductive inference produces settled beliefs. By a "belief" Peirce meant a proposition for whose consequences one takes responsibility. Belief, then, requires commitment to a particular way of interpreting reality. It exemplifies a habit of interpretation and it contrasts with doubt. Successful inquiry transforms a state of doubt into a state of belief. The fixation of belief terminates the state of doubt.[22] Humans experience doubt as:

> an uneasy and dissatisfied state from which we struggle to free ourselves and pass into the state of belief; while the latter is a calm and satisfactory state which we do not wish to avoid, or to change to a belief in anything else. On the contrary, we cling tenaciously, not merely to believing, but to believing just what we do believe.[23]

The mere fact that someone asks a particular question need not throw the mind into a state of doubt. Doubt engages interest and questions commitment to a belief which one experiences as important. Belief, moreover, need not express an indubitable proposition. It can and often does result from propositions which one does not in fact doubt, although one might, in altered circumstances, call the belief into question. Some people like to

---

[20] Peirce, *Collected Papers,* 5:365. See also Paula Rothernberg Struhl, "Peirce's Defense of the Scientific Method," *Journal of the History of Philosophy* 13 (1975) 481–90.

[21] Ibid., 5:365–8.

[22] Peirce, *Collected Papers,* 5:374–5. See also Chung-ying Cheng, "Peirce's Probabilistic Theory of Inductive Validity," *Transactions of the Charles S. Peirce Society* 1 (1966) 86–112; Chung-ying Cheng, "Charles Peirce's Arguments for the Non-Probabilistic Validity of Induction," *Transactions of the Charles S. Peirce Society* 1 (1967) 24–39; Gordon N. Pinkham, "Some Comments on Cheng, Peirce, and Inductive Validity," *Transactions of the Charles S. Peirce Society* 26 (1990) 309–23.

[23] Peirce, *Collected Papers,* 5:372–3. See also Gary Shapiro, "Habit and Meaning in Peirce's Pragmatism," *Transactions of the Charles S. Peirce Society* 9 (1973) 24–40.

argue for already accepted beliefs, but this kind of intellectual contentiousness does not advance knowledge.[24]

Nor does inferential reasoning always explain the fixation of belief. People in fact form stable habits of interpretation in a variety of ways. Peirce distinguished four principal ways in which the human mind tends to fix its beliefs: tenacity, authority, taste, and shared systematic inquiry.

The method of tenacity exemplifies intellectual stubbornness. One remains doggedly committed to one's belief despite all evidence and objections to the contrary. This method exemplifies a kind of fundamentalism and roots itself in the perceived advantages of standing by one's belief or in the perceived disadvantages of abandoning it.

> A man may go through life, systematically keeping out of view all that might cause a change in his opinions, and if only he succeeds—basing his method, as he does on two fundamental psychological laws—I do not see what can be said against his doing so. It would be an egotistical impertinence to object that his procedure is irrational, for that only amounts to saying that his method of settling belief is not ours. He does not propose to himself to be rational, and indeed, will often talk with scorn of man's weak and illusive reason. So let him think as he pleases.[25]

In practice, however, the method of tenacity tends to break down in the face of social pressure. In other words, the method of tenacity often runs head on into the second method of fixing belief, namely, the way of authority. The way of authority sanctions certain beliefs, rewards those who hold them, and punishes those who contradict them. The sanctioning authority prefers to keep people ignorant of evidence which calls sanctioned beliefs into question, and the sanctioning authority will, on occasion, use physical violence or even public execution in order to enforce a particular belief. "Cruelties always accompany this system; and when it is consistently carried out, they become atrocities of the most horrible kind in the eyes of any rational man." The way of authority enjoys more success than the way of tenacity, but in the end it never prevails because eventually some honest and courageous minds recognize the arbitrariness which attends the authoritative imposition of an unwarranted belief and prefer to throw off the yoke of intellectual tyranny.[26]

---

[24] Peirce, *Collected Papers,* 5:376. See also D. B. Burrell, "C. S. Peirce: Pragmatism as a Theory of Judgment," *International Philosophical Quarterly* 5 (1965) 521–40; Luciano Fliridi, "Skepticism and the Search for Knowledge: A Peirceish Answer to a Kantian Doubt," *Transactions of the Charles S. Peirce Society* 30 (1994) 543–73.

[25] Peirce, *Collected Works,* 5:377.

[26] Ibid., 5:378–82.

The method of taste opts among a menu of beliefs for the one which the mind finds most attractive. As Peirce's logic matured, he came to recognize a certain co-naturality between the educated mind and nature. In principle, the human mind in confronting any problem confronts an infinite number of possible theoretical explanations. The fact that investigating scientists hit upon the right hypothesis as frequently as they do suggests that in the initial fixation of belief one ought to trust one's hunches, one's interpretative instincts. In 1910 Peirce inserted the following sentence into his treatment of the fixation of belief by taste:

> This method is far more intellectual and respectable from the point of view of reason than either of the others which we have noticed. Indeed, as long as no better method can be applied, it ought to be followed, since it is the expression of instinct which must be the ultimate cause of belief in all cases.[27]

The method of taste, however, easily degenerates into the method of tenacity, and it often opts for the wrong explanation. In the end, the human mind needs a more adequate way of fixing its beliefs than tenacity, authority, or taste.

The fixation of belief through shared systematic inquiry offers the best way of fixing beliefs. Of the four methods of fixing belief, only the practice of shared systematic inquiry raises no doubts concerning its adequacy. In the long run, the authoritative imposition of belief engenders resentment and suspicion, but other minds tend either to endorse the conclusions of shared and open inquiry or at least to take them seriously. Moreover, as a method, shared, systematic inquiry works in the long run.[28]

The method of shared systematic inquiry accords well with Peirce's doctrine of logical fallibilism.[29] Fallibilism holds that the human mind has a better chance of reaching true belief if the mind in question admits that it can err than if it denies its capacity for error.

Peircean fallibilism follows logically from his theory of inference and from the evolutionary nature of the universe. In investigating any complex question, one must first decide how much of one's life needs to be devoted to the investigation. Given the limits of time and space, one must, as a consequence, formulate a hypothesis before one knows whether or not all relevant data has been taken into account. Moreover, even if one has verified a belief provisionally, one has no assurance that new facts will not

[27] Ibid., 5:383, 590–604.

[28] Ibid., 5:384–7. See also Idus Murphee, "Peirce: The Experimental Nature of Belief," *Journal of Philosophy* 55 (1963) 309–17.

[29] Peirce, *Collected Papers,* 1:135–75.

crop up which call one's conclusion into question. Nor can one rest assured that some other more comprehensive mind will not so revise the frame of reference in which one thinks about the question at issue that the novel frame of reference will force a revision of one's initially verified belief. At both points where the reasoning mind touches reality (namely, in both abductive and inductive inference), the reasoning mind can in fact err. It can both formulate and verify its hypothesis prematurely. If one adds to the human capacity for error the fact that the world in which we live gives solid evidence of evolving, then a conclusion verified in one epoch may no longer apply in a later epoch. The method of shared systematic inquiry takes the fallibility of the human mind into account by checking the limitations of one's personal experience against the experience of others, by the pooling of insight, and by creating a social context in which one can responsibly revise one's beliefs.[30]

Peirce first formulated the pragmatic maxim in an article entitled "How to Make Our Ideas Clear," published in *Popular Science Monthly* in 1878. He defined a "clear idea" as "one which is so apprehended that it will be recognized wherever it is met with and so that no other will be mistaken for it" and a "distinct idea" as one that contains nothing not clear, with the result that one can "give a precise definition of it, in abstract terms."[31] He offered his pragmatic maxim as a better method for clarifying thought than that proposed by Descartes. In enunciating the pragmatic maxim, he insisted on the conditioned character of rational beliefs, namely, that they determine "how we should act under such circumstances" as originally motivated the doubt which belief replaces. Perceptions stimulate action. Beliefs dispose one to act toward reality in a specific way. Hence, "our idea of anything *is* our idea of its sensible effects" (5.394–401). In its initial formulation, the pragmatic maxim interrelated ideas and sensations. It stated: "Consider what effects, that might conceivably have practical bearings, we conceive the object of our conception to have. Then, our conception of these effects is the whole of our conception of the object" (5.402).

When read in the light of Peirce's theory of inference, the maxim asserts that the meaning of any given hypothesis consists in the sum total of its predictable operational consequences. So understood, the maxim offers, in my judgment, a fundamentally sound interpretation of inferential meaning, but the maxim fails to deal with other kinds of meaning. In formulating the maxim, Peirce showed no concern with other forms of meaning than inference. With time he would come to recognize that think-

---

[30] Ibid., 5:574–604.
[31] Ibid., 5:389–90.

ing involves much more than the interrelation of sensations and rational inference.[32]

<h1 style="text-align:center">III</h1>

As Peirce's thought matured, his interpretation of the pragmatic maxim evolved. In his 1903 lectures on pragmatism Peirce elaborated his most systematic statement of what pragmatic thinking meant for him. By 1903, however, Peirce had recontextualized the maxim by situating it within his theory of the normative sciences. His theory of the normative sciences, moreover, functioned within his summary classification of the state of scientific knowledge at the dawn of the twentieth century.

Prior to reading Abbot's *Scientific Theism,* Peirce seems to have believed in keeping science and religion as separate from one another as possible. Abbot, however, seems to have helped him recognize that one could use logic to effect a closer wedding of religion and science. Peirce began subsequently to dream of elaborating a realistic, theistic metaphysics in dialogue with the positive sciences. As a preparation for formulating that metaphysics "architectonically" (i.e., systematically and comprehensively), Peirce decided that he needed to survey the current state of scientific knowledge. His survey led him to a logical classification of the sciences.[33]

Peirce distinguished sciences of discovery from sciences of review.[34] Evolutionary theory illustrates how a science of review organizes the results of scientific discoveries in other fields. Peirce divided sciences of discovery into mathematics, philosophy, and idioscopy. Mathematics studies logical possibility.[35] Philosophy reflects on lived experience. Peirce also called the philosophical sciences coenoscopic, from the Greek term *"koinos,"* meaning common. By that he meant that they examine shared

---

[32] See C. F. Delaney, *Science, Knowledge, and Mind: A Study in the Philosophy of C. S. Peirce* (Notre Dame, Ind.: University of Notre Dame Press, 1993); Peter Skagestad, *The Road of Inquiry: Charles Peirce's Pragmatic Realism* (New York: Columbia University Press, 1981); R. M. Martin, *Peirce's Logic of Relations and Other Studies* (Dordrecht: Foris Publications, 1980); Richard Smyth, "The Pragmatic Maxim in 1878," *Transactions of the Charles S. Peirce Society* 13 (1977) 93–111; G. Gentry, "Peirce's Early and Later Theory of Cognition and Meaning," *Philosophical Review* 55 (1946) 634–40; Winston H. F. Barnes, "Peirce on 'How to Make Our Ideas Clear,'" *Studies, I,* 53–60; Idus Murphee, "The Theme of Positivism in Peirce's Pragmatism," *Studies, II,* 226–41; Peter Ochs, "A Pragmatic Method of Reading Confused Philosophic Texts: The Case of Peirce's 'Illustrations,'" *Transactions of the Charles S. Peirce Society* 25 (1989) 251–91.

[33] See Philip P. Wiener, "Peirce's Evolutionary Interpretations of the History of Science," *Studies, I,* 143–52.

[34] Peirce, *Collected Papers,* 1:182.

[35] Ibid., 1:182–4.

human experiences.[36] The idioscopic sciences focus on a specific realm of experience and tend to employ both special methods and special instrumentation in order to examine and understand their object.[37]

The coenoscopic or philosophical sciences divide into phenomenology, the normative sciences, and metaphysics. Phenomenology categorizes descriptively the generic kinds of elements which comprise ordinary, lived experience. Phenomenology describes whatever appears in experience without making any judgment as to its ontological status.[38] The normative sciences deal critically with the way in which one ought to live. The normative sciences study the kinds of habits one needs to form in order to live fruitfully. Aesthetics studies the ideals which ought to give purpose and direction to the living of life. Aesthetics also discerns the nature of the *summum bonum,* that which gives ultimate meaning and purpose to human striving.[39] Ethics studies the kinds of habits of choice one ought to cultivate in order to live for the ideals to which one stands committed.[40] Logic studies the habits of thought which one ought to cultivate in order to think clearly about reality, so that one may make the kinds of choices which eventuate in fruitful living.[41] All the normative sciences mediate between phenomenology and metaphysics, but logic builds the final bridge between a descriptive account of what appears in experience and a metaphysical judgment about the character of reality. Let us reflect in greater detail on the way in which this division of the philosophical sciences shaped Peirce's mature understanding of pragmatic realism.[42]

Peirce's phenomenology discovered three generic kinds of elements which appear in lived, human experience. He named each element: quality, fact, and law. Peirce defined a "quality" as an instance of particular suchness. We experience qualities in the shifting kaleidoscope of feelings which make up experience: sensations, emotions, images, abstract con-

---

[36] Ibid., 1:241 and footnote.

[37] Ibid., 1:242. See also O. Bird, "Peirce's Theory of Methodology," *Philosophy of Science* 26 (1959) 187–200; Paul D. Forster, "Peirce on the Progress and Authority of Science," *Transactions of the Charles S. Peirce Society* 25 (1989) 421–52.

[38] Peirce, *Collected Papers,* 1:186, 190, 280, 535.

[39] See J. Feibleman, "Esthetics of Peirce," *Personalist* 22 (1941) 253–69.

[40] See J. Feibleman, "Individual Psychology and the Ethics of Peirce," *Journal of General Psychology* 21 (1944) 293–5.

[41] Peirce, *Collected Papers,* 1:573–615.

[42] Ibid., 1:487–8, 624–5. See also Peter Krausser, "The Three Fundamental Structural Categories of Charles S. Peirce," *Transactions of the Charles S. Peirce Society* 13 (1977) 189–215; Fred Michael, "Two Forms of Scholastic Realism in Peirce's Philosophy," *Transactions of the Charles S. Peirce Society* 24 (1988) 317–48; Edward S. Petry, "The Origin and Development of Peirce's Concept of Self-Control," *Transactions of the Charles S. Peirce Society* 28 (1992) 666–90.

cepts.[43] Viewed in itself, each quality exhibits a *sui generis* character which accounts for its particularity. Each quality is what it is.[44] Quality also endows experience with a sense of "presentness."[45] Viewed as modes of being, qualities exemplify what Peirce called "firstness."

> Firstness is the mode of being which consists in its subject's being positively such as it is regardless of aught else. That can only be possibility. For as long as things do not act upon one another there is no sense or meaning in saying that they have any being, unless it be that they are such in themselves that they may perhaps come into relation with others.[46]

Any idea or value abstracted from everything but its own essential meaning exemplifies firstness. Think, for example, of "teal," "wombat," "mountain," "2+2=4" as real possibilities and you will experience firstness.

By "facts" Peirce meant the contingent interplay of brute forces, physical action together with its physical reaction without any mediating intelligence. One experiences facts as concrete shocks of physical resistance, as physical struggle. While qualities enjoy particularity and possibility, facts exhibit concrete individuality and actuality. They make experience this rather than that.[47] Facts endow experience with concrete relatedness and with environmental rootedness.[48] When one views facts as modes of being, the reciprocity of facts, the interplay of action and reaction, justifies calling them instances of "secondness."

> An object cannot be a *second* of itself. If it is a second, it has an element of being what another makes it to be. That is, the being of a second involves Secondness. The reaction still more manifestly involves the being what another makes a subject to be. Thus, while Secondness is a fact of complexity, it is not a compound of two facts. It is a single fact about two objects.[49]

An earthquake, a volcanic eruption, a hurricane all exemplify secondness. The earthquake results from the grinding of plates, the volcanic eruption from the welling up of magma from the core of the earth, the hurricane

[43] Peirce, *Collected Papers,* 1:300–16.
[44] Ibid., 1:422.
[45] Ibid., 5:41–4.
[46] Ibid., 1:25, 524, 530ff. See also J. Dewey, "Peirce's Theory of Quality," *Journal of Philosophy* 32 (1935) 701–8.
[47] Peirce, *Collected Papers,* 1:427–40.
[48] Ibid., 5:45–58. See also T. A. Goudge, "Views of Charles Peirce on the Given in Experience," *Journal of Philosophy* 32 (1935) 533–44; T. A. Goudge, "Further Reflections on Peirce's Doctrine of the Given," *Journal of Philosophy* 33 (1936) 289–95.
[49] Peirce, *Collected Papers,* 1:526; see also 521–6. See also Jeffrey R. Di Leo, "Peirce's Haecceitism," *Transactions of the Charles S. Peirce Society* 27 (1991) 79–109; Robert A. Jacques, "On the Reality of Seconds," *Transactions of the Charles S. Peirce Society* 28 (1992) 757–66.

from the spiraling of powerful winds. Willing which does not eventuate in overt physical activity and which fails therefore to evoke a concrete factual response exemplifies a degenerate form of secondness: for example, the decisive fixation of a belief or an attitude.

By a "law" Peirce meant real generality, the habitual tendency to act in a specific way under specifiable conditions. Peirce put it this way: "In short, the idea of a general involves the idea of possible variations which no multitude of existent things could exhaust but would leave between any two not merely *many* possibilities, but possibilities absolutely beyond all multitude."[50]

Generality orients experience to a future by exemplifying a tendency to act in a predictable way. The predictability of a law links it also to the notion of "representation," since by making a prediction we represent a law to ourselves and to other minds. "A law is in itself nothing but a general formula or symbol."[51] Viewed as a mode of being, a law exemplifies what Peirce called "thirdness."

> The first is a positive qualitative possibility, in itself nothing more. The second is an existent thing without any mode of being less than existence, but determined by that first. A *third* has a mode of being which consists in the Secondness that it determines the mode of being of a law, or concept. Do not confound this with the ideal being of a quality in itself. A quality is something capable of being embodied. A law never can be embodied in its character as a law except by determining a habit. A quality is how something may or might have been. A law is how an endless future must continue to be.
>
> Now in genuine Thirdness, the first, the second, and the third are all three of the nature of thirds, or thought, while in respect to one another they are first, second, and third. The first is thought in its capacity as mere possibility; that is, mere *mind* capable of thinking, or a mere vague idea. The second is thought playing the role of a Secondness, or event. That is, it is of the general nature of *experience* or *information*. The third is thought in its role as governing Secondness. It brings the information into the mind, or determines the idea and gives it body. It is informing thought, or *cognition*. But take away the psychological or accidental human element, and in this genuine Thirdness we see the operation of a sign.[52]

A harpsichordist's ability to play, the wisdom of a great scholar, personal saintliness, the ability to read and write all exemplify thirdness.

Thirdness renders reality significant and therefore intelligible. Thirdness also finds exemplification in what Peirce called a "representamen."

[50] Peirce, *Collected Papers,* 5:103.
[51] Ibid., 5:107.
[52] Ibid., 1:536–7.

> *A REPRESENTAMEN is a subject of a triadic relation TO a second, called its OBJECT, FOR a third, called its INTERPRETANT, this triadic relation being such that the REPRESENTAMEN determines its interpretant to stand in the same triadic relation to the same object for some interpretant. . . .* The relation must therefore consist in the *power* of the representamen to determine *some* interpretant to being a representamen of the same object.[53]

By an "interpretant" Peirce meant "the significant outcome of a sign," the kind of interpretative response the sign seeks to evoke.

Thirdness comes in two degenerate forms. A sign which symbolizes through qualitative resemblance (think of a map) or a sign which symbolizes through physical interaction (think of a weathercock) each exemplify a degenerate form of thirdness. As we shall see, Peirce called the first kind of sign an "icon" and the second kind of sign an "index."[54]

Phenomenology deals with the universal qualities of things. It therefore studies experience under the aspect of firstness. The normative sciences, by contrast, relate phenomena to ends. The normative sciences, therefore, study experience under the aspect of secondness, or concrete decision.[55]

The normative sciences deal with three different kinds of goods. Aesthetics studies ideal goods as admirable, as good in and for themselves.

---

[53] Ibid., 1:541. Stephen French, "A Peircean Response to the Realist Empiricist Debate," *Transactions of the Charles S. Peirce Society* 25 (1989) 293–306; James Jacob Liszka, "Peirce's Interpretant," *Transactions of the Charles S. Peirce Society* 26 (1990) 17–62; Sandra B. Rosenthal, "Peirce's Ultimate Logical Interpretant: A Pragmatic Perspective," *Transactions of the Charles S. Peirce Society* 26 (1990) 195–210; Susan Haack, "'Extreme Scholastic Realism': Its Relation to Philosophy of Science Today," *Transactions of the Charles S. Peirce Society* 28 (1992) 19–50; Claudine Engel Tiercelin, "Vagueness and the Unity of C. S. Peirce's Realism," *Transactions of the Charles S. Peirce Society* 28 (1992) 51–82; Risto Hilipin, "On Peirce's Philosophical Logic: Propositions and Their Objects," *Transactions of the Charles S. Peirce Society* 28 (1992) 467–88; Nathan Honser, "On Peirce's Theory of Propositions: A Response to Hilipin," *Transactions of the Charles S. Peirce Society* 28 (1992) 489–504; Cheryl Misak, "Pragmatism and the Transcendental Turn to Truth in Ethics," *Transactions of the Charles S. Peirce Society* 30 (1994) 739–75.

[54] See David Savan, "On the Origins of Peirce's Phenomenology," *Studies, I*, 185–94; Isabel S. Stearns, "Firstness, Secondness, and Thirdness," *Studies, I*, 195–208; Charles Hartshorne, "The Relativity of Nonrelativity: Some Reflections on Firstness," *Studies, I*, 215–24; Charles K. McKeon, "Peirce's Scotistic Realism," *Studies, I*, 238–50; Rollin Workman, "Pragmatism and Realism," *Studies, II*, 242–53; Edward C. Moore, "The Influence of Duns Scotus on Peirce," *Studies, II*, 401–13; Manley Thompson, "Peirce's Experimental Proof of Scholastic Realism," *Studies, II*, 414–29; Victor Lowe, "Peirce and Whitehead as Metaphysicians," *Studies, II*, 430–54; Charles Hartshorne, "Charles Peirce's 'One Contribution to Philosophy' and His Most Serious Mistake," *Studies, II*, 455–74; Robert Almeder, "Peirce's Pragmatism and Scotistic Realism," *Transactions of the Charles S. Peirce Society* 9 (1973) 3–23.

[55] Peirce, *Collected Papers,* 5:122–3.

Peirce vacillated when it came to asserting the normativity of aesthetic thinking, but he came eventually to regard aesthetics as the scientific study of supreme goodness. As the science of the *summum bonum,* aesthetics defines absolute and ultimate desirability: that which one ought to desire in any and all circumstances. Ethics studies moral good: the kinds of means one ought to employ in order to live for the *summum bonum.* Logic studies the reasonable good. Logic decides what it means for one to act reasonably and rationally. Peirce discovered an organic relationship among the three normative sciences. Aesthetics teaches one what to aspire to; ethics teaches one how to orient one's choices habitually to the supreme good; logic teaches one to think clearly about reality so that one can make wise ethical choices. In the end, therefore, even logic serves the attainment of supreme goodness.[56]

Peirce's concern with the normative sciences sprang in part from the distinction which he eventually drew between speculation and life. Like Emerson and Brownson, he came to believe that thinking exemplifies the partial act, living the total act. Peirce put his insight this way: "It is the instincts, the sentiments, that make the substance of the soul. Cognition is only on its surface, its locus of contact with what is external to it."[57] Not surprisingly, the mature Peirce distinguished three kinds of reasoning: (1) necessary, deductive reasoning which can only predict the operational consequences of specific hypotheses; (2) probable statistical reasoning (or induction), which allows one to deal with a multitude of relatively insignificant risks; and (3) what Galileo called *il lume naturale,* or instinct (or abduction).

> Reason is of its essence egotistical. . . . Men many times fancy that they act from reason when, in point of fact, the reasons they attribute to themselves are nothing but excuses which unconscious instinct invents to satisfy

[56] Ibid., 5:137–50. See also Vincent C. Potter, *Charles S. Peirce on Norms and Ideals* (New Haven, Conn.: Yale University Press, 1967) 25–51; Vincent C. Potter, "Peirce's Analysis of Normative Science," *Transactions of the Charles S. Peirce Society* 1 (1966) 5–32; S. Veyama, "Development of Peirce's Theory of Logic," *Journal of Symbolic Logic* 20 (1956) 170; A. W. Burks, "Peirce's Conception of Logic as a Normative Science," *Philosophical Review* 52 (1943) 187–93; Richard S. Robin, "Peirce's Doctrine of the Normative Sciences," *Studies, II,* 271–88; Herman Parrett, *Peirce and Value Theory: On Peircean Ethics and Aesthetics* (Amsterdam: John Benjamins, 1989); Larry Holmes, "Peirce on Self-Control," *Transactions of the Charles S. Peirce Society* 1 (1966) 113–30; Thomas V. Curley, "The Relation of the Normative Sciences to Peirce's Theory of Inquiry," *Transactions of the Charles S. Peirce Society* 5 (1969) 90–106; Beverly Kent, "Peirce's Esthetics," *Transactions of the Charles S. Peirce Society* 12 (1976) 261–83; Catherine Wells Hantzis, "Peirce's Conception of Philosophy: Its Method and Its Program," *Transactions of the Charles S. Peirce Society* 23 (1987) 289–307; Helmut Pape, "Final Causality in Peirce's Semiotics and His Classification of the Sciences," *Transactions of the Charles S. Peirce Society* 29 (1993) 581–607.

[57] Peirce, *Collected Papers,* 5:628.

the teasing "whys" of the *ego*. The extent of this self-delusion is such as to render philosophical rationalism a farce.

Reason, then, appeals to sentiment in the last resort. Sentiment on its side feels itself to be the man. That is my simple apology for philosophical sentimentalism.[38]

This validation of instinctive reasonableness gave the mature Peirce an enhanced respect for common sense. Peirce the philosopher, however, sought to render common sense consciously self-critical. As we shall see below, he eventually called his version of pragmatism "critical common-sensism." Peirce's critical common-sensism would function primarily as a logical doctrine, but each of the normative sciences contributes to the critical ordering of the instinctive living of life. Aesthetics educates the heart to long for the highest goods and to spurn the baser ones. Ethics educates the conscience to choose the practical means which lead to the higher aesthetic goods. Logic renders ethical thinking self-critical and in the process it teaches one to acknowledge not only the strengths but the radical limitations of purely logical thinking. In a sense, Peirce's normative sciences rendered Emerson's *Conduct of Life* more logically precise.

In ordering one's instinctive human wisdom, the normative sciences teach one to live realistically in one's world. Logic, however, also justifies the speculative transition from descriptive philosophical thinking to metaphysics. Phenomenology reduces the elements which appear within experience to three: qualities, facts, and laws. The study of logic shows that all three function in the inferential perception of real generality.

Peirce argued that within perceptual judgments, the mind had no control over the percept, if not over the perceptual judgment itself. Both quality and fact clearly function within every perception. Facts force themselves upon the mind and defeat on occasion the mind's predictions. As a consequence, one cannot seriously doubt the actuality of secondness. The fact that qualities endow experience with presentness means that we experience them with an immediacy which also puts the reality of firstness beyond doubt. The nominalistic caste of modern philosophy, however, makes the reality of laws, of real generality, of thirdness, seem problematic to many minds. Peirce, however, argued that a sound analysis of judgments of perception forces one to conclude to the reality of thirdness as well. The mind perceives reality inferentially, and every inference characterizes a real tendency. Peirce put it this way:

If you object that there can be no immediate consciousness of generality, I grant that. If you add that one can have no direct experience of the general,

[38] Ibid., 1:631.

> I grant that as well. Generality, Thirdness, pours in upon us in our very per-
> ceptual judgments, and all reasoning, so far as it depends on necessary rea-
> soning, that is to say, mathematical reasoning turns upon the perception of
> generality and continuity at every step.[59]

The deductively clarified law which inductive inference grasps as its conclusion, abductive reason already knew, though only initially and vaguely.
Moreover, since abduction fades into perception, every perception also
grasps thirdness, however vaguely.

The fact that the human mind perceives the reality of thirdness inferentially means that the symbolic structure of the human mind corresponds
to the symbolic structure of the realities it perceives. Facts, the behavior of
things in one's world, manifest symbolically the laws or general tendencies which cause them, and those tendencies endow perceived reality with
continuity by exemplifying a tendency to act repeatedly in a specific way
under specifiable circumstances.

Peirce's semiotic, his theory of signs, makes metaphysical claims. As
a consequence, one cannot understand the intent of his semiotic without
asserting its cognitive claims about the nature of the real. Let us try to
understand why.

Peirce's semiotic recognizes three trichotomies, or classifications, of
signs. The first trichotomy categorizes the kind of reality the sign exemplifies. The second trichotomy characterizes signs by the way the sign
symbolizes its object. The third trichotomy of signs characterizes them by
the kind of reality the sign attributes to its object.

When viewed as a kind of reality, signs divide into qualisigns, sin-
signs, and legisigns. A qualisign exemplifies a quality which functions as a
sign. The quality needs embodiment in order to function as a sign, but its
embodiment has nothing to do with its character as a sign. Mathematical
ideas exemplify qualisigns. A sinsign exemplifies a significant event. (The
"sin" in "sinsign" comes from "single" and calls attention to the uniqueness
and un-repeatability of events.) An earthquake or a drop in temperature
would exemplify a sinsign. A legisign exemplifies a law, usually a law established by human fiat. All conventional signs, all legislation, all conventional rules exemplify legisigns by prescribing a certain kind of behavior.

---

[59] Ibid., 5:150; see also 5:108–50, 300–53; Nynfa Bosco, "Peirce and Metaphysicism,"
Studies, II, 345–58; Carl Hausman, "In and Out of Peirce's Percepts," *Transactions of the
Charles S. Peirce Society* 24 (1990) 271–308; Carl Hausmann and Douglas B. Anderson,
"The Telos of Peirce's Realism: Some Comments on Margolis's 'The Passing of Peirce's
Realism,'" *Transactions of the Charles S. Peirce Society* 30 (1994) 825–38; Kelley J. Wells,
"Contra Margolis's Peircean Constructivism: A Peircean Pragmatic Logos," *Transactions
of the Charles S. Peirce Society* 30 (1994) 839–60.

When viewed under the aspect of the way in which they relate to their object, signs divide into icons, indices, and symbols. Icons symbolize by resembling, or exemplifying, the same qualities as their object. A map would exemplify an icon. An index derives its significance from the fact that its object affects the sign physically. The lowering of the mercury in a thermometer, for example, functions as an index of a drop in temperature. A symbol not only has the character of a legisign but designates a law, or general tendency, operative in reality. The laws of physics or of chemistry would exemplify symbols.

The third trichotomy of signs classifies signs by the kind of reality which the sign's interpretant attributes to its object. A rheme attributes a qualitative possibility or essence. Nouns and adjectives exemplify rhemes (e.g.: "cold," "hot," "giraffe," "house"). A dicent sign attributes factual existence, or actuality. A propositional assertion about an event exemplifies a dicent sign (e.g.: "It rained yesterday"). An argument attributes real generality. Arguments contain a dicent sign which functions as its premiss, another proposition which functions as a conclusion, and a copulative proposition which links the other two propositions to one another (e.g.: "All humans are mortal. Socrates is a human. Therefore, Socrates is mortal.").

On the basis of the three trichotomies of signs, Peirce distinguished ten classes of signs: (1) a qualisign, e.g., the mathematical concept "two"; (2) an iconic sinsign, e.g., this map or diagram; (3) a rhematic indexical sinsign, e.g., a spontaneous outcry like "Help!"; (4) a dicent indexical sinsign, e.g., the turning of a weathercock; (5) an iconic legisign, e.g., the idea for a diagram prior to drawing it; (6) a rhematic indexical legisign, e.g., a demonstrative pronoun; (7) a dicent indexical legisign, e.g., a newsboy's cry, like "Extra! Extra!"; (8) a rhematic symbol, e.g., a common noun; (9) a dicent symbol, e.g., an ordinary proposition; (10) an argument, e.g., inferential thinking.[60]

---

[60] Peirce, *Collected Papers,* 2:227–64. See also C. W. Spinks, *Peirce and Triadomania: A Walk in the Semiotic Wilderness* (New York: Mouton de Gruyter, 1991); Don D. Roberts, *The Existential Graphs of Charles S. Peirce* (The Hague: Mouton, 1973); Alan R. Perreiah, "Semiotic and Scholastic Logic," *Transactions of the Charles S. Peirce Society* 25 (1989) 41–9; Robert G. Meyers, "Peirce's New Way of Signs," *Transactions of the Charles S. Peirce Society* 28 (1992) 505–21; Claudine Tiercilin, *La Pensée-signe: Études sur Peirce* (Nimes: Éditions Jacqueline Chambon, 1993); Claudine Tiercilin, *C. S. Peirce et le pragmatisme* (Paris: Presses Universitaire de France, 1993); Roger Ward, "C. S. Peirce and Contemporary Theology: A Return to Conversion," *American Journal of Theology and Philosophy* 16 (1995) 125–48; P. Weiss and A. Burks, "Peirce's Sixty-Six Signs," *Journal of Philosophy* 42 (1945) 383–8; J. Dewey, "Peirce's Theory of Linguistic Signs, Thought, and Meaning," *Journal of Philosophy* 43 (1946) 85–95; M. H. Thompson, "Logical Paradoxes and Peirce's Semiotic," *Journal of Philosophy* 46 (1949) 513–36.

As Peirce's thought evolved, he proposed several different formulations of his pragmatic maxim in an effort to distinguish his understanding of pragmatism from that of other thinkers. In his 1903 lectures on pragmatism Peirce portrayed the maxim as a way of dealing with thirdness. The pragmatic maxim, Peirce argued, implies what he called three cotary propositions. Peirce coined the word "cotary" from the Latin word for whetstone, *cos, cotis*. The cotary propositions sharpen the edge of the pragmatic maxim by clarifying its intent. The three cotary propositions make the following assertions: (1) all intellectual knowledge derives from sensory experience; (2) perceptual judgments contain general elements which enable the mind to derive from them universal propositions; (3) abductive inference shades into, or exemplifies, a kind of perceptual judgment. In other words, abductive inference expresses a perception in logical form. A true abduction grasps the law, or tendency, in reality which justifies its initial classification of explanatory data but initially and vaguely until one clarifies deductively the way the law operates.

As we have seen, the pragmatic maxim asserts that the inferential meaning of any abduction consists in the sum total of its deductively predictable logical consequences. As Peirce put it:

> If you carefully consider the question of pragmatism you will see that it is nothing else than the question of the logic of abduction. That is, pragmatism proposes a certain maxim, which, if sound, must render needless any further rule as to the admissibility of hypotheses to rank as hypothesis, that is to say, as explanations of phenomena held as hopeful suggestions; and, furthermore, this is all that the maxim of pragmatism really pretends to do, at least so far as it is confined to logic, and is not understood as a proposition in psychology. For the maxim of pragmatism is that a conception can have no logical effect or import differing from that of a second conception except so far as, taken in connection with other conceptions and intentions, it might conceivably modify our practical conduct differently from that second conception. . . . Thus, the maxim of pragmatism, if true, fully covers the entire logic of abduction.[61]

[61] Peirce, *Collected Papers,* 5:196; see also K. T. Fann, *Peirce's Theory of Abduction* (The Hague: Martinus Nyhoff, 1970); Richard J. Bernstein, "Peirce's Theory of Perception," *Studies, II,* 165–89; Richard M. Martin, "On Acting on a Belief," *Studies, II,* 212–25; Sandra B. Rosenthal, "A Pragmatic Concept of the Given," *Transactions of the Charles S. Peirce Society* 1 (1967) 74–95; B. Gresham Riley, "Existence, Reality, and Objects of Knowledge: A Defense of C. S. Peirce as a Realist," *Transactions of the Charles S. Peirce Society* 2 (1969) 34–48; Robert F. Almeder, "Peirce's Theory of Perception," *Transactions of the Charles S. Peirce Society* 6 (1970) 99–110; W. M. Brown, "The Economy of Peirce's Abduction," *Transactions of the Charles S. Peirce Society* 19 (1983) 397–411; Douglas R. Anderson, "The Evolution of Peirce's Concept of Abduction," *Transactions of the Charles S. Peirce Society* 22 (1986) 145–64; Timothy Shanahan, "The First Moment of Scientific Inquiry: C. S. Peirce on the Logic of Abduction," *Transactions of the Charles S. Peirce Society*

In other words, the pragmatic maxim asserts that only those propositions can function logically as abductions which have clearly deducible operational consequences. Peirce phrased it this way: "Any hypothesis, therefore, may be admissible, in the absence of any special reasons to the contrary, provided it be capable of experimental verification, and only insofar as it is capable of such verification."[62]

In 1905, two years after the lectures on pragmatism, Peirce offered yet a third formulation of the maxim: "In order to ascertain the meaning of an intellectual conception one should consider what practical consequences might conceivably result by necessity from the truth of that conception; and the sum of these consequences will constitute the entire meaning of the conception."[63] This phrasing of the maxim approximates more closely Peirce's original formulation in his 1878 article "How to Make Our Ideas Clear," but the 1905 formulation highlights (however cryptically) the contribution which each form of inference makes to the process of reasoning. Abduction formulates the "meaning" of an intellectual conception. Deduction predicts with logical "necessity" the operational consequences of one's hypothesis, "the entire meaning of the conception," and needs inductive validation.

In 1905 Peirce also renamed his version of pragmatism "pragmaticism" in order to distinguish it from the pragmatisms of William James and of F.C.S. Schiller. The article in which he did so, while putting into print some of the insights of the unpublished "Lectures on Pragmatism," failed to advance beyond the insights of the lectures. Peirce intended the article,

22 (1986) 449–66; Hugh Joswick, "Peirce's Mathematical Model of Interpretation," *Transactions of the Charles S. Peirce Society* 24 (1988) 108–21; J. E. Tiles, "Iconic Thought and the Scientific Imagination," *Transactions of the Charles S. Peirce Society* 24 (1988) 161–78; Edward H. Madden, "Discussing James and Peirce with Meyers," *Transactions of the Charles S. Peirce Society* 25 (1989) 123–48; Robert G. Meyers, "The Roots of Pragmatism: Madden on James and Peirce," *Transactions of the Charles S. Peirce Society* 25 (1989) 85–121; Jeremiah McCarthy, "An Account of Peirce's Proof of Pragmatism," *Transactions of the Charles S. Peirce Society* 26 (1990) 63–113; Cornelis de Waal, "The Real Issue Between Nominalism and Realism," *Transactions of the Charles S. Peirce Society* 32 (1996) 425–46. For a summary of the development of Peirce's pragmatism see also Karl-Otto Apel, *Charles S. Peirce: From Pragmatism to Pragmaticism,* trans. John Michael Krois (Atlantic Highlands, N.J.: Humanities Press, 1995). Apel does a thorough and careful analysis of the development of Peirce's pragmatic logic, although, in an understandable attempt to explain Peirce to a European audience, every now and then, in my judgment, he assimilates Peirce to German philosophers in ways in which Peirce himself might have qualified.
[62] Peirce, *Collected Papers,* 5:197.
[63] Ibid., 5:9.

however, as an introduction to a series of articles on pragmaticism. In the second article he described his pragmaticism as "critical common-sensism."[64]

He discovered in critical common-sensism six distinguishing characteristics. (1) Critical common-sensism divides propositions and inferences into the dubitable and the indubitable, and it distinguishes logical inference from non-logical associations. One holds critically propositions which one can really doubt and then verify or falsify. One tends to hold indubitable propositions uncritically. Critical common-sensism also distinguishes logical argumentation in the strict sense from the associated suggestions of a belief. A belief associated with another belief determines the latter, but unconsciously. Inferred propositions determine one another consciously. Doubt about a belief or inference always has an origin outside the doubter, usually a surprising origin.[65] (2) Critical common-sensism finds little or no change in the beliefs people hold uncritically.[66] (3) Indubitable beliefs apply to a way of life and, when rooted in instinct, they resist any attempt to doubt them.[67] (4) Indubitable beliefs tend to exhibit vagueness. A vague sign lies open to determination by some other conceivable sign. The principle of contradiction does not apply to a vague sign.[68] In other words, before one can verify or falsify a vague sign, one must clarify it. (5) Critical common-sensism attaches great importance to real (as opposed to fictive) doubt. Real doubt has an identifiable motive; fictive doubt lacks such a motive. The human mind tends to resist fictive doubt. Critical common-sensism also holds that one runs fewer risks in believing too little than in believing too much.[69] (6) Common-sensism becomes critical by subjecting to criticism its own beliefs, the beliefs of the Common Sense school of philosophy, the beliefs of those who would base logic on metaphysics, on psychology, or on any special science, and the beliefs of Kantian philosophy.[70]

---

[64] See Arthur O. Lovejoy, "What Is the Pragmatistic Theory of Meaning? The First Phase," *Studies, I,* 3–20; Justus Buchler, "What Is the Pragmatistic Theory of Meaning?" *Studies, I,* 21–33; Daniel J. Bronstein, "Inquiry and Meaning," *Studies, I,* 33–52; W. B. Gallie, "Peirce's Pragmatism," *Studies, I,* 61–74; George Gentry, "Habit and the Logical Interpretant," *Studies, I,* 75–90; Paul D. Foster, "Peirce and the Threat of Nominalism," *Transactions of the Charles S. Peirce Society* 28 (1992) 691–724.

[65] Peirce, *Collected Papers,* 5:438–43.

[66] Ibid., 5:444.

[67] Ibid., 5:445.

[68] Ibid., 5:446–50.

[69] Ibid., 5:451.

[70] Ibid., 5:453. Peirce's list of indubitable forms of knowledge apparently included sensations, unconscious feelings and abductions, attention, percepts, perceptual facts, direct action and reaction with resistant objects, perceptual judgments, the reasoning of pure mathematics, principles governing inference, instinctive beliefs, moral sentiment and instinct,

Peirce discovered the first three descriptive tenets of critical common-sensism in Scottish common-sense philosophy, but he held that pragmaticism advances beyond traditional common-sense philosophy in the fourth, fifth, and sixth tenets. In addition, pragmaticism distinguishes three modalities of thought and reality: actuality, possibility, and necessity. We know actuality by direct recollection, necessity when only one state of things corresponds to what we know, and possibility when knowledge does not exclude more than one state of things. Real actuality is the past. The future is either necessitated or contingent. Pragmaticism as a doctrine seeks to bring about the conscious control of future facts, the only facts we can control. It portrays consciousness therefore as conative and discovers in the present moment the struggle over what shall be.[71]

In two unpublished papers written in 1905 Peirce attempted to clarify the relationship between pragmaticism and critical common-sensism. He argued that pragmaticism's concern to distinguish accurately between truth and falsity, probability and improbability, renders it attentive to the matters of everyday fact which critical common-sensism takes into account in order to make inferences based on those facts,[72] for what one cannot doubt, one must necessarily hold as true.[73]

Critical common-sensism qualifies significantly the position taken by the middle Peirce that thought has no absolute starting point and must begin *in medias res.* The mature Peirce discovered in humans a relatively stable number of vague, common-sense beliefs which resist all doubt. These beliefs do not, like Descartes's *Cogito,* provide a deductive starting point for thinking about all reality, but they do provide the mind with a relatively stable number of affirmations which resist any real doubt and which endow thinking with instinctive stability.

Critical common-sensism also developed an aspect of the mature Peirce's logic of abduction, which holds that the attractiveness of a

---

especially in moments of crisis, common sense judgments, beliefs determined by other beliefs without proceeding on any general principle, factual propositions supported by overwhelming evidence. See David Savan, "Decision and Knowledge in Peirce," *Transactions of the Charles S. Peirce Society* 1 (1965) 35–51; James E. Broyles, "Charles S. Peirce and the Concept of Indubitable Belief," *Transactions of the Charles S. Peirce Society* 1 (1965) 77–89; Arnold E. Johnson, "Paper Doubt, Feigned Hesitancy, and Inquiry," *Transactions of the Charles S. Peirce Society* 8 (1972) 214–30; Robert Almeder, "The Epistemological Realism of Charles Peirce," *Transactions of the Charles S. Peirce Society* 11 (1975) 3–17; John P. Murphy, *Pragmatism from Peirce to Davidson* (San Francisco: Westview, 1990).

[71] Peirce, *Collected Papers,* 5:453–63.

[72] Ibid., 5:497–9.

[73] Ibid., 5:515; Arthur F. Smullyan, "Some Implications of Critical Common-Sensism," *Studies, I,* 111–20.

hypothesis offers one good reason for selecting it for testing. The mature Peirce had come to trust in Galileo's *il lume naturale,* a co-naturality between the mind and nature which explains the educated mind's uncanny ability to select from an infinite number of logical possibilities the one hypothesis which proves to be true. Part of the mind's instinctive co-naturality with reality consists of a set of primitive, instinctive, indubitable beliefs about life and reality which tend to prove true.

In addition to a proposition's spontaneous attractiveness, Peirce's logic of abduction identified three other reasons, or canons, for initially adopting a hypothesis for experimental testing. The canon of caution states that one should only adopt hypotheses for whose testing one has the resources of energy, time, and money. The canon of testability advises one to prefer a hypothesis which one can break up into smaller logical components for independent testing. The canon of breadth advises one to elect for testing that hypothesis which has the greatest number of implications for other realms of human inquiry.[74]

In 1906 Peirce in yet another unpublished paper reformulated for a fourth time his pragmatic maxim. He did so in the following terms:

> The *total* meaning of the predication of an intellectual concept is contained in an affirmation that, under all conceivable circumstances of a given kind (or under this or that more or less indefinite part of the cases of their fulfillment, should the predication be modal) the subject of the predication would behave in a certain general way—that is, it would be true under given experiential circumstances (or under a more or less definitely stated proportion of them *taken as they would occur,* that is, in the same order of succession, *in experience*). A most pregnant principle, quite understandably, will this "kernel of pragmatism" prove to be, that the whole meaning of an intellectual predicate is that certain kinds of events would happen, once in so often, in the course of experience, under certain kinds of existential conditions—provided it can be proved to be true.[75]

This final formulation of the maxim shifts attention from the act of interpretation to the way the interpreted reality would behave under specified circumstances. So formulated, the maxim asserts the same basic thesis as its earlier formulations, but it makes more explicit than they do the link between the maxim and real, conditioned generality. One cannot understand how some reality "would behave if" without asserting the reality

---

[74] Peirce, *Collected Papers,* 7:220–1; see also Paul Weiss, "The Logic of the Creative Process," 166–82.

[75] Peirce, *Collected Papers,* 5:467–8. See also Dennis Rohatyn, "Peirce and the Defense of Realism: The Unfolding of Pragmatic Logic," *Transactions of the Charles S. Peirce Society* 19 (1983) 45–61.

of law. This final formulation of the maxim also distinguishes between actual and possible verification and explicitly allows for verification within a range of probability.

The essay in which Peirce enunciated this final formulation of the maxim also linked it to the idea of an interpretant. The essay distinguished emotional, energetic, and logical interpretants. Emotional interpretants evoke a felt, aesthetic response. Energetic interpretants grasp commands. Logical interpretants grasp inferences. In this essay, Peirce also grounded different kinds of interpretants in different kinds of habits. Peirce then proposed pragmaticism as a method for modifying habits of belief in ways which will allow one to take better control of the world in which one lives. The essay closed by contrasting pragmaticism with the logically more vague accounts of pragmatism propounded by James and Schiller.[76]

In the same year Peirce also restated his pragmatistic doctrine of truth. He defined truth as "the conformity of a representamen to its object, *its* object, ITS object, mind you." He then explained that for a representamen to become true, "its object" must act upon it to make it true. The sign does not determine the object; the object determines the sign by acting in a specific way. Needless to say, in questions of any complexity, questions which transcend the limits of critical common-sensism, the verification of an inference always occurs in the context of Peircean fallibilism.[77]

This clarification also marked a significant advance over the thought of Peirce's middle period. The middle Peirce defined truth as that account of reality on which the scientific community would eventually agree. That definition put truth beyond the present grasp of the mind. The mature Peirce equated truth with a verified induction which events make true.

As Peirce's thought evolved, then, he claimed both more and less for his pragmatic maxim. He claimed less because, when he originally

[76] Peirce, *Collected Papers*, 5:470–96. See also T. L. Short, "Interpreting Peirce's Interpretant: A Response to Lalor Liszka and Meyers," *Transactions of the Charles S. Peirce Society* 33 (1996) 488–541.

[77] Ibid., 5:554. See also C. J. Misak, *Truth and the End of Inquiry* (Oxford: Clarendon Press, 1991); Robert Almeder, "Peirce's Thirteen Theories of Truth," *Transactions of the Charles S. Peirce Society* 21 (1985) 77–94; George A. Benedict, "What Are Representamens?" *Transactions of the Charles S. Peirce Society* 21 (1985) 241–70; Marcus G. Singer, "Truth, Belief, and Inquiry in Peirce," *Transactions of the Charles S. Peirce Society* 21 (1985) 383–406; Demetra Sfendoni-Mentzou, "Towards a Potential Pragmatic Account of Peirce's Theory of Truth," *Transactions of the Charles S. Peirce Society* 27 (1991) 27–77; Helmut Pape, "Not Every Object of a Sign Has Being," *Transactions of the Charles S. Peirce Society* 27 (1991) 141–77; Patrick F. Sullivan, "On Falsificationist Interpretations of Peirce," *Transactions of the Charles S. Peirce Society* 27 (1991) 197–219; H. S. Thayer, "Peirce and Truth: Some Reflections," *Transactions of the Charles S. Peirce Society* 32 (1996).

formulated it, he proposed it as a definition of meaning. The mature Peirce had come to see that pragmatism defines meaning in only one realm of human evaluative response, namely, in rational, inferential thinking. At the same time, the mature Peirce also claimed more for the maxim. He claimed the ability to demonstrate its truth, a demonstration which engaged all five of his philosophical sciences. From phenomenology he derived the three basic categories: quality, fact, and law. Having situated logic within the normative sciences, he then used it to move from phenomenology to metaphysics through an analysis of the act of perception which shows that in the process of thinking abductively, deductively, and inductively, the mind not only grasps secondness with the senses but perceives thirdness directly and inferentially. For Peirce the human mind perceives more than it senses because it perceives thirdness. In other words, Peircean pragmatism culminates not in the instrumental building of bridges (although it could) but in metaphysics. It seeks to give the mind more control over the world and over the course of human life, but it does so primarily by clarifying the realistic meaning of rational thought.[78]

IV

In 1890 Charles Peirce began to sketch in manuscript form his "guess at the riddle" of a sphinx-like universe. The sweep of his own philosophical vision kindled his heart with excitement. On the first page of this unpublished projected work, he penned the following observation: "And this book, if ever written, as it soon will be if I am in a situation to do it, will be one of the births of time."[79]

The published version of Peirce's "guess" took modest form. It appeared in a series of five articles in *The Monist* which probed the grounds of evolutionary theory: "The Architecture of Theories" (1891); "The Doctrine of Necessity Examined" (1892); "The Law of Mind" (1892); "Man's Glassy Essence" (1892); and "Evolutionary Love" (1893).

The first article in the series defended the legitimacy of and need for an architectonic approach to philosophical thinking through "a complete survey of human knowledge." Such a survey yields philosophically interesting "general conceptions," like the law of the conservation of energy.[80] The very existence of such rational generalizations made by scientific reason raises two

---

[78] See Peter T. Manicas, "Pragmatic Philosophy and the Charge of Scientism," *Transactions of the Charles S. Peirce Society* 24 (1988) 179–222.

[79] Peirce, *Collected Papers,* 1:354, n. *. See also John K. Sheriff, *Charles Peirce's Guess at the Riddle* (Bloomington: Indiana University Press, 1994); E. Nagel, "Charles Peirce's Guesses at the Riddle," *Journal of Philosophy* 30 (1933) 365–86.

[80] Peirce, *Collected Papers,* 6:7–9.

interrelated philosophical problems: (1) How does it come about that, out of the infinite number of theoretical possibilities available to it as an explanation of events, the scientific mind, relying on its hunches and innate common sense, can hit upon the one explanation which interprets accurately the data under investigation? (2) How does it come about that laws exist at all?[81]

The scientific evidence assembled by Darwin and by others suggested that the laws of nature result from some kind of evolutionary process. However, Peirce's survey of evolutionary theory at the end of the nineteenth century yielded four contrasting accounts of the evolutionary origins of nature's laws: (1) evolution results from the operation of mechanical principles (Spencerian evolution); (2) evolution results from heredity and sporting (Darwinian evolution); (3) evolution results from a series of incremental changes (Lamarckian evolution); and (4) evolution results from cataclysmic, environmental changes (the theory of Clarence King).[82] In his *Monist* articles, Peirce set out to refute Spencerian evolution, to evaluate the other three evolutionary theories, and to propose an account of the evolution of natural laws based in his own triadic metaphysics.

Other sciences contributed to Peirce's architectonic amassing of empirical data relevant to the formulation of a scientific metaphysics. From psychology, Peirce derived the notion of feelings (which exemplify qualitative simplicity), of sensations of reaction (which exemplify dyads), and habits of thought (which exhibit a triadic, general structure).[83] From philosophy, Peirce derived the need to reject and transcend dualistic patterns of thought. Peirce deemed that the history of philosophy offered three non-dualistic metaphysical hypotheses: monism, materialism, or idealism. Of the three, he judged that the theory of objective idealism, namely, that "matter is effete mind," offers the "one intelligible theory of the universe."[84] From mathematics, Peirce derived the concept of continuity and mathematical generalization. Mathematical generalization, since it studies possibility, experiences no constraint to conform to sensory images. Moreover, mathematical measurement requires the philosopher to give some account of space.[85] Finally, logic supplies the basic categories of firstness (that which exists independent of anything else), secondness (reaction, or existence in relationship), and thirdness (mediation between a first and a second).[86]

[81] Ibid., 6:8–12. See also Beverley Kent, *Charles S. Peirce: Logic and the Classification of the Sciences* (Kingston, Ont.: McGill-Queens University Press, 1987).
[82] Peirce, *Collected Papers,* 6:14–17.
[83] Ibid., 6:18–23.
[84] Ibid., 6:24–5.
[85] Ibid., 6:26–31.
[86] Ibid., 6:32.

With these fundamental building blocks derived from his survey of scientific knowing, Peirce set out to construct his guess at the cosmic riddle. He began by excluding a mechanistic interpretation of nature. Mechanism hopes to explain all reality by appealing to necessary laws. Those who defend mechanism often present it as an unavoidable postulate of scientific reason, but the postulation of a principle never demonstrates its truth. Like any other hypothesis, mechanism can lay no claims to any privileged, self-evident truth. A scientific postulate exemplifies "the formulation of a material fact which we are not entitled to assume as a premiss, but the truth of which is requisite for the validity of an inference." So, one must either prove the truth of a postulate by citing indicative evidence or concede its possible unverifiability.[87]

The critical philosophical mind must then ask: Does direct observational evidence support a strictly necessitarian account of the universe? Necessitarianism presupposes that certain quantities in nature have exact mathematical values, but scientific measurement never achieves exactitude. As a consequence, no appeal to exactitude of measurement can exclude a priori the presence of spontaneity in the universe. By the same token, scientific observation does not allow one to conclude that facts always conform precisely to some unchanging law. The observable adaptations in natural organisms never advance with necessary uniformity.[88]

Moreover, nothing we know scientifically precludes the possibility of chance events in the universe or rules it out as unintelligible. On the contrary, the cumulative evidence derived from the study of biological evolution suggests that the organic universe evolved through a process of diversification and specification. The necessitarian presupposes that the same laws operative at the beginning of the cosmic process operate now. On necessitarian presuppositions, then, the world at its inception should have exhibited the same complexity and diversity as it now possesses and manifests. The overwhelming preponderance of the evidence amassed so far, however, rules against such a presupposition. "Everywhere the main fact is growth and increasing complexity." The observable evidence then points to the fact that any mechanical forces operative in nature find themselves countered by an element of pure chance. Peirce called the philosophical affirmation of the reality of chance "tychism," from the Greek word *tychē,* chance. Contemporary chaos theory supports this insight.

---

[87] Ibid., 6:39–42.

[88] Ibid., 6:43–50. Peirce wrote his *Monist* articles well in advance of chaos theory, but one can assert with some confidence that its eventual formulation would not have surprised him. See James Gleick, *Chaos: Making a New Science* (New York: Viking Press, 1987).

Philosophical necessitarianism seeks to explain the operations of the mind by appealing to the mechanical laws of matter. The evidence supports belief that chance operates in the universe. Peirce found one law which governs the operations of the mind: "that ideas tend to spread continuously and to affect certain others which stand to them in a peculiar relation of affectability. In this spreading they lose intensity and especially the power of affecting others, but gain generality and become welded with other ideas."[89] Peirce called this law of the continuous spreading of ideas the law of "synechism," from the Greek verb *"synechô,"* I hold together. Without continuity within consciousness, the mind could never compare a present idea to a past one. How then does a past idea become present to the mind? If not vicariously, then by direct perception. If by direct perception, however, then something connects the past to the present by "a series of real but infinitesimal steps." In other words, "this infinitesimally spread-out consciousness is a direct feeling of its contents as spread out."[90]

The continuity of consciousness, however, also requires it to occupy time. The flow of consciousness exemplifies the directional flow of the past to the future. In that flow, the past can affect present feelings, but future feelings cannot do the same. Two states absolutely unaffectable by one another would exemplify contemporaneous existence. A state between two states affects the one and is affected by the other. Finally, every state of feeling is affectable by an earlier state.[91]

Feelings have both intensive continuity and spatial extension. The intensity of feeling implies that "when any particular kind of feeling is present, an infinitesimal continuum of feelings differing infinitesimally from that is present." One can observe the spatial extension of feeling in the wave-like motion which flows through a glob of protoplasm. Feeling, however, differs from thought, although the latter develops in continuity with feeling.[92] The spreading of a feeling to affect other feelings occupies a temporal duration and welds the feelings in question together in association. The resulting general idea exemplifies a "habit of feeling."[93]

Three different elements make up an idea: "The first is quality as feeling. The second is the energy with which it affects other ideas. . . . The third is the tendency of an idea to bring along other ideas with it."[94] As an idea spreads, its power to affect other ideas is reduced but its intrinsic

---

[89] Peirce, *Collected Papers,* 6:104.
[90] Ibid., 6:107–11.
[91] Ibid., 6:127–31.
[92] Ibid., 6:132–3.
[93] Ibid., 6:137.
[94] Ibid., 6:135.

quality remains relatively unchanged. The general idea is a living continuum of feeling felt as immediately present. Its existence refutes any nominalistic philosophical hypothesis about the nature of reality, and the general idea's pattern of growth demands that the future be influenced only by suggestions from the past.[95] In Peirce's scientific universe time cannot reverse directions.

The law of continuous spreading, therefore, governs the production of mental association. This same law operates in the development of scientific inference. The three modes of inference proceed by different habits of association, which, as we have seen, Peirce called the leading principles of each mode of inference. In abduction, "a number of reactions called for by one occasion are united in a general idea which is called out by the same occasion." In deduction, "the habit fulfills its function of calling out certain reactions on certain occasions." In other words, the ability to think deductively enables one to predict both future events and the conditions under which they will transpire. In induction, "a number of sensations followed by one reaction become united under one general idea followed by the same reaction." Induction, in other words, establishes a new habit of belief. Habit, then, exemplifies "that specialization of the law of mind whereby a general idea gains the power of exciting reactions." But mental action exhibits neither necessity nor invariance.[96]

Peirce enunciated his law of mind in five clauses:

> First, then, we find that when we regard ideas from a nominalistic, sensualistic way, the simplest facts of mind become utterly meaningless. That one idea should resemble another or influence another, or that one state of mind should do so much as be thought of in another, is, from that standpoint, sheer nonsense.
>
> Second, by this and other means we are driven to perceive, what is quite evident of itself, that instantaneous feelings flow together in a continuum of feeling, which has in a modified degree the peculiar vivacity of feeling and has gained generality. And in reference to such general ideas, or continua of feeling, the difficulties about resemblance and suggestion and reference to the external cease to have any force.
>
> Third, these general ideas are not mere words, nor do they consist in this, that certain concrete facts will every time happen under certain descriptions of conditions; but they are just as much, or rather far more, living realities than the feelings themselves out of which they are concreted. And to say that mental phenomena are governed by laws does not mean merely that they are describable by a general formula; but that there is a living idea, a conscious continuum of feeling which pervades them, and to which they are docile.

---

[95] Ibid., 6:139–42.
[96] Ibid., 6:145–8.

Fourth, this supreme law, which is the celestial and living harmony, does not so much demand that the special ideas shall surrender their peculiar arbitrariness and caprice entirely; for that would be self-destructive. It only requires that they shall influence and be influenced by one another.

In what measure this unification acts, seems to be regulated only by special rules; or, at least, we cannot in our present knowledge say how far it goes. But it may be said that, judging by appearances, the amount of arbitrariness in the phenomena of human minds is neither altogether trifling nor very prominent.[97]

Thus summarized, the law of mind throws light on the meaning of a "personality." Personality exemplifies "some kind of co-ordination or connection of ideas." One can apprehend a personality only by living it over a period of time, but the personality remains present and living at each infinitesimal interval of its development. At any moment, one apprehends one's own personality through "immediate self-consciousness," colored by the feelings of the moment. Every personality, then, exemplifies "a teleological harmony of ideas." The teleology in question operates developmentally, not mechanically and repetitiously. As a developing, general idea, every personality involves a reference to a future. Peirce believed that this understanding of personality could interpret the phenomenon of multiple personalities.[98]

The law of mind enabled Peirce to elaborate in somewhat more detail what he meant when he suggested that matter exemplifies effete mind. Sensible matter, he noted, gives evidence of consisting of molecules in swift motion and exerting enormous mutual attractions and repulsions. Moreover the impenetrability of bodies, to the extent that the human mind can observe it, gives evidence of limitation. We have no reason to suppose absolute physical impenetrability. Absolute impenetrability would have to consist of infinite repulsion at a certain distance. The kinetic theory of matter assimilates the structure of molecules to a miniature star cluster. Physical science also has evidence for the dissociation, or throwing off, of sub-molecular particles. Through the process of dissociation, molecules in sufficiently close proximity could produce perturbations in one another's internal motions.[99]

[97] Ibid., 6:150–4. See James A. Blackowicz, "Realism and Idealism in Peirce's Categories," *Transactions of the Charles S. Peirce Society* 8 (1972) 199–213; Matthew J. Fairbanks, "Peirce on Man as a Language: A Textual Interpretation," *Transactions of the Charles S. Peirce Society* 12 (1976) 18–32; Patricia A. Muoro, "Peirce on Person," *Transactions of the Charles S. Peirce Society* 20 (1984) 169–81; Robert G. Meyers, "Peirce's Doubts About Idealism," *Transactions of the Charles S. Peirce Society* 21 (1985) 223–39; Vincent M. Colapietro, "Inwardness and Autonomy: A Neglected Aspect of Peirce's Approach to Mind," *Transactions of the Charles S. Peirce Society* 21 (1985) 485–512.

[98] Peirce, *Collected Papers,* 6:155.

[99] Ibid., 6:238–45. See also Lesley Friedman, "Peirce's Reality and Berkeley's Blunders," *Journal of the History of Philosophy* 35 (1997) 253–68.

Protoplasmic substances, or life-slimes, exemplify matter as effete mind. They exist in two states of aggregation: either solid (or nearly solid) or liquid (or nearly liquid). Especially in the liquid state, they decompose when exposed to heat, and they do not pass from a solid to a liquid state by ordinary fusion. All their vital actions, moreover, take place at temperatures very slightly below the point of decomposition.[100]

If one takes solidity in the broadest sense, then all protoplasms have some solidity. They liquify only when disturbed, with the liquefaction starting from the point of disturbance and spreading progressively through the mass. With the cessation of disturbance, the protoplasm returns to its former solid, quiescent state. Some protoplasm, especially muscular protoplasm, tends to draw itself up in globular forms. Other forms of protoplasm put forth extraordinary pseudopods. Repeated liquefaction produces fatigue.[101]

Most important of all, life-slimes grow through assimilation, not through simple accretion. Frequent liquefaction increases the power of assimilating food. Protoplasms grow and waste; they also reproduce, often through the union of two sexes, although not necessarily so. Finally, protoplasm both takes habits and feels.[102]

One needs, then, a molecular hypothesis which can account for all these behavioral properties of protoplasmic life. Some of the properties appear to result from the instability of a substance as complex as protoplasm. One can explain the liquefaction of the protoplasm as the result of the dissociation of sub-molecular particles operating in an unstable compound. The return to a solid condition would, then, signify the restoration of equilibrium. The chilling of the protoplasm in a state of liquefaction can account for the changes in surface tension which produce both contraction and the extension of pseudopods. Assimilation of food could result from extreme molecular diffusion in liquefaction allowing for the restoration of molecular equilibrium through assimilation. The loss of energy which accompanies liquefaction chills the protoplasm; the restoration of equilibrium brings a recovery of heat. Loss of energy without the restoration of heat produces fatigue. The restoration of tissue through nourishment demands the delivery of the needed food with the right chemical composition, at the right spot, in the right direction, and with the correct velocity.[103]

In the course of successive liquefaction and solidification, the protoplasm throws out pretty nearly the same molecules as it draws in through assimilation.

---

[100] Peirce, *Collected Papers*, 6:246.
[101] Ibid., 6:248–9.
[102] Ibid., 6:247–54.
[103] Ibid., 6:259–60.

They will be thrown out, too, in about the same way, as to position, direction of motion, and velocity, in which they were drawn in; and this will be in about the same course that the ones last before them were thrown out. Not exactly, however, for the very cause of their being thrown off so easily is their not having fulfilled precisely the conditions of stable retention. Thus, the law of habit is accounted for, and with it its peculiar characteristic of not acting with exactitude. . . .

Now those who insist on the doctrine of necessity will for the most part insist that the physical world is entirely individual. Yet law involves an element of generality. Now to say that generality is primordial, but generalization is not, is like saying that diversity is primordial but diversification is not. It turns logic upside down. At any rate, it is clear that nothing but a principle of habit, itself due to the growth by habit of an infinitesimal chance tendency toward habit-taking, is the only bridge that can span the chasm between the chance medley of chaos and the cosmos of law and order.[104]

The activity of protoplasm, in other words, gives experimental evidence of the growth and breakdown of habits. The growth of habits in protoplasms generates uniformity; the breakdown of habits causes a regression to the state of chance spontaneity, which manifests itself in increasing diversity.[105]

For Peirce, the terms "matter" and "mind" designate the same reality but viewed alternately from the outside and from the inside. Viewed as externally acting and reacting with other things, an entity appears as matter. Viewed internally as the spread of feeling, it appears as mind, for a general idea exemplifies "a certain modification of consciousness which accompanies any regularity of general relation between chance and actions." Every general idea exhibits a certain "unity of the ego."

Personal unity would require, then, that the feelings which comprise the person exist in close enough connection to influence one another. Besides individual organismic realities, "corporate bodies who are in intimate and intensely sympathetic communion" can also exhibit a kind of personal consciousness. We find it hard to imagine in what such a corporate mind might consist, but we do encounter it experientially. At the close of his essay on "Man's Glassy Essence," the fourth of five related essays published in *The Monist,* Peirce observed:

When the thirty thousand young people of the society of Christian Endeavor were in New York, there seemed to me to be some mysterious diffusion of sweetness and light. If such a fact is capable of being made out anywhere, it should be in the church. The Christians have always been ready to risk their lives for the sake of having prayers in common, of getting together and

[104] Ibid., 6:260, 263.
[105] Ibid., 6:261–3.

praying simultaneously with great energy, and especially for their common body, for "the whole state of the Church militant here in earth," as one of the missals has it. This practice they have been keeping up everywhere, weekly, for many centuries. Surely, a personality ought to have developed in that church, in that "bride of Christ," as they call it, or else there is a strange break in the action of mind, and I shall have to acknowledge my views are much mistaken.[106]

Clearly, Peircean synechism allows not only for communicated continuity among individual persons but for the same kind of communicated continuity between human communities and God. In Pauline language the Church as a community incorporates the "mind of Christ." Indeed, the Church viewed from the outside manifests visibly the corporate mind which it exemplifies when viewed from the inside.[107]

Peirce's allusion to shared religious experience at the end of his essay "Man's Glassy Essence" prepared his invocation of Johannine theology in his final essay, "Evolutionary Love." Once grant God as a factor within the developing cosmos, Peirce argued, and one can begin to relate evolutionary theory to the theological vision of John the Evangelist. The assertion of the "ontological gospeler" that "God is love" makes sense only if God loves universally and only if love can conquer hatred and can encompass the defect of love in such a way as to lead deficient love to self-transcendence. "For self-love is no love; so if God's self is love, that which he loves must be defect of love; just as a luminary can light up only that which otherwise would be dark." Accordingly, the fourth gospel affirms that God's Son came not to judge the world but to save it; judgment results only from humanity's defect of love.[108]

> The movement of love is circular, at one and the same impulse projecting creations into interdependency and drawing them into harmony. This seems complicated when stated so; but it is fully summed up in the simple formula we call the Golden Rule. This does not, of course, say Do everything possible to gratify the egoistic impulses of others, but it says, Sacrifice your own perfection to the perfectionment of your neighbor. . . . Love is not directed to abstractions but to persons, not to persons we do not know, nor to numbers of people, but to our dear ones, our family and neighbors. "Our

---

[106] Ibid., 6:271. See also Demetra Sfendoni-Mentzou, "Peirce on Continuity and Laws of Nature," *Transactions of the Charles S. Peirce Society* 33 (1997) 646–78.

[107] See Larry Holmes, "Prolegomena to Peirce's Philosophy of Mind," *Studies, II,* 359–81; John F. Boler, "Habits of Thought," *Studies, II,* 382–400; Vincent M. Colapietro, *Peirce's Approach to the Self* (Albany: State University of New York Press, 1989); Vincent G. Potter and Paul B. Shields, "Peirce's Definitions of Continuity," *Transactions of the Charles S. Peirce Society* 13 (1977) 20–34.

[108] Peirce, *Collected Papers,* 6:287.

neighbor," we remember, is one whom we live near, not locally perhaps but in life and feeling.

Everyone can see that the statement of St. John is the formula of an evolutionary philosophy, which teaches that growth comes only from love, from I will not say self-*sacrifice,* but from the ardent impulse to fulfill another's highest impulse. . . . Love, recognizing germs of loveliness in the hateful, gradually warms it into life, and makes it lovely. That is the sort of evolution which every careful student of my essay "The Law of Mind" must see that *synechism* calls for.[109]

The Christian gospel of love stands in diametrical contradiction to the "Gospel of Greed" trumpeted and practiced in corporate America. Peirce summed up the conflict in the following terms:

Here, then, is the issue. The gospel of Christ says that progress comes from every individual merging his individuality in sympathy with his neighbors. On the other side, the conviction of the nineteenth century is that progress takes place by virtue of every individual's striving for himself with all his might and trampling his neighbor under foot whenever he gets a chance to do so. This may accurately be called the Gospel of Greed.[110]

Peirce's agapastic evolution blends his philosophical synechism with Johannine theology. An expression of his own "passionate predilection," the doctrine of agapastic evolution proclaims on the basis of a pragmatic logic of abduction that the strong feeling which the Christian gospel arouses in human hearts constitutes "an argument of some weight" in its favor. The theory of agapastic evolution addresses itself, therefore, to "the normal judgment of the Sensible Heart."[111]

In his essay "Evolutionary Love," Peirce situated his own theory of agapastic evolution with respect to other going evolutionary theories. Darwinian theory appealed to sporting, and therefore to chance, as an explanation of biological evolution. Other evolutionary theories cited cataclysm or the operation of necessary laws in order to explain biological evolution. Clearly, an explanation of evolution by an appeal to chance contradicts evolution by mechanical necessity and vice versa. Lamarckian theory appealed to habit as the principle of evolution and explained the origin of habit in mechanically induced modifications. In Lamarckian theory, habit serves a double function:"to establish new features, and also to bring them

---

[109] Ibid., 6:288-9. See also N. A. Brian Noble, "Peirce's Definitions of Continuity and the Concept of Possibility," *Transactions of the Charles S. Peirce Society* 25 (1989) 149–74; Wayne C. Myrvold, "Peirce on Cantor's Paradox and the Continuum," *Transactions of the Charles S. Peirce Society* 31 (1995) 508–41.

[110] Peirce, *Collected Papers,* 6:294.

[111] Ibid., 6:295.

into harmony with the general morphology and function of the animals to which they belong."[112] Peirce discovered a convergence between Lamarck's theory of evolution and his own account of the "law of mind." His survey of evolutionary theory revealed, therefore, three different explanations of evolution: "evolution by fortuitous variation, evolution by mechanical necessity, and evolution by creative love. We may term them *tychastic* evolution, or *tychasm, ananchastic* evolution, or *ananchasm,* and *agapastic* evolution, or *agapasm.*" The theories corresponding to these three forms of evolution Peirce dubbed tychasticism, ananchasticism, and agapasticism, respectively. He named the laws governing each form of evolution tychism, ananchism, and agapism.[113]

In elaborating his law of mind, Peirce recognized both chance and necessity as factors in the cosmic process. His refutation of necessitarianism affirmed the reality of chance. He correlated the experience of necessity with the external perception of realities ruled by an inner teleological principle, and he identified this telic principle with habit or law. In the end, however, Peirce regarded chance and necessity as degenerate forms of authentic evolutionary development and subsumed them within the larger law of agapism, since evolutionary love encompasses and seeks to elevate realities less perfect than itself.[114]

The tychastic and ananchastic development of thought illustrates their degeneracy as modes of development. Tychastic thinking develops through random departures from habitual modes of thinking, departures

---

[112] Ibid., 6:297–9.

[113] Ibid., 6:302. See also F. M. Hamblin, "Comment on Peirce's Tychism," *Journal of Philosophy* 42 (1945) 378–83; Charles Hartshorne, "Continuity, the Form of Forms in Charles Peirce," *Monist* 39 (1929) 521–34; H. G. Townsend, "Pragmatism of Peirce and Hegel," *Philosophical Review* 37 (1928) 297–303; M. Capek, "Theory of Eternal Recurrence in Modern Philosophy of Science with Special Reference to C. S. Peirce," *Journal of Philosophy* 57 (1960) 289–96; J. H. Rytina and C. P. Loomis, "Marxist Dialectic and Pragmatism: Power as Knowledge," *American Sociological Review* 35 (1970) 308–18; P. P. Wiener, "Peirce-Langley Correspondence and Peirce's Manuscript on Hume and the Laws of Nature," *American Philosophical Society Proceedings* 91 (1947) 201–28; E. H. Madden, "Chance and Counterfacts in Wright and Peirce," *Review of Metaphysics* 9 (1956) 420–32; Peter T. Turley, "Peirce on Chance," *Transactions of the Charles S. Peirce Society* 5 (1969) 241–54; John W. McNeill, "Peirce on the Possibility of a Chance World," *Transactions of the Charles S. Peirce Society* 16 (1980) 49–58; Bernard Suits, "Doubts About Peirce's Cosmology," *Transactions of the Charles S. Peirce Society* 15 (1979) 311–21; Timothy L. Alborn, "Peirce's Evolutionary Logic, Continuity, Indeterminacy, and the Natural Order," *Transactions of the Charles S. Peirce Society* 25 (1989) 1–28; Victor Cosculluela, "Peirce on Tychism and Determinism," *Transactions of the Charles S. Peirce Society* 28 (1992) 741–55; Andrew Reynolds, "Peirce's Cosmology and the Laws of Thermodynamics," *Transactions of the Charles S. Peirce Society* 32 (1996) 403–23.

[114] Peirce, *Collected Papers,* 6:305.

which lead to unforeseen results which tend to fix some ideas as habitual beliefs more than others. The ananchastic development of thought results from an externally enforced acceptance of ideas without reflection on their consequences or inner teleology, or it can also result from the unthinking acceptance of deductive conclusions irrespective of their consequences. The agapastic development of thought flows not from chance, nor from mere circumstances, nor from the force of deductive logic alone, "but by an immediate attraction for the idea itself, whose nature is divined before the mind possesses it, by the power of sympathy, that is by virtue of the continuity of the mind."[115]

Genuine agapastic development engages "a whole people or community in its collective personality." Through the mediation of community, the idea enters into "such individuals as are in powerfully sympathetic connection with the collective people." Agapastic thinking does, however, also allow for two degenerate forms which bypass the community either totally or in part as the originating source of thought. The agapastic evolution of thinking may, for example, derive from an individual mind in consequence of some striking experience or personal development of insight, even though the meaning and attractiveness of the transforming insight comes partially mediated through sympathy with some community. The conversion of St. Paul illustrates this first degenerate case of the agapastic evolution of understanding. However, sympathy with a community need not always condition novel insight. Sometimes it springs from the attractiveness of the idea itself to the mind which first proposes it. In this second case of degenerate agapastic thinking the novel insight results from "the continuity between the man's mind and the Most High."[116]

The tychastic development of thought characterizes "backward and barbarizing movements" exemplified in the negative, hostile, and sectarian attitudes of many nominally Christian movements. Purposelessness and capitulation to external circumstance characterizes the ananchastic development of thought. Think, for example, of the medieval appropriation of Aristotle as a result of the Arab invasions of the Holy Land and of Spain and of the crusades. Internal agapism or mere logical groping finds a good example in Hegelian metaphysics. Genuine agapastic development of thought manifests, by contrast, a self-directed purposiveness and transcends the powers of individual minds. The construction of the Gothic cathedrals and the achievements of shared scientific inquiry exemplify genuine cognitive agapasm.[117]

[115] Ibid., 6:307.
[116] Ibid., 6:308.
[117] Ibid., 6:316–7. See Edward C. Moore and Richard S. Robin, *From Time and Chance to Consciousness: Studies in the Metaphysics of Charles Peirce* (Oxford: Berg, 1994); Sandra

During his middle period, Peirce apparently believed that religion and science do not mix well, but during his final, mature period, with hints from Abbot, he glimpsed the possibility of harmonizing religion and science through the mediation of logic. Peirce's discovery of the non-rational character of abductive reasoning marked the transition in his thought to a more positive understanding of the relationship between religious and scientific thinking.

In his lectures on "Vitally Important Topics" delivered in 1898, Peirce insisted on the abstract and theoretical character of strictly scientific thinking. The scientific *eros* cares nothing for the practical application of its theories to life but confines its passion to the pursuit of speculation for its own sake.[118] The practical, unscientific person, by contrast, shows little interest in speculation for its own sake. In the day-to-day living of life, people rely on instinct, on what Galileo called *il lume naturale*.[119] Egotistical reason appeals to sentiment only as a last resort. Still, people tend to admire most those traits of character and behavior which spring from sentiment more than from logic. In speculative matters, sentiment shows itself instinctively conservative: it draws back from pushing any pure theory to its extreme practical limits.[120] Accordingly, in "Vitally Important Topics," Peirce severely qualified the role which instinct plays in speculative thinking, partly in response to the irrationality of James's "will to believe":

> I would not allow to sentiments or instinct any weight whatsoever in theoretical matters, not the slightest. Right sentiment does not demand any such weight; and right reason would emphatically repudiate the claim if it were made. True we are driven oftentimes in science to try the suggestiveness of instinct; but we only try them, we compare them with experience, we hold ourselves ready to throw them overboard at a moment's notice from experience. If I allow the supremacy of sentiment in human affairs, I do so at the dictation of reason itself; and equally at the dictation of sentiment, in theoretical matters I refuse to allow sentiment any weight whatever.[121]

B. Rosenthal, *Charles Peirce's Pragmatic Pluralism* (Albany: State University of New York Press, 1994); Murray Murphy, "On Peirce's Metaphysics," *Transactions of the Charles S. Peirce Society* 1 (1965) 12–25; P. P. Wiener, "Evolutionism and Pragmatism of Peirce," *Journal of the History of Ideas* 7 (1946) 321–54; K. Britton, "Introduction to the Metaphysics and Theology of C. S. Peirce," *Ethics* 49 (1939) 435–65; R. W. Sellars, "Panpsychism or Evolutionary Materialism," *Philosophy of Science* 27 (1960) 329–50; W. Donald Oliver, "The Final Cause and Agapasm in Peirce's Philosophy," *Studies, II,* 289–303; Rulon Wells, "The Nature of Peirce's Evolutionism," *Studies, II,* 304–22; Thomas Goudge, "Peirce's Evolutionism–After Half a Century," *Studies, II,* 323–41.

[118] Peirce, *Collected Papers,* 1:616–25.
[119] Ibid., 1:626–30.
[120] Ibid., 1:627, 631–3.
[121] Ibid., 1:634.

Peirce, then, carefully and correctly restricted irrationality in inferential thinking to the abductive formulation of a hypothesis. Still, Peirce recognized in sentiment a realm of genuine beliefs which have practical impact on one's daily life.[122] Like the knowledge born of scientific experiment, instinctive sentiment can grow and develop through the interaction of personal expectation and actual event. The collective wisdom of educated sentiment takes shape in common sense living.[123]

In religious matters the instinctive sentiment, the heart, reigns supreme. Indeed, apart from the instinctive perceptions of the heart, religion cannot even exist. As Peirce put it:

> If, walking in a garden on a dark night, you were suddenly to hear the voice of your sister crying to you to rescue her from a villain, would you stop to reason out the metaphysical question of whether it were possible from one mind to cause material waves of sound and for another mind to perceive them? If you did, the problem might probably occupy the remainder of your days. In the same way if a man undergoes any religious experience and hears the call of his Savior, for him to halt till he has adjusted a philosophical difficulty would seem an analogous sort of thing, whether you call it stupid or whether you call it disgusting. If, on the other hand, a man has had no religious experience, then any religion not an affectation is as yet impossible for him; and the only worthy course is to wait quietly till such experience comes. No amount of speculation can take the place of experience.[124]

While personal religious sentiments can make no speculative claims, they do enjoy a kind of practical infallibility. One's deepest beliefs suit one emotionally and practically as an individual, even though others find them trivial. Nevertheless, as soon as a sentiment assumes importance in a person's life, the one experiencing the sentiment seeks to generalize it:

> The generalization of a sentiment can take place on different sides: Poetry is one sort of generalization of sentiment, and in so far is the regenerative metamorphosis of sentiment. But poetry remains on one side ungeneralized, and to that is due its emptiness. The complete generalization, the complete regeneration of sentiment is religion, which is poetry, but poetry complete.[125]

---

[122] Ibid., 1:635–8.

[123] Ibid., 1:648, 653–4.

[124] Ibid., 1:655.

[125] Ibid., 1:676. See also Douglas P. Anderson, *Creativity and the Philosophy of C. S. Peirce* (Dordrecht: Martinus Nijhoff, 1987). I find it questionable that Peirce in the end identified finite minds with an absolute divine mind. See Robert Almeder, *The Philosophy of Charles S. Peirce: A Critical Introduction* (Toronto: Roman and Littlefield, 1980); Goerg Klawritter, *Charles Sanders Peirce: Realität, Wahrheit, Gott: Einblick in Leben und Werk des Begründers des Pragmatismus* (Würzburg: Königshausen und Neumann, 1984).

In Peirce's lectures on "Vitally Important Topics," however, theory and sentiment, heart and mind, remain in the end irrevocably sundered: "To sum up, all sensible talk about vitally important topics must be commonplace, all reasoning about them unsound, and all study of them narrow and sordid."[126]

As Peirce's thought matured, however, several circumstances converged which allowed him to effect the logical wedding of religion and science. His agapastic theory of evolution fused scientific and religious beliefs. His need to distinguish his own "pragmaticism" from the "pragmatism" of James, Schiller, and others had focused his attention on the logic of abduction, and the more he pondered the workings of the abductive mind the more he found himself forced to acknowledge its instinctive, non-rational character. This assimilation of abduction to spontaneous, instinctively held religious beliefs eventually led him to apply pragmatic logic to the clarification and verification of religious affirmations. No longer could he confine the claims of *il lume naturale* to the practical, non-speculative living of life. Rather, *il lume naturale* contributed to the initial fixation of all belief: both theoretical and practical. Appeal to *il lume naturale* justified including "instinctive simplicity" among the criteria for adopting any hypothesis for testing.

All of these themes came to written expression in Peirce's "Neglected Argument for the Reality of God." The Neglected Argument began by defining some of the key terms which functioned in the argument. By the term "God" Peirce meant "the definable proper name, signifying *Ens necessarium,* in my belief really creator of all three Universes of Experience."[127] By "the three Universes of Experience" Peirce meant the realms of quality, fact, and law.[128] By "real" Peirce meant "having Properties, *i.e.,* characters sufficing to identify their subject, and possessing these whether they be anywise attributed to it by any single man or group of men, or not."[129] By an "experience" Peirce meant "a brutally produced conscious effect that contributes to a habit, self-controlled, yet too satisfying, on deliberation, as to be destructible by no positive exercise of internal vigour." As an example of an experience Peirce cited the child who, having stuck its finger into a flame, resists thereafter any attempt to make it repeat the painful act.[130] By an "argument" Peirce meant "any process of thought reasonably tending to produce a definite belief."[131]

---

[126] Ibid., 1:677.
[127] Ibid., 6:452.
[128] Ibid., 6:455.
[129] Ibid., 6:453.
[130] Ibid., 6:454.
[131] Ibid., 6:456.

The Neglected Argument begins with the "humble argument," and the humble argument engages "musement." By musement Peirce meant "mind play," the free ranging of mind and imagination over all three realms of being: over the range of qualitative possibility, over the actuality of brute struggle in nature, over the incremental development of habit and of mind itself, over the interplay of the three realms of possibility, actuality, and purpose. Mind play follows only one rule, namely, to obey no rules, but as the mind ranges over the emergence of purpose and of mind from out of the infinite range of possibilities, as one meditates the emergence of purpose in a world of brute struggle, as the imagination freely ponders the preparation of the higher stages of evolution in the emergence of lower stages, such reflections

> inevitably suggest the hypothesis of God's Reality. It is not that such phenomena might not be capable of being accounted for, in one sense, by the action of chance with the smallest conceivable dose of a higher element; for if by God be meant the *Ens necessarium,* that very hypothesis requires that such should be the case. But the point is that that sort of explanation leaves a mental explanation just as needful as before. Tell me, upon sufficient authority, that all cerebration depends upon movements of neurites that strictly obey certain physical laws, and that thus all expressions of thought, both external and internal, receive a physical explanation, and I shall be ready to believe you. But if you go on to say that this explodes the theory that my neighbor and myself are governed by reason, and are thinking beings, I must frankly say that it will not give me a high opinion of your intelligence. But however that may be, in the Pure Play of Musement the idea of God's Reality will be sooner or later to be found an attractive fancy, which the Muser will develop in various ways. The more he ponders it, the more it will find response in every part of his mind, for its beauty, for its supplying an ideal of life, and for its thoroughly satisfactory explanation of his whole threefold environment.[132]

In writing down his personal beliefs about God, Peirce gave a descriptive example of how the musing mind works:

> I have often occasion to walk at night, for about a mile, over an entirely untraveled road, much of it between open fields without a house in sight. The circumstances are not favorable to severe study, but are to calm meditation. If the sky is clear, I look at the stars in the silence, thinking how each successive increase in the aperture of a telescope make many more of them visible than all that had been visible before. The fact that the heavens do not show a sheet of light proves that there are vastly more dark bodies, say planets, than there are suns. They must be inhabited, and most likely millions of

---

[132] Ibid., 6:465.

them with beings much more intelligent than we are. For on the whole, the solar system seems one of the simplest; and presumably under more complicated phenomena greater intellectual power will be developed. What must be the social phenomena of such a world! How extraordinary are the minds even of the lower animals. We cannot appreciate our own powers any more than a writer can appreciate his own style, or a thinker the peculiar quality of his thought. I don't mean that a Dante did not know that he expressed himself with fewer words than other men do, but he could not admire himself as we admire him; nor can we wonder at human intelligence as we do at that of wasps. Let a man drink in such thoughts as come to him in contemplating the physico-psychical universe without any special purpose of his own; especially the universe of mind which coincides with the universe of matter. The idea of there being a God over it all of course will be suggested; and the more he considers it, the more he will be enwrapt with Love of this idea. He will ask himself whether or not there really is a God. If he allows instinct to speak, and searches his own heart, he will at length find that he cannot help believing it. I cannot tell how every man will think. I know the majority of men, especially educated men, are so full of pedantries—especially the male sex—that they cannot think straight about these things. But I can tell how a man must think if he is a pragmatist.[133]

The Neglected Argument explains what a pragmaticist must think about the reality of God. The Neglected Argument subjects to an analysis in the light of Peircean pragmaticism the fruits of an act of musement (Peirce's term for mind play) which culminates in belief in the reality of God. From the standpoint of pragmatistic logic, an initial belief in the reality of God has the same logical status as any hypothesis, or abduction, formulated by the mind. Like any other hypothesis it needs deductive clarification and inductive validation. Deductive reasoning clarifies the meaning of a hypothesis by predicting its conceivable operational consequences. The logical prediction of those consequences produces a deductive argument. Inductive reasoning then tests the fruits of deductive prediction against experience. "Deduction Explicates; Induction evaluates: that is all."[134]

The religious assent to God engages the mind's educated instincts—*il lume naturale*—in the same way in which the spontaneous attractiveness of a scientific hypothesis designates it as the *logically* superior hypothesis. Pragmatistic logic next requires the believer to clarify the meaning of that religious abduction by deducing its moral consequences. Those conse-

[133] Ibid., 6:501. See also Vincent Colapietro, "Notes for a Sketch of a Peircean Theory of the Unconscious," *Transactions of the Charles S. Peirce Society* 31 (1995) 482–506.
[134] Peirce, *Collected Papers,* 6:466–75. See also Bowman L. Clarke, "Peirce's Neglected Argument," *Transactions of the Charles S. Peirce Society* 8 (1977) 277–87.

quences include the commitment to collaborate with the divine creative process by maximizing the growth of life and value and to resist the forces of evil which thwart the divine creative intent. Finally, one tests one's belief in God by actually living out its practical, moral consequences.[135]

Peirce believed that anyone could appropriate the humble argument. Indeed, he believed that most people come to rational faith in God by some such mental process. His Neglected Argument consisted in validating logically the legitimacy of such a belief. Those who seek to debunk religious faith by appealing to scientific arguments need to realize that from the standpoint of sound scientific method, belief in God on the basis of the humble argument has as much legitimacy as the scientist's espousal of a hypothesis about specific natural events. The spontaneous attractiveness of belief in God endows it with initial logical plausibility and makes it logically preferable to unbelief. Moreover, the deductive clarification and lived moral validation of belief in God exemplify the same sound logical principles as scientific experimentation. One tests the truth of religious hypotheses by living them.[136]

In the end, then, logic effects the wedding of religion and science. The same human mind thinks about scientific and religious questions but thinks analogously about both because religion involves more than speculative understanding. "Religion is a life, and can be identified with a belief only provided that belief be a living belief—a thing to be lived rather than said or thought." Christianity inculcates a religion of universal love: love of God and love of neighbor. The aims of Christianity, then, coincide with the aims of agapastic evolution. A religion of love requires communitarian embodiment and expression. Moreover, despite the imperfections of the Church, Christianity in its evolutionary thrust seeks to bring all people and the whole of creation within the ambit of divine and human love. One tests the truth of Christianity by living it. Such a test, Peirce argued, not only makes good religious sense, it also makes good logical sense.[137]

[135] Peirce, *Collected Papers,* 6:474–93.
[136] Ibid., 6:486–91.
[137] Ibid., 428–51. See also Charles Hartshorne, "Critique of Peirce's Idea of God," *Philosophical Review* 40 (1941) 516–23; R. G. Meyers, "Truth and Ultimate Belief in Peirce," *International Philosophical Quarterly* 11 (1971) 87–103; Paul Weiss, "Essence of Peirce's System," *Journal of Philosophy* 37 (1940) 253–69; Yuri K. Melville, "The Conflict of Science and Religion in Charles Peirce's Philosophy," *Transactions of the Charles S. Peirce Society* 1 (1966) 33–50; Richard L. Trammel, "Religion, Instinct, and Reason in the Thought of Charles S. Peirce," *Transactions of the Charles S. Peirce Society* 8 (1972) 3–23; Dennis Rohatyu, "Resurrecting Peirce's Neglected Argument for God," *Transactions of the Charles S. Peirce Society* 18 (1982) 66–74; Douglas R. Anderson, "Three Appeals in Peirce's Neglected Argument," *Transactions of the Charles S. Peirce Society* 24 (1990)

Peirce recognized the scandal of Christian sectarianism, but, in contrast to Enlightenment thinkers who looked to reason to overcome sectarian divisions among humans, Peirce looked to the law of universal love to heal a divided Church.

> Without a church, the religion of love can have but a rudimentary existence; and a narrow, little exclusive church is almost worse than none. A great catholic church is wanted. . . . Let us endeavor, then, with all our might to draw together the whole body of believers in the law of love into sympathetic unity of consciousness. Discountenance as immoral all movements that exaggerate differences, or that go to make fellowship depend on formulas invented to exclude some Christians from communion with others. . . . Doubtless, a lot of superstition clings to the historical churches; but superstition is the grime upon the venerable pavement of the sacred edifice, and he who would wash that pavement clean should be willing to get down on his knees to work inside the church.[138]

Peirce saw that the logic of pragmaticism requires both Catholics and Protestants to advance beyond the ringing anathemas of both the Reformation and the Counter-Reformation to reconciliation through dialogue and through shared inquiry. In other words, when applied to the churches, the logic of pragmaticism requires overcoming Christian sectarianism through ecumenical dialogue and through consensus rooted in a shared inquiry and in shared religious experience.[139]

V

One does not normally associate the name of Charles Sanders Peirce with American Transcendentalism, and yet the mature Peirce conceded that "some cultured bacilli" of the Transcendental virus had probably invaded his mind and "after long incubation" had resurfaced in his thought

---

349–61; Michael L. Raposa, "Peirce and Modern Religious Thought," *Transactions of the Charles S. Peirce Society* 27 (1991) 341–69; C. F. Delaney, "Peirce on the Hypothesis of God," *Transactions of the Charles S. Peirce Society* 28 (1992) 725–39; Peter Ochs, "Charles Peirce's Unpragmatic Christianity: A Rabbinic Appraisal," *American Journal of Theology and Philosophy* 9 (1988) 41–73; Peter Turley, "Peirce's Cosmic 'Sheriff,'" *Journal of the History of Ideas* 36 (1975) 717–20; Edwin Hubbard, "Peirce's Attempt at a Verifiable Definition of God," *American Journal of Theology and Philosophy* 16 (1995) 149–71; Robert S. Corrington, "Peirce's Ecstatic Naturalism: The Birth of the Divine in Nature," *American Journal of Theology and Philosophy* 16 (1995) 173–87.

[138] Peirce, *Collected Papers,* 6:443, 445, 447. See also Estanislao Arroyabe, *Peirce: Eine Einfürung in sein Denken* (Königstein: Forum Academicum, 1982); Gerard Deladalle, *Foundations of Semiotics* (Amsterdam: John Benjamins, 1987).

[139] Peirce, *Collected Papers,* 6:450–1; see also John E. Smith, "Religion and Theology in Peirce," *Studies, I,* 251–67; Walter P. Krolikowski, "The Peircean Vir," *Studies, II,* 257–70.

"modified by mathematical conceptions and by training in physical inves-tigations."[140] Peirce need not have alluded to "Concord Transcendental-ism" at the beginning of his essay on "The Law of Mind," The fact that he did so gives solid evidence that he saw some kind of analogy between his mature metaphysics and the concerns of the "Concord Transcendental-ists." In order to understand better what Peirce meant by those cultured Transcendental bacilli, one needs to situate him within the Transcendental critique of Enlightenment modernism.

In his youth Peirce knew both Emerson and Parker as regular guests at his father's table. Did the mature Peirce owe any intellectual debts to ei-ther Transcendental thinker? In comparing and contrasting Peirce's thought, on the one hand, with that of Emerson and Parker, on the other, I in no way intend to suggest that Peirce himself reflected explicitly on all the issues in New England Transcendentalism discussed in this final sec-tion of the present chapter. Unlike the history of ideas which gives an ac-count of the actual genesis and development of thought, a dialectical study of ideas like this one compares and contrasts interpretative frames of ref-erence in ways which may or may not have occurred to the thinkers stud-ied. The comparison and contrast seeks to highlight the advantages and disadvantages of the frames of reference under dialectical study.

I doubt, for example, that Peirce either studied or understood the method of discernment which structures virtually all of Emerson's pub-lished works. Nevertheless, Peirce's theory of the normative sciences does correct unexamined and illegitimate postulates of Emersonian discernment. Emerson assumed that the phenomenological description of experience yielded an insight into the metaphysical structure of the universe. Peirce's logic argues, correctly in my judgment, that in all philosophical thinking the normative sciences of aesthetics, ethics, and logic need to mediate be-tween phenomenology and metaphysics. In other words, in order to grasp the nature of reality one must first put into order one's psyche, one's con-science, and one's mind. Unhealed psychic aberrations can all too easily betray one into confusing reality with the rationalization of one's neuroses or psychoses. A morally degenerate conscience can all too easily betray one into confusing reality with the rationalization of one's own selfishness, and, until one understands how the mind ought to work, one can all too easily mistake one's own intellectual befuddlement for reality.

In other words, Peirce's philosophical logic helps explain why Emerson's saturnalia of faith failed. Emerson fallaciously and uncritically assumed that he needed only to describe his Neo-Platonic metaphysics to others for them to grasp its truth self-evidently in their own subjectivity.

[140] Peirce, *Collected Papers*, 6:102.

In the process, Emerson presented a seriously flawed philosophical hypothesis based on an equally flawed epistemology and logic as the equivalent of a verified induction, or, worse still, as a self-evident account of reality without need of rational justification. No wonder his audiences left his lectures scratching their heads.

We need not rehearse here and in detail the flaws in Emerson's Neo-Platonic hypothesis. Suffice it to say that the multiple dualisms in Emerson's vision of the cosmos—cosmic dualism, spirit-matter dualism, operational dualism, subject-object dualism, and individualism—rendered his metaphysical vision problematic in the extreme. When the mature Emerson realized that others found his Platonic hypothesis unintelligible, he amplified and qualified that hypothesis with his philosophy of bias. The philosophy of bias explained to him satisfactorily the failure of other minds to share his personal philosophical prejudices at the same time that it rationalized his failure to criticize in a truly systematic way his own flawed philosophical assumptions. The philosophy of bias blamed the failure of Emerson's saturnalia of faith on a capricious nature rather than on his own skewed and unverifiable philosophical assumptions. The narrow bias of other people's minds, the mature Emerson argued, kept them from grasping the truth of Neo-Platonic metaphysics with the same subjective self-evidence as he himself. Whether or not Peirce intended his attack on "the spirit of Cartesianism" to include Emerson, clearly the sage of Concord had caught that spirit.

Like Abbot, Peirce saw that a metaphysics of relationship overcomes philosophical dualism, but Peirce's fallibilism kept him from acquiescing as facilely as Abbot did in a pantheistic explanation of cosmic relationship. Peirce seems to have conceived the relationship of God to the cosmos in more traditional terms as the relationship of creator to creature. Moreover, while Peirce affirmed some kind of continuity between uncreated Mind and created minds, he left the precise nature of that relationship vague.

However, if Peirce eschewed Emersonian pantheism, other themes in Emerson's Transcendentalism did achieve qualified, philosophical restatement in Peirce's mature philosophy. In both his Transcendental and Post-Transcendental periods Emerson had insisted on the superiority of aesthetic insight to the objectifying, linear logic of positive science. Emerson rooted aesthetic insight in subjectivity and called it intuitive. Peirce, as we have seen, began his philosophical career with a rejection of all forms of subjectivistic intuitionism, but as his thought matured he realized that in his attack upon intuitionism he had failed to do justice to the aesthetic dimensions of human experience. The middle Peirce seems to have equated human thinking with inferential reasoning on sense data. Moreover, he seems also during his middle period to have endorsed James's fallacious reduction of feeling to sensation. The mature Peirce saw that he needed to coordinate his pragmatic logic with his theory of the normative sciences. He also saw that, when he did so, he made logic serve aesthetic insight and responsible moral living. Among the normative sciences, aesthetics, as the science of the *summum bonum,* sets the ultimate goals of human living which clarity of thought seeks to enhance, while ethics teaches how to live for ultimate good.

The mature Peirce avoided falling into the Emersonian trap of exalting intuitive, imaginative insight over rational, inferential insight, but he did come to recognize that common sense, which for him probably included imagination, memory, and concrete reasoning, made realistic cognitive claims. Moreover, in formulating his normative sciences, Peirce did endorse in a general sort of way the thesis which Emerson argued in *The Conduct of Life,* namely, that the experience of beauty yields an insight into the ideals which make the living of life worthwhile. In a sense, Peirce's normative sciences endowed the argument of *The Conduct of Life* with a logical precision which that argument badly needed. In other words, the mature Peirce came to realize that, when one purifies imaginative intuition from any fallacious claims to grasp reality self-evidently within subjectivity alone, then aesthetic insight does yield a solid, realistic insight into the ultimate purpose of human living. If so, then aesthetic insight grasps thirdness in its thrust to achieve the *summum bonum.* In this qualified sense, Peirce did endorse in logically corrected form two fundamental Emersonian insights: (1) living constitutes the total act, thinking the partial act, and (2) moral living seeks the ultimately Beautiful.

Peirce confessed to having contracted some cultured Transcendental bacilli in the introduction to his article on "The Law of Mind" published in *The Monist* in 1892. If Emerson ever formulated a "law of Mind," he did so in *Nature.* Emerson's version of that law asserted: "1. Words are signs of natural facts. 2 Particular natural facts are symbols of particular spiritual facts. 3 Nature is the symbol of spirit."[141] Peirce's summary statement of "the Law of the Mind" asserted:

> Logical analysis applied to mental phenomena shows that there is but one law of mind, namely, that ideas tend to spread continuously and to affect certain others which stand to them in a peculiar relation of affectability. In this spreading they lose intensity, and especially the power of affecting others, but gain generality and become welded with other ideas.[142]

[141] Ralph Waldo Emerson, *The Complete Works of Ralph Waldo Emerson,* Centenary Edition, 14 vols. (Boston: Houghton, Mifflin & Co., 1903–04) 1:25.
[142] Peirce, *Collected Papers,* 6:104.

Clearly the two formulations have little in common philosophically. Nevertheless, Peirce, like Emerson, conceived reality in symbolic, revelatory terms. Peirce's semiotic developed his triadic metaphysics, and that metaphysics acknowledged some kind of symbolic continuity between God and God's creation. Moreover, from his youth Peirce, like Emerson, saw in nature a revelation of its divine source. To be sure, Peirce developed these themes very differently from Emerson, but they echo fundamental Emersonian concerns.

Peirce's logic of relatives also helped ground a relational account of reality, and that relational metaphysics echoed in a much more sophisticated and nuanced manner Emerson's sense of organic, cosmic interrelatedness. Emerson's dualistic caste of mind prevented him from offering a philosophically consistent account of cosmic relatedness, but Peirce's relational metaphysics succeeded better in that speculative enterprise by replacing dualism with a defensible philosophical relationism.

Like Emerson and with much greater philosophical acumen, Peirce repudiated Enlightenment nominalism and replaced it with a metaphysical and epistemological realism. Peirce's realism has a historical, developmental character largely absent from Emersonian Platonism, but in the debate between nominalists and realists, both men came down four-square on the side of realism.

Finally, Emersonian Transcendentalism gave epistemological pride of place to the creative imagination. As Peirce's own thought matured, he reformulated, qualified, and restated this basic Emersonian insight. One suspects that in glorifying the creative imagination, Emerson merely rationalized the intuitive bias of his own personality, which gravitated spontaneously to imaginative rather than to logical forms of thinking. Paradoxically, Peirce, whose personal bias went in exactly the opposite direction, found himself led on the basis of his logical analysis of inferential thinking to agree, after significant qualification, with the general thrust of Emerson's thought on this point. Having decided that inference holds the key to logic and that inference divides into three irreducible kinds—abductive, deductive, and inductive—Peirce found himself forced to acknowledge the non-rational, creative, imaginative character of abductive thinking. He called the workings of the creative inferential imagination *il lume naturale,* musement, common sense, or mind-play. Moreover, he came to acknowledge that common sense not only includes aesthetic experience but also has more to say about the practical living of life than abstract inferential logic. Still, instead of asserting the cognitive superiority of imaginative thinking to inferential reason, as Emerson had, Peirce's epistemology recognized a truth in both perceptions of reality. Peirce acknowledged that the aesthetic appeal of a hypothesis endows it with an initial logical normativity, but, in contrast to William James's "will to believe," Peirce insisted that all hypotheses adopted on passional grounds need deductive clarification and inductive verification in conformity with strictly logical, inferential principles.

Peirce's philosophy corrected Emerson's on other crucial points as well. With the mature Emerson Peirce acknowledged the finitude of the individual mind, and like the mature Emerson Peirce looked to a community of minds to accomplish creatively what no single individual can do. In Emersonian Transcendentalism the Over Soul supplies the metaphysical glue which holds society together. In the Emersonian universe personal bias requires individual geniuses to espouse and to embody historically an expressive individualism which absolves them of all social commitments which threaten to compromise that creative bias. Peirce's fallibilism led him to value communal consensus over individual judgment.

As we have already seen, Peirce's attack on privileged powers of intuition which grasp truth within subjectivity alone undercut the methodological and epistemological foundations both of Parker's Enlightenment fundamentalism and of the Enlightenment fundamentalism which flourishes in the contemporary American academy. Between Brownson and Peirce, however, one can detect some areas of at least remote convergence. Neither Peirce nor Brownson felt constrained to choose between reason and Christianity. Both preferred the analogical to the dialectical imagination. Both espoused a kind of vitalism. Brownson derived his vitalism from Leroux; Peirce's depiction of matter as effete mind amounted to an endorsement of a form of panpsychism. Both Brownson and Peirce rejected subjectivism and other forms of dualism. Both Peirce and Brownson defended a triadic construct of human knowing, although Brownson never conceived anything comparable to Peirce's logic and semiotic. Peirce's logic and his epistemology also corrected Brownson's complete failure to give a philosophical account of rational forms of knowing. Both thinkers rejected nominalism and defended a form of realism, although Peirce's developmental realism, which he articulated in his Law of Mind and in his evolutionary theory, corrected the implicit essentialism in Brownson's Platonic realism. Moreover, as we have seen, that essentialism kept Brownson from dealing adequately with the historical development of religious doctrine. Here again Peirce succeeded where Brownson failed. Both Peirce and Brownson valued human and religious community as important counters to social individualism, but, while Brownson's commitment to community bore fruit in both a theology and a political philosophy, Peirce developed neither. In theology and political philosophy, then, Brownson helps complement Peirce.

Peirce read and admired Abbot's *Scientific Theism.* Peirce also endorsed Abbot's refutation of Kantian conceptual nominalism. Peirce, however, never committed himself to the speculatively dubious task of justifying philosophically Emersonian pantheism as Abbot did. In a sense, Abbot dedicated his entire speculative career to overcoming the dualisms in Emerson's pantheism and to replacing Emersonian intuition with the logic of science. Peirce never manifested the a priori commitment to Emersonian Transcendentalism which characterized Abbot's thought, but, paradoxically, Peirce in the end did more epistemological justice to the kind of imaginative thinking which Emerson valued than Abbot.

Both Abbot and Peirce valued scientific thinking, but, while Abbot admired science as an outside observer, Peirce pondered the implications of scientific method as an impressive practitioner of that method. Both Abbot and the young Peirce believed that the syllogism lay at the heart of logic, although Peirce's conversion to a logic of relatives caused him to qualify this early belief. Abbot, however, never reflected on logical issues with the single-minded passion which Peirce exhibited. Moreover, in the end, Abbot seems never to have assimilated what Peirce meant by a logic of relations and by abduction, deduction, and induction. For Abbot the syllogism always involved the subsumption of the concrete individual under a universal genus whether one argued inductively from individual to genus or deductively from genus to individual. In other words, from Peirce's perspective Abbot's philosophy failed to emancipate itself completely from the "spirit of Cartesianism." Like Descartes, Abbot sought to ground his system in an unrevisable, self-grounding deductive principle. Instead of the Cartesian *cogito,* Abbot's first deductive principle asserted: "human knowledge exists." Peirce knew better than to construct a metaphysics on deductive inference alone, and he finally appealed to his critical commonsensism in order to endow human thought with cognitive stability.

Both Abbot and the mature Peirce sought to effect the wedding of religion and science, but they did so differently. Abbot argued for the compatibility between scientific thinking and what he called "free religion." By "free religion" he meant a form of naturalistic pantheism. Peirce used his pragmatistic logic in order to justify the fixation of religious belief through musement, and he incorporated Johannine themes into his account of agapastic evolution. Moreover, Peirce placed his hope for the future of religion in the reform of the Christian Church, in overcoming superstition and sectarian denominationalism through shared inquiry, and in thus creating a truly universal, Catholic Church.

While both Abbot and Peirce defended a form of metaphysical realism, Peirce seems never to have endorsed in his own thought Abbot's doctrine of *universalia inter res*. That doctrine rationalized Abbot's pantheis- tic subsumption of the finite, created universe into the divine "All-Thing." Peirce's laws would appear to develop with more autonomy than either Abbot's pantheism or his *universalia inter res* would seem to allow, for, if habits of choice explain decision, the fact that in Abbot's syllogistic phi- losophy each concrete individual exemplifies identically the same law or general tendency means that a single law must account for the choices of historically distinct individuals. The idea makes little sense.

Both Emerson and Parker struggled to respond to the religious skep- ticism which British empiricism entailed and to which David Hume gave eloquent expression. Emerson turned to Platonic realism as a philosophi- cal alternative to Hume; Parker turned to Schleiermacher. Peirce initially confronted Enlightenment nominalism in the work of its most sophisti- cated proponent: Immanuel Kant. As a young man Peirce immersed him- self in Kant's thought so thoroughly that he could recite large passages of *The Critique of Pure Reason* by heart. His logical studies of the syllogism, however, emancipated him from the trammels of Kantian conceptual nom- inalism. Having proven to his own satisfaction the logical irreducibility of abduction, deduction, and induction, Peirce realized that Kantian tran- scendental logic recognized only one form of inference: deduction. That realization relativized the cognitive claims of *The Critique of Pure Rea- son*, for it meant that in writing his critiques Kant had only proposed an unverified philosophical hypothesis about how the human mind thinks. Worse still, Kant had presented a fallible philosophical abduction about scientific thinking as a verified induction at the same time that he called it a transcendental deduction. By Peirce's standards one could hardly come up with a more confused formula for inferential thinking.

Moreover, Peirce's inferential logic convinced him that far from grounding scientific insight, as it claimed to do, *The Critique of Pure Rea- son* explained scientific thinking away and replaced it with conceptual nominalism. Scientists, Peirce recognized, seek to understand the laws op- erative in the cosmos. They expect the way in which things behave in na- ture to correct their fallible scientific hypotheses about the laws which explain their behavior. On Kant's nominalistic principles, science must impose on concrete natural facts a generality which derives exclusively from the subjectivity of the human mind. In other words, Peirce's study of Kant led him to recognize a fundamental contradiction at the heart of En- lightenment modernism: the Enlightenment exalted scientific thinking as a universal human panacea, but, by grounding science in a nominalistic British empiricism, Enlightenment modernism made scientific thought philosophically unthinkable. Only the rejection of all forms of nominalism, whether classical or conceptual, could render the fact of scientific insight intelligible. Science becomes really possible only when one recognizes with Peirce that one perceives thirdness, real generality in acting realities, and does so both inferentially and instinctively.

While Peirce's logic of inference validated with very significant qualification the scientific enterprise which Enlightenment modernism so prized, the fallibilistic implications of his pragmatic logic of inference called into question the naive optimism with which the Enlightenment had portrayed the transformative potential of the scientific enterprise. Enlightenment modernism predicted that science would usher in a cultural millennium of unparalleled joy, peace, and prosperity. Peirce had his doubts. His conviction concerning the finitude and fallibility of the human mind made him much less sanguine about the future of science than Enlightenment rhetoric warranted. Science, he believed, seeks primarily theoretical understanding rather than social and environmental transformation. Moreover, instead of assuming that the practical application of scientific insight automatically ensures human progress, Peirce's theory of the normative sciences required that applied science conform to ultimately sound moral principles and aesthetic ideals. Brownson abandoned the Enlightenment myth of unlimited social progress through science by rediscovering the reality of original sin. Peirce's logic pricked the same Enlightenment bubble with greater philosophical effectiveness by criticizing science from within, from critical reflection on the inherent limitations of fallible scientific thinking. In other words, in his philosophical validation of scientific thinking, Peirce showed that Enlightenment optimism about what science can accomplish sprang in large measure from ignorance of the way in which scientific thinking actually works.

Peirce's pragmatic logic also led him to repudiate another important Enlightenment fallacy: subjectivism. The fact that Enlightenment *philosophes* looked to Locke's philosophy in order to justify scientific thinking only dramatized the fact that those same *philosophes* had failed finally to understand how scientists think. Not only did British empiricism endorse a nominalism which made scientific insight unintelligible, but that same British philosophy endorsed a subjectivistic account of human knowing which made the grasp of reality as such impossible. As Hume understood full well, Lockean epistemology restricts the objects of knowing to ideas. However, if scientists can explain the laws of nature, they must have the capacity to understand more than just ideas. British empiricism may have restricted human knowing to the cognitive grasp of subjective ideas, but Peirce's pragmatic logic required scientists to interact realistically with natural events if they ever hoped to understand the real laws which govern those events. The scientific mind uses ideas, but it uses them precisely in order to grasp the operational significance of events. One must interact with those events in order to understand what they signify. In the process, one must let the predicted behavior of events verify or falsify one's abductive perception of the law which governs them.

Peirce's pragmatism and his theory of the normative sciences also called into question another key presupposition of the Enlightenment: its separation of the theoretical, scientific understanding of nature from moral thinking. As we have seen, the American Enlightenment effected that separation by grounding ethical insight in the subjective intuition of moral truth quite apart from anything science might have to say about the nature of the real. As the ability of the human mind to grasp moral truth self-evidently within subjectivity alone gave way under skeptical attack, Enlightenment philosophy tended to regard ethical thinking as the expression of irrational, subjective feelings which defy all rational analysis or justification.

Peirce's pragmatic logic blurred too neat a philosophical distinction between theory and practice. The logical meaning of any abduction consists in the sum total of its operational consequences. The verification of any theoretical scientific abduction requires that one interact practically with the things one is trying to understand. Columbus could prove his hypothesis about the roundness of the earth only by hiring the Niña, the Pinta, and the Santa Maria and by sailing west. The interplay of thought and action in scientific investigation did not compromise in Peirce's mind the theoretical intent of scientific thought. Rather, it proved that apart from active, practical interaction with the realities under scientific investigation, the human mind can draw no verified, speculative conclusion concerning their reality.

Peirce's normative sciences further blurred the distinction between theory and practice, but they did so on different grounds from logical pragmaticism. Peirce's normative sciences subordinate ethics to a realistic, aesthetic insight into the ends ultimately worth embracing practically. The normative sciences also subordinate the logical search for truth to the ethical pursuit of sound ideals for living. Science seeks theoretical understanding, but the responsible thinker must see to it that the practical application of science actually enhances the quality of human living.

Peircean logic also circumscribed the role of science in another way. In his lectures on "Vitally Important Topics" Peirce argued in effect that anyone who would attempt to live life on the basis of abstract inferential insight alone would act like either a fool or a lunatic. Abstract inference can enhance the clarity and control with which the human mind approaches the world, but in the end people live their lives on the basis of common-sense thinking and educated instincts. Given the limits of what science can do, the invocation of common sense in the living of life made good logical sense to Peirce. This logical conclusion struck a serious blow at any Enlightenment rationalism which would attempt to ground the living of life in scientific reason alone.

While Peirce's logical fallibilism undercut the exorbitant claims which the Enlightenment made for scientific thinking, that fallibilism never degenerated into an epistemological relativism. If the human mind takes the time to think clearly about events by invoking the pragmatic maxim, the world will teach it how to think realistically about the cosmos through the way in which events behave. Moreover, from the standpoint of the scientific investigator, belief engages commitment to a particular explanation of reality until one encounters a good reason for calling that belief into question. Factual evidence which contradicts that belief, a contradiction between the belief in question and other beliefs to which one stands committed, or the development of a more adequate way of thinking about reality can all call one's original commitment to a specific belief into question.

Besides Peirce's understanding of belief as a proposition to whose consequences one stands practically committed, his critical common sensism also prevented his fallibilism from degenerating into epistemological relativism. The fund of common-sense beliefs which one cannot bring oneself to question also lends cognitive stability to human thought. From the philosophical foundation laid by critical common-sensism, the reasoning mind can begin to identify areas of inquiry affected by *real* doubts and can begin to deal *realistically* with those doubts.

Peirce's fallibilism and his logic of relations both have social consequences which call into question the legitimacy of Enlightenment individualism. The Enlightenment portrayed individuals as atomic units unrelated except by artificial and rescindable social acts. Peirce's logic of relations grounded a relational, realistic metaphysics which recognized three different kinds of relationship: qualitative, conceptual, cognitive relationships; factual, environmental, and social relationships; and dynamic, real, general relationships toward the future. In a relational universe, persons must first discover their real relatedness in order to make sound judgments about the kinds of relationships they ought to forge through consensus. Peirce's fallibilism also required that one acknowledge the irreducibly social, dialogic character of thought. For Peirce, commitment to the truth has as its pragmatic consequence commitment to a community of shared inquiry, just as lived religious belief requires commitment to a religious community dedicated to understanding, asserting, and embodying the truth about God and about the deity's relation to the world.

The Transcendentalists mounted a critique of Enlightenment modernism by seeking in intuitive forms of knowing a cognitive alternative to scientific rationalism. Peirce's critique of Enlightenment modernism derived its suasive force from the fact that it rooted itself in critical reflection on the actual practice of the kind of scientific thinking which Enlightenment modernism exalted without fully understanding. Moreover, Peirce's logic and his pragmatic realism undercut the religious skepticism bred of Enlightenment nominalism by effecting a wedding of religion and science more convincing than that proposed by Abbot. Abbot's wedding of religion and science in the end required consent to the pantheistic metaphysics it defended. Peirce, with greater wisdom, wedded religion and science by showing that one and the same human mind reasons about religious and secular realities and by arguing that a sound understanding of how the logic of science works sanctions rather than undercuts religious belief.

In this chapter I have been arguing that Peirce's pragmatistic realism offered a more adequate philosophical criticism of the speculative shortcomings of Enlightenment modernism than anything articulated by classical Transcendentalist philosophy and theology. The chapter which follows examines selected themes in the thought of Josiah Royce which expand and build on the postmodern foundations which Peirce constructed.[143]

---

[143] See F. I. Carpenter, "Charles Sanders Peirce: Pragmatic Transcendentalist," *New England Quarterly* 14 (1941) 34–48; Charles Hartshorne, "Charles Sanders Peirce: Pragmatic Transcendentalist," *New England Quarterly* 14 (1941) 49–63; C. W. Morris, "Peirce, Mead, and Pragmatism," *Philosophical Review* 47 (1938) 109–27; J. H. Muirhead, "Peirce's Place in American Philosophy," *Philosophical Review* 37 (1928) 460–81; H. A. Patin, "Pragmatism, Intuitionism, and Formalism," *Philosophy of Science* 24 (1957) 243–52; J. Buchler, "Peirce's Theory of Logic," *Journal of Philosophy* 36 (1939) 197–215; R. J. Roth, "Is Peirce's Pragmatism Anti-Jamesian?" *International Philosophical Quarterly* 5 (1965) 541–63; Richard Rorty, "Pragmatism, Categories, and Language," *Philosophical Review* 70 (1961) 197–223; J. P. Diggins, "Ideology and Pragmatism: Philosophy or Passion?" *American Political Science Review* 64 (1970) 899–906; Paul Weiss, "Charles Sanders Peirce: Founder of Pragmatism," *Sewanee Review* 50 (1942) 184–92.

Chapter 11

JOSIAH ROYCE: ABSOLUTE PRAGMATISM

*I strongly feel that my deepest motives and problems
have centered on the Idea of the Community,
although this idea has only come gradually to my clear
consciousness.*

—Josiah Royce

I

On January 24, 1848, James W. Marshall, the foreman of John C. Sutter, a Swiss entrepreneur who owned an inland empire in the Sacramento Valley in California, was inspecting the race for the sawmill which Sutter had Marshall constructing on a fork of the American River in the foothills of the Sierra Nevada mountains. In the mill race, Marshall discovered a large nugget of gold. Sutter, who was destined to lose his empire to the squatting argonauts who swarmed to California in search of the yellow metal, tried to keep the discovery a secret, but by the following year the news got out. Among the forty-niners who inundated the California gold fields came the parents of Josiah Royce. On November 20, 1855, his mother, Sarah Royce, gave birth to him in Grass Valley, California, in the heart of the California gold country. The child bore his footloose father's name and had three sisters.

A deeply religious woman and a cultural leader in the town of Grass Valley, Sarah Royce taught at the local school, where Josiah joined the other children under his mother's demanding tutelage. A strong-minded woman with passionate intellectual interests and high intellectual standards, Sarah also saw to the boy's instruction at home. After emerging as the leading philosopher of religion in the United States, Royce attributed his skill in dialectical argumentation in part to his endless disputes with his sister nearest him in age. When their intellectual gymnastics grew wearying to the rest of the family, Sarah would impose silence on Josiah for an hour, a discipline which did nothing to dampen his enthusiasm for argumentation.[1]

Josiah grew up during the Civil War but had little understanding of the national tragedy unfolding on the battlefields of the east. However, the assassination of President Lincoln did make a strong impression on him and stir his youthful patriotic ardor. In 1866 the Royces moved to San Francisco where Josiah attended both grammar and high school. The young Josiah's tendency to lecture his classmates, whom he regarded as less informed than himself on most topics, did nothing to improve his popularity among his peers. In the big city of San Francisco, the red-headed, freckled, countrified Josiah became the butt of his comrades' abuse. He remembered this youthful ordeal as education in the meaning of original sin.

In 1871 he crossed San Francisco Bay first to live in Oakland and then to begin his college studies at the infant University of California in the Berkeley hills. There the scientist and naturalist Joseph LeConte and the poet E. R. Sill shaped young Josiah's intellectual interests. LeConte had studied under Louis Agassiz and expounded Darwinian theory. LeConte would one day support John Muir in the latter's public debate about the geological formation of Yosemite valley. Muir had taken on in print Josiah Whitney, a colleague of LeConte and head of the team which first surveyed the Sierra Nevada range. Muir, the self-educated naturalist and high school drop-out, correctly attributed the majestic cliffs of Yosemite to glaciation.

At Berkeley, Josiah Royce began reading J. S. Mill, Herbert Spencer, and other thinkers in the British empiricist tradition. Between 1875 and 1876 the young Royce, with the financial assistance of benevolent businessmen in San Francisco, did a year of graduate studies in philosophy in Germany, first in Heidelberg, then in Leipzig, and finally in Gœttingen. There he immersed himself in the work of Immanuel Kant, Johann Gottlieb Fichte, and Arthur Schopenhauer. In 1876 he began a two-year fellowship at the newly opened Johns Hopkins University. While at Hopkins Royce made a life-long friend in the person of William James. After completing his doctorate at Hopkins, Royce returned to California where he taught for four years in the English department of his old alma mater. In 1880 Royce married Katherine Head.

---

[1] See Sarah Bayliss Royce, *A Frontier Lady: Recollections of the Gold Rush and Early California*, ed. R. H. Gabriel (New Haven, Conn.: Yale University Press, 1932).

Royce and James corresponded during Royce's years at Berkeley. Royce found California an intellectual desert and wrote James inquiring about the possibility of returning to the east coast to teach philosophy. In 1882, when James went on sabbatical, Royce took his place on the philosophy faculty of Harvard University. During the following year Royce filled in for another member of the Harvard faculty, and in his third year in Cambridge, after the publication of *The Religious Aspect of Philosophy*, he joined the Harvard philosophy department, never to leave it until his death.

In 1886 Royce published a history of the vigilante movement in San Francisco from 1846 to 1856. This historical study and a western novel, *The Feud of Oakfield Creek: A Novel of California,* published in 1887, testify to Royce's personal fascination with California and with his own western roots.[2]

In 1888 Royce experienced a personal breakdown. His doctor suggested a health cruise. Royce spent a year sailing to Australia and to New Zealand.[3] Until Royce returned, Francis Ellingwood Abbot replaced him on the Harvard faculty. On resuming teaching, Royce undertook to direct the thesis of the young George Santayana. Between 1890 and 1891 he and Abbot became embroiled in a public philosophical altercation in which William James took Royce's side, while C. S. Peirce defended Abbot. Royce and Peirce knew one another's work, and the two had corresponded, but Peirce's public support of Abbot led to a temporary estrangement between Royce and Peirce.

In 1892 Royce's immersion in German philosophy during his year abroad as well as his subsequent philosophical studies bore fruit in *The Spirit of Modern Philosophy,* an appreciative interpretation of the development of continental philosophy during the nineteenth century.

In 1895 Royce returned to Berkeley where he delivered a paper on the topic "The Conception of God." Three colleagues responded: S. E. Mezes from the University of Texas and J. LeConte and G. H. Howison, both of the University of California at Berkeley. In 1895 Howison published the first edition of Royce's address and of the panel's responses under the title *The Conception of God.* Howison's objections about Royce's vagueness concerning the reality of finite individuals, however, prodded Royce into

---

[2] See John K. Roth, "Josiah Royce's Provincialism," *Social Consequences of Religious Belief,* ed. W. Garrett (New York: Paragon House, 1989) 66–79; John K. Roth, "Philosophical Theology and Provincialism: Reflections on the Thought of Josiah Royce," *God, Values, and Empiricism: Issues in Philosophical Theology,* ed. W. Peden and L. Axel (Macon, Ga.: Mercer University Press, 1989) 187–94.

[3] See Frank Oppenheim, *Royce's Voyage Down Under: A Journey of the Mind* (Lexington: University Press of Kentucky, 1980).

writing a long supplementary essay clarifying his position. A second edition of *The Conception of God* eventually appeared. It reproduced the first edition but appended Royce's long essay.[4] The ever-prolific Royce followed this book with another in 1898: *Studies of Good and Evil*, a series of essays on the living of life and the doing of philosophy.

In January 1899 Royce delivered the first series of the prestigious Gifford Lectures at the University of Aberdeen in Scotland. He followed them the next year with a second series. He subsequently published the lectures as a two-volume study in philosophical metaphysics entitled *The World and the Individual*. Volume one dealt with four philosophical conceptions of being; volume two, with a theory of knowledge, nature, humanity, and the moral order. Peirce read *The World and the Individual* with much appreciation and regarded this as Royce's "great work" until Royce published *The Problem of Christianity* in 1913. After reading *The World and the Individual,* Peirce subsequently voiced his views in a letter to Royce but urged the author to study logic because he "needed it so much." Royce took Peirce at his word and immersed himself in logical studies, including the logic of Peirce himself. Royce's study of Peirce transformed him into a Peircean pragmaticist. Indeed Peirce, who deplored William James's nominalistic reading of his pragmatic philosophy, came to regard Royce as the only other contemporary American pragmatist. Royce published numerous articles in philosophical logic. In fact, so thoroughly did he follow Peirce's advice that when his health failed in 1912 he found himself forced to choose between logic and the philosophy of religion.

Royce and James spent a lifetime arguing philosophy as colleagues on the Harvard philosophy department. Moreover, Royce seems to have daunted James with his prolific publications. In 1900 Royce published *The Conception of Immortality.* He followed it in 1903 with *Outlines of Psychology,* in 1904 with *Herbert Spencer: An Estimate and Critique,* in 1908 with *The Philosophy of Loyalty and Race Questions, Provincialism, and Other American Problems,* and in 1911 with *William James and Other Essays on the Philosophy of Life.* In 1906 Royce lectured at Johns Hopkins University. The lectures were published posthumously as *Lectures in Modern Idealism.*

Royce's decision to focus on the philosophy of religion bore fruit in a series of three interrelated books. The first, *The Philosophy of Loyalty,* undertook a systematic criticism of American individualism and reflected Royce's growing focal interest on community, a focus which he developed in part as a result of his study of Peircean pragmatism. The second book, *The Sources of Religious Insight,* which appeared in 1912, replied in a systematic

---

[4] See John J. McDermott, "The Confrontation between Royce and Howison," *Transactions of the Charles S. Peirce Society* 30 (1994) 779–802.

way to James's *Varieties of Religious Experience.* Royce first delivered *The Sources* as a series of lectures at Lake Forest University, Illinois, in 1911.

Royce's essay "Principles of Logic," while written in 1910, did not appear in print until 1913 as a contribution to the volume *Logic of the Encyclopedia of the Philosophical Sciences.* This essay set out the logical principles guiding both *The Sources of Religious Insight* and Royce's greatest religious work, *The Problem of Christianity,* also published in 1913. Prior to its publication Royce had delivered *The Problem* as a double series of lectures at Manchester College, Oxford.

In 1914 Royce accepted the Alford Professorship of Natural Religion, Moral Philosophy, and Civil Polity at Harvard University. The outbreak of the World War I during the same year distressed Royce deeply. In 1914 Royce published *War and Insurance* and followed this book with another, *The Hope of the Great Community,* published in 1916. Royce, the great philosopher of community, died on September 14 of the same year in a world convulsed by global conflict.[5]

Of all the thinkers studied in this little book, only Royce reflected explicitly on the idea of modernity. He did so in his masterwork *The Problem of Christianity.* In the first volume of that work Royce argued, correctly in my estimate, that any criticism of modernity needs to deal simultaneously with the interrelated set of philosophical and theological issues which the Enlightenment and its aftermath raise.

If the subtleties of Peirce's philosophy defy summary in a single brief chapter, the scope and complexity of Royce's philosophical achievement make the attempt to encapsulate his thought within a few pages even more hopeless. This chapter, therefore, like the last one, proposes a much more modest goal. It focuses primarily on those themes in the later Peircean phase of Royce's philosophy which relate most obviously to the development of a constructive critique of modernism. Accordingly, after a brief summary of themes from Royce's early philosophy, the four sections of this chapter examine the following issues in the mature Royce: his critique of individualism in *The Philosophy of Loyalty;* Royce's contribution to the logic of relations in *Principles of Logic;* his response to James and to James's phenomenology of religious experience in *The Sources of Religious*

[5] See John Clendenning, *The Life and Thought of Josiah Royce* (Madison: University of Wisconsin Press, 1980); Frank Oppenheim, "Josiah Royce's Intellectual Development," *Idealistic Studies* 6 (1976) 85–104; Robert V. Hine, *Josiah Royce: From Grass Valley to Harvard* (Norman: University of Oklahoma Press, 1991); Bruce Kuklick, *Josiah Royce: An Intellectual Biography* (Indianapolis: Bobbs-Merrill, 1972); Bruce Kuklick, *The Rise of American Philosophy: Cambridge, Massachusetts, 1860–1930* (New Haven, Conn.: Yale University Press, 1977).

Insight; and the pragmatic vision of Christianity which he developed in *The Problem of Christianity.* This section begins with a brief summary of Royce's early ethics, theory of knowledge, and metaphysics.

II

In *The Religious Aspect of Philosophy,* published in 1885, Royce subjected to a preliminary analysis the foundations of moral and religious commitment. He identified the object of moral reasoning as ethical ideals. He conceded that anyone who defends moral idealism needs to respond to legitimate rational objections to the possibility of normative thinking. Royce conceded that neither subjective intent nor the accidental outcome of moral commitment offers ethics an adequate speculative justification. Neither can the de facto historical evolution of morality make normative claims. Nor can human sympathy in and of itself provide an adequate norm for conscientious, moral striving. In the end, the young Royce grounded moral idealism in the following maxim: *"Act always in the light of the completest insight into all the aims that thy act is to effect."* Since human wills espouse moral ideals, the ethical maxim implicitly commits one to seek the reconciliation of one's personally espoused ideals with conflicting ideals espoused by others. From the beginning, then, Royce envisioned moral reasoning as a social, dialogic process implicitly rooted in community. A reasonable morality rules out the possibility of reconciling conflicting moral ideals on the basis of caprice. Rather, a reasonable morality seeks to discover a universal moral will to which all may conscientiously consent. As a consequence, moral reasoning takes one to the threshold of religious assent.[6]

---

[6] See Josiah Royce, *The Religious Aspect of Philosophy: A Critique of the Bases of Conduct and of Faith* (New York: Harper & Brothers, 1958) 1–226. For a masterful study of Royce's mature religious thought which demonstrates the close connection between it and Royce's mature logic see Frank Oppenheim, *Royce's Mature Philosophy of Religion* (Notre Dame, Ind.: University of Notre Dame Press, 1987). See also Edward A. Jarvis, *The Conception of God in the Later Royce* (The Hague: Martinus Nijhoff, 1975); Daniel S. Robinson, *Royce and Hocking: American Idealists* (Boston: Christopher Publishing House, 1968); Gabriel Marcel, *Royce's Metaphysics,* trans. Virginia and Gordon Ringer (Chicago: Regnery, 1956); Clifford Barrett, *Contemporary Idealism in America* (New York: Russell and Russell, 1964); H. L. Chouragia, *A Comparative Study of the Philosophy of Josiah Royce and Radhakrishnan* (New Delhi: Oriental Publishers and Distributors, 1979); Thomas F. Powell, *Josiah Royce* (New York: Washington Square Press, 1967); Tribuhwan Nath Sharan, *The Religious Philosophy of Josiah Royce* (New Delhi: Oriental Publishers and Distributors, 1976); George Douglas Straton, *Theistic Faith for Our Time: An Introduction to the Process Philosophy of Royce and Whitehead* (Washington, D.C.: University Press of America, 1979).

Conflicting speculative claims about God, however, force the honest thinker to confront the reality of religious doubt. Doubt in turn raises the possibility of error. Royce's argument for the reality of God began with a search for the conditions for the possibility of erroneous judgment. Royce argued that the inevitable fallibility of all finite human judgments requires the existence somewhere of a standard for deciding between truth and error. Royce contended that the finitude of human intentions in judging requires an infinite judge in order to authenticate our judgments as either true or erroneous. In other words, the very possibility of doubt requires the existence of a divine All-Knower, a divine mind which comprehends all truth and all error and which distinguishes correctly between them. The reality of the All-Knower endows the human search for moral truth with religious significance, since in the end God functions as the ultimate arbiter among human ethical claims and systems.[7]

In *The World and the Individual,* Royce gave systematic elaboration to these early philosophical positions. The first volume of this monumental work dealt with four metaphysical conceptions of Being: realism, mysticism, critical realism, and Royce's own qualification of critical realism. In dealing with the four conceptions of Being, Royce insisted on the intimate relationship between metaphysics and epistemology. In other words, he recognized that any adequate, philosophical account of Being, of reality, must also explain the human mind's capacity to grasp reality. Realism sins by seeking to divorce reality from cognition by an illegitimate objectification of Being. Mysticism sins in the opposite direction by equating being with a cognitive immediacy which transcends both the world of senses and the world of conception. The positions defended by both realism and mysticism force philosophical consideration of the ancient metaphysical question of the one and the many. Realism fragments reality into a multiplicity of entities unrelated to thought, while mysticism, by circumscribing reality to the Transcendent, reduces multiplicity to mere illusion.[8]

The truth about reality, Royce argued, lies somewhere between the extremes of realism and mysticism. The realist allows only external, objective meanings; the mystic ends logically in despair of ever knowing a world of multiplicity. Critical realism asserts that the mind can grasp the specific conditions for the possibility of genuine knowing. For the critical realist, "Being" means "to be valid, to be true, to be the measure of ideas." In its

---

[7] Royce, *The Religious Aspect of Philosophy,* 227–484. See also John E. Skinner, *The Logocentric Predicament: An Essay on the Problem of Error in the Philosophy of Josiah Royce* (Philadelphia: University of Pennsylvania Press, 1965).

[8] Josiah Royce, *The World and the Individual,* 2 vols. (New York: Dover Publications, 1959) 1:1–195.

Kantian formulation, however, critical realism excludes as contradictory any knowledge of the individual as such. Royce argued that a distinction between internal and external meaning allows one to avoid this unacceptable Kantian conclusion. Ideas, which exemplify internal meaning, drive to concrete embodiment as external meaning. Thinking displays purpose, and purpose holds the key to cognitive correspondence. Ideas select the objects of thought and make them the focus of attentive and purposive expectation. The empirical content of an idea gives it, as a consequence, concrete embodiment and singles it out from other objects as an object of exclusive conscious intention. That exclusivity makes it "this object and no other."

These insights led Royce to define Being in the following terms: "What is, or what is real, is as such the complete embodiment, *in individual form and in final fulfillment* of the internal meaning of finite ideas." Having examined the first three conceptions of being—realism, mysticism, and critical realism—Royce presented his fourth conception of Being as "empirical" in the sense that it takes into account the physical world, social relationships, time, mathematical conceptions, and moral truth. The fourth conception of being also includes the All-Knower, for the world expresses, embodies, and fulfills Divine Thought. The All-Knower encompasses the universe by grasping the totality of abstract possibility and embodied meaning. The All-Knower, as a consequence, exemplifies a self-represented, infinite system of truth. In an extended supplementary essay, Royce also attempted to reply to Bradley's thesis that the Absolute reduces all finite realities to mere appearances. He appealed to a logic of infinite multitudes in order to argue that finite individuals can exemplify genuine reality within the absolute All-Knower.[9]

The second volume of *The World and the Individual* invoked the fourth conception of Being in formulating an account of the world, of human nature, and of the moral order. Royce argued that one can reduce all descriptive categories about the world to one of the following: likeness, difference, the ordered series, the ordered system, and the relationship "between." A logical class of objects, M, will lie between two other such classes, A and B, when class M includes all the objects common to both A and B and is included within the class of objects which is either A or B. Nature, which evolves, provides human experience with its common object. Habit manifests itself in nature in identifiable rhythms. We experience time perceptually as irreversible succession and conceptually as purposive striving. Finite, temporal beings, limited in their time-span, never know the whole of what they perceive in their dissatisfied striving.[10]

[9] Ibid., 1:473–588.
[10] Ibid., 2:75–204.

Each human self occupies a place in the order of nature. Viewed empirically each self consists of a certain totality of facts, but the self also includes the feelings, thoughts, desires, memories, emotions, and moods which make up each individual experience.

In social contacts, each self experiences both an Ego and its Alter. The Ego, moreover, knows itself only in contrast to an Alter. The self has an essentially ethical character. Neither a substance nor a thing, the self exemplifies a meaning embodied in a conscious life. The self involves the validity of a system of laws and relationships, but the self exemplifies more than a law since it ultimately incarnates a divine purpose.[11]

The Absolute is the larger Self which comprehends and includes every finite self and which provides each finite self with its ultimate goal or purpose for living. Every self of necessity seeks the Absolute, for every finite intention seeks to know the divine Other which defines its true individuality, its true moral destiny. We sin when our choices consciously contradict the self we know we ought to become. Because evil exists in the very fabric of things, the Absolute wills both our moral freedom (and therefore our ability to sin) and our atonement for evil choices. Future atonement makes sense of present evil. Moreover, the fact that all things exist in relationship means that one can regard nothing with moral indifference. Every sin has consequences for the other members of the cosmos. "Personality" therefore has of necessity ethical connotations. A person is a conscious being whose life, temporally viewed, seeks its completion through deeds while this same life, eternally viewed consciously, attains its perfection by means of the present knowledge of the whole of its temporal striving. God exemplifies a person who attains eternal perfection through morally significant striving. God enjoys consciousness of time but not in time. Humans too exemplify persons, but no finite individual finds ultimate fulfillment within space and time. The lives of those who die exist therefore in continuity with an afterlife which fulfills their finite, temporal existence.[12]

III

Before Royce reached his "Peircean insight" he had already sketched a preliminary metaphysics, theory of knowledge, and ethics. His self-

---

[11] Ibid., 2:204–99. See also James Harry Cotton, *Royce on the Human Self* (Cambridge, Mass.: Harvard University Press, 1954); Vincent Buranelli, *Josiah Royce* (New York: Twayne Publishers, 1964); Clifford Barret, *Contemporary Idealism in America* (New York: Russell & Russell, 1964) 111–41.

[12] Royce, *The World and the Individual,* 2:300–452. See also Joseph Philip Howard, *The Principle of Individuation in the Philosophy of Josiah Royce* (New Haven, Conn.: Yale University Press, 1916).

immersion in the thought of Peirce led him, however, to qualify in significant ways his early philosophical thinking.

At the beginning of the twentieth century the pragmatic and idealistic realism of Peirce and Royce offered a speculative alternative to the therapeutic individualism of William James, the philosophical nominalism of James and of George Santayana, and the naturalism of Santayana and of John Dewey. Against James's individualism, Royce, building on Peirce, developed a metaphysics of community. Against James's theistic nominalism and Santayana's atheistic nominalism, Royce, following Peirce, defended a pragmatistic realism. Against Santayana, Royce and Peirce defended the reality of God, the need for atoning love, and the moral necessity for divine saving grace. Secular culture in the United States opted on the whole to follow the lead of James, Santayana, and Dewey, and the nation continues to this day to pay the moral price of that fatal option.

In the 1980s, *Habits of the Heart* anatomized the moral bankruptcy of the therapeutic and utilitarian individualism of middle- and upper-class America.[13] Early in this century, however, Royce had already prescribed a plausible antidote to the virus of individualism. He called the antidote "loyalty."

Royce defined "loyalty" in a preliminary way as "the willing and practical and thoroughgoing devotion of a person to a cause."

> A man is loyal when, first, he has some *cause* to which he is loyal; when, secondly, he *willingly* and *thoroughly* devotes himself to this cause; and when, thirdly, he expresses his devotion in some *sustained and practical way,* by acting steadily in the service of his cause. Instances of loyalty are: The devotion of a patriot to his country, when this devotion leads him actually to live and perhaps to die for his country; the devotion of a martyr to his religion; the devotion of a ship's captain to the requirements of his office when, after a disaster, he works steadily for his ship and for the saving of the ship's company until the last possible service is accomplished, so that he is the last man to leave his ship, and is ready if need be to go down with his ship.[14]

The genuinely loyal person sustains such a commitment not only in the face of opposition but also when confronted with failure and rejection. Loyal commitment engages the affections but requires more than just emotional involvement. Authentic loyalty demands decisive commitment and self-discipline. It exemplifies practical dedication to an ideal which transcends narrow, private, or sectarian interests. Causes which engage loyalty unify, integrate, and stabilize social living.[15]

---

[13] Robert N. Bellah et al., *Habits of the Heart: Individualism and Commitment in American Life* (Berkeley and Los Angeles: University of California Press, 1985).

[14] Josiah Royce, *The Philosophy of Loyalty* (New York: Macmillan, 1908) 17.

[15] Ibid., 1–24.

Loyalty endows personal commitment with clarifying self-awareness. Commitment to an ethical cause requires the surrender of self-will and of personal selfishness. That same commitment excludes moral capricious ness. A cause sufficiently universal in its scope to qualify as moral requires one to transcend pleasure, pain, and any crudely pragmatic consideration. Such a cause provides an individual with a personal as well as a social plan for creative living.

> Loyalty, then, fixes our attention upon some one cause, bids us look with-out ourselves to see what this unified cause is, shows us this some one plan of action, and then says to us, "In this cause is your life, your will, your opportunity, your fulfillment."
>
> Thus loyalty, viewed merely as a personal attitude, solves the paradox of our ordinary existence, by showing us outside of ourselves the cause which is to be served, and inside of ourselves the will which delights to do this service, and which is not thwarted but enriched and expressed in such service.[16]

One lives creatively as a person by dedicating one's life to realizing the ideal to which one stands committed. Such loyalty has social consequences because it simultaneously commits one to the community of those who share one's cause. The loyal person stands ready to sacrifice everything for the cause which claims that person's commitment. Authentic loyalty comes in many forms which correspond to the various ideals and communities to which different individuals commit themselves. Royce acknowledged domestic, religious, commercial, and professional forms of loyalty, but the cause which engages authentic loyalty transcends not only the individuals but the communities committed to the ideals which claim them. Dedication to a lost cause expresses the ultimate degree of loyal commitment.[17]

An exaggerated individualism contradicts authentic, moral, loyal living. Such individualists oppose a morality of loyalty because they fallaciously imagine that it encroaches on individual freedom. In fact, freedom to live for a transcendent, all-consuming cause exemplifies a high kind of liberty. Individualists can in fact espouse a misguided form of loyalty. While genuine loyalty creates and strengthens social ties, individualism

---

[16] Ibid., 42. See also James Harry Cotton, *Royce on the Human Self* (Cambridge, Mass.: Harvard University Press, 1954); E. Karl Theo Humbach, *Das Verhältnis von Einzelperson und Gemeinschaft nach Josiah Royce* (Heidelberg: Beiheften zum Jahrbuch Für Amerikastudien, 1962); Ralph di Pasquali, *The Social Dimensions of the Philosophy of Josiah Royce* (Rome: Pontifico Ateneo Antoniano, 1961); Wayne Proudfoot, "Conceptions of God and the Self," *Journal of Religion* 55 (1975) 51–75; Peter Fuss, "Royce on the Concept of the Self: An Historical and Critical Perspective," *American Philosophy from Edwards to Quine,* ed. Robert W. Sahahn and Kenneth R. Merrill (Norman: University of Oklahoma Press, 1977).

[17] Royce, *The Philosophy of Loyalty,* 24–52, 295–7.

manifests its moral bankruptcy by inspiring cliquishness, selfishness, social fragmentation, and moral isolation. Blind loyalty can also degenerate
into different forms of social oppression, but individualism offers no antidote to such a perversion of true loyalty. On the contrary, individualism
exalts personal self-will, the lust for power, and the vindication of personal
right over social obligation. It fallaciously pits the good of the individual
against the common good of all.[18] In the end, the individualist needs to
learn that one becomes a true individual by dedication to a cause. As
Royce observed:

> In view of such considerations, when I listen to our modern ethical individ-
> ualists,—to our poets, dramatists, essayists who glorify personal initia-
> tive—to our Walt Whitman, to Ibsen, and, above all, when I listen to
> Nietzsche,—I confess that these men move me for a time, but that ere long
> I begin to listen with impatience. Of course, I then say, be indeed au-
> tonomous. Be an individual. But for Heaven's sake, set about the task. Do
> not forever whet the sword of your resolve. Begin the battle of real individ-
> uality. Why these endless preliminary gesticulations? "Leave off thy gri-
> maces," and begin. There is only one way to be an ethical individual. That
> is to choose your cause, and then to serve it, as the Samurai his feudal chief,
> as the ideal knight of romantic story his lady,—in the spirit of all the loyal.[19]

Human causes differ in what they seek to accomplish. As a consequence, sometimes causes conflict. If loyalty exemplifies the highest
moral ideal, the conflict of loyalties exemplifies the worst moral evil, and
only loyalty to the cause of loyal living overcomes that conflict. Those
loyal to loyal living commit themselves to overcoming moral conflicts
among apparently conflicting human causes and to reconciling those
causes in a shared moral consensus or in moral unanimity. Loyalty to loyalty requires lived tolerance of authentic causes other than one's chosen
cause, and such loyalty creates social communion. Not only does loyalty
to loyalty measure the moral authenticity of one's devotion to one's own
cause, but it makes loyalty morally contagious and encourages its spread.[20]

> Since no personal good that your fellow can possess is superior to his own
> loyalty, your own loyalty to loyalty is itself a supremely benevolent type of
> activity. And since your fellow-man is an instrument for the furtherance of
> the cause of universal loyalty, his welfare also concerns you, in so far as, if
> you help him to a more efficient life, you make him better able to be loyal.
> Thus benevolence is an inevitable attendant of loyalty. And the spirit of loy-
> alty to loyalty enables us to define wherein consists a wise benevolence.

18 Ibid., 52–101.
19 Ibid., 98.
20 Ibid., 101–46.

Benevolence without loyalty is dangerous sentimentalism. Thus viewed, then, loyalty to universal loyalty is indeed the fulfillment of the whole law.[21]

Loyalty to loyal living in oneself and in all other loyal persons creates the human conscience and unifies both personal and communal living through commitment to a single integrating purpose. One's cause defines one's moral personality. Conflicts of conscience reflect the apparent conflict of loyalties, but the resolution of one's conscience reconciles conflicting moral ideals into a unified plan for ethical living. Those who would live moral lives must commit themselves to some cause, because the refusal to espouse any cause easily and inevitably degenerates with time into an unauthentic commitment to non-commitment. Then the decision not to decide transforms itself into a sin of omission. Having decided which cause to espouse, the loyal conscience serves that cause until the cause succeeds or until further loyalty would amount to disloyalty.[22] Royce put it this way:

> My causes must form a system. They must constitute in their entirety a single cause, my life of loyalty. When apparent conflicts arise amongst the causes in which I am interested, I shall deliberately undertake, by devices which we shall hereafter study in these lectures, to reduce the conflict to the greatest possible harmony. Thus, for instance, I may say, to one of the causes in which I am naturally bound up:—
> "I could not love thee, dear, so much,
> Loved I not honour more."
> And in this familiar spirit my loyalty will aim to be, even within the limits of my own personal life, an united, harmonious devotion, not to various conflicting causes, but to one system of causes, and so to one cause.[23]

Can one teach loyal living? One can legitimately exhort others to live loyal lives, but one cannot tell them which cause they must espouse. Rather, one can point out to others fields of loyal endeavor or elucidate the consequences of disloyal living. Disloyalty always breeds estrangement and social alienation, while loyal living breeds the opposite: mutual commitment and social communion. Still, within limits, one can both inspire and train humans in the practice of loyalty, especially during adolescence, but only in life-long adult fidelity does loyalty manifest the full scope of responsible human devotion. Effective leaders inspire loyalty, even to lost causes. A lost cause brings grief and the hope for a better future, but fidelity to a lost cause expresses the noblest and final test of true religious devotion.

[21] Ibid., 145–6.
[22] Ibid., 149–60.
[23] Ibid., 132–3.

> Loyalty means giving the Self to the Cause. And the art of giving is learned by giving. Strain, endurance, sacrifice, toil,—the dear pangs of labor at the moments when perhaps defeat and grief most seem ready to crush our powers, and when only the very vehemence of labor itself saves us from utter despair,—these are the things that most teach us what loyalty really is.[24]

In the end, one learns the meaning of loyalty only by living it. Inspiring leadership and the idealization of causes educates the conscience and prepares it for committed, loyal practice.[25]

Genuine causes make demands and require sacrifices of those who espouse them. One's particular moral cause situates one within the total scheme of the universe. The loyal thus serve "a real whole of life, an experiential value too rich for any expression in merely monetary terms." Loyalty to life commits one as well to loyalty to truth, and commitment to truth can function as a cause in its own right. In addition, loyalty to truth orients one to a transcendent reality which goes beyond any particular true affirmation or act of verification. Loyalty to truth also bears fruit in a metaphysics, in a theory of the whole, in an account of the nature of reality.[26]

> Any special idea of mine may be wrong, even as any loyal deed may fail, or as any cause may become, to human vision a lost cause. But to deny that there is truth, or that there is a real world, is simply to say that the whole truth is that there is no whole truth, and that the real fact is that there is no fact real at all. Such assertions are plain self-contradictions. And on the other hand, by the term "real world," defined as it is for us by our ideal needs, we mean simply that whole of experience in which we live, and in unity with which we alone succeed.
>
> Loyalty, then, has its own metaphysic. This metaphysic is expressed in a view of things which conceives our experience as bound up in a real unity with all experience,—an unity which is essentially good, and in which all our ideas possess their real fulfillment and success. Such a view is true, simply because if you deny its truth you affirm that very truth under a new form.[27]

Like loyalty to loyalty, loyalty to truth has an ultimate and therefore a religious dimension. Religious loyalty seeks to embody an eternal, moral truth. Indeed, one may describe religion as "the interpretation both of the eternal and of the spirit of loyalty through emotion" and through suitable imaginative activity. As a consequence, all those who serve morally transcendent truth qualify as religious.[28] Hear Royce himself:

[24] Ibid., 296–7.
[25] Ibid., 198–298.
[26] Ibid., 301–48.
[27] Ibid., 345–6.
[28] Ibid., 351–98.

Hence, when religion, in the service of loyalty, interprets the world-life to us with symbolic detail, it gives us indeed merely symbols of the eternal truth. That this truth is indeed eternal, that our loyalty brings us into personal relations with a personal world-life, which values our every loyal deed, and needs that deed, all this is true and rational. And just this is what religion rightly illustrates.[29]

Royce's philosophy of loyalty inculcated a form of moral idealism, but it did more than that. It sought to balance ideal loyalty to a cause with realistic commitment to a concrete community of loyal persons who share those ideals. In addition, the philosophy of loyalty countered the chauvinism which so easily plagues finite human communities with loyalty to the universal community of the loyal and to the universal good of humankind. At the heart of loyal living lay the ongoing and simultaneous balancing of these three intimately interrelated commitments. As Royce developed his mature religious philosophy, he would deepen and expand the critique of individualism which he sketched in his philosophy of loyalty. In writing *The Philosophy of Loyalty,* Royce probably thought of it as an essay in ethics. However, viewed from the standpoint of Peirce's normative sciences, *The Philosophy of Loyalty* well exemplifies what Peirce meant by aesthetics, for the book reflects normatively about the kinds of ideals which make life worth living and on the kinds of habits which enable one to embrace those ideals.[30]

IV

Although Royce did not publish *Principles of Logic* until 1913, he had completed its writing in 1910. As a consequence, his logical reflections in *Principles* provides a methodological context for his mature religious philosophy.

At the beginning of *Principles of Logic,* Royce distinguished between logic as a normative science and logic as a principle of order. As a normative science, logic divides into "formal logic" and "applied logic." Formal logic enunciates general normative principles for correct thinking,

---

[29] Ibid., 396–7.

[30] See Peter Fuss, *The Moral Philosophy of Josiah Royce* (Cambridge, Mass.: Harvard University Press, 1965); Donald William Dotterer, "Josiah Royce's Philosophy of Loyalty: A Hermeneutical Tool for Pauline Theology," *American Journal of Theology and Philosophy* 7 (1986) 149–63; John K. McCreary, "Psychological and Religious Idealism in Royce," *Journal of Religion and Psychical Research* 4 (1981) 138–42; Bennett Ramsey, "The Ineluctable Impulse: 'Consent' in the Thought of Edwards, James, and Royce," *Union Seminary Quarterly Review* 37 (1983) 303–22; Griffin Trotter, *The Loyal Physician: Roycean Ethics and the Practice of Medicine* (Nashville: Vanderbilt University Press, 1997).

while "applied logic" studies the methods appropriate to different speculative disciplines. Royce proposed to reflect on logic not as a normative science, but as a science of order. Viewed as a science of order, logic studies "the Types of Order, which characterize any realm of objects which a thinker has actually succeeded in mastering, or can possibly succeed in mastering, by his methods."[31]

Royce found the seeds of a logical science of order already present in Socratic logic. Socratic concern with proper definition led to a systematic analysis of correct classification. Careful study of the evidence which attaches to certain notable propositions led to an examination of the modes of inference. Socratic logic, as Plato developed it, recognized that universals, Ideas, form a system and that one can make inferences because truths have momentous objective relationships to one another. As a consequence, the order and connection of rational processes must reflect the order and connection of reality itself.[32]

Modern logic presupposes that the mind gains understanding inductively, on the basis of experience and of controlling systems of facts. Modern logic requires, therefore, a system for classifying facts and builds in part on the foundations laid by Socrates, but modern scientific logic distinguishes descriptive methods which compare and contrast corresponding stages in the natural evolution of processes from statistical method. Statistical method tries to uncover uniform patterns in nature whose explanation initially eludes us. Statistical method raises the question of the correlation of series of phenomena.[33]

The statistical correlation of facts requires their classification with respect to a feature or features in which they vary, like the varying size of organisms and their organs. Statistical method then enumerates the members of the different classes of things under study, insofar as enumeration promises to advance inquiry. One then arranges the enumerations in orderly series with respect to the questions one raises concerning them and the laws to which one believes them subject. The comparison of different series tends to show how two or more aspects of the phenomena under investigation vary together. One might, for example, study how human mortality varies with age, or how the mean temperature of the earth varies with respect to latitude, or how the size of an organism varies with respect to heredity or environment. The correlation of different series of facts enables the statistician to deal with aggregates, or blocks, of facts which ap-

---

[31] Josiah Royce, *Principles of Logic* (New York: Book Sales Ind., 1981) 9–13. See also Andrew Reck, "Interpretation," *Continuum* 2 (1964) 455–63.

[32] Royce, *Principles of Logic,* 13–15.

[33] Ibid., 15–19.

pear to exemplify identifiable laws. Clearly, the operational procedures of statistical method, by invoking concepts like "number," "series," and "correlation," give methodological prominence to the concept of order in general, as do more classical forms of logic.[34]

Statistical reasoning also engages the notion of "probability." The degree of probability of any statistical argument depends upon two key factors: the number of sampled instances and the fairness of the sample. From a logical standpoint, statistical reasoning raises the question of the legitimacy of generalizing from a limited sample of relevant data. Some logicians justify statistical generalization by appealing to the uniformity of nature or to the principle that every occurrence has a sufficient reason. These justifications, however, fail finally to justify statistical reasoning, for while nature does display uniformities, one may differ in one's account of which patterns constitute uniformity. The judgment about uniformity, therefore, requires the prudential assessment of which facts count as important and which do not. Similarly, the principle of sufficient reason fails to explain why only a few laws, or sufficient reasons, can claim to govern nature. Neither argument, therefore, adequately justifies assigning a definite degree of probability to any given statistical series.[35]

Royce endorsed Peirce's argument that the *determinate constitution* of any given set of facts provides the natural and indispensable presupposition for all probable, statistical reasoning. Grant the determinate constitution of any set of facts, and a "fair sample" of the data in question will yield a probable, but only a probable, account of their actual constitution. For example, by random sampling one can establish the probable content of cargoes, the probable constitution of populations, or of any other collection. Randomness of selection justifies calling a sample "fair."[36]

One can argue statistically to the probability of hypotheses provided one formulates one's hypothesis "in terms of certain conceptual order systems whose exactness of structure far transcends, in ideal, the grade of exactness that can ever be given to our physical observations themselves." One's hypothesis anticipates the occurrence of a specific observable fact or facts. The hypothesis, therefore, focuses the investigator's attention on selected facts conceived of as relevant. Deductive reasoning provides the rationale for statistically verified patterns in nature. One could, for example, predict an eclipse of the moon on the basis of statistical evidence alone, but lunar theory calls the investigator's attention to the ideal consequences of a more general theory of gravitation. A hypothesis suggests an

---

[34] Ibid., 18–20.
[35] Ibid., 22–4.
[36] Ibid., 24–30.

interpretation of the laws governing a particular set of facts. A hypothesis will tend to advance knowledge to the extent that it provides an extensive, exact, and systematic sampling of facts which flow from the hypothesis deductively. In other words, the statistical validation of a hypothesis derives from the exactness, the order, and the systematic character of the concepts which define the meaning of the hypothesis. In the inductive validation of hypothetico-deductive thinking, therefore, the order of the precise quantities under investigation plays a crucial role.[37]

Any theory of logic as a science of order needs to offer an account of different kinds of rational order. Initially, one must distinguish ideal and actual measurement. Actual measurement can only approximate the ideal standard to which it seeks to conform. The mind both creates and finds different types of order in the world. In creating an ideal system of measurement one must discover the forms which characterize all activity which exemplifies a specific kind of order. In logic viewed as a science of order, the category "relation" plays a fundamental role. Qualities, normally expressed as adjectives, distinguish different kinds of objects from one another: qualities like hard, sweet, bitter, warm, cold, etc. Relations accrue to realities whose characteristics designate them as belonging to an ideal or real collection of objects. Indeed, as we shall see, relation links all the elements of logic—individuals, sets, classes, and levels—with decision functioning in the logical identification of individuals. In other words, relationship implies membership in a collection.[38]

Dyadic relationships divide into symmetrical and non-symmetrical. The terms of a symmetrical relationship exemplify equality. Thus, if a=b, then, b=a. In totally asymmetrical relationships, the two terms cannot simultaneously enjoy the same relationship. Greater and less exemplify such asymmetrical relationships. In addition, dyadic relationships divide into transitive and intransitive relationships. For example, let "R" signify relation. One may then define transitivity in the following manner: if (a R b) and (b R c), then it always follows that (a R c), no matter what a, b, and c exemplify. Both symmetrical and asymmetrical relations can exhibit transitivity. "Greater than" and "superior to" exemplify transitive, asymmetrical relationships, while "opposed to" or "contradictory of" exemplify symmetrical but non-transitive relationships. In other words, symmetry of relationship need not entail transitivity. Some relations exclude all transitivity. For example, if a begets b and b begets c, then a cannot beget c. Finally, one may classify dyadic relationships by the number of objects to which one of the two related terms may stand related. For example, if a

[37] Ibid., 30–4.
[38] Ibid., 35–8.

begets b, a can also subsequently beget c, d, e, etc. Similarly, one may owe debts to more than one creditor. The categories "symmetry," "non-symmetry," "transitivity," "non-transitivity," and "multiplicity of objects" apply as well to triadic, tetradic, and other polyadic relationships. Addition (a + b = c) exemplifies a triadic relationship.[39]

The idea of "relation" necessarily implies the idea of "class." Logically defined, the idea of "class" implies (1) a relationship of belonging or not-belonging to an identifiable set, (2) the assertion or denial of the relationship of belonging, and (3) a norm for determining which assertions qualify as true and which as false. From the stand point of logic, one may define as an "individual" an entity identifiable throughout some process of investigation as unique within the range of that investigation and therefore unreplaceable by any other reality. Pragmatic motives cause the mind to designate some realities as logical individuals. The identification of individuals therefore expresses a decision of the will at the same time that it makes possible all orderly mental activity. One cannot class individuals with other individuals until one has identified them. As a consequence, all classification involves volition, decision, choice. "Apart from some classifying will, our world contains no classes." All classification engages volition, but classification exemplifies precise, not arbitrary, logical relationships because it expresses the will to act rationally.[40]

The transitive relationship of *subsumption* grounds all syllogistic reasoning. For example, if one can subsume q under p, then whatever conforms to the norm of p conforms to the norm of q. Equality exemplifies a transitive relation of subsumption. In other words, if p subsumes q, and q subsumes p, then p equals q and vice versa. As a consequence, the norms of rational thinking all exemplify a theory of logical order. What Royce called the "epsilon relation," however, differs from the relationship of subsumption. By the "epsilon relation" Royce meant the relation of an individual to the class to which it belongs and of which it is a member. The same relationship can apply to a set, or class, of classes. Non-transitivity characterizes the epsilon relation, while transitivity characterizes the relationship of subsumption.[41]

The concepts of "relation," "relational properties," and "classes" have enabled mathematicians and students of logic to define in exact terms a vast range of order systems. These order systems exhibit not only dyadic but triadic relationships, both simple relations of correlation and functional relationships. Symmetrical relations, especially symmetrical, transitive

[39] Ibid., 37–47.
[40] Ibid., 47–51.
[41] Ibid., 51–3.

relationships, make it possible to classify and so ground the most exactly definable classifications in any science of order. Among different logical series, a series of levels, like contour lines or isobars on a map, rank among the most important.

The human mind must *generate* logical systems of order. The most important laws of an ordered universe deal, in general, with *levels* of order and depend on the concepts of "class" and "relation." Indeed without the concepts class and relation, no rational activity could ever take place. We experience classifiable objects, and we experience them as classifiable. We also experience physical and psychical relationships as constituting the world. Still, we actively construct ideal relational systems and classes for dealing with experienced relationships and classes. "Working hypotheses" consist of constructed relational systems and classes which successfully interpret experienced relationships and classes and so enable us to deal successfully with the world. In addition to "working hypotheses," however, Royce discovered another logical class of propositions which he characterized as self-reinstating. He called the defense of such propositions "absolute pragmatism." Royce characterized absolute pragmatism in the following way:

> There are *some* truths that are known to us *not* by virtue of the special successes which this or that hypothesis obtains in particular instances, but by virtue of the fact that *there are certain modes of activity, certain laws of the rational will, which we reinstate and verify, through the very act of attempting to presuppose that these modes of activity do not exist, or that these laws are not valid.* Thus, whoever says that there are no classes whatever in his world inevitably classifies. . . .
>
> *In brief, whatever actions are such, whatever types of action are such, whatever results of activity, whatever conceptual constructions are such, that the very act of getting rid of them, or of thinking them away, logically implies their presence, are known to us indeed both empirically and pragmatically (since we note their presence and learn of them through action); but they are also absolute. And any account which succeeds in telling what they are has absolute truth. Such truth is a "construction" or "creation," for activity determines its nature. It is "found," for we observe it when we act.* . . .
>
> Now theories and hypotheses may be merely suggested to us by physical phenomena, so that, if we had different sensations from our present ones, or if our perceptions followed some other routine than the observed one, we should have no need for these hypotheses and resulting theories. In so far, the hypotheses are contingent and the theories have only conditional value. . . .
> But such logical facts as the difference between *yes* and *no,* are not dependent on the contingent aspect of our sensations, but on our rational consciousness of what we intend to do or not to do. Such facts have not the contingency of

the empirical particulars of sense. And some modes of action, such as affirmation and denial, are absolute modes.[42]

Royce concluded, therefore, that any logical theory of order contains
some necessary elements and laws as well as some empirical, contingent
phenomena. As a consequence, giving an account of the necessary classes
and relations constitutes the central problem of any logical theory of order.
Some pragmatists, like William James, maximize empirical and contingent relationships in their theory of order; others, like Royce himself, recognize a realm of ideal, possible objects which constitute a system of
order which conforms to laws like the law exemplified in the relationship
of yes and no. These relations and laws have an absolute validity and constitute a system which Royce called "system sigma."

> *This system has an order which is determined entirely by the fundamental
> laws of logic, and by the one additional principle thus mentioned.* The new
> principle in question is precisely analogous to a principle which is funda-
> mental in geometrical theory. This is the principle that, between any two
> points on a line, there is an intermediate point, so that the points on a line
> constitute, for geometrical theory, *at least a dense series.* In its application
> to the entities of pure logic, this principle appears indeed at first sight to be
> extraneous and arbitrary. For the principle corresponding to the geometrical
> principle which defines the dense series of points, does not apply at all to
> the logical world of propositions. And, again, it does not apply with *ab-
> solute* generality to the objects known as classes. But it *does* apply to a set
> of objects, to which the foregoing repeated reference has been made. This
> set of objects may be defined as, "certain possible modes of action that are
> open to any rational being who can act at all, and who can also reflect upon
> his own modes of action."[43]

Since decision functions in the generation of logical systems of order,
the logical analysis of systems must also deal with modes of action.
Modes of action, Royce argued, obey the same general laws to which
propositions and classes submit. For example, the "mode of action" which
we call "to sing" or "singing" has a contradictory mode of action expressed by "not to sing" or "not singing." The phrase "to sing and dance"
results logically from the modes of action "to sing" and "to dance." Similarly, between two modes of action the relation of inclusion may or may
not obtain; and modes of action can contradict one another. System sigma
exemplifies a logical system of order which one cannot question without
abandoning the very conception of rational activity itself. Hence, its denial
necessarily involves a rational contradiction and therefore reinstates the

[42] Ibid., 63–5.
[43] Ibid., 72–3.

reality denied. System sigma, therefore, plays a fundamental role in the active generation of all other logical systems of order. This polyadic system of logical classes and relationships subtends "all the order systems on which the natural sciences depend for the success of their deductions."[44]

Royce's *Principles of Logic* built consciously on the foundations laid by Peirce's pragmaticism. Both men viewed logic as both a normative science and as a science of order. In dealing with logic as a science of order, both endorsed and developed a logic of relations. Royce explicitly endorsed Peirce's logical explanation of statistical probability. In Royce's handling of hypothetico-deductive method, one finds an implicit endorsement on Royce's part of Peirce's inferential logic. Both Royce and Peirce recognized the importance of choice within logical thinking and rejected the notion of a speculative reason which does not rest on fallible prudential options. Both thinkers reflected extensively on the logic of both the dyad and the triad, and both acknowledged the fundamental importance of triadic relationships in inferential thinking.

Despite Royce's assimilation of Peirce's ground-breaking logical insights, three logical notions articulated in *Principles of Logic* give it a distinctive Roycean flavor: the epsilon relation, absolute pragmatism, and system sigma. The epsilon relationship suggests that the relationship of inclusion exemplifies the most fundamental logical relationship. This insight gave logical support to the metaphysics of community which Royce would develop in *The Problem of Christianity*. That metaphysics built creatively and constructively on Peirce's logical and metaphysical turn to community.

Royce's absolute pragmatism also suggests a way of bridging an approach to logic as a science of order and logic as a normative science. In speaking of absolute pragmatism, Royce is asserting a logical rather than a strictly metaphysical absoluteness. He is arguing that reinstating logical principles enjoy an unconditioned character. By reinstating logical principles Royce means a logical principle whose denial implicitly reaffirms what one denies. The unconditioned absoluteness of such principles endows them with logical normativity. System sigma explores the relationships among these logical absolutes. In other words, unlike Peirce, Royce continued to assert something like an unconditioned ground and starting point for human thought.

While Royce attributes logical rather than metaphysical absoluteness to reinstating logical principles, anyone familiar with his thought immediately suspects that lurking behind system sigma lies Royce's divine Absolute, the All-Knower who alone grasps in an eternal insight the totality of all rela-

[44] Ibid., 72–7; see also C. I. Lewis, "Types of Order and System Sigma," *Philosophical Review* 26 (1916) 407–19.

tionships of truth and falsity. The Problem of Christianity would transform the All-Knower into the Interpreter Spirit, the "final interpretant" of Peirce's philosophy. Moreover, Royce would discover the divine interpreter at work in the Pauline communities of the apostolic Christian Church.[45]

V

Royce's analysis in 1908 of the dynamic thrust of loyal, ethical living culminated in an insight into the ultimately religious character of all genuine loyal living. In 1912, in *The Sources of Religious Insight,* Royce addressed the question of religious experience directly. In writing *The Sources,* Royce also undertook to criticize in a systematic way William James's *The Varieties of Religious Experience.* In *The Varieties,* James had bracketed the historical and social dimensions of religion and focused on individual religious experience. Moreover, James had also suggested that the unconscious gives one privileged access to religious experience. Royce's emphasis on religious insight expressed his concern to shift the discussion of religious experience to conscious human awareness. Moreover, Royce began his exploration of human religious awareness by calling attention to the radical limits of individual religious experience.

By an "insight" Royce meant a certain kind of human understanding. Insight yields a unified, synthesizing grasp of unity in diversity. It makes the one who experiences the insight intimately present to the reality which the insight discloses. Moreover, besides a synthesizing unity, an insight yields a range and coherence of understanding. It can occur in any human speculative endeavor, but it also occurs in religious contexts.[46] Royce, then, offered the following summary definition of an insight:

> Insight is knowledge that makes us aware of the unity of many facts in one whole, and that at the same time brings us into intimate personal contact with these facts and with the whole wherein they are united. The three marks of insight are breadth of range, coherence and unity of view, and closeness of personal touch.[47]

An insight acquires a religious character when it concerns itself with the problem of human salvation. All great religions assert that humanity needs saving, even though different religions offer different accounts of how salvation occurs. One asserts the possibility of salvation when one holds that among human aims one aim or complex of aims has more importance than all others. Human belief in the possibility of salvation has

---

[45] See Mary Briody Mahowald, *An Idealistic Pragmatism: The Development of the Pragmatic Element in Royce* (The Hague: Martinus Nijhoff, 1972).
[46] Josiah Royce, *The Sources of Religious Insight* (New York: Scribner's, 1912) 5–9.
[47] Ibid., 5–6.

deep roots in each person's heart. Salvation engages human choice and moral striving. Those who forfeit salvation miss the real meaning of life. As a consequence, religious doctrines of salvation always have a practical dimension to them: they offer not only an understanding of the meaning of salvation but identify the means required to reach salvation.[48] Royce summarized what he meant by a religious insight in the following terms: "Religious insight means, then, for my present purposes, *insight into the need and into the way of salvation.*"[49]

Religious insight engages individual commitment and belief. People can grasp the saving meaning of life in a solitary encounter with a saving deity, as James argued in *The Varieties*. In the end, however, religion raises problems and questions which transcend the scope of finite, individual human consciousness. Individual religious experience interrelates three related concerns: a personal ideal of life, a felt need for personal salvation, and a longing for communion with some saving power. The personal search for salvation engages loyalties and requires a plan of life which sets the individual in relationship with a Deliverer. Every practical plan of life, however, has of necessity social ramifications. As a consequence, no individual reaches salvation alone. One can grasp the ultimate meaning of life only in and through social communion with others. Authentic religious insight, therefore, calls the individual religious person beyond self-preoccupation and social isolation to commitment to and in community. The isolated individual bereft of a saving community can only yield an insight into the human need for salvation, not into the effective means of attaining it.[50] Royce put it this way:

> If one principal source of our need of salvation is the natural narrowness of our view of the meaning of our own purposes and motives, and the consequent fickleness and the forgetful inconsistency with which we usually live out our days, it seems right, in searching for a way that may lead toward salvation, to get such help as we can by looking to your normal social experience for whatever guidance it can give.[51]

Shared social experience offers, then, a second important source of religious insight. Shared religious consciousness, however, comes in many different forms. Often the claims of different religious communities conflict. As a consequence, the search for religious insight in community forces one into dialogue with those whose religious convictions differ from one's own. Active participation in such a religious dialogue forces

---

[48] Ibid., 9–26.
[49] Ibid., 17.
[50] Ibid., 26–34.
[51] Ibid., 55.

believers to face their own conflicting religious attitudes. It also forces them to face the narrowness and finitude which mars most human opinions, including religious opinions.

Salvation, however, requires an integrated perception of the scope and meaning of life, even though the achievement of such a vision, even in a community which searches for salvation, happens only momentarily and partially. The partial and fragmented character of individual religious experience forces one to join with others in searching for salvation, but the fragmented and sectarian character of shared religious experience requires one to confront next the fact that no human community can save itself. We experience collective as well as personal guilt and dissolution. Shared religious experience advances the individual along the road to salvation, but the fact that religious communities also need salvation means that shared religious experience, like individual religious experience, teaches a community to look beyond itself for the source and reality of salvation.[52] Royce summarized the matter this way:

> I conclude, then, for the moment thus: Social experience seems to lie on the way to salvation. Normally the way to salvation, if there be any such way, must lead through social experience. But when our social experience shows us any such way upward it does so, if it truly does so, because human social life is the hint, the likeness, or the incarnation of a life that lies beyond and above our present human existence. For human society as it now is, in this world of care, is a chaos of needs; and the whole of social order groans and travails together in pain until now, longing for salvation. It can be saved, as the individual can be saved, only in case there is some way that leads upward, through all our turmoil and our social bickerings, to a realm where that vision of unity and self-possession which our clearest moments bring us becomes not merely vision but fulfillment, where love finds its own, and where the power of the spirit triumphs.[53]

Human reason contributes to the vision of unity for which humans long both personally and communally. Not all religious beliefs have irrational or subconscious grounding. Rational reflection on the ultimate meaning of life yields conscious and intentional religious insight. Analytic reason formulates hypotheses, predicts their operational consequences, and then verifies or falsifies their truth or determines their degree of probability. Human reason, however, functions synthetically as well as analytically, and synthetic reason ponders all the relevant sides of any given

---

[52] Ibid., 37–75.

[53] Ibid., 75; see also James Collins, "Josiah Royce: Analyst of Religion as Community," *American Philosophy and the Future,* ed. Michael Novak (New York: Scribner's, 1968) 199–200.

question in a search for a frame of reference which will integrate the best of every position examined. Synthetic reason takes into account the spontaneous hunches of the individual mind, but in the end it seeks a meaningful insight into the very nature of reality.

Synthetic reason serves the human need for salvation when it provides to personal and communal self-understanding the integrating insight which reconciles conflicting religious beliefs. A reconciling insight moves consciously beyond sectarian limits and viewpoints. Ultimately, synthesizing reason seeks the reconciliation of all viewpoints in a unified, world-transcending grasp of all reality. Such an insight would supply the condition for the existence of the world as we know it. The search for religious insight orients one ultimately, therefore, to the world-transcending reality of God, for only the divine mind reconciles all conflicting viewpoints in a single synthetic vision.[54] Royce summarized the contribution which reason makes to religious insight in the following manner:

> To assert then that there is no largest view, no final insight, no experience that is absolute, is to assert that the largest view observes that there is no largest view, that the final insight sees that there is no such insight, that the ultimate experience is aware that there is no ultimate experience. And such an assertion is indeed a self-contradiction. . . . In every error, in every blunder, in all our darkness, in all our ignorance, we are still in touch with the eternal insight. We are always seeking to know even as we are known.[55]

The human search for salvation, however, engages more than the human mind. It involves decision as well, for authentic religious knowing must always bear fruit in authentic religious practice. Therefore, decision, the practical living of life, offers a source of religious insight which complements that of reason. Every opinion expresses an attitude of will, and opinions need testing in the arena of practical living. However, if the source of salvation must transcend, encompass, and integrate ourselves and our world, then moral striving will yield a religious insight only to the extent that it adjusts the human will to the will of the divine Deliverer. Moral insight, therefore, goes beyond the verification or falsification of individual religious beliefs. A religiously significant moral insight must show religious seekers the place assigned them in the universal scheme of things by the absolute will of One who saves them, for only such a practical, lived recognition of one's role and place in the divine scheme of things yields salvation. Humans experience the absoluteness of choice and of opinion on a regular, day-to-day basis. Deeds once done remain there-

---

[54] Royce, *The Sources of Religious Insight,* 79–116.
[55] Ibid., 114–5.

after absolutely irrevocable. So do the beliefs which motivated them. The knowledge and will of a Divine Deliverer would enjoy not only that kind of absoluteness but also the absoluteness of eternity and of world-encompassing comprehension.[56]

Religion and morality have an intimate relationship to one another, but they also differ. The moral conscience asks: "What ought I to do?" Moral reasoning concerns itself primarily with rights and duties. Religion, however, concerns itself with the *summum bonum,* with the highest good in life which endows all other goods with saving significance. In forming the moral conscience, one must consult the experience of others, but society, which tends to counsel moral accommodation and compromise, rarely provides an adequate response to the moral question. Authentic moral living requires a selfless and ultimate dedication which makes one ready to brave death itself, if necessary, for the realities and values to which one stands committed. In other words, authentic moral living engages loyal commitment, and loyalty to loyalty, the commitment to advance always the cause of loyal living in oneself and in others, universalizes moral striving by creating a common moral will. That commitment allows for none of the "moral holidays" which William James attributed to belief in metaphysical absolutes. Loyalty to loyalty transforms human moral striving into yet another source of religious insight by revealing the need for human moral behavior to conform itself to a transcendent, universal will which reconciles in itself all genuine loyalties.[57] As Royce put it:

> The divine will wills in us and in all this world, with its endless past and its endless future, at once. The divine insight is not endless future, at once. The divine insight is not lifeless. It includes and surveys all life. All is temporal in its ceaseless flow and in its sequence of individual deeds. All is eternal in the unity of its meaning.
>
> To assert this, I insist, is not to deny our freedom and our initiative. The divine will wills me, precisely in so far as it wills that, in each of my individual deeds, I should then and there express my own unique, and in so far free, choice. And to assert, as I do, that the divine will wills all "at once" is not to assert that it wills all at any one moment of time, but only that the divine will is expressed in the totality of its deeds that are done in all moments of time.[58]

Many people view the reality of evil as an obstacle to religious faith, but, under certain conditions, even the experience of suffering can yield religious insight. We spontaneously admire those who struggle against evil,

[56] Ibid., 119–61.
[57] Ibid., 165–210.
[58] Ibid., 160–1.

and the destruction of evil plays an important role in any religious insight. The struggle against evil, however, takes on religious meaning only when those who struggle have the assurance that they act in union with a Divine Principle who surveys and controls the real nature of things. Evil in and of itself, of course, offers no religious enlightenment; but experiences of evil which yield life-giving consequences can and do give a religious insight into salvation. Such experiences suggest that evil itself can serve a higher purpose and even function in a necessary way in the achievement of saving purpose. Those who meet God in suffering do not thereby cease to regret evil. Instead, through their willingness to endure an evil fortune they discover in and through suffering deeper relations that give life its purpose, a purpose which in the end only sorrow itself can engender.[59] As Royce insisted, in such experiences of evil and suffering the achievement of good in some real sense presupposes the existence of evil:

> Now such sorrows, such idealized evils, which are so interwoven with good that if the precious grief were wholly removed from existence, the courage, the fidelity, the spiritual self-possession, the peace through and in and beyond tribulation which such trials alone make possible, would also be removed— they surely show us that the abstract principle: "Evil ought to be abolished," is false. They show us that the divine will also must be made perfect through suffering. Since we can comprehend the meaning of such experiences only through resolute action, through courage, through loyalty, through the power of the spirit, they in no wise justify sloth, or mere passivity, or mystical idleness. The active dealing with such sorrow gives, as [William] James himself once asserts, a new dimension to life. No experiences go further than do these to show us how, in our loyalty and in our courage, we are becoming one with the master of life, who through sorrow overcomes.[60]

The limitations of human consciousness function as a perennial source of sorrow. Every limited human effort to reach religious understanding seeks for a comprehensive form of insight which belongs properly only to God. The divine consciousness enjoys genuine reality, but the fact that it transcends nature puts it beyond direct, empirical investigation. The divine consciousness, however, ultimately endows the world with a unity of meaning. The community of the loyal, therefore, united in the one divine Spirit provides a final and important source of religious insight.

> The Cause for any such devoted servant of a cause as we have been describing *is some conceived, and yet also real, spiritual unity which links many individual lives in one, and which is therefore essentially superhuman, in exactly the sense in which we found the realities of the world of reason*

[59] Ibid., 213–54.
[60] Ibid., 253.

to be superhuman. Yet the cause is not, on that account, any mere abstraction. It is a live something: "My home," "my family," "my country," "my service," "mankind," "the church," "my art," "my Science," "the cause of humanity," or, once more, "God's will,"—such are names for the cause.[61]

The community of the loyal united, whether consciously or unconsciously, in the reconciling divine Spirit exemplify the invisible church. Some loyal people may in addition belong to visible churches as well, and that membership goes beyond social convention because it expresses a life of loyalty lived according to one's best lights.[62]

> The invisible church is to be to us a source of insight. This means that we must enter into some sort of communion with the faithful if we are to enjoy the fruits of their insight. And, apart from one's own life of loyal service itself, the principal means of grace—that is, the principal means of attaining instruction in the spirit of loyalty, encouragement in its toils, solace in its sorrows, and power to endure and to triumph—the principal means of grace, I say, which is open to any man lies in such communion with the faithful and with the unity of the spirit which they express in their lives. It is natural that we should begin this process of communion through direct personal relations with the fellow-servants of our own special cause. Hence, whatever is usually said by those who belong to any section of the visible church regarding the spiritual advantages which follow from entering the communion of their own body may be accepted, from our present point of view, as having whatever truth the devotion and the religious life of any one body of faithful servants of the unity of the spirit may give to such statements when applied precisely to their own members. But to us all alike the voice of the invisible church speaks—it sustains us all alike by its counsels, not merely in so far as our own personal cause and our brethren of that service are known to us, but in so far as we are ready to understand the loyal life, and to be inspired by it, even when those who exemplify its intents and its values are far from us in their type of experience and in the manner of their service.[63]

In *The Sources of Religious Insight,* Royce by his own testimony wrestled with the following fundamental question: What conditions would make a saving, historical revelation of God really possible? He called this question the "religious paradox" and he formulated the paradox in the following terms:

> The paradox is that a being who is so ignorant of his duty and of his destiny as to need guidance at every point, so weak as to need saving, should

[61] Ibid., 199–200.
[62] Ibid., 257–97.
[63] Ibid., 291–2.

still hope, in his fallible experience, to get into touch with anything divine. The question is how is this possible? What light can my individual experience throw upon vast problems such as this?[64]

One can, perhaps, summarize Royce's resolution of the religious paradox in the following terms. Individual experience yields an insight into one's need to transcend individual experience if one hopes to find salvation. In a like manner, shared religious experience reveals that communities of individuals who seek salvation, while they assist the individual on the path to salvation, themselves need to be saved. Synthetic reason can reveal to communities of faith the fact that salvation must come from a world-transcending, eternal, all-encompassing reality. The need to make absolute choices in the search for salvation reveals the need for a Deliverer even more absolute. Loyalty to loyalty opens the path to salvation by committing one to all those who seek the ultimate source of saving purpose. Evil and suffering unite humans to the divine Deliverer who suffers in and with them. Finally, the communion of all the people united through genuine loyalty of the divine Spirit, whatever their concrete religious or moral affiliation, can disclose to bewildered and sinful humans both the possibility and the reality of salvation.

Both *The World and the Individual* and *The Sources of Religious Insight* began to deal in a preliminary fashion with the Christian doctrine of atonement. In *The Problem of Christianity* Royce would ponder in greater detail the Christian message of salvation and its relevance to "the modern mind." In *The Problem* Royce would also propose a metaphysical interpretation of Christian religious experience.

VI

In pondering the problem of Christianity Royce explicitly addressed the question of modernity. By "the problem of Christianity" Royce meant whether "modern" minds can still consent with heartfelt belief to the central ideas which animate Christian religion. By "modern" minds he meant people who confront reality as the intellectual heirs and stewards of contemporary western civilization. In *The Problem of Christianity* Royce would present Christianity as a religion in search of a metaphysics and he would argue that a Peircean pragmatic realism provides the kind of metaphysical underpinnings which make Christianity intellectually credible in a contemporary context. If, as I am suggesting in this study, one discovers in Peirce a systematic critical dismantling of the least tenable aspects of Enlightenment modernism, then one can interpret Royce as saying (even

---

[64] Ibid., 25.

though he himself would probably not have put it this way) that a sound insight into Peirce's constructive postmodernism renders Christianity intellectually credible to a contemporary mind critically responsive both to Christian religious experience and to the historical development of religious and philosophical speculation.

Royce therefore proposed to approach Christianity with a measure of critical distance. In writing *The Problem of Christianity* he did not assume the persona of a Christian apologist or evangelist. At the same time, he rejected the carping adversarial position which Enlightenment thinkers tended to assume all too uncritically. Instead, he proposed to reflect on Christianity as a friendly philosophical critic and witness to its religious importance.[65]

Royce recognized that one cannot dissociate Christianity from its founder, but he believed that before one can deal speculatively with the person of Jesus one needs to probe the religious concerns and experiences of the first Christian community. Royce's own reflections focus especially on the Pauline communities, and indeed the Pauline letters probably offer the most detailed insights into one major communitarian strain in apostolic Christianity.[66] Royce recognized that the Pauline communities rooted themselves ultimately in Jesus' teachings concerning love, but he also believed that Paul the apostle explored the social implications of that doctrine more thoroughly than any other New Testament writer. Paul recognized that a community cannot function as a community without a common purpose, a common life, and a common mind. Moreover, through the mutual loyalty of its members, the Pauline communities grew in a shared sense of consciousness and of purpose.

In the letters of Paul and elsewhere in the New Testament, Royce discovered three recurring religious ideas, each of which named a fundamental dimension of the shared religious experience of Pauline Christians: (1) that one can achieve salvation only through membership in a community, (2) that everyone suffers under a burden of guilt, and (3) that without entering into the atonement no one achieves salvation. In the first section

---

[65] Josiah Royce, *The Problem of Christianity,* ed. Jesse A. Mann, 2 vols. (Chicago: Regnery, 1968) 1:3–45.

[66] Disagreement over the character of the Christian community divided the early apostolic Church. The roots of the disagreement seem to stretch to Jesus himself, who ordinarily confined his ministry to Palestinian Jews. When Jesus encounters Samaritans and Gentiles in the gospels, they initiate the encounter. These confrontations with faith-filled Gentiles and Samaritans may have caused Jesus to expand his vision of God's kingdom to include them in the long run. However, the fact that the Jesus movement did not explicitly target non-Jews left the first community of disciples divided as to the status of non-Jewish Christians within the community.

of *The Problem of Christianity* Royce undertook to reflect on each of these
central Christian ideas for the light which each throws on the religious experience of the first Christians and on all genuinely loyal living.

The Christian insistence that the path to salvation lies through membership in a community in no way detracted from individual uniqueness.
The Pauline communities acknowledged the unique giftedness of each individual, but they also required that each member of the community use
those gifts in order to render loving service to one another. Mutual, loving
service transformed the members of the Pauline churches into "the body
of Christ," an organic communal reality which both encompasses and transcends the individuals who compose it. Moreover, individual participants
experience organic membership in that communal body as both a present
experience and a divine creation. In other words, Royce found incarnate in
the Pauline communities precisely the kind of loyalty which Royce's philosophy of loyalty had attempted to describe. Moreover, Christianity uni-
versalized loyalty by excluding no one in principle from its loving
concern, and that universality manifested its moral authenticity.[67]

In Royce's own words:

> But in Paul's teaching, loyalty, quickened to new life, not merely by hope,
> but by the presence of a community in whose meetings the divine spirit
> seemed to be daily working fresh wonders, keeps indeed its natural relation

---

The most conservative position, exemplified in the mother Church in Jerusalem, required circumcision and submission to the Torah on the part of Gentile converts to Christianity. The letter of James may represent this particular strain in the apostolic Church.
Petrine Christians baptized Gentiles without circumcising them and seem to have then accorded them thereafter a status within the Christian community analogous to "God-seekers,"
i.e., to Gentiles who converted to Judaism. However, Petrine Christians tended to believe
that one chose the better path if one embraced the entire Torah but interpreted it in the light
of Jesus' teachings. In the Petrine communities, then, uncircumcised Gentiles followed a
less perfect path, even though they belonged to the kingdom of God. Matthew's Gospel represents the Petrine tradition. Paul the apostle did not require circumcision of Gentile converts and argued that baptism endows all Christians, whether Jew or Gentile, with an equal
ecclesial status. Paul, however, recognized the divine origins of Torah and believed that
those who submitted to circumcision remained bound by the Law in its entirety. The
Pauline letters reflect life in this particular group of local churches. The most radical of the
apostolic Christians, sometimes called Hellenists, argued that Jesus had abrogated and replaced both the Torah and the Jerusalem Temple, which no longer enjoyed any binding
force. The letter to the Hebrews and the Gospel of John probably reflect the influence of
this fourth strain in apostolic ecclesiology. See Raymond E. Brown and John P. Meier, *An-
tioch and Rome: New Testament Cradles of Catholic Christianity* (New York: Paulist Press,
1982); Raymond E. Brown, *The Churches the Apostles Left Behind* (New York: Paulist
Press, 1984).

[67] Royce, *The Problem of Christianity,* 1:49–106.

to the militant virtues, is heroic and strenuous, and delights in metaphors
derived from the soldier's life. It appears also as the virtue of those who love
order, and who prefer law to anarchy, and who respect worldly authority
And it derives its religious ideas from the prophets.

But it also becomes the fulfillment of what Jesus had taught in the par-
ables concerning love. For the Apostle, this loyalty unites to all these stern
and orderly militant traits, and to all that the prophets had dreamed about
Israel's triumph, the tenderness of a brother's love for the individual brother.
Consequently, in Paul's mind, love for the individual human being, and loyalty to the divine community of all the faithful; graciousness of sentiment,
and orderliness of discipline; are so directly interwoven that each interprets
and glorifies the other.[68]

Christian belief in a universal moral burden of guilt also articulated,
Royce believed, another perennial dimension of the human condition. In
his autobiographical musing Royce had characterized the systematic hazing he had encountered as a school boy in San Francisco as his own
schooling in the meaning of original sin. Moreover, in explaining that universal moral burden Royce appealed to the shared, social character of
human experience. Human conduct results from trained, hereditary dispo-
sitions, but society trains one to form one's conscience by its institutions
and expectations. Society both nurtures and challenges the growing individual. Social intercourse also nurtures growth in self-awareness. One defines oneself consciously over against other selves. Moreover, one does so
in a social context inevitably fraught with conflict and tension. Conflict inspires mutual criticism, and mutual criticism in turn heightens one's own
sense of individuality. However, given the instinctive character of human
egocentrism, individuality inevitably degenerates into individualism and
sets the individual in opposition to the laws, customs, and values of one's
nurturing community. Royce argued that the social character of human experience renders the conflict between individualism and collectivism
morally inevitable. Given human finitude and fallibility, that conflict also
makes mutual betrayal morally inevitable. In proclaiming the universal
moral burden of the individual, the Pauline Christians merely named a
perennial woe of the human condition.[69]

Royce observed:

In the modern world the habit of forming a high grade of individual consciousness has now become settled. . . . The result is that the training of
the cultivated individual, under modern conditions, uses, on the one hand,
all the motives of what Paul calls "the flesh,"—all the natural endowment of

[68] Ibid., 1:100–1.
[69] Ibid., 1:109–59.

man the social being,—but develops this fleshly nature so that it is trained
to self-consciousness by emphasizing every sort and grade of more skillful
opposition to the very social will that trains it. Our modern world is therefore peculiarly fitted to illustrate the thesis of Paul's seventh chapter of the
epistle to the Romans.[70]

The human need for salvation, which gives the religious quest its
name and purpose, flows necessarily from the moral inevitability of social
and moral betrayal. The first Christians proclaimed that guilty humans can
find salvation only by faithful loyalty to one's beloved religious community. Because a community exemplifies a living, composite organism, one
can make the community as such into the object of loyal fidelity and
commitment. Christianity, however, insisted that saving loyalty, even as it
embraced the members of one's immediate community, must transcend all
racial, regional, or national concerns. Loyalty to a universal community
which embraces every individual and excludes none in principle creates
the realm of grace which mediates salvation to morally burdened, individual humans. Loyalty to one's community as such both evokes and receives
the loyalty of each member, just as it evokes and treasures the diversity of
individual gifts which unites all the members in an organic, spiritual bond
of consciousness and life. Loyalty, Royce believed, can and does come in
many forms, but loyalty reaches its highest expressions in religious loyalty. The universal scope of authentic religious loyalty grounds its saving
impact by healing the social divisions which inevitably result from human
social conflict. Introduction into the ambit of that loving loyalty creates
the realm of saving grace which annuls the moral burden of sinful individuals.[71]

Royce described the Christian experience of saving grace in the following terms:

> Other religions have been inspired by loyalty. Other religions have identi-
> fied a community with a divine being. And, occasionally,—yes, as the world
> has grown wiser and more united, increasingly,—non-Christian thinking
> and non-Christian religion have conceived an ideal community as inclusive
> as mankind, or as inclusive as the whole realm of beings with minds, how-
> ever vast that realm might be.
>
> But historically speaking, Christianity has been distinguished by the con-
> creteness and intensity with which, in the early stages of its growth, it
> grasped, loved, and served its own ideal of the visible community, supposed
> to be universal, which it called the Church. It has further been contrasted
> with other religions by the skill with which it gradually revised its views of

[70] Ibid., 1:147–8.
[71] Ibid., 1:163–213.

the divine nature, in order to be able to identify the spirit that, as it believed, guided, inspired, and ruled this Church, with the spirit of the one whom it had come to worship as its risen Lord.[72]

The experience of sin and repentance presupposes a functioning human conscience. The conscience affirms and embraces the ideals which make moral claims on human conduct. Different individuals conceive those ideals differently, but every conscience, as Royce has asserted in *The Religious Aspect of Philosophy,* affirms and submits to some ideal. Sin consists in personal disloyalty to those ideals which one acknowledges as personally binding. The betrayal of shared moral ideals does more than violate the conscience, however; for it also betrays the community which shared commitment to those ideals helps create. Social conflict makes such treason morally inevitable, but, once the act of betrayal occurs, it remains thereafter historically irrevocable. No future act or event can undo the treachery.[73]

Royce described the kind of betrayal he meant in the following manner:

> The hell of the irrevocable: all of us know what it is to come to the border of it when we contemplate our own past mistakes or mischances. But we can enter it and dwell in it only when the fact "This deed is irrevocable," is combined with the further fact "This deed is one that, unless I call treason my good, and moral suicide my life, I cannot forgive myself for having done."
>
>   Now to use these expressions is not to condemn the traitor, or any one else, to endless emotional horrors of remorse, or to any sensuous pangs of penalty or grief, or to any one set of emotions whatever. It is simply to say: If I morally value myself at all, it remains for me a genuine and irrevocable evil in my world, that ever I was, even if for that one moment only and in that one deed, with all my mind and my soul and my heart and my strength, a traitor. And if I ever had any cause, and then betrayed it,—such an evil not only was my deed, but such an evil forever remains, so far as that one deed was done, the *only* value that I can attribute to myself precisely as the doer of that deed at that time.[74]

The traitor may learn to acquiesce in the fatal irrevocability of an act of personal and social treachery, but only forgiveness of the treachery has the capacity to reconcile the repentant traitor with those whom he or she has betrayed. Treachery ruptures social bonds. It ruptures not only personal but communal bonds, and only the betrayed beloved has the capacity to forgive the traitor and the treachery in a way that can reestablish the

[72] Ibid., 1:195–6.
[73] Ibid., 1:217–67.
[74] Ibid., 1:264–5.

ruptured social ties. Forgiveness embodies loyalty sustained in the face of betrayal and treachery. It cannot undo the treacherous deed, but it can re-create the life-giving, saving, social ties which treachery shatters. Such forgiveness expresses the victory of the creative will. It has the capacity to transform treachery into a *felix culpa* which makes the world better than if the treachery had never occurred. The forgiveness of personal and of so-cial betrayal brings new life out of moral death, new bonding among those formerly alienated by sin and betrayal. Pauline Christians found in the atoning forgiveness of their beloved religious community a force of love so powerful, so deep, and so all-encompassing that no baseness or treach-ery, however deep or tragic, exceeded its power to heal and annul in a crea-tive act of forgiveness.[75]

Royce looked to atoning love to redeem treachery:

> When treason has done its last and most cruel work, and lies with what it has destroyed,—dead in the tomb of the irrevocable past,—there is now the opportunity for a triumph of which I can only speak weakly and in imper-fectly abstract formulas. But, as I can at once say, this of which I now speak is a human triumph. It forms part of the history of man's earthly warfare with his worst foes. Moreover, whenever it occurs at all, this is a triumph, not merely of stoical endurance, nor yet of kindly forgiveness, nor of the mystical mood which, seeing all things in God, feels them all to be good. It is a triumph of the creative will. And what form does it take amongst the best of men, who are here to be our guides?
>
> I answer, this triumph over treason can only be accomplished by the com-munity, or on behalf of the community, through some steadfastly loyal ser-vant who acts, so to speak, as the incarnation of the very community itself. This faithful suffering servant of the community may answer and confound treason by a work whose type I shall next venture to describe, in my own way, thus: First, this creative work shall include a deed, or various deeds, for which only just this treason furnishes the opportunity. Not treason in general, but just this individual treason shall give the occasion, and supply the condition of the creative deed which I am in ideal describing. Without just that treason, this new deed (so I am supposing) could not have been done at all. And hereupon the new deed, so concretely practical in the good which it accomplishes, that, when you look down upon the human world after the new creative deed has been done in it, you say, first: "This deed was made possible by that treason; and, secondly, *The world as transformed by this creative deed, is better than it would have been had all else remained the same, but had that deed of treason not been done at all.*"[76]

[75] Ibid., 1:271–322. See also Linell E. Cady, "Alternative Interpretations of Love in Kierkegaard and Royce," *Journal of Religious Ethics* 10 (1982) 238–63.

[76] Royce, *The Problem of Christianity,* 1:306–8.

Despite the limitations and sinfulness of its members, the Christian community aspires to a universality which makes place in it for every individual, since it regards each individual as an object of divine love. Moreover, the "creative deed" of atoning forgiveness of which Royce speaks includes and expresses a divine forgiveness and creativity which acts in and through the creative forgiveness of the atoning community. In the Pauline churches, the Spirit of God bound the members of each local community to one another and transformed them also into loyal members of the universal Church which sought to include all within the saving realm of divine grace which it embodied. However, the union of all people in a single religious family under God, bound to one another in an atoning and compassionate love, functions in Christian religious experience as an ideal that is betrayed again and again by the members of the Christian community. The ideal of universal love motivates Christian religious loyalty, but the constant betrayal of that ideal requires the ongoing redemption of those who betray it through the atoning love of the beloved community. In the ongoing history of sin and atonement, of treachery and reconciling forgiveness, the divine Spirit triumphs again and again over human weakness and malice.[77]

If, then, by "the modern (or postmodern) mind" one means the contemporary heirs and stewards of human culture and civilization, then Royce's argument in *The Problem of Christianity* challenges them to acknowledge that Christian religion has perennial relevance and believability because it addresses perennial and universal elements in the human condition. Christian religious faith makes moral demands and Christianity developed its own mystical tradition. Still, the Christian doctrine of life offers more than just a morality or a mysticism. It offers a perennial religious challenge to humans by insisting that they can find salvation in no other way than through active participation in a community of universal atonement. Only that lived, loyal participation can give human life ultimate meaning and purpose. Only such a community provides the realm of saving grace which can heal human sinfulness and treachery and endow it with saving meaning.[78]

Royce summed up the relationship of Christianity to modernity in the following terms:

---

[77] Ibid., 1:327–80; see Frank Oppenheim, "Graced Communities: A Problem in Loving," *Theological Studies* 44 (1983) 604–24.

[78] Royce, *The Problem of Christianity,* 1:383–425. See also Linell E. Cady, "Royce and Postmodern Theology," *American Journal of Theology and Philosophy* 9 (1988) 149–64; Linell E. Cady, "A Model for Public Theology," *Harvard Theological Review* 80 (1987) 193–212.

Assertions are indeed sometimes made to the effect that the Church, in all its various forms and divisions, or in very many of them, is already rapidly losing touch, or has already hopelessly lost touch, with the modern world; and that here the process of estrangement between the Church and modern life is constantly accelerated. Some observers even venture to predict a rapid dwindling of all or most of the ecclesiastical institutions of Christendom in the near future. I suppose all such extreme assertions to be hasty and unwarranted. What we can see is merely this: that if the future of Christianity depended upon its institutions rather than upon its ideas, the result of changes that lie before us would be doubtful.

But our study of the Christian ideas has shown that the deepest human strength of this religion lies precisely in these ideas themselves. By the might of these ideas early Christianity conquered the Roman world. In the light of these ideas European civilization has since been transformed; and by their spirit it still guides its life. These Christian ideas,—not their formulations in the creeds,—not their always inadequate institutional embodiment,—and of course not any abstract statement of them such as our philosophical sketch has attempted,—these ideas constitute the sword of the spirit with which the Christian religion has to carry on its warfare. What makes its contest with the world of the future hopeful is simply the fact that, whatever creed or institution or practice may lose its hold on the modern mind, the Christian doctrine of life is the expression of universal human needs,—and of the very needs upon whose satisfaction the very life of every social order depends for its worth and for its survival.[79]

Christianity embodied and continues to embody a religious experience, but, Royce insisted, that religious experience raises important philosophical questions which have crucial metaphysical implications. In the second half of *The Problem of Christianity* Royce undertook to explore those questions and implications.

At first blush Christianity seems to contradict important dimensions of human experience. The embodied character of human life and experience makes it inevitably separate and diverse. I can never experience personally your toothache, nor can you experience directly my physical pain. Even though at a conscious level humans can share ideas and ideals, they can never share directly and immediately one another's insights and aspirations. I cannot think your thoughts for you. Choice also engages individual human needs, wants, preferences, and commitments, but you cannot make my choices for me. While common sense may argue on these and similar premises that individual human independence and initiative have ultimate value and importance, the fact remains that human communities can and do come to act with a common intelligence and with a com-

---

[79] Royce, *The Problem of Christianity,* 1:395–6.

mon purpose. Moreover, in the second half of *The Problem of Christianity* Royce set out to demonstrate philosophically how human communities can come to act in precisely this manner.[80]

Every community exemplifies a temporal and spatial process. It has a history. Moreover, the ongoing recall of that history endows it with a shared sense of identity and solidarity. In re-appropriating the past, both individuals and communities come to a sense of their actual identity. Every act of recall, however, engages human interpretation. Through the process of interpretation, the present moment expands to include the past. In order to retrieve the past we need to interpret it correctly. The shared interpretation of a community's history endows that community with a common memory, and that memory empowers the community to face the future in shared expectation and hope. Communities, then, come to consciousness of themselves as communities by reaching consensus about their common origins and common hopes. In Christianity the shared, ecclesial memory of Jesus' death and resurrection simultaneously grounds both Christian faith and Christian hope.[81]

While shared memories and shared hopes contribute in significant ways to creating shared community consciousness, the Pauline Christians of the first century recognized that other factors contribute in significant ways to shared, communal awareness. Only by actively collaborating in the practical realization of the common future to which they aspire can communities come to full shared consciousness as communities. Active collaboration in making actual the shared future to which a community aspires makes a distinctive contribution to shared communal self-awareness. Such effective collaboration requires the orchestration of all the gifts and talents individually and corporately embodied in the community in question. Effective practical collaboration requires mutual sensitivity and mutual flexibility. It expresses a shared feeling for the community as a whole. In addition, effective community leadership floats. The community requires different kinds of leaders in different kinds of situations. Different kinds of leadership engage different kinds of personal gifts and therefore the gifts of different individuals within the community. The vision which inspires spontaneous communal collaboration has an inherently aesthetic character. The beauty and excellence of the cause which draws a community together must inspire the kind of enthusiastic loyalty which long-term collaboration requires. Moreover, the moral inevitability that some members of the community will over the long haul betray the community and

[80] Ibid., 2:3–37.
[81] Ibid., 2:37–72.

its ideals requires that the ideal of atoning love, which forgives in advance any betrayal, lie at the heart of the community's shared ideals.[82]

At this point in his argument, Royce summarized the problem of Christianity in the following terms:

> If our results are in any way positive, they may enable us to view the problem of Christianity, that is, the problem of the religion of loyalty, in a larger perspective than that which human history, when considered alone, determines. The favorite methods of approaching the metaphysical problems of theology end by leaving the individual alone with God, in a realm which seems, to many minds, a realm of merely concepts, of intellectual abstractions, of barren theories. The ways which are just now in favor in the philosophy of religion seem to end in leaving the individual really alone in his intuitions, his lurid experiences of sudden conversion, or his ineffable mysteries of saintly peace.
>
> May we hope to gain by a method which follows the plan now outlined? This method, first, encourages a man to interpret his own individual self in terms of the largest ideal extension of that self in time which his reasonable will can acknowledge as worthy of the aims of his life. Secondly, this method bids a man consider what right he has to interpret the life from which he springs, in the midst of which he now lives, as a life that in any universal sense cooperates with his own and ideally expresses its own meaning so as to meet with his own, and to have a history identical with his own. Thirdly, this method directs us inquire how far, in the social order to which we unquestionably belong, there are features such as warrant us in hoping that, in the world's community, our highest love may yet find its warrant and fulfillment.[83]

Having established the conditions under which communities of people come to share a common conscious sense of identity and of purpose, Royce the idealist found in Peirce's pragmatic realism systematic philosophical grounding for a philosophy of community. He found in Peirce's triadic understanding of both experience and reality a decisive refutation of a dyadic epistemology which reduces human cognition to the subjective interrelation of concrete percepts and abstract concepts. Royce found such an epistemology in both William James and Henri Bergson, but Immanuel Kant and the British empiricism which inspired his philosophy also defended this indefensible theory of knowledge. Royce correctly pointed out that such an epistemology lacks the categories to interpret the social dimensions of human knowing and so offers an inadequate account of how humans think and grasp reality. By reducing knowing to subjective cognition, such thinkers overlook the fact that knowing

[82] Ibid., 2:72–105.
[83] Ibid., 2:104–5.

always and necessarily involves interpretation. Grasping an interlocutor's communicative intent involves much more complex processes of knowing than the subjective interrelation of percepts and concepts In the end, moreover, interpretation engages and governs all human social relationships. We need to interpret ourselves to ourselves and to one another. We need to interpret one another to ourselves.[84]

The act of interpretation, as Peirce saw clearly, always involves three terms, not two. A triadic understanding of the cognitive relationship derives its warrant from a sound logic of relations. In every act of interpretation, someone must explain some reality to some interlocutor. When we explain ourselves to ourselves, we interiorize dialogic patterns of thinking which we acquire through social interaction with other minds. Interpretation has a temporal structure: it relates a past and a present to a future. Even more, interpretation structures conscious temporal processes: we experience and perceive time interpretatively. In addition, interpretation always involves signs and symbols. A sound understanding of interpretation, therefore, requires the development of a semiotic, a systematic theory of social, symbolic behavior. The social character of interpretation also renders it dialogic. In a dyadic construct of human knowing, the verification of a concept in a percept terminates the cognitive act. In a triadic understanding of cognition, however, the process of interpretation never ends. Every interpretation invites and ever requires further interpretation. Moreover, one grasps more in interpretation than concrete sensible facts. One grasps communicating selves as well as the ideas and ideals which they communicate. As a consequence, a life of interpretation has simultaneously a social and an ideal dimension.[85]

Royce described the world of interpretation thus:

> Metaphysically considered, the world of interpretation is the world in which, if indeed we are able to interpret at all, we learn to acknowledge the being and the inner life of our fellow-man; and to understand the constitution of temporal experience, with its endlessly accumulating sequence of significant deeds. In this world of interpretation, of whose most general

---

[84] Ibid., 2:109–39; see also Frank Oppenheim, *Royce's Mature Ethics* (Notre Dame, Ind.: University of Notre Dame Press, 1993); Frank Oppenheim, "A Roycean Road to Community," *International Philosophical Quarterly* 10 (1970) 341–77; John E. Smith, *Royce's Social Infinite* (New York: Liberal Arts, 1950); M. L. Briody, "Community in Royce: An Interpretation," *Transactions of the Charles S. Peirce Society* 5 (1969) 224–47; Donald William Dotterer, "Josiah Royce's Philosophy of Loyalty: A Hermeneutical Key for Pauline Theology," *American Journal of Theology and Philosophy* 7 (1986) 149–63; David Willis-Watkins, "The Community's Congruent Loyalty to Jesus Christ," *Faithful Imagining* (1995) 187–201.

[85] Royce, *The Problem of Christianity*, 2:139–63.

structure we have now obtained a glimpse, selves and communities may exist, past and future can be defined, and the realms of the spirit may find a place which neither barren conception nor the chaotic flow of interpenetrating perceptions could ever render significant.[86]

In the development of shared communal awareness, the ongoing process of interpretation plays an indispensable role. Even an elementary human cognitive act like comparison engages interpretation, because in every comparison a mediating idea tells one in what respect the compared realities agree or differ. Simple acts of interpretation enjoy the same triadic structure as more complex acts. In a dyadic construct of cognition one can only verify or falsify ideas. In a triadic construct of cognition, interpretation has the power to mediate among conflicts of opinion and belief. The ongoing process of interpretation uses one idea to make sense out of other ideas. As a consequence, the will to interpret, the decision to come to terms with alien ideas and patterns of thought, expands consciousness. Because we deal with life through interpretation, the will to interpret enhances personal self-possession through social dialogue. Social dialogue enhances personal mastery over life at the same time that it allows individuals to share insights and to appropriate the shared perceptions of the communities to which they belong. The interpretation of another's intent always has a hypothetical or abductive character which subsequent dialogue will verify or falsify, but, beyond the mere verification and falsification of personal beliefs, the will to interpret expresses the search for common meaning. The will to interpret therefore embodies the will to community. Hence, the will to interpret also expresses and embodies mutual loyalty in the communal search for truth and for shared social identity.[87]

Royce described that search in the following terms:

> The mere form of interpretation may be indeed momentarily misused for whatever purpose of passing human folly you will. But if the ideal of interpretation is first grasped; and if then the Community of Interpretation is conceived as inclusive of all individuals; and as unified by the common hope of the far-off event of complete mutual understanding; and, finally, if love for this community is awakened,—then indeed this love is able to grasp, in ideal, the meaning of the Church Universal, of the Communion of Saints, and of God the Interpreter.
>
> Merely to define such ideals is not to solve the problem of metaphysics. But it is to remove many obstacles from the path that leads toward the light.[88]

---

[86] Ibid., 2:160–1.
[87] Ibid., 2:167–221.
[88] Ibid., 2:220–1.

Engagement in the ongoing process of interpretative dialogue presupposes a will to interpret. One can conceive the will to interpret in a
number of different ways, but Royce argued that only one way meets the
demands and challenges of lifelong interpretation of oneself and one's
world. The first conception of the will to interpret expresses "the will to
live." Royce found this notion well exemplified in the philosophy of
Arthur Schopenhauer and of William James. The will to live expresses the
desire to be oneself, whoever one happens to be, and to achieve one's aims
and goals in life. The will to live, therefore, engages us with our fellow
humans. Social interaction causes us to interpret those with whom we interact on an analogy with one's own personal experience. The will to live
endows each idea with its own vital thrust. It asserts itself over against
other ideas as long as it can maintain itself. The second conception of the
will to interpret exemplifies "resignation." Resignation negates the will to
live. Royce found the doctrine of resignation well exemplified in southern
Buddhism. The resigned will has no interest whatever in the competing
ideas of the pragmatic will to live. It seeks instead processes of pure conception and of pure perception which constitute the object of the mystical
quest. In the end, however, Royce questioned whether a doctrine of resignation can generate a satisfactory account of human salvation. Royce
found philosophical adequacy only in the third conception of the will to
interpret. The third conception provides a doctrine of life which coincides
with the Christian doctrine of life.

> The attitude of will which Paul found to be saving in its power, just as to his
> mind it was also divine in its origin, was the attitude of Loyalty. Now loy-
> alty, when considered from within, and with respect to its deepest spirit, is
> not the affirmation of the will to live of which Schopenhauer spoke. And
> loyalty is also not the denial of the will to live. It is the positive devotion of
> the Self to its cause,—a devotion as vigorous, as self-asserting, as articulate,
> as strenuous, as Paul's life and counsels always remained. . . .
>
> Now this third attitude of will, as we found in dealing with the whole
> Christian doctrine of life, has in any case its disposition to imagine, and also
> practically to acknowledge as real, a spiritual realm,—an universal and di-
> vine community.[89]

The communitarian character of Christian commitment provides the
only principle on which the process of interpretation can build. As Royce
explained:

> Whatever my purposes or my ideas,—whatever will to live incites me to
> create and to believe, whatever reverses of fortune drive me back upon my

[89] Ibid., 2:309–11.

own poor powers, whatever problems baffle me, through their complexity and my ignorance, one truth stands out clear: Practically I cannot be saved alone; theoretically speaking, I cannot find or even define the truth in terms of my individual experience, without taking account of my relation to the community of those who know me. This community, then, is the real whatever is real. And in that community my life is interpreted. When viewed as if I were alone, I, the individual, am not only doomed to failure, but I am lost in folly. The "workings" of my ideas are events whose significance I cannot even remotely estimate in terms of their momentary existence, or in terms of my individual successes. My life means nothing, either theoretically or practically, unless I am a member of a community.[90]

Authentic loyalty to a community, of necessity then, incorporates the will to interpret, and the will to interpret seeks to create the shared consensus which mediates shared communal awareness. As a consequence, any theory of knowledge which fails to explain the act of interpretation or which rules it out in principle fragments human society in tragic and destructive ways. The will to consensus also roots itself in a critical epistemological realism. Those committed to the process of interpretation seek to come to terms with reality at the same time that they seek a realistic mutual understanding of one another. Spiritual union, as the apostle Paul saw, creates a unified, organic social reality animated by a common life. We grasp the real world when we reach a true interpretation of our problematic situation. The goal of every attempt to understand lies in the future. A community of interpretation which would grasp the real seeks implicitly to encompass the whole time process in a unity of meaning. If the shared will to interpret ever grasped the universe perfectly, it would also yield a perfect self-understanding on the part of the community of interpretation which the will to shared interpretation creates. Such a community would embody the universal community which Christianity aspires to become.[91]

Royce summed up his metaphysical argument in the following terms:

> The metaphysical doctrine just set forth in outline can be summed up thus: The problem of reality is furnished to us by a certain universal antithesis of two Ideas, or, if one prefers the word, by the antithesis of two Selves. The first thesis of this doctrine is that Reality—the solution to this problem—is the interpretation of this antithesis, the process of mediating between these two selves and of interpreting each of them to the other. Such a process of interpretation involves, of necessity, an infinite sequence of acts of inter-

---

[90] Ibid., 2:312–13.

[91] Ibid., 2:221–76. See also Frank Oppenheim, "Four Practical Challenges of the Mature Royce to Californians and Others," *Transactions of the Charles S. Peirce Society* 30 (1994) 803–24; John E. Smith, "Experience, God, and Classical American Philosophy," *Journal of Theology and Philosophy* 14 (1993) 119–45.

pretation. It also admits of an endless variety within all the selves which are thus mutually interpreted. These selves, in all their variety, constitute the life of a single Community of Interpretation, whose central member is that spirit of the community whose essential function we now know. In the concrete, then, the universe is a community of interpretation whose life comprises and unifies all the social varieties and all the social communities which, for any reason, we know to be real in the empirical world which our social and our historical sciences study. The history of the universe, the whole order of time, is the history and the order and the expression of this Universal Community.[92]

A sound understanding of such a process of interpretation of necessity requires a semiotic, a theory of signs. Peirce saw and Royce agreed that "the universe consists of real signs and of their interpretation." We live in an inherently symbolic universe. We must learn to read signs; and we must learn to read, to interpret, the universe correctly. The universe includes the reality of the will, of striving, and of decision. In a symbolic metaphysical realism Royce found the ultimate inspiration of a sound pragmatism. A semiotic realism offers in the end a metaphysical interpretation of reality in general, a metaphysics of community. Moreover, the world of ideas and the world of decision interact constantly. "Each idea therefore expresses and, as far as it can, embodies its own will to live." As a consequence, human volition will never find ultimate satisfaction in mere resignation. Once one acknowledges the symbolic character of the real, then the loyal will to interpret the minds symbolically incarnate in the expression, gestures, and overt acts of communication which make up the fabric of human interaction takes on the character of a moral imperative. We grasp the reality of the world and of other minds when they in fact interpret to us our own existence. The facial expressions of another person, therefore, exemplify more than a brute fact, as a dyadic construct of the human mind would seem to suggest. Such concrete facial expressions and gestures embody feelings, attitudes, beliefs, intent. We experience them, therefore, not as brute facts but as signs, as symbolic expressions of the minds of living persons. Every mind we encounter, therefore, reminds us of the inherently symbolic character of the universe we inhabit. The world has its interpreter: proximately, the minds which inhabit it and understand it, ultimately and absolutely the divine Spirit of the universal community which encompasses, understands, and interprets all. Royce put the matter this way:

> Our Doctrine of Signs extends to the whole world the same fundamental principle. The World is the Community. The world contains its own interpreter. Its processes are infinite in their temporal varieties. But their interpreter, the

[92] Royce, *The Problem of Christianity,* 2:272–3.

> spirit of this universal community,—never absorbing varieties or permitting them to blend,—compares and, through a real life, interprets them all.[93]

In other words, in an absolute pragmatism which builds on Peirce's seminal insights, Royce discovered the metaphysical vision which makes philosophical sense of Christian religious experience.[94]

Royce had no intention of reducing the Christian gospel to "a complex of metaphysical ideas." He saw clearly through that particular fallacy of the Enlightenment. Still, he argued that a metaphysics of community, rooted in his absolute pragmatism, did interpret fundamental and essential dimensions of Christian religious experience. If, however, a realistic, social semiotic grasps a fundamental truth about Christianity, then the Christian community can only understand itself authentically as a community of interpretation coterminous in aspiration with the whole of reality.

In order to dramatize this point, Royce suggested a mental experiment. Imagine a Pauline Christian of the first century miraculously transported to the twentieth century and confronted with the post-Reformation Church. What processes of interpretation would one have to contrive in order to explain to such a person that the Church fragmented into denominational sects which he confronts embodies in this century the Church which he knew and experienced in the first century? Granted that this Pauline Christian had studied some philosophy, Royce argued that he or she would recognize in Royce's vision of the Church as a universal religious community of interpretation rooted in the divine, interpreter Spirit a vision with which to identify.[95]

---

[93] Ibid., 2:324.

[94] Ibid., 2:279–325.

[95] Ibid., 2:329–79; see also Jacqueline A. Kegley, *Genuine Individuals and Genuine Community: A Roycean Public Philosophy* (Nashville: Vanderbilt University Press, 1997); Jacqueline A. Kegley, "Josiah Royce, A Source of New Insight for Religion Today," *Religious Studies* 18 (1982) 211–24; Jacqueline A. Kegley, "The Divine Relativity and the Beloved Community," *The Philosophy of Charles Hartshorne,* ed. L. Hahn (Lassalle, Ill.: Open Court, 1991); Frank Oppenheim, "The Idea of Spirit in the Mature Royce," *Transactions of the Charles S. Peirce Society* 19 (1983) 381–95; Elisa Buzzi, *Individuo e communità nella filosofia di Josiah Royce* (Milan: Vita e Pensiero, 1992); Humbach, *Das Verhältnis von Einzelperson und Gemeinschaft nach Josiah Royce;* Robert Corrington, "Beyond Experience: Pragmatism and Nature's God," *American Journal of Theology and Philosophy* 14 (1993) 147–60; Edward A. Jarvis, "Josiah Royce's Idea of Ultimate Reality and Meaning," *Ultimate Reality and Meaning* 3 (1980) 168–86; John E. Smith, "Creativity in Royce's Philosophical Idealism," *Contemporary Studies in Philosophical Idealism,* ed. John Howie and Thomas O. Buford (Cape Cod, Mass.: Claude Stark & Co., 1975) 197–215; John E. Smith, "Royce, the Absolute, and the Beloved Community," *Meaning, Truth, and God,* ed. Leroy S. Rouner (Notre Dame, Ind.: University of Notre Dame Press, 1982) 135–53; John J. McDermott, "Josiah Royce's Philosophy of the Community: Danger of the Detached Individual," *American Philosophy and the Future,* 153–77.

In *The Problem of Christianity* Royce candidly acknowledged the indebtedness of his thought to Peirce's ground-breaking philosophical insights. He sent a copy of *The Problem of Christianity* to Peirce in homage and gratitude. Peirce, who would within weeks die painfully of cancer in extreme poverty and isolation, received the book with deep emotion, and in his final letter to his friend and colleague the dying Peirce seems to have endorsed in a general sort of way what Royce had written. Given Peirce's reticence about his personal religious beliefs and attitudes, *The Problem of Christianity* could conceivably offer a helpful clue to unraveling the riddle of Peirce's own personal religious commitment.

VII

I have already suggested ways in which Royce's *Principles of Logic* both endorsed and expanded Peirce's logic of relations. The mature Royce developed Peirce's pragmaticism in other ways as well. His philosophy of loyalty complemented Peirce's theory of the normative sciences. His critique of William James on religious experience in *The Sources of Religious Insight* developed in significant ways Peirce's philosophy of community, as did *The Problem of Christianity*. In addition, in writing *The Problem* Royce began to explore the theological implications of both his philosophy of loyalty and his metaphysics of community.

Royce's philosophy of loyalty expands Peirce's theory of the normative sciences by developing the ethical idealism which the early Royce enunciated. In my judgment, however, Royce's insight into loyalty exemplifies what Peirce would have recognized as an essay in his normative science of aesthetics. The ideals which engage the human conscience must first capture and claim the human heart. While Royce never developed in any intentional way a normative aesthetics, by rooting ethical thinking in spontaneously attractive ideals Royce, in my judgment, implicitly conceded Peirce's point that normative thinking about ideals and finally about supremely desirable ideals sets the moral agenda for the human conscience. Moreover, with Peirce, Royce recognized that concern with the *summum bonum* endows moral striving with a religious dimension.

In *The Sources of Religious Insight* Royce acknowledged William James's contribution to the philosophy of religion in his *Varieties of Religious Experience,* but in the same study Royce correctly took James to task for his religious individualism, his religious irrationalism, and his dipolar nominalism. While conceding to James that individual experience does yield religious insight, Royce argued against James that a single individual's religious experience can never provide an adequate source of religious insight since it mostly yields negative insights. The isolated individual remains lost without a saving community of grace. On reading *The Varieties of Religious Experience,* Peirce wrote James that the logic of the position he had developed in that work required him to join some religious community. James never did. Royce could not bring himself to identify with one of the mainline churches, as Peirce had, but Royce worshiped regularly with a community of friends and colleagues. In insisting on the lost character of individual religious experience and on the inevitable communitarian dimensions of the religious search for salvation, Royce corrected James's thought in needed ways which people in this country have, unfortunately, too often tended to ignore.

In addition, Royce, like Peirce, suspected the irrationalism of James's approach to religious belief. Both thinkers resisted James's attempt to ground metaphysical thinking in subjective temperamental preferences of the psyche. In so speaking, James echoed and further popularized fallacies of Enlightenment thinking. Moreover, in *The Sources* Royce deliberately set out to provide an alternative to James's attempt to ground religious faith in the individual unconscious. One must acknowledge, Royce insisted, the role which conscious thought and reason plays in human religious experience. Royce read Peirce's Neglected Argument for the reality of God with appreciation and appropriated musement as an indispensable method for the conscious exploration of human religious experience. Convinced that the human unconscious provides a weak and unpredictable guide in the fixation of religious beliefs, Royce saw correctly that the responsible fixation of religious belief requires a rationally defensible conception of the reality of God which interprets not only conscious personal experience but social experience as well.

Moreover, in *The Sources* Royce, once again building on Peirce's triadic realism, correctly taxed the philosophical nominalism exemplified in James's di-polar construct of experience. To the end of his life, James failed to transcend the Enlightenment nominalism of John Locke. James persisted in interpreting human cognition as the subjective interrelation of concrete percepts and abstract concepts. Royce, like Peirce, recognized that James's conceptual nominalism could do justice neither to the social nor to the religious dimensions of shared human experience.

The Problem of Christianity deepened and expanded the seminal insights which Royce had reached in *The Sources of Religious Insight.* In *The Problem,* Royce developed a cogent account of the conditions for the possibility of shared communal awareness. Moreover, he argued both correctly and persuasively that his philosophy of loyalty interprets the way in which the Christian conscience functions.

In *The Problem of Christianity* the reader also finds an initial attempt to explore the theological implications of Peirce's triadic theory of signs and of his pragmatistic metaphysical realism. *The Problem* argued with sound insight that Christianity began as a religious experience in search of a metaphysics and that only a metaphysics of community and a communal morality of loyalty can do philosophical justice to that experience.

In Royce's decision to approach Christianity constructively as a friendly critic, the intellectual impulse which began in the American Enlightenment in a sense came full circle. Enlightenment philosophy in young America took an adversarial stance toward Christianity on the naive and false assumption that Christianity and Calvinism coincided. Transcendentalism began and evolved as a movement which attempted to come to terms with the least tenable philosophical and religious assumptions of the American Enlightenment. In Brownson, American Transcendentalism evolved to the point that he found himself both philosophically and theologically at home with Roman Catholicism. The figures of Brownson and of Abbot both brought the Transcendental tradition to the threshold of Peircean pragmatism. In Peirce's thought one finds a systematic dismantling of the least tenable presuppositions of Enlightenment thinking, a postmodernism before postmodernism became fashionable. Both Peirce and Royce recognized an affinity between a metaphysical realism, pragmatically understood, and traditional Christian faith. Peirce converted from Unitarianism to the Episcopal Church. Royce, who seems to have viewed himself as a member of the invisible Christian Church, explored the theological implications of Peirce's thought.

Moreover, in the philosophies of both Peirce and Royce one finds a formula for moving beyond the scandal of the Protestant Reformation and the Catholic Counter-Reformation. Both movements had shattered Christendom into warring sects, and the scandal of sectarianism had provided the American Enlightenment with one of its legitimate criticisms of the Christian church. Sectarianism implicitly contradicts the universalism which Christian faith requires of its members. Royce especially recognized the challenge which an accelerating technological culture posed for the mainline churches. Moreover, he did not anticipate that any of the denominations would in the end triumph decisively over the others. Both Royce and Peirce saw that the Christian Church can move beyond the scandal of denominationalism only if Christians of every denomination commit themselves to overcoming religious sectarianism by shared systematic inquiry into the origins, the meaning, and the destiny of the entire Christian community. Together the thought of Peirce and Royce laid sound speculative and theological foundations for serious ecumenical dialogue among the Christian churches. As a prelude to such dialogue, Royce urged the established Christian churches to simplify their religious beliefs by rediscovering the fundamental ideas on which Christianity rests, to stop trying to get the better of one another, and to live in responsive fidelity to the Spirit of the Beloved Community, who must teach erring mortals how best to heal the wounds of sectarianism.[96]

The Enlightenment *philosophes* correctly taxed the papacy for espousing a monarchical understanding of Church government. In *The Problem of Christianity* Royce, in my judgment, put his finger on one of the important theological keys to moving the Catholic tradition beyond papal monarchicalism. At the Vatican Council II the Catholic church grasped that key, even though in the wake of the council the more reactionary wing of the Catholic Church mislaid it. With Royce I find an important theological strategy to move Catholics beyond the least defensible aspects of medieval hierarchicalism and papal monarchicalism. The Catholic Church needs to re-appropriate and to grasp the implications of a Pauline theology of the Church as a Pentecostal community created by the gifts of the Spirit. Whether creative and constructive minds in the Catholic community will use that key to unlock the mysteries of ecclesiology only the future can tell.

The time has come to cull the fruits of this dialectical study of religious thought in the United States. In the following chapter I will argue that together Peirce and Royce laid sound philosophical foundations for a constructive postmodernism which responds to the least tenable aspects of deconstructionist postmodernism and which offers new metaphysical and epistemological foundations for contemporary theological thinking.

---

[96] Royce, *The Problem of Christianity,* 2:421–32.

Chapter 12

TOWARD A CONSTRUCTIVE POSTMODERNISM

In a perceptive article, Thomas Guarino has identified five major challenges which deconstructionist postmodernism poses for contemporary theology. (1) Deconstructionist postmodernism repudiates all foundational thinking rooted in ontology. If you want to get deconstructionist postmoderns' goats, accuse them of talking onto-theology. (2) The rejection of all forms of ontological realism fuels the deconstructionist postmodernist's repudiation of theological truth. (3) The repudiation of ontology has important consequences for the interpretation of texts. In deconstructionist postmodernism, texts enjoy historical stability but their meanings do not. (4) The postmodern rejection of metaphysical ontology makes it impossible for human language to grasp reality or to disclose reality. (5) Because deconstructionist postmodernism regards cultural-linguistic systems as incommunicable, it limits all thinking, including theological thinking, to intra-systemic coherence.

Guarino discovers some virtue in the postmodern critique of theology. He suggests that it challenges theologians to open themselves to the unfamiliar, to the "Other." In other words, postmodernism reminds theologians of the otherness of God and cautions an incautious theological mind not to make facile claims about the reality of God and about divine and natural law.

When push comes to shove, however, Guarino discovers totalitarian tendencies in deconstructionist postmodernism. He describes it as "a totalizing discipline" which inculcates "an (a)systematic view of reality." At the heart of this (a)systematic theory of the whole lies the deconstructionist postmodern's systematic rejection of all foundational ontology.[1] As I have already indicated, "postmodernism" means many different things to

---

[1] See Thomas Guarino, "Postmodernity and Five Fundamental Theological Issues," *Theological Studies* 57 (1996) 654–85.

different people, but any postmodernism which fits Guarino's description would require a response. In my judgment the rejection of all foundational ontology exemplifies what Royce calls a reinstating proposition, for in denying the possibility of ontology one makes an ontological statement. One asserts that the nature of all being precludes the human mind's ability to make true statements about it. One cannot have one's cake and eat it too. If deconstructionist postmodernism wants to reject what it calls the human mind's illegitimate universalizing tendencies, then deconstructionist postmodernism cannot indulge in the luxury of making sweeping, universal generalizations about reality, including the universal generalization that no one can make generalizations about reality. Here we encounter one of many indications that a deconstructionist postmodernism will go the way of other fads which have set academic hearts atremble by inevitably deconstructing itself.

Still, while deconstructionist postmodernism continues to absorb significant portions of the academy, one needs to respond to the speculative challenge it poses. Like most movements, much postmodernist thinking shows its strength more in what it rejects than in what it affirms. Some forms of philosophical ontology deserve rejection. Classical metaphysics claimed to offer the mind not only a universal insight into reality but one which enjoys a priori necessity. If Peircean fallibilism has it right (and I for one believe that it does), then a metaphysical theory about reality in general may aspire to universality but it can claim no a priori necessity. Postmodernism would also correctly reject, in my judgment, any metaphysics based on Kantian transcendental logic and on the turn to the subject. The narrow analysis of human subjectivity and of the structures of intentionality provides a woefully inadequate foundation for reaching an insight into the nature of reality in general, as Immanuel Kant saw both clearly and correctly. Moreover, Kantian transcendental logic, as Peirce recognized, offers a sure-fire plan for confused thinking because it treats an abduction like an induction while calling it a deduction.

A rejection of the inflated claims of classical metaphysics and of any metaphysics built on transcendental logic and the turn to the subject does not, however, disprove the human mind's capacity to grasp reality. Nor does it rule out in principle the legitimacy of constructing a working metaphysical hypothesis. A working metaphysical hypothesis needs to avoid tautology. To define "Being" as "that which is," as many Thomistic metaphysicians do, advances human thought not one iota. Any testable metaphysical hypothesis needs to characterize reality by attributing to it clearly defined traits capable of inductive testing. It then needs to test those traits against both lived experience and detailed scientific investigations into the real.

All testable metaphysical hypotheses develop a root metaphor for reality. Some metaphysicians, like Plato and Aristotle, compare reality to an idea. Others, like René Descartes, compare reality to a machine. Others compare reality to an event or to an organism. I myself like to explore the consequences of comparing reality to an experience.

A logically defensible metaphysical hypothesis can claim no necessity, but it does aspire to universality by offering a philosophical interpretation of reality in general. The fact that a metaphysical hypothesis ambitions a universally applicable account of reality means that its deductively predicted operational consequences all function within the realm of interpretation. In other words, a successful or working metaphysical hypothesis will encounter no reality it cannot interpret.

A metaphysical hypothesis qualifies as a "working hypothesis" when it meets four identifiable criteria. First, any working hypothesis needs to exhibit logical consistency. A root metaphor for reality in general provides the basis for a metaphysical theory of the whole, but a metaphor differs from a theory. Having decided on a testable metaphysical metaphor, one needs to define it philosophically and technically, and one must also define clearly and consistently any other terms which function in one's metaphysical hypothesis. If the affirmations one makes about reality contain no logical contradictions, then one's working theory of the whole has passed its first test, namely the test of logical consistency. A logically inconsistent theory would contradict itself and take back with one hand what it gives with another. People can, of course, contradict themselves if they choose to; they do it all the time. But internal contradiction in a metaphysical hypothesis gives one solid evidence that the people who propound it do not know what they are talking about. The deconstructionist who makes the metaphysical generalization that one cannot make any metaphysical generalizations illustrates this logical lesson rather neatly.

The second logical criterion for a metaphysical hypothesis qualifying as a "working hypothesis" is that the theory of the whole aspires to universality, even though it cannot, on fallibilistic principles, claim a priori necessity. A theory of the whole offers the human mind a synthetic insight, a way of thinking in a unified manner about oneself, one's world, and the reality of God. As a consequence, besides avoiding logical contradictions, a metaphysical theory of the whole needs to define all the key terms it uses to speak about reality in such a way that those terms imply one another. They will imply one another if they remain unintelligible apart from one another.

As the philosophical and theological critique of Enlightenment modernism advanced in the United States, it quite correctly censured the dualistic caste of Enlightenment patterns of thought. As we have already seen, one thinks dualistically when one conceives of two interrelated realities in such a way that one can no longer grasp or understand adequately how they relate. As we have also seen, the Enlightenment propounded several dualisms. Enlightenment modernists endorsed the dualistic fallacy of subjectivism by depicting all human knowing as the relationship within human subjectivity of concrete percepts and abstract concepts. If human knowing only interrelates subjective percepts and concepts and does nothing else, then, as both Peirce and Royce correctly pointed out, one cannot account for either scientific knowing or true common sense judgments. Nor can one explain the social dimensions of knowing unless, as Brownson, Peirce, and Royce correctly insisted, one recognizes the triadic character of human knowing.

Enlightenment modernists also propounded the fallacy of individualism when they depicted human persons as atomic units who enjoy only artificial relationships to one another established by rescindable social contracts. As Brownson recognized and argued persuasively, a social contract like the federal constitution must in fact articulate the historical constitution of the nation it governs by interpreting correctly both how its citizens have related historically to one another and how they ought to relate to one another in the future. In other words, morally defensible social contracts may create some new social relationships, but they also acknowledge the reality, the givenness, of others. Moreover, contracts which acknowledge real, morally binding rights and duties may also exhibit an ethically unrescindable character. Enlightenment modernists in young America often acquiesced in a spirit-matter dualism which they inherited from medieval and classical philosophy, although some, like Jefferson and Palmer, correctly recognized that Lockean epistemology logically entailed a metaphysical materialism. Spirit-matter dualism rested in turn on another fallacy, namely, on essentialism. In one of its classical philosophical formulations, the essence fallacy reifies ideas as metaphysical principles.

Besides endorsing a host of philosophical fallacies, Enlightenment modernists in young America tacitly acquiesced in the theological dualisms which Calvin inherited from Augustine and not only endorsed but exacerbated. Augustine viewed nature and grace in dualistic, essentialistic terms. He depicted human nature as so intrinsically corrupt that it could perform no virtuous act without the help of divine grace. This overly pessimistic view of human nature helped ground Calvin's determinism and predestinationism. In the evangelical scheme, either grace or the devil rides the human will and rules out the possibility of freedom of choice, and, since God alone grants the free and unmerited gift of supernatural grace, a Calvinist Jehovah decides how each human will choose from one moment to the next. As Enlightenment *philosophes* correctly objected, in a Calvinist universe, only God exercises free choice and moral responsibility and does so in morally reprehensible ways by arbitrarily saving some and damning others.

In rejecting a theological doctrine of total human depravity, however, the thinkers of the Enlightenment swung to the opposite extreme of declaring the innocence and total integrity of human nature. In other words, instead of critiquing Augustine's dualistic portrait of nature and of grace, they implicitly endorsed it by assuming naively and unnecessarily that one must choose between either total human innocence and total moral depravity. It did not take long for the idea of human fallenness to reinstate itself in young America, even though popular culture tended to endorse an Enlightenment myth of the American Adam. The mature Emerson defended a Platonized, dualistic account of the fall, while Brownson discovered that, in choosing the middle ground between total human depravity and total human innocence, the Council of Trent had developed an intellectually defensible understanding of original sin. Enlightenment modernism proposed another false option when it presented a Deism in which God abstains from any intervention in human history, including a liberating one, as the only speculative alternative to a Calvinistic doctrine of divine predestination.

Perhaps I digress. I have been using Enlightenment modernism as a good example of how not to formulate a metaphysical hypothesis. Any fallible theory of the whole which acquiesces in the fallacies of both dualism and essentialism will necessarily fail by obscuring the way in which things really relate to one another and by endowing reality with an essential fixity which renders history and cosmic evolution difficult, if not impossible, to understand. Postmodernism correctly insists that any anthropology or theory of knowing must acknowledge the developmental, historical character of humanity and of human thinking. As the philosophical critique of Enlightenment modernism advanced in young America, that critique developed a metaphysical strategy for avoiding both dualism and essentialism by conceiving reality from the very beginning in relational terms which include the possibility of both positive and negative relationships. A metaphysics of relationship promises to succeed in giving an account of any real relationship instead of pretending dualistically that it does not exist. A metaphysics of relationship also recognizes that, while essences function positively in human evaluative responses to reality, the realities which they disclose have an inherently relational character. A metaphysics of relationship promises to meet the logical criterion of coherence, for, if one conceives reality in relational terms from the very beginning, then logical consistency requires that the key terms in any philosophical theory of the whole all imply one another because they all designate different aspects of a complex relational whole.

The criteria of logical consistency and of logical coherence test the way in which one goes about formulating a sound metaphysical hypothesis, a philosophical theory of the whole which ambitions universal applicability but which confesses with contrite fallibilism that it might in the end prove metaphysically inadequate. A metaphysical hypothesis will qualify as a "working hypothesis" if it meets two other criteria: the criteria of applicability and of adequacy. A world-hypothesis qualifies as applicable if it can in fact interpret some realities. It interprets those realities successfully if in fact it applies to them in the sense in which one has defined it philosophically. Clearly, an inapplicable theory would have no metaphysical interest, because while it might aspire to universal applicability, it would fail finally to encounter anything in the universe of which it can make sense. Besides applying to some things, a "working" metaphysical hypothesis must not encounter any reality which it cannot interpret. If it does, then, it cannot offer a universalizable interpretation of reality and needs revision before it can promise to do so.

I derive the criteria of logical consistency, coherence, applicability, and adequacy from the thought of Alfred North Whitehead. I have, moreover, argued elsewhere that his own world hypothesis, the philosophy of organism which he formulated systematically in *Process and Reality,* fails finally to meet those criteria because it acquiesces in a fatal fallacy of Enlightenment modernism, namely, in conceptual nominalism.[2] The thought of both Peirce and Royce make it clear that a constructive transcending of the limitations of Enlightenment modernism needs to defend some form of metaphysical and epistemological realism. Both Peirce and Royce saw clearly that one cannot separate one's metaphysical theory of the whole from one's epistemology, since knowledge constitutes a part of reality which one's theory of the whole seeks to interpret and because any metaphysical theory about reality in general needs to justify its cognitive applicability and adequacy. Peirce laid the philosophical foundations for a critical metaphysical and epistemological realism. Royce built both philosophically and theologically on those foundations.

The fecund philosophical foundations which Peirce laid and which Royce endorsed and developed have the capacity to generate more than one kind of world hypothesis. With hints from Whitehead and from John Dewey, I have been constructing a metaphysics of experience on the foun-

[2] See Donald L. Gelpi, *The Turn to Experience in Contemporary Theology* (Mahwah, N.J.: Paulist Press, 1994) 52–89.

dations which Peirce and Royce laid. A metaphysics of experience takes experience as its root metaphor. If in addition that metaphysics builds on Peirce, then it must define experience in triadic, realistic terms, as indeed I have done. I define "experience" metaphysically as a process composed of relational elements called feelings, and I discover in the higher forms of experience three kinds of feelings: particular values (what Peirce called "qualities"), concrete decisions (what Peirce called "facts"), and general tendencies (what Peirce called "laws"). Autonomously functioning tendencies count as selves, and selves capable of conversion count as human persons. Alejandro Garcia-Rivera, a friend and colleague on the faculty of the Jesuit School of Theology at Berkeley where I teach, is currently moving Peirce's thought in a different metaphysical direction. Alex has developed a theological aesthetic by putting Peirce and Royce in dialogue with Hispanic theology and plans to develop a theology of nature. Since we both build on Peirce and Royce, our metaphysical systems tend to converge rather than to contradict one another. Robert Lassalle-Klein, of the same faculty, is exploring the relationship between Peirce's pragmaticism and Ignatio Ellacuria's theory of historicization.

A fallibilistic metaphysical theory needs, as Peirce also saw, verification both in lived experience and in multi-disciplinary thinking. One needs to test one's world-hypothesis both against all the realities encountered in experience and against detailed scientific studies of limited aspects of reality which the specialized, idioscopic sciences undertake. In dealing with the results of idioscopic investigations of different realms of reality, a successful metaphysical theory must meet the following speculative challenges.

First, it must successfully interpret the verified results of the idioscopic sciences. It will interpret those results successfully if one's theory applies to them in the sense in which one has defined that theory philosophically. For example, I have argued in other works that the metaphysics of experience which I defend can successfully interpret the results of individual and social psychology.[3]

Second, a successful metaphysical theory must contextualize the results of the idioscopic sciences. By that I mean that it must provide an over-arching frame of reference within which to situate those results. For example, in the same works to which I just referred I have argued that my fallibilistic, philosophical construct of experience does in fact provide a comprehensive frame of reference within which to situate successfully different developmental psychological theories. One situates a theory by

[3] See Donald L. Gelpi, *Experiencing God: A Theology of Human Emergence* (Lanham, Md.: University Press of America, 1987); Donald L. Gelpi, *Inculturating North American Theology: An Experiment in Foundational Method* (Atlanta: Scholars Press, 1988).

identifying the realm of experience which it addresses and how that realm of experience relates to other realms of experience. Jean Piaget, for example, focuses primarily on speculative human development, Lawrence Kohlberg on moral development, James Fowler on religious development, and Eric Erickson on affective development. Not only does the metaphysics of experience which I defend give an account of each of these forms of development, but it also studies how they mutually condition one another.

Third, a metaphysical theory needs to criticize the questionable presuppositions on which different idioscopic hypothesis may rest. One may mount two kinds of criticisms of the theories proposed by the idioscopic sciences. One criticism draws on the normative sciences in order to criticize the ideals or immoral attitudes they can tacitly inculcate or the logical and methodological fallacies which they can tacitly invoke. A metaphysics which includes a theory of knowledge can also call into question unjustifiable assumptions which idioscopic theories make about reality in general. Not a few contemporary scientists in this country and elsewhere continue to espouse a form of Enlightenment fundamentalism. When they do, they need their philosophical come-uppance.

A deconstructionist postmodernism may complain that realistic metaphysical claims close off intellectual development and freeze reality in indefensible ways. A metaphysical theory like Peirce's, however, which espouses a contrite fallibilism and which acknowledges the evolving, developmental character of the universe, does neither. Peircean fallibilism not only recognizes but even insists that one must call any theory into question as soon as one has good reason to do so, whether that theory springs either from the coenoscopic, philosophical sciences or from the focused, idioscopic sciences. Fallibilism acknowledges three such good reasons for challenging an abduction: a contradiction in one's own theory, facts which call that theory into question, or the development of a better frame of reference for thinking about reality than that which one now employs. A fallibilistic metaphysics enjoys all the open-endedness which any postmodernist can reasonably demand.

Moreover, by conceiving reality in relational, functional, developmental terms rather than in the substantialist, essentialist, and static terms of classical Greco-Roman metaphysics, not only does a metaphysical theory which builds on a Peircean realism interpret history philosophically, it also offers a working metaphysical hypothesis about the nature of historical reality.

At the same time, a fallibilistic metaphysical realism which builds on the foundations laid by Peirce and Royce avoids the epistemological relativism in which much deconstructionist postmodernism currently wallows all too promiscuously. Three elements in Peircean fallibilism keep it from degenerating into an epistemological relativism: Peirce's account of belief, his critical common-sensism, and his realism. By a belief, a Peircean pragmaticist means a proposition to whose consequences one stands committed. The verification or falsification of propositions requires belief, for, unless one stands by the consequences of any proposition, one has no way to measure its rational truth or falsity. If one does stand behind those consequences, one can test any deductively clarified abduction's truth or falsity against the way reality behaves. However, until one falsifies a belief or comes up with a better hypothesis, one maintains one's commitment to the beliefs one has.

Besides the commitment which belief requires, Peirce's logical fallibilism also avoids relativism by endorsing a critical common-sensism. As we have seen, critical common-sensism takes doubt very seriously and argues that, if we attempt to subject our learned beliefs to real doubt, some of them successfully resist that effort. In other words, we all find ourselves committed to a certain number of beliefs which we cannot truthfully call into question.

A third component in Peirce's philosophy prevents fallibilism from degenerating into relativism: namely, metaphysical and epistemological realism. The pragmatic maxim implicitly asserts what Peirce insisted on explicitly elsewhere: that if we take the time to formulate hypotheses about reality with clear operational consequences, then reality will teach us what kinds of laws it obeys by either behaving or failing to behave in the manner in which we predict. Verification transforms a hypothesis into a habitual belief.[4]

Peirce suspected that different cultures would find the same fundamental common-sense beliefs indubitable. In other words, he proposed his critical common-sensism as a testable, cross-cultural hypothesis. The nominalistic caste of much of deconstructionist postmodernism which reduces individuals and communities to unrepeatable surds devoid of any commonality fosters an indefensible cultural relativism. Deconstructionist

[4] See Guy Debrock, "Peirce, A Philosopher for the Twenty-first Century: Part I, Introduction," *Transactions of the Charles S. Peirce Society* 28 (1992) 1–18; Thomas Olshewsky, "Peirce's Antifoundationalism," *Transactions of the Charles S. Peirce Society* 29 (1993) 401–9; Kai Nielsen, "Peirce, Pragmatism, and the Challenge of Postmodernism," *Transactions of the Charles S. Peirce Society* 29 (1993) 513–60; John J. Stuhr, "Can Pragmatism Appropriate the Resources of Postmodernism? A Response to Nielsen," *Transactions of the Charles S. Peirce Society* 29 (1993) 561–72; James Jacob Liszka, "Good and Bad Faith: A Response to Nielsen," *Transactions of the Charles S. Peirce Society* 29 (1993) 573–9; Susan Haack, "Reflections of a Critical Common-sensist," *Transactions of the Charles S. Peirce Society* 32 (1996) 359–73; Victorino Tejerra, "Has Habermas Understood Peirce," *Transactions of the Charles S. Peirce Society* 32 (1996) 107–25.

postmodernism tends to presuppose that one cannot understand alien cultures or communicate realistically across cultures despite the fact that people do both all the time. This cultural relativism and the tacit, indefensible metaphysical nominalism on which such cultural relativism rests simply dramatize the fact that so-called deconstructionist postmodernism—like Enlightenment modernism—acquiesces uncritically in the presuppositions of the dialectical imagination which the Enlightenment inherited from Protestantism and which Protestantism adapted from an indefensible Augustinian dualism.

Cultures do not differ *toto caelo* from one another as some deconstructionist postmoderns would have us believe. Cultures rhyme. They resemble one another analogously and must of necessity do so. By "culture" I mean anything touched and changed by symbolic human communication. Cultures exemplify different kinds of interrelated social symbols, but they rhyme, or resemble one another analogously, because every culture seeks to meet the same generic kinds of elemental human needs and humanely enhanced living. Cross-cultural studies tend to verify this suggestion and give the lie to the cultural relativism which deconstructionist postmodernism is currently seeking to foist on the incautious academic fadist.

In his study of the theological challenges of contemporary postmodernism, Thomas Guarino correctly argues that an adequate theological response to the intellectual challenge posed by contemporary postmodernism requires the formulation of "an historically and ideologically sophisticated foundationalism." By a "foundationalism" Guarino means a form of critical metaphysical realism which can offer a basis for constructive Christian theological thinking. I endorse his suggestion and I have written this book in order to call attention to the fact that much of the critical philosophical and metaphysical thinking for which Guarino calls has already happened. Indeed, if academics in the United States knew their own cultural and philosophical tradition better, I suspect that postmodernism would not be enjoying its present vogue on many campuses and in many academic departments.

Moreover, the triadic, social, realistic metaphysics which Peirce developed can indeed support Christian theological thinking, as Royce demonstrated in *The Problem of Christianity* and as I have argued in just about every theological book I have written. In writing *The Problem of Christianity,* Royce recognized that he had failed to deal with the christological issues raised by Christianity, but he believed that he had laid necessary speculative foundations for resolving disputed christological questions. In *The Divine Mother* and in the christology which I hope soon to publish, I have in effect not only endorsed Royce's claim but have also sought to build constructively on the theological foundations which he laid. Moreover, I take growing satisfaction in seeing others in the theological generation which follows mine doing the same kind of thinking.

No one need, then, feel threatened by the failure of intellectual nerve which a deconstructionist postmodernism seeks to inculcate and rationalize. The human race seems to indulge in this kind of intellectual, *fin du siècle* decadence every thousand years or so. The critique of Enlightenment modernism which Transcendentalism began and which Peircean pragmatism brought to a climax has already traced the path around both modernism and a deconstructionist "postmodernism" which tacitly endorses the same kind of indefensible nominalism as many an Enlightenment *philosophe*.

At the beginning of what many historians call "the American century," the intellectual community in the United States faced an important crossroad. It could have opted with Peirce and Royce for a postmodern version of Christian theism or it could have chosen to perpetuate the least tenable aspects of Enlightenment modernism. On the whole the academy tended to make the latter option. The American secular academy too often popularized a nominalistic empiricism superficially refurbished as therapeutic individualism and scientific naturalism. The manipulation of the media by international capitalism, the supine acquiescence of politicians in Enlightenment slogans, and the capitulation of the churches to the privatization of religion have all conspired far too effectively to produce a nation of Enlightenment fundamentalists entrapped in the outdated presuppositions of an outdated eighteenth-century philosophy. As a consequence, as *Habits of the Heart* has persuasively argued, at the close of the American century American consciences too often languish in a corrosive individualism which leads down one ethical blind alley after another. Instead of fulfilling the Enlightenment promise of unlimited human progress, technology has mushroomed into the fatal cloud which devastated the cities of Hiroshima and Nagasaki. In a shrinking planet, we find ourselves confronted with the specter of a world-wide ecological crisis engineered by Enlightenment technology and possessing a destructive potential perhaps as massive in its human consequences as thermonuclear war.

The Transcendental critique of Enlightenment modernism which culminated in the pragmatisms of Peirce and of the mature Royce continues to offer this nation a chance to readjust its perceptions of reality in a manner which allows it to continue to embrace the best ideals of American republican government while discarding the false options propounded by the fallacious dualisms of eighteenth-century Enlightenment modernism. Only history will tell whether this nation's intellectual, cultural, and political leaders will have the wisdom to build constructively on the best insights of the American intellectual tradition while discarding its demonstrated follies.

INDEX

356 *Varieties of Transcendental Experience*

Locke, John, viii, 19–21, 28, 39, 40,
52, 63, 64, 73–6, 84, 100, 114, 130,
139, 148, 223, 284, 336, 342
logic, viii, 58, 62, 74, 75, 81, 94, 102,
103, 129, 130, 162, 171, 173, 199,
217, 218, 224, 229–32, 235, 237,
238, 241, 243, 248, 249, 252, 254,
259, 265, 269, 270, 272, 274,
277–87, 292, 293, 303–11, 329,
335, 340, 341, 344, 346
long run, the, 241
love, 15, 78, 95, 102, 103, 144, 177,
266, 274–6, 298, 319, 321, 322,
325, 328; evolutionary, 266–9
loyalty, 183, 298–303, 311, 315–22,
324, 327, 328, 331–3, 335, 337

Madison, James, 29, 31, 32, 182
Manicheism, 80
Maréchal, Joseph, 175
materialism, 109, 114, 166, 207, 259,
342
mathematics, 103, 227, 228, 250,
254 n. 70, 259, 260, 296
Mather, Cotton, 3, 4, 59–61, 181
Mather, Increase, 59–60
matter (material), 40, 51, 54, 82, 84,
87, 93–5, 106, 108, 109, 111, 117,
131, 132, 141, 142, 165, 191, 193,
213, 223, 224, 259, 261, 263, 265,
274, 281, 342
Mayhew, Jonathan, 62
meaning, 242, 244, 245, 252, 253,
258, 295–7, 312, 315, 316, 325,
330, 332, 339
mechanism (*see also* necessitarianism), 20, 207, 213, 216, 259–61,
267
memory, 113, 127, 168, 169, 194, 279,
297, 327
Menzes, S. E., 291
metaphor, root, 341, 344
Metaphysical Club, the, vii, 200–2,
207, 229
metaphysics (ontology), vii, ix, xi, 92,
94, 99, 110, 112, 133, 148, 149,
163, 168, 170, 172, 175, 188, 200,

218, 221, 224, 231, 232, 243, 244,
249, 250, 254, 258, 259, 277, 278,
280, 282, 286, 287, 295, 297, 298,
302, 310, 318, 326, 328, 330,
333–5, 337, 339–46, 348
method, x, 106, 112, 126, 206, 207,
209, 210, 240, 241, 244, 277, 282,
328, 346, 347
Michelangelo Buonarroti, 105, 115,
122
middle class, 7, 14, 16, 17, 77, 81, 298
Mill, John Stewart, 290
millenarianism, 25, 45, 57, 83, 180,
181, 284
mind, 14, 63, 68, 74, 102, 108, 124,
127, 141, 148, 151, 168, 173, 203,
208–10, 213, 215, 216, 220, 221,
232, 237, 238, 241, 242, 246, 250,
256, 258, 259, 261–3, 265, 266,
268, 269, 272–4, 278, 279, 281,
283, 284, 287, 306, 314, 318, 319,
322, 325, 333; mind play, 273, 280
miracle, 48, 53, 63, 144, 177
modernity, v, ix, xii, 71, 73, 75, 77, 85,
91, 92, 94, 100, 115, 131, 133,
191–3, 195, 199, 200, 225, 277,
283, 284, 287, 293, 318, 322, 325,
326, 341–4, 348, 349
monism, 217, 259
monophysitism, 178
monotheism, 141, 142, 149
Monroe, James, 25, 42
Montaigne, Michel de, 109, 111, 112
Montesquieu, Baron de la Brede et de,
19, 21
morality, 76, 83, 133, 139, 140, 143,
145, 146, 189, 199, 217, 223, 279,
284, 284, 291, 294, 299–303, 311,
314, 315, 321, 322, 323, 325, 327,
333, 335, 337, 343, 346
moral sense (sentiment), 28, 37, 41
motion, 110, 111, 113
Muir, John, 90, 91
musement, 273, 274, 280, 282, 336
mystery, 15, 48, 164, 328
mysticism, 91, 93, 110, 112, 146, 227,
295, 296, 325, 331